| DATE | | | |
|---|---|---|---|
|  |  |  |  |
|  |  |  |  |
|  |  |  |  |
|  |  |  |  |
|  |  |  |  |
|  |  |  |  |
|  |  |  |  |
|  |  |  |  |
|  |  |  |  |
|  |  |  |  |
|  |  |  |  |
|  |  |  |  |

*The*
*Psychology of*
*Human Aging*

# The Psychology of Human Aging

MARGUERITE
D. KERMIS

## Theory, Research, and Practice

*Canisius College*

ALLYN AND BACON, INC.   *Boston   London   Sydney   Toronto*

*Series Editor: Bill Barke*
*Production Editor: Elaine Ober*

*Photographs by Frank Siteman* © *MCMLXXXIII*

REF
BF
724.55
.A35
K47
1984

**Library of Congress Cataloging in Publication Data**

Kermis, Marguerite D., 1948–
    The psychology of human aging.

    Bibliography: p.
    Includes index.
    1. Aging—Psychological aspects.   2. Aged—Psychology.
3. Aged—Mental health services.  I. Title.
BF724.55.A35K47   1984     155.9'37     83-15593
ISBN 0-205-08093-6

*Printed in the United States of America*
*10 9 8 7 6 5 4 3 2 1   88 87 86 85 84 83*

*For George
May we be together
until the white wings
of time scatter our
days*

## Chapter 4
## Research and Methodology in Aging     75

## Chapter 5
## Physiology of Aging  93

## Chapter 6
## Aging and Health    *126*

## Chapter 7
## Sensory Processes and Psychomotor Response    *159*

## Chapter 8
## Cognitive Processes        186

## Chapter 9
## Personality and Adjustment   216

## Chapter 10
## Psychiatric Disorders   249

## Chapter 11
## Mental Health Interventions      *285*

$A$ textbook such as this inevitably reflects my own values and experiences, as well as the influences that shaped my thinking. My concern with aging as a field of inquiry grew from two major sources, one personal and one academic. The personal concern arose from my contact with vital grandparents who were an integral and colorful part of my childhood. My academic interest was nurtured in the Life-Span Developmental Psychology doctoral program and All-University Gerontology Center of Syracuse University. Additional concerns in psychological aging were shaped by postdoctoral work in preventive medicine at the University of Buffalo Medical School, and are continually fueled by my teaching, practice, and research activities. The focus of this text on theory, research, and practice in aging reflects these multiple facets of my gerontological background.

This textbook is designed to provide an introduction and overview of current knowledge and concerns in psychological aging. It is written for students who have had no previous specialized background in gerontology. While it is intended primarily as a textbook for undergraduates, graduate students or practitioners who want a comprehensive introduction to the subject will also find it useful.

*The Psychology of Human Aging* presents a comprehensive exposure to diverse topics in psychological aging. For this reason, many areas not traditionally covered in undergraduate psychology courses are broached, such as health policy, preventive medicine, and brain aging. In addition, within each topic considerable breadth of supporting materials is presented. While length limitations prevent me from fully developing such ancillary materials, I have suggested additional readings wherever possible which might serve to answer any additional questions the reader might have.

*The Psychology of Human Aging* is organized in terms of a general introduction to aging concerns and realities (chapters one through four) and three major topical areas: physical aging (chapters five and six), cognitive and sensory processes (chapters seven and eight), and personality and adjustment (chapters nine through twelve). In each chapter an effort is made to introduce theoretical aspects, then follow the way in which each was investigated, and conclude with implications of the research on practice. This organization has grown from my extensive training experience with gerontological practitioners, who maintain that there is little literature which makes an effort to integrate research and practice in aging. I have made an attempt to do so in this textbook.

Psychological aging is a groundbreaking area filled with excitement and challenge for the student and professional alike. However, it is also a rigorous, multidisciplinary area which many students may find conceptually difficult at the outset. To overcome this potential problem, I have attempted to write a book that is student-oriented and readable, but also scholarly. Some of the features which should support my efforts in this direction are:

1.   The writing style is clear and straightforward.

2. The textbook includes numerous case studies of psychological aging as well as practical applications of the research the reader encounters.

3. Each chapter is organized in a hierarchical manner, moving from theory to research to practice.

4. Each chapter begins with thought questions to focus the student's reading and conceptualization of the material.

5. There is a summary at the end of each major section within the chapter and a final conclusion section to each chapter.

It is my hope that the students and professionals who read this book will gain an appreciation of the complexity of issues in psychological aging, as well as an awareness that there are no easy answers to many of the aging dilemmas introduced here. However, I also hope that those who read it will feel a sense of both enthusiasm and competence to begin to undertake the challenge of continued inquiry.

# Acknowledgments

As always in such a project, many people have contributed to the creation and writing of this book. Canisius College has provided the ambience and resources for the initial ideas to develop. My departmental chairman and friend, Donald Tollefson, has allowed me the freedom to explore its promise. Jerome Dusek, my mentor, showed me how the process of inquiry could be translated into the classroom as well as into the writing of textbooks. He also gave me my first opportunity to do serious writing and taught me much about writing for the reader's understanding.

Allyn and Bacon—through my editors Bill Barke and Elaine Ober, its staff, and excellent reviewers—has helped to bring the promise to fruition. Also of immense help in this project were Martha Hicks-Courant and the staff at Editing, Design, and Production, Inc. Frank Siteman, the photographer whose photos illustrate the text, has also been an integral part in the book's effectiveness. The visual images he has created beautifully capture the promise and pathos of aging.

Of course, no textbook is really possible without the input of students. My students at Canisius College have strongly influenced this effort by their questions and concerns. It is my hope that other students will profit from their efforts.

Finally, I would like to thank my family. My parents have been very supportive in this project, and their pride in my efforts has been a great incentive. It is impossible to adequately thank my husband, George, for his support and love in this process. He has always encouraged me to develop my ideas and capabilities. He has believed in me at times when I doubted, and this confidence has been an immeasurable contribution to this effort. He has made this, and all things I do, possible and joyous.

*The*
*Psychology of*
*Human Aging*

Aging and old age are phenomena that all of us are familiar with and many of us have definite ideas about. The process of growing older acts as a common denominator. It is something that all of us are undergoing but most of us take for granted until some marker event, such as the first gray hair or achy twinge, reminds us of it. Consolations in this awareness are the realizations that everyone else is moving along at the same rate (although most others appear to age faster than we do) and that we don't feel psychologically any different than we ever did.

It frequently emerges in classes and lectures that some people have fairly negative expectations of what old age is like. These negative views of old people possibly reflect a person's contact with seriously ill aged persons or perhaps indicate the prevailing social stereotypes of what old age is. Gerontologists may be disturbed by such negative attitudes but often respect the speaker's candor. Many persons hold such beliefs but never verbalize them openly. They silently attribute such characteristics as the following to old age:

Old people are all sick.
Old age is a time of helplessness and hopelessness.
Old people have nothing to offer any longer.
Old people are obsolete.
Old people become exactly like children.

Other people may think that such statements are true about the majority of old people but that the vital, intact elders they know are exceptions to the rule. They quietly believe the prevalent social stereotypes, and when they themselves show "symptoms" of old age, they begin to act the part, or become anxious or depressed, because they feel they are "failing."

The truth of what old age is rarely duplicates the feared specter of senility, ill health, aloneness, and institutional placement believed by many Americans to reflect old age. As will be seen in Chapter 2, only five percent of elderly Americans live in institutions such as nursing homes, psychiatric hospitals, or homes for the aged. However, although our most negative expectations of old age are unlikely to be realized, they are visions of the future that haunt many of us.

As students interested in the psychology of aging, we must remember that our visions of reality guide us. Whether these perceptions are true is irrelevant; we live according to our illusions. To a large extent, the reality that confronts today's elderly and the elderly of the future—ourselves, should we live long enough—is determined by what we believe old age to be.

In this textbook we will study the current knowledge about the process of aging and the people who constitute today's elderly. We will also consider the factors believed to affect the way in which individuals and groups of people born at similar times (also called *cohorts*) age. These predictive factors must be understood before any effective intervention programs can be designed to improve the quality of life of aging persons.

*Aging and old age are phenomena with which all of us are familiar.*

**In Search of a Psychology of Aging**

For each of us the process of aging is untrodden territory. None of us has ever individually aged before. So, too, are you students reading this textbook pioneers in studying the psychology of aging. Only a few years ago the majority of students who earned undergraduate degrees from institutions of higher learning never had an opportunity to study adult development in the process of acquiring a formal education. Even fewer had an opportunity to study any aspect of aging. For various reasons the prevailing practice was to limit the research and study of human behavior to considerations of the activities of young adults and occasionally of infants, children, and adolescents.

In fact, next to white rats and pigeons, young adults (i.e., college sophomores taking introductory psychology) have been and continue to be the most studied creatures of all time. The psychological behavior of the college student is often the baseline against which every other group is referenced. This has led at times to severe misunderstandings about the process of aging. For example, from a study comparing college students (eminently accessible to researchers) with institutional-

*For each of us the process of aging is untrodden territory.*

ized elderly people (also extremely accessible to researchers), one could assume that aging is a fairly negative event; elderly people would be portrayed as more mentally and physically infirm than younger people, as well as socially isolated. In contrast, were researchers to compare healthy, community-dwelling elderly people with healthy, community-dwelling young people, the results would present an entirely different and more positive portrait of old age. This positive view of normal aging might be even more pronounced were the researchers to compare healthy, community-dwelling elderly people with institutionalized elderly people. In this sort of research methodology, the different actions of normal aging and aging combined with disease become fairly obvious.

Perhaps an "old" humorous story will make this point clearer:

> Once upon a time there was a man who had gone to a good party and had
> had quite a bit to drink. As he approached his home through a dark alley, his
> keys slipped from his hand and fell to the ground. He searched for the keys but
> could not find them in the dark. Then he noticed light at the corner of the
> alley and went over there to look for his keys under the light.
>
> Eventually a policeman came by, saw him groping on the ground, and
> asked him what he was doing. "I lost my keys," the man said. "Did you lose
> them here?" asked the policeman. "No, sir," he answered, " but this is where
> the light is."

Research on human development has tended to be conducted "where the light is";
hence our focus on college students and institutionalized old people. Traditionally
it has been easier and more efficient to obtain research subjects through institutional linkages than otherwise. This has greatly benefited psychology as a science,
but it has left enormous gaps in our knowledge of developmental processes in
general and aging in particular.

During the past twenty years, however, a number of factors have combined to
significantly increase interest in the study of aging and the aged. For example, there
has been a rapid increase in the number and percentage of elderly people in the
general population. This rapid increase has changed the perception of services,
programs, and health benefits required to maintain quality of life as a person grows
older. An awareness of the difficulties faced by many elderly people has led to
enhanced interest in and study of old age, there has also been a gradual increase in
the study of the characteristics, problems, and behavior of people who have ceased
to be adolescents but are not yet elderly. Thus, interest in the study of adult
development and aging has increased rapidly, far more rapidly indeed than the
increase in the number of persons who are qualified by training to work with
elderly populations.

The material contained in this textbook is designed to contribute to a balanced
view of the aging process and the aged population. It includes discussion not only
of the current state of knowledge about aging, but also of the impact of social
attitudes and values on researchers, service providers, and the general population. It
is important to note at the outset that our personal values and the values of society
significantly affect the questions we ask and the answers we accept about aging.
This material should lead you, the reader, to develop an objective awareness of
both the benefits and the liabilities of growing old, for that is your future and the
future of each of us fortunate to survive our youth.

As will be discussed, the gradual deterioration of perception, mobility, health,
and income tend to accompany increasing age. However, these changes are very
gradual and are adjusted to successfully by many elderly persons. In fact, these
changes are so well compensated for by the increase in experience and efficiency
that come with age that the majority of elderly people are not significantly

impaired by them (Lesnoff-Caravaglia, 1980). Some active old people may even be in better physical condition than younger persons leading a sedentary life. Buster Crabbe, a former Olympic swimming champion and movie Tarzan, and Jack Lalanne, the TV exercise program host, are excellent examples of the positive effects of lifetime physical fitness.

The two following vignettes illustrate other examples of common successful adaptation:

> Mrs. A, age 82, was having a great deal of difficulty finding the right retirement living complex to meet her needs. She had always been an avid swimmer and therefore desired year-round swimming pool access. One difficulty was that she liked to take her daily two-mile swim nude!
>
> Mr. C was a 76-year-old man I met on a ski lift one evening. He was quite bent in his upper back and knees, which gave him the perfect stance for downhill skiing. When asked if he had ever broken any bones, he replied "Look, honey, when I leave the hospital, I say 'Don't make the bed!' "

These cases illustrate the happy and full late life experienced by many elderly people. To a large extent, this success reflects good mental and physical health. There are certainly old persons who do not have such a successful experience. However, although it is important for us not to dismiss the causes and consequences of their desperate plight, it is also vital for us to realize that they are not the majority of elderly people. Old age is a time of adaptation and change. Nevertheless, there are great individual differences among the elderly (Birren & Renner, 1977).

In addition to needing basic knowledge and skills pertaining to aging, the student of geropsychology needs to develop a sensitivity to elderly people. This text therefore stresses an appreciation of individual differences and a sense of the range of concerns, interests, needs, and life-styles presented and expressed by elderly people. The composite image presented should thus contribute to the development of an appreciation of the vitality and competence of elderly people.

Finally, it is to be hoped that this text will enable you, the student of the psychology of aging, to develop a conceptual framework and a set of principles around which to organize your information and experience as well as to apply to the realities of old people. In addition, you should develop a sensitivity to your and others' fears, preconceptions, stereotypes, and myths about aging and the aged. These issues and the related feelings they tend to foster will be explored continually and intensively throughout this text.

Psychology is the study of human behavior in all its various forms. The psychology of aging, geropsychology, focuses on the behavior of individuals involved in the processes of postmaturity development. This study has as its focus certain broad

**The Psychology of Aging**

areas and their psychological repercussions, such as sensory and motor processes, perception, motivation, intellectual functioning, emotions, personality development, health, and psychopathology.

The study of the psychology of aging seeks to answer three main questions regarding these general topics (Birren & Renner, 1977):

In what ways do the elderly differ from young people, and how do persons change as they grow older?

How do we account for these differences or changes?

What are the consequences, if any, of these age-related differences and changes?

With the answers to these questions, geropsychologists will be able to construct the reality, causes, and implications of behavioral changes associated with aging.

Increasingly the problems and realities of aging are being approached by life-span developmental psychologists, psychologists who view the behaviors exhibited in late life as having evolved from earlier behaviors. From the life-span perspective, a person's behavior is a function of past, present, and future events (Baltes & Schaie, 1973; Goulet & Baltes, 1970). Past factors include the person's basic physiological endowment and early social and cognitive environment. Present factors include current interpersonal, family, group, and cultural influences. The future environment, real or imagined, is also a powerful determinant of an individual's pattern of development (Erikson, 1963; Lowenthal, 1977). Myths about aging and a person's expectations and goals are other important determinants of present behavior. The life-span perspective thus emphasizes the continuous process of change from conception to death and its impact upon the person undergoing that change (Nash, 1978; Overton & Reese, 1973; Riegel, 1973b).

This text is written from a life-span and developmental perspective, the latter of which is characterized by the following (Nash, 1978; Overton & Reese, 1973):

Concern with normal rather than abnormal behavior.

Maturity and old age viewed as integral parts of the life span.

The belief that each behavior at any age level reflects earlier development and experience.

The view of later development as necessary to any evaluation of the success of early adjustment.

Consideration of the whole person from a multidisciplinary perspective.

Developmental psychologists may also discuss pathology in development, such as mental disorders or physical illness, but they believe these topics can best be discussed and understood after a clear presentation of normal developmental processes.

If the emphasis is on developmental processes, why would a psychologist be interested in focusing on one part of the life cycle, such as old age? Many reasons could be suggested for such a choice.

*Old age has certain social transitions associated with it, such as retirement, role change, and loss of confidants. Such transitions often lead old people to engage in introspection or life review.*

First, practical considerations, such as the sheer amount of data involved in a thorough discussion of adult development, might suggest late life as a focus for an understanding of life in its entirety.

Second, some problems and issues have a higher probability of occurring in old age than in youth, and the psychologist might choose to specialize in such issues. For example, coping with aloneness, isolation, disability, and multiple chronic illnesses is more frequently a problem in late life than at any other stage of the life cycle. If one is interested in the effects of cumulative stresses or losses and the way humans adapt to or cope with them, late life is an optimal focus.

Third, old age is also associated with certain social transitions and their attendant psychological consequences, such as retirement, change of residence, income reduction, role change, and the loss of confidants. Psychologists interested in social transitions might well choose old age as an area of primary concern.

Finally, the number of old people has grown rapidly in this century, increasing the role of care givers or service providers such as long-term care administrators, geriatric practitioners, pension planners, and legislators, whose task it is to ensure that elderly people maintain independence and an adequate quality of life for as long as possible.

**Psychological Issues in Aging**

Various social and health issues related to old age are of interest to psychologists because of their impact on the aging person's psychological functioning. These issues focus on age stereotyping and definitions, mental and physical changes as they affect individual competence, and cognitive ability. These controversial concepts are briefly introduced in this section; they will be considered in more detail in their respective chapters.

### Definitions and Stereotypes

There are many variations in the definitions by which our society and other societies establish oldness. Some researchers believe that aging commences with conception or birth. Others think aging is the progressive loss of functions and capabilities that occurs after maturity (Finch & Hayflick, 1977). Still others consider aging relative, asserting that chronological age is not a good predictor of anything because of the great individual differences found in aging populations (Botwinick, 1973).

There is considerable disagreement on these points. Chronological age is in fact viewed by many researchers as the best predictor of any organismic variable, imperfect as it is. However, there is more than one type of age. Researchers have introduced four definitions, including chronological age. The three other sorts of age are psychological age, which indicates the degree of cognitive competence and personality development an individual has attained; social age, which reflects societal expectations and norms relating to progression through the life cycle; and biological age, a measure of the individual's physiological function (Birren, 1964).

This disparity in definition suggests a major difficulty in any discussion of psychological phenomena related to age. For example, considerable skill is required to disentangle the effects of disease processes, social and environmental changes, or long-standing personality patterns from normal aging. How researchers go about this is discussed in Chapter 4. If these factors are not disentangled, psychologists (or any professionals or individuals) may well find themselves discussing pathology as though it were normal aging. This is an important concern for persons attempting to assess the validity of universal aging phenomena.

### Mental Health and "Senility"

Defining the normality of physical and mental health for elderly persons is often very difficult. The dividing line is rarely sharp, regardless of whether we are focusing our attention on the physical or mental health of an aged person. There is much to be learned about the cause-and-effect relationships among life experiences, physical status, and socioeconomic factors. Researchers by no means agree on the origin of the symptoms we call *senility,* which include confusion, disorientation, and apathy. The label *senility* implies that the cause of the symptoms is an irreversible, untreatable change in brain tissue. Some researchers are convinced that these symptoms are manifestations of changes in brain structure and biochemical function in the aging brain (Coyle et al., 1982; Sloane, 1980). Others associate the manifestations of such symptoms with the effects of loneliness and social isolation (Blazer, 1980); the lack of stimulating contacts with others is implicated in that socially isolated persons may react to their isolation with apathy, withdrawal, loss of interest, and even confusion (Pfeiffer, 1977). The symptoms of "senility" may also include depression, which so parallels some aspects of dementia (organic brain disorder) that it has been called *pseudodementia* (Blazer, 1980). This will be discussed further in later chapters. There is no agreement on which symptoms of so-called senility should be ascribed to the effects of diseases such as Alzheimer's, presumed to have no causal relationship with aging, and which should be attributed to normal aging (Sloane, 1980).

Certain people continue to be creative and productive well past the age of sixty-five. Outstanding contributions by statesmen, jurists, and researchers quickly

*We find old people everywhere who enjoy life, participate in activities, and maintain a life-style compatible with contentment, satisfaction, and pleasure. In general, meaningful activity— such as we see here— enhances life's satisfaction and quality.*

come to mind. Such people as Pablo Casals, Pablo Picasso, B.F. Skinner, Carl Rogers, and even George Burns are visible examples of such continued productivity. We can also think of many warm and helpful relationships among grandparents, their children, and their grandchildren. We find old people everywhere who seem to be able to enjoy life, participate in activities, and maintain a life-style compatible with contentment, satisfaction, and pleasure.

Given gerontology's early emphasis on institutionalized elderly people, however, we still do not know all the factors that contribute to or enable old people to live such a life. Preliminary findings indicate that successful aging is related to health status, previous life experiences, current social and economic factors, and expectancies of what one's future will be like (Botwinick, 1978; Neugarten, 1977). It is also related to preventive health care and personal choice in one's life (Fries & Crapo, 1981). There is, however, much about this interaction among complicated factors that we still do not understand.

### Physical Health and Disease

We are unable to say with certainty why elderly persons seem more vulnerable than young persons to certain types of disease, mainly those of a chronic nature (Kart et al., 1978). Immune system mechanisms are unquestionably involved in these age-associated conditions (Fries & Crapo, 1981; Hickey, 1980; Lesnoff-Caravaglia, 1980). Some body processes show no change with age, and others decline gradually. In contrast, some capacities, such as certain aspects of vision, may decline very early in life. We will discuss the psychological impact of these changes in Chapters 5, 6, and 7.

There are of course great individual differences in the timing, pattern, and severity of aging changes. People age at different rates. In addition, their abilities, problems, attitudes, and expectancies differ. Combined, these factors lead to a great degree of differentiation among groups of old people. Individual differences in the body's resilience and in adaptive capacities force us to appraise the assets and liabilities of each old person rather than of the elderly as a group. However, for many people, both professionals and laypersons, this is not an easy or usual task.

Obviously, as people live longer, they are exposed to more stresses and are more likely to contract various diseases. Degenerative processes such as arteriosclerosis and osteoarthritis have had more time to affect older than younger people. Furthermore, death is more imminent the longer one lives. Nevertheless, the maintenance of good emotional and physical health is related to many factors, and the relative importance of any single factor varies from one individual to another. It is not sound judgment to conclude inevitable decline and a poor prognosis merely because a person is chronologically old. This text explores the psychological effects of belief in such statements on the elderly and on those of us in transit to old age.

### Cognitive Competence

A key issue in the field of geropsychology is cognitive competence. A persistent myth about old age is that people become both less intelligent and less able to learn

*Old people are often able to learn new things; it just takes longer for them than for young persons.*

as they age. Experimental aging research has demonstrated that this myth is false. However, there is no doubt that changes in cognitive processes occur with age (Botwinick, 1977; Kausler, 1982; Siegler, 1980).

In considering cognitive aging, it is essential to keep in mind the circumstances under which testing, interviewing, counseling, and other professional psychological activities are done. Motivation often determines a person's degree of cooperation, and this affects results. Evaluating the results of psychological tests in elderly people must be done with care. The elderly may see no value to the testing, finding it either demeaning or anxiety-producing because of its evaluative context (Botwinick, 1977). These attitudes may well lower performance by increasing rigidity and cautiousness (Botwinick, 1977; Kausler, 1982).

Much study of learning capacities has revealed that old persons are often able to learn new things but that it takes longer for them than for younger persons

(Botwinick, 1977; Kausler, 1982). Elderly people are also still able to perform various tasks with the same degree of efficiency as before; however, performance diminishes when an old person is expected to perform a task in a given time to meet a "normal" or laboratory standard (Botwinick, 1977; Siegler, 1980).

Measurement of intelligence is not simple. Most standard intelligence tests currently used are dependent on education, i.e., they are biased in favor of young persons, who have had more extensive formal education and formal test-taking experience than elderly persons. In the case of elderly people who have had little formal education, the tests do not represent intellectual ability. It is possible for a person to have a great capacity to deal with the problems of daily living and yet score low on some intelligence tests. Old people have a store of experience from which they can draw to provide solutions to various problems. This resource may be tapped only by problems or questions of living and not by the usual tests of intelligence (Gardner & Monge, 1977; Monge & Gardner, 1972).

Memory, especially for recent events, eventually tends to be impaired with increasing age (Kausler, 1982). The explanation for this is not entirely clear, as will be seen in Chapter 7. Some memory impairment is due to central nervous system

*Persons whose reflexes are slowed down may learn to drive their cars more slowly and carefully.*

changes (Bartus et al., 1982; Coyle et al., 1982). Other selective memory loss may have to do with recall of events that occurred in a happier period of life, or the retention of remote memory may reflect that things formerly made a more profound impression on the individual (Lachman & Lachman, 1980). Whatever the explanation, mild to severe memory disturbances are common among elderly people, although severe disturbance usually indicates some sort of psychopathology (Kahn & Miller, 1978).

### Sensory Competence

In general, both sensory and motor functions become impaired with advancing age (Botwinick, 1978; Kart et al., 1978). Hearing, sight, taste, smell, and touch, as well as balance, are affected, but compensations are possible. Hearing aids, eyeglasses, bright lamps, walking canes, and so on may help. A slowing down of motor activity and responses is also noticeable, but as with sensory impairment, compensation is often possible. The person whose reflexes are slowed down may learn to drive his car more slowly and carefully than before, or he may hold on to the handrail when walking down a flight of stairs. These precautions minimize the possibility of accidents. Although it takes longer to do a particular task than it used to, the old person may still accomplish what needs to be done and usually has the extra time required, at least in the real world outside of laboratory experiments.

### Psychiatric Illness in the Elderly

Myths and issues such as those presented above have considerable impact on the psychological function of those who already are or are becoming old. All of us, and our society in general, tend to live by our myths or expectations, which help shape who we are and who we become. If the prevailing views of old age focus on negative experiences, illness, and inevitable "senility," those may well become our shared future. This pattern is nowhere more evident than in our beliefs about psychiatric disorders and senility in the aged.

The mental health of the elderly is an area of research and concern for psychologists studying aging (Blazer, 1980). Aged persons present a variety of complaints and clinical syndromes that are diagnosed as mental illness. These symptoms show varying patterns of onset. Personality disorders and psychological symptoms that manifested themselves earlier in the person's life may persist for many years and be carried over into late life. These disorders do not shorten life, but they may limit the quality of life possible. Sometimes one sees an accentuation of symptoms as a person ages, but regression or stabilization may also occur. Elderly psychotic patients are often described as "burnt out," since their symptoms may diminish with age. We also speak of psychologically normal people "mellowing" with age. Conversely, the aggressive, hostile, demanding person may persist or worsen in these characteristics because they are permanent personality traits.

In contrast to long-standing symptoms are sudden-onset symptoms, which may be associated with organic disorder. An individual may also show depression or other functional disorder for the first time in late life because of increased stress or decreased ability to deal with stress. Not all symptoms seen in old age are those of organic impairment (dementia); they may be related to stress or loss and therefore be remediable.

The severity of the symptoms of any psychiatric disorder in an elderly person, whether depression or dementia, varies. Some persons show only minimal symptoms until they are subject to stress. The stress of going to a hospital, the loss of a loved one, or pressure to perform a task rapidly may aggravate these symptoms. In the absence of external stress, the symptomatology may go unnoticed. Furthermore, a person living a relatively simple life may show few manifestations of psychiatric disorder, whereas a person in a situation in which important decisions have to be made quickly may have more obvious difficulty. A retired farmer or blue-collar worker does not contend with the same kinds of problems as a seventy-year-old business executive trying to keep up with younger associates.

There are no psychological disorders found only in old age, nor does old age implicitly guarantee the presence of disabling organic brain disease. A person who is old chronologically does not inevitably have a poor prognosis for mental health. Often the opposite is true; having survived many stressful periods and problems, an elderly person may have a surprising reserve of resilience and adaptability. Old persons often respond well to minimal therapeutic efforts or support.

Mental illness in the aged is a complex phenomenon that is difficult to understand and conceptualize, as is normal aging. Diagnosing the extreme states is not difficult, but differentiating "normal" aging from mental distress or distinguishing between health and illness is sometimes problematic (Birren & Sloane, 1980). In addition, according to the developmental model, criteria for abnormality change throughout the life span. It is the task of geropsychologists of the future to make these distinctions easier for gerontologists in the years to come.

### Ageism

Many of the topics discussed in the past few pages as the domain of geropsychologists are related to some common stereotypes about growing old. The National Council on the Aging (NCOA) has suggested that certain stereotypes persist in our culture:

Old people are all alike.
Old people are all poor.
Old people are all sick.
Old people are all depressed.
Old people are a drag on everyone else.
Old people can't function in society.
Old people all live alone.
Old people all die in institutions.
If we live long enough we will all become senile.

Additional research (Schonfield, 1981) suggests that these negative stereotypes may not be held by many persons in the United States and that if they are, they may be directed only at a small group of old people. This research further implies that attitudes toward aging are multidimensional, situational, and applied to only a minority of the elderly.

Nevertheless, whether believed by many or a few, these stereotypes are a total falsification of the existence of many old people. Unfortunately there are people who fit the most negative stereotypes of what growing old is like. Furthermore, for many people, especially socially isolated persons who have no significant other to affirm their humanity, the myth of aging may become a self-fulfilling prophecy as it is internalized. Even old people who have avoided the self-fulfilling prophecy are affected by stereotypes about aging. In either case, stereotyping can lead to a compromised quality of life for the aged and aging.

It is the general purpose of this text to confront the facts about psychological aging; to indicate successful and unsuccessful patterns of aging and suggest interventions to improve the quality of life; and to erase myths about aging, which are destructive not only to those who are old now but also to those of us in the process of aging. Age is a relative and multifaceted concept. Our current conceptions of age functions should be clearly stipulated in terms of the society and historical time being considered. Individual differences and cohort differences make aging a process of continuous evolution. Persons who are old today may well show different patterns of aging than persons born in 1984, an era of low infant mortality, enriched foods, extensive educational opportunities, increased industrial pollution, and so on. Our definitions and "universals" may need to be re-evaluated in the future and the truth of current developmental functions of old age reassessed.

**General Directions of the Text**

What is important for the psychologist interested in aging, and the student approaching the field, is not so much an infallible body of knowledge as a manner of asking the correct questions. The three questions we stated earlier in this chapter as core to the psychology of aging are vital to the establishment of a science of psychological aging. However, their answers are not static laws etched in stone. Aging, like the people going through its process, is a continuously evolving phenomenon. History, biology, personal health and experience, socioeconomic status, education, and countless other variables all affect its manifestations. This text therefore attempts to integrate relevant material from other fields into the discussion of psychological aging.

It is hoped that this approach will be both challenging and satisfying to you, the student. Specific data about aging, which may change, are not as important as a framework within which to approach the subject—an emphasis on the whole person, the ecological system in which the person lives, and the behavior that originates from interaction between the person and the environment. Individuals

*Each old person experiences old age and its physical consequences differently.*

interested in the psychology of aging should not ask what the deteriorations associated with aging are but rather how, in the face of almost continuous change, old people manage to cope so well. It is up to you to help this aspect of the psychology of aging unfold.

*Why is a knowledge of demographics useful to students of the psychology of aging?*

*How can population statistics be translated into social and psychological characteristics of a group of people?*

*What sorts of effects do early experiences have on a person's health status in late adulthood?*

*Why is self-assessment of health such an important predictor of general emotional and physical health?*

*What sorts of health needs will the elderly of the future have?*

$P$OPULATION aging is a world-wide phenomenon, occurring in the highly industrialized countries of the Western world as well as in less developed countries with agrarian economies. Especially within this century, the number of old persons and their proportion to the population as a whole have increased significantly. This demographic event has led indirectly to the definition of old age as a social problem.

The secular (or world-wide) trend toward decreased mortality is due to various factors, some of which were well underway before the twentieth century started. Economic improvements such as increased agricultural efficiency and superior crops and livestock led to a better diet. Diet, of course, is essential to health maintenance. Transportation was improved, which helped eliminate famines due to local food shortages. Medical advances such as antibiotics and immunization helped control infectious diseases of childhood, which had killed many children during the first year of life. Public health projects such as improved water supply, sanitary sewers, and spraying with insecticide to control malaria helped prevent the occurrence of many diseases formerly present in pandemic proportions. Added to these factors was a demographic trend toward lower birth rates. This combination of decreased fertility and increased life expectancy has led, and will continue to lead, to the rapid aging of the world population.

When the number of elderly persons was few, there was a place for them in the social structure. Past traditions and social values supported them. Urbanization and the secularization of our society have increased both mobility and social change. Our current social value systems stress the importance of the individual over responsibility to the social group. This has led to a breakdown in the traditional approaches to human needs, especially the needs of the elderly (United Nations, 1975).

This chapter deals with the overall status of the elderly in the United States. It considers who elderly Americans are and their numbers, places of residence, and health. Population statistics relating to minorities, morbidity, and mortality are discussed. This chapter deals with *group* data, which of necessity obscure individual patterns of aging. There are many similarities among the elderly, but there are

*Flu vaccination is one of many ways in which both the young population and senior citizens are now protected from disease. Preventive medicine has changed the causes of death in this century.*

also many traits, acts, and conditions that vary widely. The older a group of adults born at the same time becomes, the more dissimilar its members grow in terms of physical ability, life-style, and so on. Aging does not take its toll at the same chronological age for all people.

The discussion of demographics in this chapter may initially appear to be extraneous to the study of the psychology of aging. However, it provides us with statistical grounding for our critical evaluation of theories, myths, and behaviors associated with aging in our culture. Demography is concerned not just with numbers but with the concepts behind these numbers and their implications. Demographics can give students of psychological aging the basis for refuting some of the myths associated with the behavior of old adults, such as the myth that if we live long enough, we will all become irreversibly "senile" (i.e., exhibit irreversible memory loss, confusion, and behavioral regression necessitating institutionalization). Approximately eighty percent of institutionalized persons suffer from some sort of mental difficulty. However, these mental difficulties need not be either organically caused or irreversible.

*Past traditions and social values supported the elderly. Support systems differ among ethnic groups.*

Demographics can present useful information to the research psychologist, clinician, or applied psychologist. It essentially presents an overview of the problems and capacities of old persons, thereby allowing us to respond to some of the myths and realities of aging that will confront us as we deal with old age and its psychological implications.

By way of contrast to the demographic data presented later in this chapter, a description of the stereotypical elderly person, as derived from the National Council on the Aging (NCOA)/Louis Harris survey (Harris & Associates, 1975), is given below:

> Typically he's a man in his sixties.
>
> Not so long ago, he was a productive member of society. But as he approached sixty-five, his job brought him less and less satisfaction. His work suffered, he had more than his share of on-the-job accidents, and his number of sick days increased. He looked forward to forced retirement with growing eagerness.
>
> He used to live in his own home, but he can't get around as he once did, his savings are almost gone, and he will most likely live out his days in an institution for the aged.
>
> Although his needs are fewer than when he was young, he's becoming a drain on the country's resources; still, after so many years of stress, he feels he deserves a little peace and quiet.
>
> He gets depressed more than he used to, and his sex life is a thing of the

past. Like most people over sixty-five, he's apt to forget things, make foolish remarks, and throw tantrums. He accepts these changes because, after all, this is second childhood, a time for disengagement.*

This is a grim, familiar portrait of old age in the United States. For many elderly persons, it is also a highly inaccurate portrait, if not a total falsification. Many people are poor, lonely, and sick in their old age. Elderly persons have inadequate housing, nutrition, and health care out of all proportion to their numbers. However, the above description is still a blatantly distorted image that contributes to ageism, possibly the biggest problem of old age in our culture.

Ageism is prejudicial discrimination against the elderly merely because they are "old." Like the other "isms," such as sexism or racism, ageism imposes behavioral and attitudinal expectations on a particular minority group, in this case old people, because of society's misinformation about them or fears of them. To psychologists interested in aging, ageism is particularly important insofar as it affects the behavior of old people. Knowledge of the statistics describing the real world of elderly people can counteract ageism. These statistics are presented in this chapter.

**The Aging Population**

Health and long life appear to be a universal goal for most individuals and societies. This goal has come progressively closer to being realized as life expectancy has increased over the last century. Each day five thousand persons reach the age of sixty-five in the United States and become classified as "old." Together they add 1.8 million people to the ranks of the elderly each year. Conversely, each day 3,600 people older than 65 die. They total 1.1 million people a year. The aged population thus shows a net growth of 1,400 people per day or 511,000 people per year (Lowy, 1979).

Mortality is measured by demographers in two different ways: the *crude death rate* is the annual number of deaths in a group per one thousand of the total population, whereas *age-specific death rates* are death rates in specific age groups. For geropsychologists the second measure, which considers age composition, is far better than the first. In less developed countries the infant mortality rate is very high and life expectancy is low, whereas in the Western industrialized countries the reverse is true. This difference in age composition is depicted in Figure 2-1. Bangladesh presents a very different age pyramid from the United States. In Africa the average life expectancy (ALE) is 46 years and 147 persons in 1,000 die before the age of 1, whereas in Europe the ALE is 71 years and only 20 persons in 1,000 die before the age of 1 (McHale et al., 1979).

Crude death rates do not consider the relative placement of ages at risk for death in a particular culture. Crude death rates may be similar in the above examples, but the ages with the highest death rates are broadly disparate. As can be seen in Figure 2-2, the age pyramids in the more developed countries (MDC) and less developed

*Louis Harris & Associates, Inc. *The myth and reality of aging in America.* Washington, D.C.: National Council on the Aging, 1975

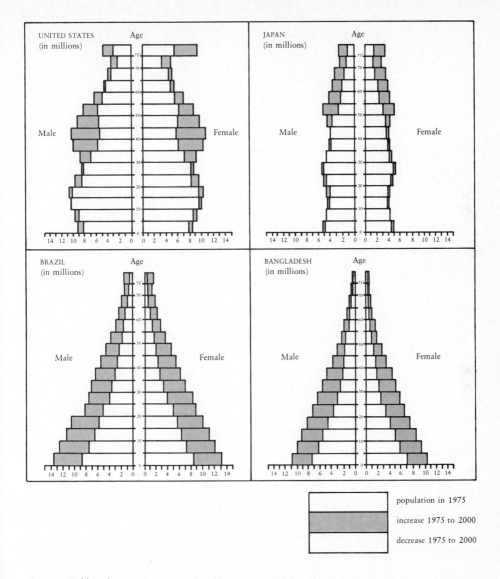

(Source: World Bank projections, 1978 (Brazil, Japan, Bangladesh); U.S. Bureau of the Census (U.S.). Cited in: McHale, M.C., McHale, J., & Streatfield, G.J. *Children in the world.* Washington, D.C.: Population Reference Bureau, 1979, p. 17)

*Figure 2-1  Number of people in United States, Japan, Brazil, and Bangladesh by age and sex in 1975 and 2000*

countries (LDC) are very different. The MDC pyramid is almost a vertical rectangle, indicating similar death rates for all age groups, whereas the LDC graph resembles more typically the traditional pyramid shape. The LDC graph shows the

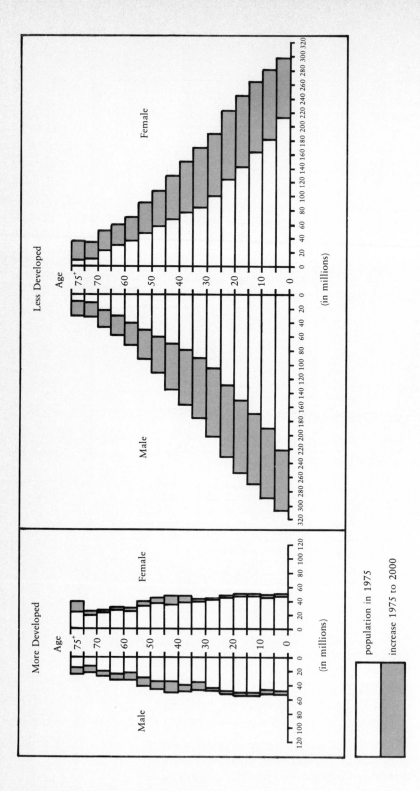

(Source: United Nations Population Division, WP 60. Cited in: McHale, M.C., McHale, J., & Streatfield, G.J. *Children in the world*. Washington, D.C.: Population Reference Bureau, 1979, p. 16)

*Figure 2–2  Number of people in more developed and less developed regions of the world by age and sex in 1975 and 2000*

high infant mortality and comparatively low adult death rates that are typical of the poorer countries. The numbers of people being born and dying in the LDCs and MDCs also differ. Birth rates are higher and the number of survivors to old age lower in the LDCs.

Of fifty million deaths worldwide per year, twenty-five percent are children under the age of one, and fifty percent are children under the age of five. Most of these infant deaths occur in the poor countries of Africa, Asia, and Latin America. Such high death rates for infants proportionally lower the rates for older adults and decrease the number of persons surviving to old age. Death rates similar to those of the LDCs were found in the United States in 1900. As shown in Figure 2-3, the death curve in 1900 in the United States was U-shaped because of the high infant mortality. In contrast, the 1950 curve was more J-shaped and did not accelerate as quickly. This was indicative of declining infant mortality as well as lower death rates for each subsequent age group.

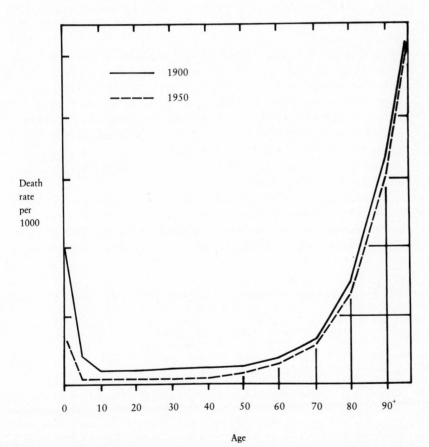

*Figure 2-3   A comparison of death curves for 1900 and 1950*

**Average Life
Expectancy**

As stated, the rapid increase in life expectancy is largely a twentieth century phenomenon. Since 1900, the part of the population older than sixty-five has increased much more rapidly than the rest of the United States population. In 1900, for example, there were only three million people older than sixty-five (approximately 4% of the total population), whereas in 1980 there were approximately twenty-five million people older than sixty-five (11% of the total population). It is expected that in the year 2000 there will be 31.8 million people older than 65, and that in 2030, when the last of the World War II baby boom children reach 65, there will be 55 million old people in our society.

There are seven times as many elderly people in the United States today than there were in 1900. Moreover, the population older than seventy-five years of age has increased by thirty-seven percent and is the fastest growing segment of our society (Cutler & Harootyan, 1975). Clearly, we are an aging society.

ALE is a hypothetical mortality projection based on age-specific death rates for a particular age group per one hundred thousand persons (Wrong, 1977). The actual length of life of the members of the group may vary; ALE is just a projection of the statistically probable number of remaining years for a person of any given age. ALE is not the potential life span of a species; life span is the number of years a species would be capable by heredity of surviving were conditions ideal. Researchers have estimated that the potential life span for humans is 120 to 150 years.

Table 2-1 shows that ALE at birth in the United States has increased approximately twenty-four years since 1900. However, life expectancy at age 65 has increased only 3.3 years in the same time. These developments are due to secular trends and socioeconomic contingencies. Both the number and the percentage of elderly persons have increased for several reasons, though not as a result of an increase in potential life span. Most of the increases in life expectancy have occurred early in the life cycle.

Decreased infant mortality rates have increased the percentage of persons fulfilling their life potential. Immigration has contributed to the number of elderly persons. In 1900 the mean number of immigrants entering the United States per year was 780,000, most of whom were then young. Today the average number of

*Table 2–1   Average life expectancy at birth and at age 65 in the United States, for various years: 1900–2000*

| Age | 1900 | 1939 | 1949 | 1955 | 1959 | 1970 | 1976 | 2000 |
|---|---|---|---|---|---|---|---|---|
| At birth | 47.3 | 63.7 | 68.0 | 69.6 | 69.9 | 70.9 | 73.1 | 74.1 |
| At age 65 | 11.9 | 12.8 | 12.8 | 14.2 | 14.4 | 15.2 | 16.0 | 16.8 |

(Sources: United States Public Health Service. National Center for Health Statistics. *Vital Statistics of the United States: 1970. Vol. II—Mortality*, Part A. Washington, D.C.: U.S. Government Printing Office, 1974, Tables 5–1 and 5–5; Siegel, J.S. Prospective trends in the size and structure of the elderly population, impact of mortality trends and some indications. *Current Population Reports*, 1979, 78)

immigrants per year is 290,000. A decreased birth rate has also increased the percentage of elderly persons in the population (Cutler & Harootyan, 1975). Because these factors have largely run their course, and because all the people who will be old in the next seventy-five years are alive today, some relatively safe projections can be made about maximum percentages of elderly people in the population in the future (barring any unforeseen calamaties).

The percentage of elderly people in the population is expected to be 12.3 percent in the year 2000 and 14.9 percent in the year 2025. The percentage is expected to decline thereafter. There will probably be no further rapid increases in life span until the degenerative diseases of middle and late life are conquered. Mortality rates in the MDCs are already so low that reductions equal in magnitude to those seen early in this century are impossible (Wrong, 1977). It is also suspected that the secular trend toward decreased mortality rates may be peaking and even reversing in the LDCs.

> The fact that the far more rapid mortality declines in underdeveloped countries have resulted from the importation of Western medical techniques not independently developed as part of an overall social and economic modernization raises questions about their permanence. People may be saved by modern medicine from infectious diseases and yet die of starvation. The greatest gains in mortality control in the West were achieved after the birth rate had begun to decline; the achievement of even more rapid gains where habits of high fertility persist and birth rates have been long higher than they were in the preindustrial West intensifies a population pressure that is already a primary cause of the poverty and economic disadvantages of many non-Western areas. Unless these areas can make the transition to low levels of fertility in time, the recurrence of famine and ensuing social and political unrest may not only prevent further declines in mortality, but may even wipe out the gains that have already been made.*

In summary, our current ALE, although still increasing, is drastically decreasing its rate of ascent.

At all ages men have a higher mortality rate than women. More men are born than women, but from birth on women have a higher survival rate (Table 2-2). The reasons for this are not certain. Some researchers speculate that the X chromosome is larger than the Y chromosome, which determines male gender. It is assumed that the extra genetic material present in the X chromosome provides some protection for females; for example, estrogen is thought to protect against coronary heart disease. It has been suggested that an immunity factor activated prenatally is

**Sex Differences in Life Expectancy**

*Wrong, D.H. *Population and society* (4th ed.). New York: Random House, Inc., 1977, pp. 45-46. Copyright © 1977 by Random House, Inc.

Table 2-2   *Sex ratios by age (males per 100 females)*

| Age group | Males |
|-----------|-------|
| Conception | 140 |
| Birth | 105 |
| 18 yrs. | 100 |
| 25–44 yrs. | 95 |
| 45–64 yrs. | 92 |
| 65+ yrs. | 69 |
| 65–74 yrs. | 74 |
| 75+ yrs. | 64 |
| 85+ yrs. | 48 |

(Adapted from: U.S. Bureau of the Census. *Census of population: Characteristics of the population.* Washington, D.C.: U.S. Government Printing Office, selected years)

directed against the Y chromosome, which is foreign to the mother's genetic make-up. Some sociologists have implicated stress in the higher mortality rates in males than females. However, these explanations are all speculative, and the exact cause of the differential life expectancy is unknown (Cutler & Harootyan, 1975).

Life expectancy statistics have not always favored females. In 1900, for example, for every one hundred men aged sixty-five there were only ninety-eight women. Between 1930 and 1950 the rates shifted to favor female survival, and it is projected that in the year 2000 there will be sixty-seven men for every one hundred women over sixty-five (Siegel, 1979). This trend is partially due to decreased maternal mortality and male occupational differences. However, it also relates to different morbidity, or illness, rates for males and females.

A final part of this picture, consequently, is to look more carefully at sex ratios in the context of mortality data. If . . . men are dying at a faster rate than women, then a combination of mortality rates and sex ratios will be able to describe those causes of death most responsible for those differences. Although war deaths have contributed to the proportionately low numbers of surviving men in older age groups, the sharp decline in the sex ratio since 1930 has been largely due to the increase in male deaths caused by the degenerative diseases. Men have suffered more from the "major killers" during the last four decades. By 1969 the male death rate for heart disease, cancer and other causes was much higher than for females.[*]

Sex ratio differences in cause of death are presented graphically in Table 2-3. As may be seen, more deaths are caused by cerebrovascular disease and arteriosclerosis

[*]Cutler, N.E., & Harootyan, R.A. Demography of the aged. In D.S. Woodrull & J.E. Birren (Eds.), *Aging: Scientific perspectives and social issues.* New York: Van Nostrand Reinhold, 1975, p. 52

*Table 2-3   Sex ratio by cause of death in the United States: 1969 (male to female ratio)*

| Cause of death | Ratio (male to female) |
| --- | --- |
| All causes | 1.350 |
| Diseases of the heart | 1.396 |
| Cerebrovascular disease (stroke) | 0.876 |
| Malignant neoplasms (cancer) | 1.259 |
| Influenza and pneumonia | 1.302 |
| Bronchitis, emphysema, and asthma | 3.984 |
| Arteriosclerosis | 0.807 |
| Accidents (all types) | 2.377 |

(Adapted from: United States Public Health Service, National Center for Health Statistics. *Vital statistics of the United States: 1969. Volume II—Mortality*, Part A. Washington, D.C.: U.S. Government Printing Office, 1974, Table 1–8)

*Elderly women outnumber elderly men.*

in women than in men. However, men have significantly higher death rates for all types of accidents and all other diseases, especially respiratory diseases, for which their rate is four times higher than that of women.

The mortality rate differential is of course reflected in the increased life expectancy of women. The ALE for children born in 1975 is 77.2 years for females and 69.4 years for males. A female born in 1971 can expect to outlive a male born in the same year by approximately seven years. A woman now aged sixty-five can expect to live another sixteen years, whereas a man can expect to live only another thirteen years. One result of these gender differences in life expectancy and mortality, in addition to the tendency of men in our society to marry younger women, is that the majority of women older than sixty-five are widowed, and conversely, that the majority of men older than sixty-five are married.

These statistics have profound implications for service delivery, program design, and crisis intervention for the elderly. Most elderly program recipients or consumers are and will continue to be women, the real income of whom is often very low. Given that income level is correlated with mental and physical health, elderly women are especially at risk of developing health problems.

**Minority Elderly**

In general, minority status in our society is associated with decreased life expectancy, increased mortality at all ages, and increased morbidity. One cause of these demographic trends is discrimination, which denies minority group members access to health services. Poverty is also a factor. Socioeconomic deprivation often leads to poor nutrition, which in turn leads to increased disease and decreased productivity, which in turn makes escape from poverty increas-

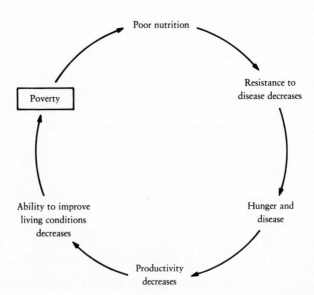

*Figure 2–4  The cycle of poverty*

ingly difficult. This cycle is presented in Figure 2-4. Inadequate housing, poor
water sanitation, and unsanitary sewage disposal, all associated with poverty,
increase infant mortality rates and lower life expectancy among the poor.
Minority group members are frequently found in low socioeconomic groups, so
these factors may well contribute to their decreased life expectancy.

Black Americans, Mexican Americans, and American Indians constitute the
largest minority groups in our society; they are considered below.

### American Blacks

Only 7.8 percent of all American blacks are over 65 years of age, compared to 11
percent of the total United States population. The ALE for blacks, 60.1 years,
shows a slight upward trend. A black male born in 1975 can expect to live to be
63.6 years old; a black female born in 1975 can expect to live to be 72.3 years old.
However, a larger percentage of blacks than of whites live to be older than seventy
once they reach sixty-five. Given the low ALE of blacks, which is largely due to
poverty and its concomitants, blacks who live beyond the age of seventy are strong
survivors.

The NCOA has stated that elderly blacks are often believed to be in "triple
jeopardy" in that they are poor, black, and old. Research has found that the triple
jeopardy concept may not apply in all cases (Jackson & Wood, 1976). It appears
that there is no difference between black and white aged persons regarding

*For a black person to live
beyond seventy requires a
strong constitution. Black
elderly are, in fact, the
strongest of survivors.*

employment, unemployment, and retirement. However, this is not a positive statement. To be old is to lose one's connection with the work force for either race. In this respect ageism does not penalize one race more than another.

The double jeopardy of being black and poor does produce some negative effects and racial differences in patterns of aging. As shown in Table 2-4, the median income of aged blacks is approximately half the median income of aged whites. Over half of all elderly blacks had incomes below $3,000 in 1973, as compared to less than one fourth of aged whites surveyed. It is probable that these percentages have not changed appreciably since that time. Such low incomes reflect a lifetime of relative deprivation, which means that elderly blacks as a group are less likely than elderly whites to have savings, own their own homes, or be able to secure adequate health care. It is clear that any improvement in the economic condition of elderly blacks, and of the aged in general, would lead to an improvement in general quality of life.

As may be seen in Table 2-5, lack of money is the most serious concern of aged blacks. Except for loneliness, the other serious problems are all clearly influenced by poverty. The causes of loneliness are less obvious, but this problem may also be affected by poverty in that, with decreased health and income, mobility declines and isolation increases.

Table 2–4   1973 Personal income for public 65 and over†

| Income | Percentage of public 65 and over | Percent white | Percent black |
|---|---|---|---|
| Under $1000 | 3 | 2 | 7 |
| $1000 to $2999 | 24 | 21 | 50 |
| $3000 to $4999 | 29 | 29 | 24 |
| $5000 to $6999 | 14 | 15 | 8 |
| $7000 to $9999 | 14 | 15 | 4 |
| $10,000 to $14,999 | 9 | 9 | 3 |
| $15,000 to $19,999 | 3 | 3 | — |
| $20,000 to $24,999 | 1 | 1 | * |
| $25,000+ | 1 | 1 | * |
| Not sure/refused | 24 | 24 | 22 |
| Median income in thousands | $4.5 | $4.6 | $2.6 |

(Adapted from: Harris poll/NCOA, 1976, selected tables)
*Less than 0.5%.
†Income for people 65 and over who are heads of household and their spouses is total household income. Income for people 65 and over who are not heads, nor spouses of heads, includes only the income that is available to them and their spouses personally to spend and not income that belongs to other members of the household.

Table 2–5    Problems of persons over 65

| Problem | Blacks (%) | Whites (%) |
|---|---|---|
| Not enough money | 75 | 36 |
| Fear of crime | 65 | 46 |
| Poor health | 70 | 48 |
| Not enough education | 56 | 22 |
| Not enough job opportunity | 28 | 10 |
| Loneliness | 45 | 27 |
| Poor housing | 37 | 7 |
| Not enough medical care | 47 | 21 |
| Not enough clothes | 27 | 5 |
| Not enough to do | 33 | 15 |
| Not feeling needed | 28 | 18 |
| Not enough friends | 22 | 14 |

(Adapted from: Jackson, M., & Wood, J.L. *Aging in America: Implications for the black aged.* Washington, D.C.: National Council on the Aging, Inc., 1976, p. 28)

Loneliness in the black aged may also reflect the reinforcement social interaction provides for people unable to afford other entertainment. A high percentage of elderly blacks are lonely; however, as may be seen in Table 2-6, loneliness is not a particularly salient negative factor for aged blacks.

There is consensus about what constitute the worst features of being old for blacks and whites. Illness, physical deterioration, slowing down, and financial difficulties are all perceived as problems by both blacks and whites. Blacks are more

Table 2–6    The worst things about being 65 and over by race

| Problem | Blacks (%) | Whites (%) |
|---|---|---|
| Poor health | 27 | 34 |
| Slowed down | 20 | 21 |
| Financial problems | 16 | 13 |
| Loneliness | 8 | 10 |
| Being neglected | 5 | 5 |
| Forced to retire | 14 | 8 |
| Fear of death | 2 | 6 |
| Physical deterioration | 6 | 9 |

(Adapted from: Jackson, M., & Wood, J.L. *Aging in America: Implications for the black aged.* Washington, D.C.: National Council on the Aging, Inc., 1976, p. 27)

likely to be upset by retirement—possibly because of its negative financial impact—and less fearful of death than whites. However, the perceived quality of life for aged blacks and whites is not appreciably different. In conclusion, it appears that

> Poverty has negatively influenced their lives, and it should be dealt with as such, but it has not had the devastating, all-determining effect as the double-jeopardy hypothesis implies . . . The Black aged have problems— more so than many other groups in American society. Yet it is also a group that exhibits a variety of strengths, strengths surely needed as its members continue to face barriers of race and age.*

### Mexican Americans

The statistics on Mexican American aging are less accurate than those available for American blacks. However, it appears that similar detrimental effects of minority status exist for Mexican Americans, only four percent of whom are believed to be older than sixty-five. The ALE estimated for Mexican Americans in Colorado is 56.7 years, indicating that life expectancy for Mexican Americans is lower than for either blacks or whites.

### American Indians

In 1980 there were 1.4 million American Indians. Despite more than a century of governmental control and supervision, we have only estimates of the age stratification of American Indians. It is currently estimated that approximately six percent of Indians survive to the age of sixty-five and that life expectancy is between forty-four and forty-six years. The 1971 White House Conference on Aging estimated that sixty-three percent of elderly Indians have inadequate heat and that twenty-one percent have no electricity. Poverty is one of the biggest factors in the high mortality rate of American Indians. The poorest people in the land, over half of all families have incomes below $2000 per year.

Nutrition, transportation, housing, and health care are substandard on many reservations. Infant and maternal mortality are also high. All of these factors combine to produce a seriously depressed quality of life and life expectancy for American Indians.

**Residence**

Although elderly people are found in all geographic locations in our country, they are mostly concentrated in just a few areas. Five states, California, Illinois, New York, Pennsylvania, and Texas, each have more than one million elderly persons, a

---

*Jackson, M., & Wood, J.L. *Aging in America: Implications for the black aged.* Washington, D.C.: National Council on the Aging, Inc., 1976, pp. 37-38

*Most elderly persons live in family settings; 11.4 million are married and live at home with their spouses.*

total of approximately one third of the United States population of persons over sixty-five. New York City alone has over one million elderly persons. Sixty percent of all elderly blacks live in the South. Most elderly persons live in the inner cities, some live in rural areas, and few live in suburban areas.

More than twelve percent of the populations of Arkansas, Iowa, Nebraska, South Dakota, Kansas, and Missouri is made up of elderly people, and approximately seventeen percent of the populace of Florida is older than sixty-five. Aside from Florida, these states are highly rural and agricultural. There has long been a trend for younger people in such areas to migrate to cities for jobs, leaving a high proportion of elderly persons behind. Fixed income and economics have made it difficult for elderly persons to make such migrations, either from rural areas to the cities or from the inner cities to the suburbs.

Most elderly persons live in family settings. At any given time ninety-five percent, approximately 21.3 million, of all persons older than sixty-five are living in their own homes, and this percentage has been increasing since 1965. Of this number 5.8 million (30%) live alone, 11.4 million are married and live with their spouses, and 4.1 million live with relatives or nonrelatives in a family setting. There are sex differences in these living arrangements based on differences in ALE. For example, seventy-seven percent of all old men are married and living with their wives, whereas only thirty-eight percent of old women are married and living with their spouses. Approximately two and a half times more elderly women live alone than elderly men.

Since ninety-five percent of all the elderly live in family settings, only five percent of the population over sixty-five live in institutions. This number is deceptive, however; nineteen percent of people older than eighty-five live in institutions. Furthermore, if old people who spend any time in institutions —nursing homes, mental hospitals, or homes for the aged—are included, the number goes up to twenty-five percent. Nevertheless, only fifteen percent of the elderly die in institutions. The number of elderly living in a family situation decreases as age increases for several reasons. Health status worsens with age, spouses die and leave no one to care for the remaining partner, and the cost of home care increases as health status declines.

## Income

In 1977 about one in seven persons sixty-five years old and over (3.2 million persons) had incomes below the poverty level. Although the total number of poor people in the United States has not changed much since 1970, the number of elderly poor has dropped by about 1.5 million, or from one fourth of that age group in 1970 to about one seventh in 1977. This is partially due to changes in the social security system, additional health care benefits, and pension plans (U.S. Department of Commerce, 1979a, 1979b).

However, although only twenty percent of the elderly are poor or near poor, many experience some financial difficulty. Direct income is reduced after retirement. The perceived loss of many who used to have substantial salaries may be greater than that of persons who have always been poor. In 1979 the median income was $16,000 per year for all United States families but $9,000 for families over sixty-five. The 1979 average yearly income was approximately $6,000 for men and $4,000 for women. Maintaining a household is particularly difficult for elderly women, who are frequently alone and whose income is often marginal.

In general, inflation has left people on fixed incomes hard-pressed financially. Biannual cost of living increases tied to consumer price indices have helped alleviate some of these financial concerns. Medical expenses, however, are still increasing and cutting into the budgets of the elderly even with Medicare and Medicaid. Both prescription and over-the-counter drugs produce large, and often unnecessary, monetary outlays. Unless an elderly person is at the poverty level and qualifies for Medicaid, Medicare covers only partial medical costs. Moreover, many physicians and hospitals want patients to pay them directly and then seek reimbursement from the insurer. This leads many old people to avoid seeking medical help.

It is generally harder for elderly people than for young people to save money. A young person may walk to work or take the bus, but an old person may find this difficult. Walking or taking public transportation makes an old person vulnerable to falls, crime, and other traumas. Young people may save money by lowering the heat in their homes. Old people's bodies do not regulate temperature as well and are more susceptible to hypothermia, a condition of low body temperature that can lead to death. Old people find it difficult to borrow money, should the need arise. It is also hard for old persons desiring employment to find even part-time work.

In summary, although the majority of old people in our society are not legally poor, many of them do have financial difficulties. Furthermore, if perceived as severe, economic constraints may affect mental and physical health as well as mobility and overall quality of life.

**Education**

Closely associated with an age group's relative socioeconomic status is the level of education attained by its members. Lack of education is correlated with low-paying jobs and low lifetime earnings. Table 2-7 shows the years of school completed by persons sixty-five years of age and over by race, sex, and Spanish origin. Elderly blacks are less likely to have completed as much education as whites of the same age. Both blacks and whites aged sixty-five and over also have generally completed less formal education than younger age groups.

According to general census data, approximately ten percent of the total population above sixty-five years of age has had less than five years of formal education and is therefore functionally illiterate. Forty-eight percent of the elderly have completed eight years or less of schooling. Only twenty percent of the elderly have completed high school. Approximately fifteen percent have had a college-level education.

*Table 2-7    Years of school completed by persons 65 and over by race, Spanish origin, and sex: March, 1978\**

| Years of school completed | All races | | White | | Black | | Spanish origin | |
|---|---|---|---|---|---|---|---|---|
| | Male | Female | Male | Female | Male | Female | Male | Female |
| | 9,170 | 13,298 | 8,249 | 12,067 | 819 | 1,111 | 233 | 286 |
| *Elementary* | | | | | | | | |
| Less than 5 yrs | 989 (10.8%) | 1,163 ( 8.7%) | 649 ( 7.9%) | 818 ( 6.8%) | 307 (37.5%) | 305 (27.5%) | 96 (41.2%) | 136 (47.6%) |
| 5–7 yrs | 1,505 (16.4%) | 1,838 (13.8%) | 1,264 (15.3%) | 1,524 (12.6%) | 215 (26.3%) | 289 (26.0%) | 40 (17.2%) | 59 (20.6%) |
| 8 yrs | 1,959 (21.4%) | 2,867 (21.6%) | 1,861 (22.6%) | 2,697 (22.4%) | 78 ( 9.5%) | 158 (14.2%) | 27 (11.6%) | 27 ( 9.4%) |
| *High school* | | | | | | | | |
| 1–3 yrs | 1,371 (15.0%) | 2,219 (16.7%) | 1,280 (15.5%) | 2,027 (16.8%) | 84 (10.3%) | 179 (16.1%) | 21 ( 9.0%) | 20 ( 7.0%) |
| 4 yrs | 1,746 (19.0%) | 3,118 (23.4%) | 1,549 (20.0%) | 2,980 (24.7%) | 82 (10.0%) | 113 (10.2%) | 26 (11.2%) | 26 ( 9.1%) |
| *College* | | | | | | | | |
| 1–3 yrs | 740 ( 8.1%) | 1,166 ( 8.8%) | 707 ( 8.6%) | 1,126 ( 9.3%) | 33 ( 4.0%) | 36 ( 3.2%) | 7 ( 3.0%) | 8 ( 2.8%) |
| 4 yrs or more | 859 ( 9.4%) | 926 ( 7.0%) | 838 (10.2%) | 894 ( 7.4%) | 21 ( 2.6%) | 30 ( 2.7%) | 15 ( 6.4%) | 9 ( 3.1%) |

(Source: U.S. Department of Commerce, Bureau of Census, Current Population Survey data)

*Noninstitutionalized population in thousands. N.B. Persons of Spanish origin may be of any race.

This low level of education affects the quality of life of old persons. There may be a serious information gap between them and their younger children and grandchildren. They may not understand or be able to read about certain health care advances or public health programs. Their real earnings have suffered, and they are not competitive in the job market. It is probable that the old age of today's better educated youth will be considerably different from that of their forefathers.

**Health Demographics**

The demographics of health in the United States can be encapsulated in the following statements:

Americans are living longer today than at any other time in our history.
The elderly as a group are more likely than young persons to suffer from chronic, disabling conditions. However, the majority of elderly persons lead active lives and remain in their own households.

Health status varies as widely in old age as at any other time in the life cycle. Granted, old people are more likely than young people to have health problems, and a minor problem quickly alleviated in youth may persist in old age. However, the extent of individual differences in patterns of aging and disease increases as one moves through the life cycle (USDHEW, 1977). Individual differences become the rule rather than the exception in old age.

Interest in the health status of elderly adults has grown in recent years because of their rapid increase in absolute number and proportion of the population. Interest has also grown because of increased utilization of health services by the elderly. Medical costs have been escalating, and public funds are paying for a growing proportion of these costs for the elderly. It is important for us to be aware of the health needs and status of the elderly if we are to meet their stated needs and adequately assess future health needs.

### Causes of Death

In 1975 the death rate in the United States was 8.9 deaths per 1,000, the lowest ever recorded in this country. This figure was down almost three percent from 1974. In this same year the age-adjusted death rate for men was 1.8 times that for women, and the death rate for nonwhites was 1.4 times that for whites. Three fourths of the deaths in 1975 were caused by coronary heart disease, which accounted for forty-four percent; cancer, which accounted for eighteen percent; and cerebrovascular disease, or strokes, which accounted for thirteen percent. The death rates for death from coronary heart disease and cerebrovascular disease have been decreasing while the number of cancer deaths has been increasing. A substantial decrease in deaths from coronary heart disease alone accounted for fifty-five percent of the decline in mortality rate from 1950 to 1975 and for sixty-one percent of the decline from 1965 to 1975 (USDHEW, 1977). The importance of these three degenerative diseases to mortality is demonstrated by the following:

*Medical costs have been escalating, and public funds are paying for a growing proportion of these costs for the elderly.*

Given current death rates in the United States . . . the elimination of tuberculosis would yield a gain of only 0.1 years in life expectancy at birth and even less at age 65. However, if the major cardiovascular-renal diseases (all diseases of the heart arteries and strokes) were completely eradicated today, life expectancy at birth would increase by 10.9 years and by 10.0 years at age 65! In heart disease alone the corresponding gains would be 5.9 and 4.9 years respectively.*

The life-time probabilities of a person dying from these diseases further emphasize their importance as causes of death. A person born in 1975 has a sixty-one percent probability of dying from cardiovascular disease and a fifteen percent probability of dying from cancer. Because these diseases are degenerative and have a slow course, deaths due to them are concentrated in the oldest age groups. Thus, a high proportion of deaths due to these diseases in the elderly are continuations of trends begun much earlier.

Age differences in causes of death are depicted in Table 2-8. Coronary heart disease and cancer account for a high proportion of deaths beginning at age 35, and

*Cutler, N.E., & Harootyan, R.A. Demography of the aged. In D.S. Woodruff & J.E. Birren (Eds.), *Aging: Scientific perspectives and social issues.* New York: Van Nostrand Reinhold, 1975, pp. 42-43

*Table 2–8    Age differences in major causes of death*

*Childhood and early adulthood*
1. Accidents, homicides, suicides
2. Cancer

*Ages 35–44*
1. Accidents, etc.
2. Coronary heart disease
3. Cancer

*Ages 45–54*
1. Coronary heart disease
2. Cancer
3. Accidents, etc.

*Ages 55–64*
1. Coronary heart disease (38% of deaths in this age group)
2. Cancer (29%)
3. Cerebrovascular disease (6%)
4. Accidents, etc.

*Ages 65+*
1. Coronary heart disease (44% of deaths in this age group)
2. Cancer (18%)
3. Cerebrovascular disease (13%)

(Adapted from: USDHEW. *Health United States 1976–1977.*
Washington, D.C.: Public Health Service, 1977)

cancer is a major cause of childhood deaths as well. Cerebrovascular disease joins the top three in the fifth decade of life, and this pattern persists unchanged into old age. Percentages of deaths for the diseases shift, indicating the deaths of susceptible populations and the time course necessary for significant changes of a degenerative nature to occur. It is clear that although the major degenerative diseases may not manifest serious symptoms until old age, prevention efforts should be directed at early and middle-aged adults.

### Disability

Morbidity and disability data have not been available for as many years as mortality data. For example, data on the incidence and prevalence of illness among institutionalized elderly have existed only since 1965. Data such as these, however, have provided knowledge about the effects other than death of the major degenerative diseases.

Short-term disability is measured by the number of days during the year people have had to modify their usual behavior because of illness. There are three levels of short-term disability: days of restricted activity, days in bed, and days lost from work. In 1965 workers older than sixty-five lost eight workdays owing to illness. In 1975 elderly workers lost only four workdays. During this same decade, the proportion of elderly workers in the work force decreased from sixteen to twelve percent. The decreased disability could mean that healthier people continued to work while those in poor health retired earlier as retirement benefits improved.

Long-term disability, i.e., continued limitations caused by chronic diseases, increased from forty-two percent in 1965 to forty-seven percent in 1975. However, age-specific disability rates did not change. The increase appears to be due to a tremendous upsurge in the number of people older than seventy-five, the group most likely to suffer from multiple chronic disorders. The limitations of mobility due to chronic disease remained unchanged from 1965 to 1975; twenty percent of the elderly suffered from some chronic disease impairment leading to long-term disability. These data are in agreement with the assessment of the National Health Survey:

> It has been suggested that prolonging the lives of older people will produce a dependent, badly impaired elderly population. However, death rates for people 65 years of age and over certainly declined from 1965 to 1975, but the limited data available do not indicate any increase in disability among noninstitutionalized elderly people.*

As stated, most deaths and disability among the elderly are caused by disease conditions that have existed for many years or are due to long-term personal habits or environmental conditions. Medical care for the elderly may ameliorate these symptoms, but prevention must begin early in adult life.

### Chronic Conditions

In 1975 four percent of all people sixty-five and older were in long-term care facilities or institutions. Generally, the population of long-term care institutions is older than the population of elderly living in the community; in 1975 eighty-three percent of institutionalized adults were older than seventy-five, whereas only thirty-eight percent of the noninstitutionalized elderly were this old. The elderly nursing home resident usually has multiple chronic conditions and functional impairments. Of nursing home residents in 1975, almost two thirds were classified as senile, thirty-six percent had coronary heart disease, and fourteen percent had diabetes. Orthopedic problems were commonplace. About one third were bedfast or chairfast, and about one third were incontinent. Sensory impairments were also very common, with visual and auditory problems afflicting approximately half of all nursing home residents.

*USDHEW. *Health United States 1976–1977*. Washington, D.C.: Public Health Service, 1977, p. 8

The most common primary diagnoses among institutionalized elderly persons in 1975 were hardening of the arteries, senility, stroke, and mental disorders. Symptoms of all of these may give rise to severe functional impairments. Although the same disorders were found among community-living elderly, the incidence of multiple chronic conditions was considerably lower in this group. Some frequently reported chronic conditions for community-living elderly in 1975 were arthritis, vision and hearing impairments, heart conditions, and hypertension. Only fourteen percent of noninstitutionalized elderly were not aware of having any chronic disease. However, laboratory findings have indicated significant pathology for many elderly people who are not aware of having diabetes, hypertensive heart disease, or coronary heart disease. The prevalence of some chronic diseases may thus be higher than our statistics indicate (USDHEW, 1977).

Regardless of the actual numbers, a prevalence of chronic conditions does not necessarily mean a prevalence of disabling conditions. The impact of chronic disease varies widely, as will be discussed in Chapter 5.

### Mental Health

Mental and emotional illness escalates with age, especially in persons with depressive disorders. Organic (physically based) disorders account for about twenty-five percent of new admittances of elderly persons to mental hospitals. Mental health will be considered in greater detail in Chapter 10.

Suicide, a problem associated with both depression and poor health, is one of the ten leading causes of death among the elderly. In 1977 the suicide rate for persons sixty-five and older was twice that for persons twenty-four and younger. The elderly accounted for twenty-five percent of all suicides carried out in the 1970s. These numbers indicate that the elderly are significantly overrepresented in the ranks of suicides. Furthermore, these statistics may underestimate the problem, since questionable cases and seeming accidents are not included in the numbers.

There are significant gender differences in age at suicide. The peak age for women is between forty-five and fifty-four, an age associated with menopause, the "empty nest syndrome," and midlife crisis. The peak age for black males in 1978 was between twenty-four and thirty-four. In contrast, the number of suicides for white men rises steadily with age, the highest percentage occurring among those older than eighty-five. Rolelessness following retirement, death of a spouse, and overall poor health probably contribute to the high rates among white men over sixty-five.

### Self-Assessment of Health

Good health for anyone of any age does not necessarily mean the complete absence of impairments or disease but only that any disorders that exist do not interfere with physical or social functioning. Illness is both a social and a physical phenomenon. There are great individual differences in the effects of disease on functioning. An individual's self-assessment of health may be as important as that person's actual medical status in predicting general emotional state and behavior.

The prevalence among the aged of chronic conditions and impairments may give the impression that most elderly persons view themselves as being in poor health and disabled. This is not the case. The majority consider themselves in good health compared to people their own age (Table 2-9). Although the number of people believing themselves to be in good or excellent health is lowest for those older than sixty-five, it is still almost seventy percent.

Self-assessment of health by elderly people corresponds to medical examination results in about seventy percent of the cases (USDHEW, 1977). It also correlates highly with other measures of health status and utilization of health services. People who rate themselves as in poor health are more likely to suffer from activity-limiting chronic conditions and relatively frequent acute conditions or disability days than persons who rate their health as excellent. The former also utilize more medical services than the latter (USDHEW, 1977).

**Summary**

The prevalence of chronic conditions and the duration of acute conditions increase with age, especially after the age of seventy-five. Stress due to changing life conditions such as retirement, inability to live independently, or the death of family members or friends may also occur more frequently with age. Nevertheless, the vast majority of old persons lead full, satisfying lives and are functioning members of their communities.

It is likely that the experience of old age will improve after the year 2000. Educational level is increasing and pensions are mandatory, which should make income levels higher. Although certain social and economic problems are likely to be precipitated by age changes in our population structure, tomorrow's elderly will probably be able to deal with these difficulties.

Past increases in ALE at birth appear to have leveled off and may begin to reverse themselves in the future (Siegel, 1979). Any further increases in ALE at birth and at

*Table 2-9  Self-assessment of health according to age\**

| Age | Level of health | | | |
| | Excellent | Good | Fair | Poor |
|---|---|---|---|---|
| All ages | 48.6 | 38.4 | 9.7 | 2.8 |
| Under 15 yrs. | 59.9 | 35.3 | 3.7 | 0.4 |
| 15–44 yrs. | 52.5 | 38.2 | 7.3 | 1.4 |
| 45–64 yrs. | 35.9 | 41.5 | 16.1 | 5.9 |
| 65 yrs. & over | 28.6 | 40.3 | 21.5 | 8.6 |

(Source: Division of Health Interview Statistics, National Center for Health Statistics: Data from Health Interview Survey. Cited in: USDHEW. *Health United States 1976–1977*. Washington, D.C.: Public Health Service, 1977)

\*Data are based on household interviews of a sample of the civilian noninstitutionalized population.

*Although some elderly are poor and lonely. . .*

age sixty-five will undoubtedly occur among males, decreasing the divergence between males and females. The current large difference is a function of both the biological advantage of women and the life-styles, roles, and personal habits of the sexes. However,

> even if men are afforded improved environmental "opportunities" or the environmental circumstances for females become more prejudicial to their health, a substantial difference in favor of women is expected to continue for several decades. (Siegel, 1979)

Other potential gains in ALE may be achieved by minority group members. This could occur through a decrease in the birth rates of these groups, a lowering of infant mortality, and the provision of improved health care, housing, and social services for minority group members of all ages. Like the male-female divergence, however, differences in life expectancy between minority groups and whites are unlikely to be resolved in the near future. Significant changes will have to occur in the number of births as well as deaths in minority groups for the ALE of minorities to approximate that of whites in the United States.

*. . . this is a highly inaccurate portrait of many old persons in the United States.*

Statistics are not mere black marks on white paper. They describe the lives and realities of people and events. To a large extent the problems associated with the aging of our population reflect the processes of modernization, defined by historians as a fundamental transformation of Western civilization (and American civilization) begun during the eighteenth century. Key elements of this transformation are the industrialization, technological innovations, bureaucratization, professionalism, urbanization, and immigration found in Western cultures (Achenbaum, 1983).

Demographically, modernization has involved a decreased birth rate as successive cohorts of American women have consciously limited the number of children they have; increased ALE at birth; the aging of the population, especially in recent decades; and changes in the family's allocation of power, resources, and production responsibilities (Achenbaum, 1983). Modernization's social and demographic changes have been associated with a growing negative image of elderly persons as pathological, useless, and obsolete. This negativity has largely been a result of the growing number and percentage of old people since 1920 (Achenbaum, 1983).

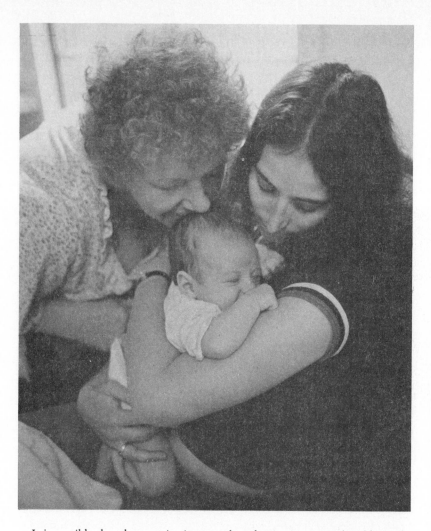

*Different generations age
differently.*

It is possible that the negative impact of modernization upon the old may be counteracted as statistics that are positive in nature, such as those presented in this chapter, become available and are disseminated to the public. A return to more traditional social values, always a persistent undertone in the United States (Achenbaum, 1983), may reaffirm the value of old people as repositories of knowledge of traditions and special skills.

In the final analysis, demographic data provide information that allows us to better design programs or interventions that may improve the utility and quality of life of various groups of people, including the elderly. Demographics does not cause the occurrence of such events as we have been describing. It merely describes people, things, and events and enumerates them for researchers and students to use.

*What sorts of factors lead us to seek the key to the aging process?*

*What factors tend to increase longevity in humans? Are these obtainable in our modern industrial society?*

*Which of the theories of biological aging best explains the influence of psychosocial factors on biological aging processes?*

*Why have there been difficulties with theories of aging, whether biological, psychological, or sociological?*

*Would a world in which the processes of aging were stopped and/or death were eliminated be a totally positive place?*

*Why do we study the processes of aging?*

---

HUMANS have always been intrigued by the process of aging and the possibility of controlling it and perhaps even of eliminating death. Despite centuries of profound human concern, however, aging remains poorly understood yet excessively theorized about.

Some biologists claim that the asymptomatic decline associated with aging is the result of integrated familiar disease activities that are simply unrecognized. Such a view might be compared to the prescientific belief that aging was disease. Other biologists feel that, since the incidence of chronic disease begins to accelerate radically in the fourth decade of life, some irreversible time-dependent process predisposes the organism to disease and multisystem deterioration. In this case, aging is not disease but is caused by an unknown factor producing both disease and decrement. The validity of these alternatives has yet to be determined by contemporary medical science (Fries & Crapo, 1981).

Psychological theories of aging present equally diverse viewpoints. According to Freud, personality is established in childhood and shows mainly negative directional changes in old age. Erikson postulated the growth of personality throughout the entire life span. Cumming and Henry said that successful aging is typified by disengagement from roles and society, and Maddox that activity is the key element of prolongevity.

Although control of the negative aspects of disease and deterioration is a rational goal of science, the utility and ethics of controlling the natural, primary aging process are difficult issues. In a world in which resources are limited and declining, the limitless extension of our life cycle becomes at least problematic. Why then should we research and theorize about the nature of aging? Because, like the mountain, it is there? Or should our exploration of the processes of aging start with a question of value, such as "Can we improve the quality of life in the life span allotted each of us?" This is a question everyone interested in aging must answer, but only after careful consideration of the implications of research goals for the individual, his society, and the world in which all must live. In the study of aging, as in many pragmatic research areas, the scientist may not stay forever in his ivory tower without impunity; if he does, he, like Faust, may suddenly find that his research controls him rather than he it.

This chapter considers questions relating to theories of aging. Theories are derived from at least two sources. First, a theory reflects the philosophical beliefs of the theorist as derived from personal experiences and the *Zeitgeist* of the sociohistorical milieu. Second, a theory is based at least partially on the existence of observable events, i.e., events that lend themselves to quantification, exploration, and prediction. This chapter begins with a discussion of the phenomena of longevity and long-lived peoples, upon which theories of aging have been based. The nature of theories—what they are used for and what makes a good one—is considered next. The theories themselves are then addressed, beginning with the biological factors assumed to influence longevity and concluding with the psychosocial factors influencing the expression of the biological substrate. Finally research difficulties associated with testing the validity of theories are discussed. The implications of longevity for human social existence are also explored.

## Long-Lived Peoples

Every society has among its members people considered to be "old." In the past such individuals may have been few in number; however, they still caused questions about longevity to be asked. Such long-lived persons may also have caused envy in people who were afraid of death and the physical and mental decrements they believed preceded it. Attempts to avoid old age have led to fraud, pseudoscientific research, and outright quackery. A good example of such research distortion may be found in the study of centenarians, people who live to be older than one hundred.

### The Centenarians

The 1980 census revealed that people over one hundred years of age constitute the most rapidly growing segment of our population. In 1970 alone there were 106,000 Americans over one hundred years of age. Such individuals are broadly scattered between the boundaries of our nation—some in cities, some in rural areas, some in the mountains of West Virginia, and some in nursing homes in Buffalo, New York, and other large cities. However, there are areas of the world in which centenarians have been believed to cluster in very large numbers.

Centenarians have frequently been seized upon for study and in many cases have been used to advertise products a manufacturer hopes to associate with longevity; one yogurt company used elderly Russian Cossacks to advertise its product. In all cases the studies and marketing methods used have emphasized specific factors present in the population and overlooked the complex interaction of variables necessary to produce true prolongation of life.

Media studies in the late 1960s focused on three groups of people among whom centenarians were an abnormally high percentage: the natives of Vilcabamba,

*Every society has among its members people considered to be "old."*

Ecuador; the Hunzukuts of the Karakoram Range in Kashmir, which is on the border of India and China not far from the mythical Shangri-la; and the Abkhazians of the Republic of Georgia of the U.S.S.R. (Busse & Blazer, 1980). Initial reports of the ages and numbers of centenarians, although greatly exaggerated, were seized upon by many as a great scientific find. Claims of vodka, yogurt, and vegetable protein as "miracle drugs" to prolong life surfaced at that time and continue to be part of longevity's folklore.

In reality the advanced ages of people were fabricated. The oldest person living in Vilcabamba, for example, is now assumed to be approaching one hundred. In all three cases the high percentage of old people was caused by an outflux of young people rather than by an increase in the numbers of old persons. Birth records in such rural areas were unavailable, so verification of ages was not possible. Medvedev, a Russian geneticist who studied the Abkhazians, believed a major cause of the hoax among these people to be the falsification of age records by men deserting from the army or dodging Soviet draft proscriptions in World War II. This explanation is supported by a rapid increase after World War II in the number of persons claiming to be centenarians and in the greater numbers of old men than of old women (usually women have far greater longevity than men). A combination of these factors led Medvedev to label all three cases hoaxes. His findings have since been supported by other researchers (Busse & Blazer, 1980).

Despite the lack of centenarians in these three areas of the world, the inhabitants' longevity was noteworthy. People from these areas who would have been classified as "old" by many societies did not physically resemble stereotypically "old" people. They were extremely healthy, with low levels of heart disease and serum cholesterol levels. Their heart rates after exercise were low, as were their blood pressure measurements. They played productive roles in their societies. In summary, there were factors at work in these three societies that were conducive to a healthy old age, if not an unusually long life span.

### Aging in Natural Environments

In natural environments some people age more slowly than and outlive other people. A number of factors, including biological or genetic features, aspects of the physical environment, and psychosocial determinants, are believed to contribute to group differences in longevity. However, knowing what these factors are is not the same as controlling them or determining their relative contributions. In natural environments these factors are inextricably interrelated or interdependent. They may exert their effects simultaneously or synergistically; in other words, it may be necessary for all to be present in some degree for one to work.

To carry out sound methodological studies of the determinants of longevity one must vary each factor individually and systematically. With humans this is morally and technically impossible. Instead, the researcher interested in longevity must wait for the rare occasions on which two populations differing in only one dimension can be compared, or the researcher must use multivariate studies involving the interaction of variables. A difficulty with multivariate studies is that they indicate relationships but not causes of behaviors or events. Another alternative is to use an animal model to manipulate factors experimentally. This technique is discussed more fully in Chapter 5. In any case researchers must specify as clearly as possible the variables they consider to be involved in determining the longevity of their subjects. Without such specifications misinterpretation or misapplication of results may result in faddish cures or outright quackery.

Geriatrics and gerontology have long been the target of pseudoscience, as is discussed in Chapters 4 and 5. Elixirs and infusions have been advocated periodically as cures for the illnesses and inevitability of old age. A brief review of suggested rejuvenation techniques should demonstrate the necessity of using the scientific method in studying the causes of aging.

The sorceress Medea, who appeared in Greek literature, believed that the key to eternal youth was a mixture of ram's blood, a snake skin, an owl's flesh, roots, herbs, grass, and so on. Upon receiving this mixture, the ancient King Aeson was said to have leapt up from his sick bed. Pope Innocent VIII (1432-1492) died instantly when the blood of a youth was transfused into his veins. The Russian physician Elie Metchnikoff (1845-1916) believed that removing the large intestine and consuming large amounts of yogurt would prevent aging (Busse & Blazer, 1980). Medvedev describes how pseudoscience was used by Lysenko, a Soviet bureaucrat, to gain political power from 1937 to 1964. Lysenko had a strong influence on the planning of agricultural production and general science under Josef Stalin. One of his disciples, a woman named O.B. Lepeshinskaya, developed a rejuvenation technique in 1949 that involved taking soda baths. Believers in her methods moved from taking baths to drinking soda water to taking soda enemas. Her techniques were not based on research but rather on conjecture (Busse & Blazer, 1980).

Research that can potentially affect an area of concern, fear, or bias in the general populace is open to such misguided application. Even today theories of aging are often translated by the popular press into cures and over-the-counter remedies that are sold to an unsuspecting public. Vitamin E and lecithin are but two examples of "longevity potions" in popular use. However, whether they work is not clearly understood by either laypersons or scientists. Researchers of aging processes should be aware of the possible popularization of their results by a gerontophobic public.

Research on the causes and processes of aging has progressed to a point at which preliminary assessments of the validity of theories can be made. The manipulation of certain factors has a decided impact upon the life span of an organism, whether animal, vegetable, or mineral. These factors and the theories explaining their mechanisms may be placed in three categories: biological or genetic, physical environmental, and psychosocial. It is important for geropsychologists to be aware of these factors as they affect the elderly individuals they study.

As already mentioned, aging is a complex process involving the interweaving of biological, historical, and psychosocial factors. When psychologists manipulate a cognitive variable, for example, they elicit a response involving elements of all the variables involved in aging. The cognitive stimulus is input through a physical medium and acted upon in the brain. The personal and social history of the individual affects that individual's perception of and ability to respond to the stimulus. The supportiveness or anxiety-producing characteristics of the environment, the individual's past successes with cognitive stimuli, and the individual's mental state at the time are all psychosocial factors affecting performance. The individual's overall health and physical functioning also have an effect on performance. The complexity of his interaction may be seen clearly in Figure 3-1.

It is methodologically acceptable to look only at overt behaviors and not to deal with the underlying complexities influencing them. However, anyone interested in

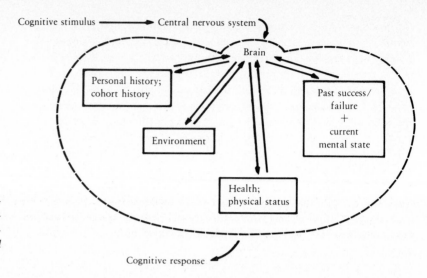

Cognitive stimulus ⟶ Central nervous system

Brain

Personal history; cohort history

Past success/ failure + current mental state

Environment

Health; physical status

Cognitive response

*Figure 3–1   The decision-making sequence: The relationship between the central nervous system and cognitive responses*

the nature of aging processes should be aware of the possible factors influencing them.

## Why Have Theories and Research?

Research on aging has three main values: cultural, scientific, and practical. From the cultural viewpoint, a society that did not question mortality would be sterile. Issues of quality and quantity of life span have profound cultural implications. For example, a society in which the life span was extended dramatically with no concern for the meaningfulness and personal utility of activities performed during that extended life would soon find itself with changed values and wasted human resources. Science fiction stories such as *Logan's Run* or *Lost Horizon* detail explicitly the hollowness and intergenerational competition that could result from a radical extension of human life.

Birren and Renner (1977) discuss the obligations of human beings as members of a species hopeful of survival and emphasize the utilization of the experiential resources of old people.

We can look at the aging of mankind as a species, or look at the aging of individuals. In the latter case one may study the . . . aging individual whereby his failing body may house a mind expanding in wisdom. Survival of such a person must be the result of a balance between the somatic vulnerabilities and the capacity of the nervous system for executive management of behavioral choice as well as maximization of the declining functions of the body through an integrative role over vegetative processes. . . . This implies that the executive portion of the nervous system that is consciously involved with voluntary activity, is directing behavior toward achievement of a balance that

*Old people are valuable, usable resources who can improve their own lives, the lives of their families, and the life of their society.*

is congruent with a lifetime of experience, a unique set of values and personality. The effort to establish a personal equilibrium among the forces that surround us results in some of us becoming wise as we grow old, more valuable to ourselves, to others, and to the broader flow of events that comprise a history of human destiny.*

It is therefore valuable for us as a culture to attempt to determine the factors involved in ensuring the maximum adaptability of aging humans and then to use the storehouse of memories, cognitions, and experiences the elderly possess.

The cultural utility of aging research can easily be extended to a practical utility. Old people are valuable, usable resources who can improve their own lives, the lives of their families, and the life of their society. Part of the aim of gerontological research and theories is to determine the capacities and skills of older people.

*Birren, J.E., & Renner, V.J. Research on the psychology of aging: Principles and experimentation. In J.E. Birren & K.W. Schaie (Eds.), *Handbook of the psychology of aging.* New York: Van Nostrand Reinhold, 1977, p. 35. Copyright © 1977 by Van Nostrand Reinhold Company. Reprinted by permission of the publisher

**The Scientific Utility of Aging Research**

As stated, aging is a multidirectional change involving the physical, psychological, and social spheres of a person's existence. The key word in this description is *change* or *process*. Aging is not a steady state, nor is it inevitably a process of deterioration and decrement. Behavior can take many directions at all stages of the life cycle.

Geropsychological research focuses on the time trajectories of change in aging behaviors, specifically on the chain of events occurring after maturity with some generality in the population. Age per se is often used by laypeople and in the past was often used by researchers as the primary explanation for aging behaviors. People were said to die of "old age" or to experience a decrease in IQ because of age rather than because of the actual causes of such changes, such as poor health, decreased motivation, and anxiety. Regressive or decremental aging behaviors are in fact unrepresentative of adult behavior changes (Baltes & Willis, 1977).

> The conclusion . . . that aging change is change toward slowness, less behavior, less acquisition, less performance and greater dependency. . .may be a function of the theoretical orientations applied rather than a representative assessment of the universe of aging change itself. (Baltes & Willis, 1977, p. 138)

The scientific value of theories and research lies in their ability to give shape to the core body of gerontological knowledge. Aging theories and research are not absolutes; rather, they are directives to the acquisition of knowledge and organizers of its structure.

Three interrelated tasks are involved in the making of a science: the generation, dissemination, and utilization of knowledge. Theories of aging should therefore lead to a body of knowledge that facilitates the description, explanation, and modification or optimization of aging behaviors (Baltes & Willis, 1977). In contrast, research on aging has four main functions:

To test hypotheses
To generate new hypotheses
To explain and predict behavior
To test alternate theories (Dusek, 1977)

If the hypotheses generated by such research are supported, the truth value or validity of gerontologic knowledge is enhanced. If the hypotheses are not supported, the research is questioned, the myth is dispelled, and the alternative view is explored. In either case the objectivity and validity of the science are strengthened.

> It is important for gerontologists to fully recognize that research has to concentrate on strategies which indeed allow for the direct assessment of change and change processes rather than time-specific interindividual changes. (Baltes & Willis, 1977, p. 138)

The methodologies involved in such assessment of change are discussed in Chapter 4.

Our current theories of aging, whether biological or psychological, are incomplete. They do not tell us about age-related functional changes, nor do they tell us about the plasticity and modifiability of aging behaviors. To a certain extent these theories are weak because we have no general theory of aging describing how behavior becomes organized over time but only theories that explain or predict limited aspects of behavior. A unifying theory of aging would need to consider biological, behavioral, and social factors, as well as interactions of the three. Biological variables affect life-span susceptibility as well as the body's ability to function. Behavioral and social variables determine a person's behaviors independent of the length of the person's life. Interactive variables determine the nature of age or developmental functions (Birren & Renner, 1977). These developmental functions may be defined as:

> the form or mode of the relationship between the chronological age of the individual and the changes observed to occur in his responses over some specified dimension of behavior over the course of his development to maturity. (Wohlwill, 1973, p. 32)

Many researchers believe the key to aging is in the interactive variables. However, little research or theoretical effort has been directed at these factors because few researchers are trained in all three areas. Multidisciplinary training or teams will undoubtedly be required to explore these complex contingencies more fully.

Given these considerations, it is unlikely that any one theory will fully explain the aging process and aging behaviors. There are many theories, and though a number of these are unlikely to be valid, they may not be discarded until there is a way to test them credibly. With technological and methodological improvements some theories can be experimentally tested. Until then, however, geropsychologists should be familiar with the nature of aging theories, which have a marked effect on the types of experiments performed.

Theories, which usually follow a number of observations, generally play two major roles. First, they systematize the observations into some organized pattern. Second, they develop a rational explanation of how or why the observed phenomenon occurs (Shock, 1977a). Given the complexity of aging, different theories address discrete aspects of the process. Each of these theories may be valid and worth studying in its own right but may not explain the cause of the aging process. Each has its positive and negative aspects, but none is likely to be *the* theory of aging. It still remains for some researcher to integrate successfully the disparate natures of these theories into a core explanation of aging.

## The Biological Theories

In senescence, the final biological stage in any organism's life, degenerative processes cause the organism to break down faster than the body's repair mechanisms can function. The breakdown leads to decreased adaptability and the decreased ability to survive. No one dies of "old age." Death in normal aging is due to disease or to failure of a specific organ or organ system, such as the heart, brain, kidney, or circulatory or respiratory system (Fries & Crapo, 1982).

The senescence of a number of body functions, organ systems, and cells occurs universally among humans and animals. However, there are great individual differences in the onset, timing, and duration of these deteriorative changes. Different species show different patterns of aging, and each has its maximum life span. The maximum life span of a species is generally seen as the upper limit of the survival potential of its members. As can be seen in Figure 3-2, the probability of death in humans increases exponentially after age thirty-five to forty, the approximate end of reproductive capacity in human females.

Each species has evolved its own life span in its own particular ecosystem. As may be seen in Table 3-1, there is considerable diversity in life spans from species to species.

Certain factors are correlated with the differences in life span. Some appear to be genetic, whereas others are more directly environmental. Generally lab-reared animals live longer than wild-reared animals because of the absence of predators, and controlled nutritional programs. Females of all species usually live longer than males, though there are exceptions (e.g., stallions outlive mares) (Rockstein et al., 1977). Body size is also correlated with life span. Again, there are exceptions; dogs do not live as long as cats. A restricted diet tends to increase the life span, but diet is combined with activity and is therefore difficult to assess independently. Finally, decreased body temperature is generally correlated with an increased life span in reptiles but usually not in mammals; however, hibernating bears have a shorter life span than would be expected on the basis of temperature, and alligators, reptiles with a high body temperature, live a long time. In the final analysis it appears unlikely that temperature has any major effect on longevity.

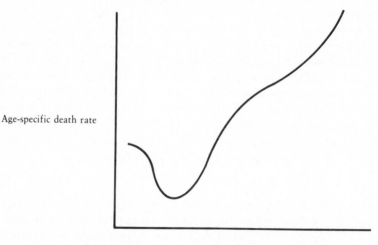

Age-specific death rate

Figure 3-2   The probability of death as a function of age

Age of organism

*Table 3-1    Specific longevity, growth, and reproductive values for various mammalian species*

| Species | Life span | | Length of gestation (mos) | Age at puberty (mos) |
| | Mean (mos) | Maximum (mos) | | |
| --- | --- | --- | --- | --- |
| Human | 849 | 1380 | 9 | 144 |
| Chimpanzee | 210 | 534 | 8 | 120 |
| Domestic cattle | 276 | 360 | 9 | 6 |
| Domestic dog | 180 | 408 | 2 | 7 |
| Cat | 180 | 336 | 2 | 15 |
| Mouse | 18 | 42 | 0.7 | 1.5 |
| House rat | 30 | 56 | 0.7 | 2 |

(Adapted from: Rockstein, M., Chesky, J.A., & Sussman, M.L. Comparative biology and evolution of aging. In C.E. Finch & L. Hayflick (Eds.), *Handbook of the biology of aging.* New York: Van Nostrand Reinhold, 1977, p. 9)

### Evolutionary Considerations

It is clear from the presence of postmitotic tissues in the body that aging has evolved. In postmitotic tissues, the cells no longer divide or reproduce and are therefore fixed populations. Nerves and muscles are examples of such tissues. The existence of fixed postmitotic cells in the human nervous system makes it possible for memory, problem-solving skills, and self-concept to exist. However, the presence of these cells in parts of the body such as the brain, kidney, and heart may contribute to senescence.

Generally senescence and death follow the end of the reproductive period. The time of onset varies with the species. For example, the pacific salmon dies after spawning, but the trout, sturgeon, herring, and sardine live for many years after this. Asiatic elephants and humans die long after their menopause (Rockstein et al., 1977).

Aging does not appear on initial inspection to be a desirable phenomenon for species survival. If evolution were to favor a gene for longevity, it would offer survival advantages during the period of maximum reproduction, and death would occur shortly after reproduction and parenting had ended. The life expectancy of humans extends to some thirty years after this time.

Researchers suspect that human longevity is an artifact of civilization rather than of genetics because the processes of senescence begin before reproduction ends. The gene for longevity in humans favors early maximum reproductive capability and late-life weakness and senescence. It must therefore be that the long life expectancy of humans is evolutionarily tied to the benefits an elderly person confers on the reproducing members of society. Elderly persons have productivity, inventiveness, leadership, and the ability to communicate accumulated cultural and behavioral values, all of which have survival value to the human species (Rockstein et al., 1977). Genetic and cultural factors thus have a combined impact on increased life span.

### Intrinsic Versus Extrinsic Determinants of Longevity

Some factors favor the intrinsic (genetic) and some the extrinsic (environmental) theories of aging, but the consensus is that both sorts of factors must be considered in biological theories of aging.

Few people would question the effect of the genetic code on longevity. Parental age at death correlates closely with offspring age at death. The role of genetics is also supported by studies in which fraternal twins were found to die an average of 75.2 months apart whereas identical twins died 38.5 months apart (Rockstein & Sussman, 1979). These studies cite the dramatic example of twin sisters who had very different life-styles.

> One sister had married a farmer, raised a large family and had lived the greater part of her adult life in the country. Her sister had remained single and lived in a large city, earning her living as a dress-maker. Both sisters suffered a massive cerebral hemorrhage on the same day at the age of sixty-nine; they died twenty-six days apart.*

Extrinsic factors modify the genetic code. Once normal offspring are born, external factors affect the full expression of the genetic program for longevity. Country dwellers can expect to outlive their urban cohorts by over five years. A nonsmoker can expect to outlive a two-pack-a-day cigarette smoker by twelve years. Diet, radiation, air pollution, and stress all negatively affect human longevity.

> A married person living in a rural area who is a nonsmoker can expect to live about twenty-two years longer than a city dweller who smokes, is unmarried and lives alone.*

These factors point to the need to distinguish between primary and secondary aging. Primary aging is a biological process caused by heredity, whereas secondary aging consists of defects and disabilities caused primarily by trauma from the environment and disease. Most elderly people cope successfully with both sorts of aging.

A normal person is someone who copes successfully with the environment. In the context of aging, normality may be defined as successful coping with defects and disabilities. Successful aging is dealt with in the discussion of psychological theories of aging that appears later in this chapter.

### Biological Themes

As stated, there is no single holistic theory of aging. Nonetheless there are themes that are common to different theories:

*Rockstein, M., & Sussman, M. *Biology of aging.* Belmont, CA: Wadsworth, 1979, p. 29

*Country dwellers can expect to outlive their urban cohorts by over five years. Recent research has also suggested that people with pets live longer than people without pets.*

Aging is a genetically programmed process.
Aging results from the accumulation of physical insults over time.
Aging is a result of both of the above processes.

Current consensus is that the third view is the most likely (Rockstein & Sussman, 1979). Regardless of its standpoint in that regard, however, any biological theory of aging must describe phenomena that meet three general criteria:

The aging phenomena under consideration must be evident universally in all members of a given species.
The process must be progressive with time.
The process must be deleterious in nature, leading ultimately to the failure of the organ or system.*

*Rockstein, M., & Sussman, M. *Biology of aging.* Belmont, CA: Wadsworth, 1979, pp. 37-38

Any phenomenon that meets these three criteria may legitimately be explored as a possible cause of aging.

All biological theories of aging, regardless of their emphasis on a genetic or environmental cause, focus to some extent on genetic structure. One class of biological theories focuses on how good function is disrupted by faulty DNA specification of enzyme production. This is an essentially genetic argument. Another theoretical focus is on the changes that occur with time in cellular protein. In this nongenetic approach the consideration is on cellular and tissue level changes. Physiological theories, a third approach, focus on the interaction among cells, tissues, and organ systems of the organism. Researchers taking this approach are aware that the ultimate explanation may lie at the molecular level, but they choose to place their emphasis on system integration (Shock, 1977a).

Some of the current biological theories of aging are presented below. They are summarized in Table 3-2.

### Genetic Theories

As stated, genetic theories of aging emphasize the subcellular changes that occur in DNA and RNA and their subsequent inability to correctly form enzymes necessary for cell function. The pertinent parts of the cell are detailed in Figure 3-3.

The general genetic theory was discussed earlier in this chapter. The essential tenets of this broad-based approach are that the genetic code sets the upper limit of the human life span, but that phenotypes may be altered by environmental factors such as radiation, drugs, and smoking. This theory does not discuss the specific nature of deviations from the genetic program. Rather it considers the broad impact of inherited tendencies on the life span and the evolutionary origins of the aging process. This theory has been called the *counterpart theory* by some gerontologists (Rockstein & Sussman, 1979).

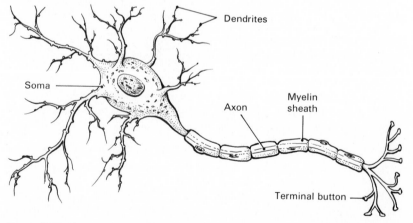

*Figure 3–3   The principal structures of a multipolar neuron*

(Source: Carlson, N.R. *Physiology of behavior*, Second edition. Boston, MA: Allyn & Bacon, 1981, p. 19)

*Table 3-2   Classification and focus of theories of aging*

| Classification | Name | Summary |
| --- | --- | --- |
| Genetic | General genetic theory | The genetic code sets the upper limit of the human life span; aging has evolutionary origins. |
| | Cellular genetic theory | DNA damage leads to faulty enzyme production and eventual cell death. |
| | Somatic mutation theory | Radiation of dividing cells causes chromosomal damage and eventual cell death. |
| | Cellular error theory | Aging and cell death result from formation of inappropriate m-RNA, which causes transcription errors in enzyme production and eventual cell death. |
| Nongenetic | Accumulation theory | Aging results from the build-up of metabolic wastes in cells. |
| | Free radical theory | Free radicals cause mutation of chromosomes and eventually cell death; they also attach to the cell membrane, causing it to leak and malfunction. |
| | Cross-linkage theory | Connective tissue changes caused by fibers cross-linking act to decrease optimal tissue function. |
| Physiological | Wear and tear theory | The organism simply wears out after the passage of stress, work, and time. |
| | Homeostatic imbalance theory | With age homeostatic mechanisms break down and bodily systems lose their ability to function together. |
| | Immunological theories | The immune system becomes increasingly incompetent with age, leading to increased disease incidence and increased autoimmune responses. |

The *cellular genetic theories* focus on DNA damage and its effect on cell function. Breaks in the DNA chain or alterations in the position of the links cause altered messages to be sent to those parts of the cell that are involved in enzyme production. This makes the manufacture of enzymes impossible, a condition that leads to the death of the cell.

The *somatic mutation theory* emphasizes the effects of radiation on the body (Curtis & Miller, 1971). X-rays delivered in sublethal doses have been found by some researchers to accelerate the aging process. However, research has raised questions about the validity of this theory. The effects of radiation have a different locus from the effects of aging. Aging predominantly affects the postmitotic cells of the body, whereas radiation affects dividing cells. Furthermore, the mutational effects of radiation are too small to account for aging. In addition, most cells contain the mechanisms to repair DNA molecules damaged by radiation.

The *cellular error theory* of aging (Crowley & Curtis, 1963; Orgel, 1963) claims that aging and cell death result from errors in the creation of an exact copy of the genetic code, i.e., the formation of inappropriate messenger RNA (m-RNA). According to this view aging results from errors in the enzymes involved in transcription and translation within the cells. Proponents of this theory claim that an exponential increase in cellular errors over time leads to what is known as an "error catastrophe," which in turn leads to the death of the cell.

Cellular loss is critical in areas of the body such as the fixed postmitotic cells of the brain and central nervous system. Cell loss in such areas as the hypothalamus, which is believed to be the location of the aging clock, may well lead to the loss of system integrity and equilibrium and thus to death. Critics claim that this theory may be overly simplistic. There are many steps between DNA and the final product; errors might occur at any point, not just in the m-RNA sequence. Moreover, the transfer processes are still unknown, and it is therefore impossible to specify where an error occurs. However, RNA differences have been discovered between young and old persons, and the theory is testable with new technology.

An important distinction between the error theory and the somatic mutation theory is that the error theory discusses production errors that lead to the transmission of faulty messages and the subsequent production of faulty enzymes whereas the somatic mutation theory deals with chromosomal damage.

The genetic theories are difficult to dispute. The genetic code is undoubtedly involved in aging. Some gerontologists even suggest the existence of deliberate biological programming for senescence (Busse & Blazer, 1980). According to this view the memory and capability for terminating a normal cell's life are stored in that cell. Cancer cells are believed to lose their memory and die naturally only when the organism dies. Support for the genetic theories comes from the medical profession and the work of Leonard Hayflick (1977).

The belief that biological aging has a cellular basis receives medical support from two rare genetic disorders, Hutchinson-Guilford syndrome (also known as *progeria*) and Werner's syndrome (Hayflick, 1977). Progeria is a rare disorder with a usual age of onset between nine and thirteen years. Symptoms include severe deceleration of growth and generalized atherosclerosis of all major blood vessels, including the aorta and the coronary vessels.

Werner's syndrome is similar to progeria but manifests itself later. The average life expectancy of Werner's syndrome victims is forty-seven years. Ten percent of all patients develop neoplasms, and all develop symptoms including graying hair and hair loss, juvenile cataracts, atherosclerosis, arteriosclerosis, and osteoporosis. In addition persons with Werner's syndrome are typically of short stature and prone to diabetes.

The exact causes of these disorders are unknown, but it is clear that they involve genetic malfunction. The diseases are more correctly said to mimic aging rather than to be cases of accelerated aging. In either case they lend support to the idea that genetic mechanisms are involved in the processes of aging.

Hayflick's work emphasizes the finite growth of mitotic cells in the body. Normally cells go through approximately fifty divisions before dying, and it is assumed that they accumulate progressive errors in DNA and RNA materials as they age. Aging according to Hayflick's theory is caused by cells being lost in critical locations faster than they can be replaced.

The main criticism of genetic theories is that they tend to become popularized into the statement that "death occurs when a crucial number of cells are lost." This is a gross oversimplification of the aging process. In general the cellular processes discussed by the genetic theories are the key to aging. Even without disease cells show finite growth (Hayflick, 1977). Thus the key to longevity does not lie in disease prevention alone. Specific genetic manipulations must be designed if the human life span is to be dramatically increased.

### Nongenetic Cellular Theories

The nongenetic theories of aging focus on aspects of intra- and intercellular function. They are more concerned with factors affecting cellular function than on the processes of DNA-RNA transfer within the cells. These theories discuss the effects of extracellular substances such as waste products and free molecules on the cell's function. They are in contrast to the genetic theories, which emphasize internal changes of the genetic code as they cause aging. Both sorts of theories deal with cell function, but each has a different locus for its discussion of cause.

The *accumulation theories* present yet another explanation of aging. According to these theories, aging is due to a buildup of metabolic waste products in each cell. These waste products interfere with normal cell function and eventually result in the death of the cell. There is considerable empirical support for these theories; various deleterious waste substances have been found to increase over time in the body's tissues.

Lipofuscin, one such waste product, is a highly insoluble fatty substance that in large quantities interferes with cell function and causes cell death. Lipofuscin makes up approximately one third of the total volume of the heart muscle in very old persons (Shock, 1977b). Many researchers reason that such a large volume of muscle occupied by an inert substance can have only a negative effect on physiological function. Studies of the impact of lipofuscin and other waste products are only in the rudimentary phases but are expected by many researchers to produce fruitful outcomes. However, a difficulty with this area of research is that it is not clear whether such waste substances are causes or effects of aging. In addition, it appears that there are large individual differences in the extent of waste accumulation, although in persons with high concentrations of such substances there appears to be a strong correlation between the amount of waste product present and aging behaviors. A final difficulty is that lipofuscins accumulate only in nondividing cells, i.e., in fixed postmitotic cells, and thus seem unlikely determinants of the aging process.

The *cross-linkage theory* (Bjorksten, 1974), a relatively new theory, posits an association between increased intracellular transport and changes in connective tissue with age, in particular changes in elastin and collagen. Bjorksten, an industrial polymer chemist, first noted that the protein gelatin used in ditto machines was irreversibly altered (denatured) by chemicals such as formaldehyde. He found that collagen and elastin become stiff with age and change in composition. Since collagen constitutes twenty-five to thirty percent of all body protein and surrounds the blood vessels and cells, such changes could have a profound impact on physiological function. This theory is not yet proved but is generating extensive research effort (Shock, 1977a, 1977b).

The *free radical theory* is a special case of the cross-linkage theory. Free radicals are chemical components of the cell that arise through the action of oxygen as by-products of normal cell processes (Rockstein & Sussman, 1979). They are highly reactive chemically and therefore exist for only a short period of time. Free radicals are especially reactive with unsaturated fats, which make up the cell membrane. Cell membranes begin to leak if enough free radicals accumulate on them. By causing chromosomes to mutate, free radicals also damage normal cells. They are also self-perpetuating; when a free radical combines with a molecule, other free radicals are released.

The free radical theory has sparked extensive research in longevity. It appears that vitamins C and E are naturally occurring antioxidants (antioxidants prevent the oxidation process leading to free radicals). This finding has helped support the popular argument that vitamins extend the life span. Butylated hydroxytoluene (BHT), a food preservative, has also been found to have antioxidant and free-radical inhibiting properties. When fed to mice, it has been found to extend their life span significantly. Much study is needed before such claims can be made about humans.

### Physiological Theories

Physiological theories of aging deal with the breakdown in system integration and function that tends to occur with age. Such theories are more likely to explain effects of aging on the whole body rather than to deal with the cellular origins of aging changes. It may be that some of these whole-body changes give rise to molecular changes, but the reverse is equally plausible. For psychologists concerned with aging behavior, theories that deal with the organism as a whole are potentially most useful and appropriate to behavioral intervention.

The *wear and tear theory*, or *stress theory* (Selye, 1956), is essentially a common-sense theory stating that at some point an organism simply wears out. Like machines, humans slow down and eventually stop after a certain amount of work. There are of course differences between people and machines in this regard, one being that machines do not repair themselves whereas living tissue does. The

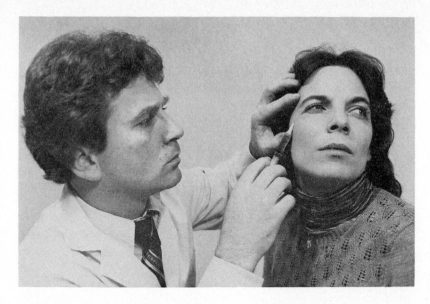

*In an effort to "counteract" aging, some people endure collagen injections.*

repair processes of humans seem to slow as they age, but nonetheless they continue to function.

The wear and tear theory is not supported by research despite its popularity with the public. The effects of physical stress and hard work may be removed by periods of rest. Chemical stresses in which hormone defenses are engaged for long periods of time may lead to physical breakdown or death. However, this is not a usual case and is therefore not an adequate model for normal aging.

The best support for this theory comes from animal research on the interaction of metabolic rates and aging. Underfeeding and cold temperatures slow down metabolic rates. Underfed and cold animals (such as animals in hibernation) engage in less activity than normal and therefore "wear out" more slowly. As mentioned, however, this is not a universal finding among all species, nor is it the case indefinitely.

The wear and tear theory has been extended by virtue of its logic to organ transplants and tissue replacements. The reasoning is that worn-out parts can be replaced, keeping the human "machine" going indefinitely; hence the emphasis on heart transplants, liver transplants, kidney transplants, plastic prosthetic devices, and so on. A problem with this logic is that dying appears to be more strongly associated with the physiological integration of organ systems than with single organs. A person who has had a simultaneous heart and kidney transplant cannot live indefinitely if his or her vascular system is plagued by atherosclerotic deposits or arteriosclerotic lesions.

A second physiological theory that is of great utility to psychologists is the *homeostatic imbalance theory* (Miller & Shock, 1953). This theory focuses on the finding that homeostatic mechanisms tend to break down with age. Old organisms universally have greater difficulty than young organisms maintaining physiological equilibrium. With age, less stress is necessary to upset the balance, which once upset is hard to regain. Such homeostatic mechanisms as blood sugar levels, body temperature, exercise heart rate, and blood pressure are all affected by this decreased ability to maintain physiological balance. The theory states that aging is due to an increase in homeostatic faults. Eventually there is imbalance even under ideal conditions. Death results when maintaining an equilibrium becomes impossible.

The homeostatic imbalance theory is of interest to psychologists because homeostasis is affected by psychosocial as well as physical or chemical stresses. A person who feels helpless or hopeless is under psychological stress, which produces the same physiological response as a chemical stressor would. The human stress response, or "fight-or-flight" response, is nondiscriminating, i.e., it is elicited by any type of noxious stimulus. As such, it can result in serious damage to or even death of the organism. The nature of psychological stresses is explored in greater detail in Chapter 11.

The homeostatic imbalance theory does not deal with physiological causes, which are left to the genetic and nongenetic theories to assess. The homeostatic imbalance theory also does not describe psychological stresses, which are left to psychological theories. However, the homeostatic imbalance theory does link the psychological, social, and physical aspects of aging and as such is a useful model.

The final theories discussed here are the immunological theories; the *autoimmune theory* and the general *immune theory* (Adler, 1974; Walford, 1969). Immunological breakthroughs, including the control of infectious diseases, are partially responsible for the rectangularly shaped survivorship curves described in Chapter 2. As our knowledge of the diseases of aging has increased, we have commensurately gained knowledge of normal, healthy aging, as well as of what techniques can be used to retard or alleviate aging and which are most fruitful.

The immune system is a possible key to the processes of aging. Normal immune processes decline with age, and this decline is accompanied by an increase in the diseases affecting human tissues. If medical science could delay, lessen, or prevent decreased immune system function, it could delay, lessen, or prevent some of the serious diseases of late adulthood.

The immune system protects the body against foreign invaders, such as viruses, bacteria, fungi, and one's own somatic cells undergoing neoplastic changes, by seeking out and destroying them (Makinodan, 1977). There are two types of immunocompetent cells: B cells, which are developed in the bone marrow and are blood borne; and T cells, which develop in the thymus and are responsible for the cell-mediated response. The latter cells are responsible for the rejection of foreign cell tissue and organ grafts, and for immunity against cancer cells (Makinodan, 1977). The immune theory states that the increased infection, autoimmune responses, and cancer we see with age are caused by decreased immune system competence.

The autoimmune theory is ancillary to the above theory. The exact mechanism by which the immune system turns against the organism's own cells (i.e., the autoimmune response) is not clearly understood. Two plausible explanations have been suggested by researchers. The first is that the host cells harbor viruses and express viral antigens on their surface late in life. The immune system in turn makes antibodies against these antigens, and autoimmune disease results. The second explanation is that the virus-infected cells may be immune cells that upon late-life transformation recognize other noninfected cells as foreign (Makinodan, 1977).

According to both immunological theories, the immune system in aging and disease is suppressed against invaders and expressed against the organism itself. There appears to be a great deal of empirical support for these theories. In humans and long-lived mice the onset of decline in normal immune functions begins shortly after sexual maturity, when the thymus begins to atrophy. Persons on immuno-suppressive therapy after tissue or organ transplant are eighty times more vulnerable to cancer than persons not taking immunosuppressants. Moreover, cessation of use of certain types of immunosuppressive drugs leads to the rejection of certain types of cancerous tumors. In addition, deaths due to cardiovascular disease and cancer are much higher among aged persons with antinuclear autoantibodies (antibodies that attack the nucleus of the person's own cells) than among elderly persons without such antibodies (Makinodan, 1977). The consensus among researchers is that decreased immunocompetence predisposes elderly persons to a wide array of diseases. Although these theories have considerable support, however, they are not theories of normal aging but rather of disease incidence in old age.

### Conclusions

The biological theories of aging are all based on the premise that aging has a single underlying cause. Implicit in this assumption is that there are ways to delay the onset, lessen the severity, and prevent the diseases of aging and perhaps even prevent aging itself. An additional goal of theorists of aging is that their theories be productive, i.e., that they increase research quality and output.

Underlying biological research on aging are the following questions, posed by Richard Adelman in *The Handbook of the Biology of Aging* (1977):

In which cell population(s) or which tissue(s) is localized the origin of any phenomenon that characterizes an aging organism?
What does aging do to the functional capability of crucial cells?
What is the biochemical basis of the modification?
At what age is the modification first expressed?
What molecular events lead to the modification?
In what ways does this relate to the potential vigor and life span of the species?
Can these events be tampered with and at what cost?

Consistent application of these questions to theoretical considerations should bring researchers closer to a single comprehensive theory of aging and its biological processes.

**The Psychosocial Theories**

While the biological theories attempt to explain the physical basis of aging, the psychosocial theories deal with the behavioral causes and effects of those processes. The intent of the psychosocial theories is not so much to tie age to behavior as it is to link behavior to events that need time to occur. According to these theories, aging behaviors have some correlation with age but are not caused by age. Age per se does not cause anything to happen. *Developmental functions*, as these time-related behaviors are called, describe the relation between age and changes in specific behaviors as a person grows toward maturity and senescence. Developmental functions by definition refer to individual, not group, relations between time and behavior (Wohlwill, 1973). Given this qualification, psychosocial theories of aging have been limited in their ability to describe modal patterns of age-related behavior, since the individuals studied often do not fit into generalized behavioral categories.

The psychosocial theories, like the biological theories, have a prescriptive function. They attempt to define the behaviors related to "successful aging" and increased longevity. In many cases, however, successful aging is defined as increased years of life rather than increased quality of life, and this blurring of the distinction between the two variables is often concealed from the reader of the research. Therefore, all such research must be read critically. Biases about the definitions of successful aging always affect the experimenter's interpretation of findings.

Perhaps because of the difficulties described above, there is no integrated psychosocial theory of aging. However, the major tasks of such a theory, like the tasks of the biological theories, have been carefully delineated. They include the following:

To identify the degree and nature of psychosocial factors associated with change across the adult life course.

To measure the effects of frustration or fulfillment of these change agents at various stages of the life cycle on the individual's adaptive level.

To assess the extent to which fulfillment in one area may compensate for frustration in another. (Lowenthal, 1977)

Several theories have attempted to perform these tasks with varying degrees of success. Two of the most ambitious have been the disengagement theory (Cumming & Henry, 1961) and activity theory (Maddox, 1970). Other broad-based social theories include those of Erikson (1963) and Lowenthal (1977). These theories are considered in later chapters.

Personality theorists such as Freud, Jung, and Adler have also had a significant impact on the study of psychological aging. The remainder of this chapter discusses the ways in which these theories have affected our understanding of psychosocial development late in life.

### Psychological Theories

Except for Erikson, who deals extensively with postmaturational personality changes, all traditional personality and psychosocial theorists discussed here emphasized early development and merely touched on late life. In many cases it remained the task of others to extrapolate their theories to late life (Kastenbaum, 1978; Neugarten, 1977).

The psychoanalytic theory of Sigmund Freud has had a significant impact on the clinical psychology of aging—perhaps by default. Freud himself dealt mainly with young adults and seemed to feel that his techniques could be applied most profitably to that age group. Following suit, psychologists and psychiatrists, as well as the entire mental health system, have traditionally avoided elderly clients.

The psychoanalytic model of Freud is essentially a Darwinian biological survival model, i.e., it posits that people strive to satisfy needs in a world of restricted resources. Since needs or goals are mostly found in the external world, a person must adapt to the world, but such adaptation often has costs such as anxiety or neurosis. Psychoanalytic theory posits that the early failures of adaptation have long-enduring results; this approach therefore concentrates on early developmental history.

Freud believed that personality was relatively formed in childhood and stable after the reawakening of sexuality during adolescence. He did not specifically deal with late adulthood, but his theory may be extrapolated to that stage. As will be seen in later chapters, biological changes occur fairly predictably in late life. Sensory abilities decline fairly quickly, energy decreases, arousal mechanisms change, and all the involuntary systems of the body begin to slow.

Freud postulated that the normal balance between id (the primitive, hedonistic aspect of personality) and ego (the rational self) was upset by biological changes such as the above. According to psychoanalytic theory, the id is physiologically derived from the smooth muscle (involuntary) and endocrine systems. With age these systems, and therefore also the biological basis for the id, decline. In contrast, the ego is founded on our contact with the external world, i.e., it is based on our sensory apparatus, mobility, memory, and imagination, all of which, especially the first, are necessary for adaptation. These skills show a more rapid decline with age than the endocrine and smooth muscle functions.

A consequence of these biological changes is that the organs supporting the id decline less quickly than those supporting the ego (Fig. 3-4). As a result of this discrepancy, old people often show an increase in anxiety because of their unconscious fear that they are losing control. To compensate for this, they frequently develop "ego rigidity," i.e., they become restricted in their responses to situational changes. If this rigidity does not provide relief from anxiety, they may well regress to more primitive defenses and behavior in a continued attempt to regain a sense of control.

Ego rigidity may be seen in a Freudian framework as an adaptive behavior rather than as mere stubborness. Reducing one's options means that one has fewer intricacies to learn and that less energy needs to be spent manipulating and sorting out factors, and it is thus easier to maintain control. Many old people face a number of changes in health, social milieu, and cognitive ability. These changes

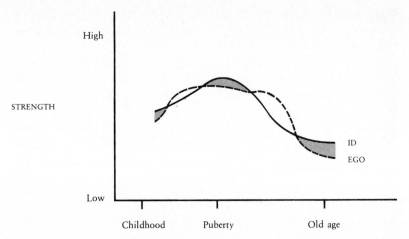

High

STRENGTH

ID

EGO

Low

Childhood　　　Puberty　　　Old age

*Figure 3-4　Relative strength of the id and ego throughout the life cycle*

place pressure on them, and the anxiety associated with such pressure may force them to hold onto patterns of behavior that were successful in dealing with problems they had at the height of their personal strength. Patterns that brought gratification at earlier stages of the life cycle may no longer be optimal for dealing with the environment, but they provide a needed association with earlier days of greater potency. From a psychoanalytic perspective, rigidity serves a function in that it allows the ego to conserve energy needed to cope with new social problems and decreasing ego strength.

Other analysts drawn from the psychoanalytic tradition also addressed themselves to the personality work of late life. Carl Jung, for example, believed that human beings are motivated by a desire to achieve selfhood. As persons move into middle and late life they show an increase in introversion and a reorganization of values toward the inner self. For Jung, old age is not just a time of reworking the past or regressing. It is rather a time for completion and integration of the personality. Jung believed that men would assume more feminine traits and women would become more accepting of their masculine self as they attempted to develop their self-potential in late life. Jung's views thus presaged the conclusions of the disengagement theorists as well as the work of Gutmann (1964; 1971), which is discussed in Chapter 9.

The theorist drawn from the psychoanalytic tradition who has had the largest impact on gerontology is Erik Erikson. Erikson postulated that personality evolves out of the life-long resolution of various psychosocial crises. For Erikson there are eight crises that must be resolved. Four of these—trust versus mistrust, autonomy versus shame, initiative versus guilt, and industry versus inferiority—are psychological work to be completed in childhood. Identity versus role confusion is the task of adolescence. Intimacy versus isolation must be resolved in early adulthood, and generativity versus stagnation remains for middle age.

The final stage of Erikson's theory, ego integrity versus despair, presents the culmination of personality growth. This is the stage of old age. In it people must

*In the stage of old age, people must evaluate their lives critically and arrive at an assessment that will give them satisfaction and acceptance.*

draw to closure all the various strands of their lives. They must evaluate their lives critically and arrive at an overall assessment that will give them satisfaction and acceptance. The productivity and intimacy gained in the earlier adult stages make this closure possible. The person who is alone or without meaningful accomplishments inevitably despairs.

From Erikson's perspective of late-life psychosocial development, in contrast to Freud's view, the need for personal growth continues up to the moment of death. Erikson's optimistic views have been supported by research on successful aging, which is presented in Chapter 9.

Psychological theories of aging, including those presented here, have tended to focus on certain aspects of behavior rather than on the whole structure of personality with its continuities and adaptations. Freud focused on sexual and biological drives as behavioral determinants. According to his view, when these drives are blocked or altered in relative balance, anxiety and neuroticism occur. Psychoanalytic theory thus presents a fairly negative portrait of old age. In contrast, Jung and Erikson present a more positive view. Jung emphasizes increasing interiority and passivity in old age, and Erikson expands on this view, seeing movement toward ego integrity as a person's life draws to a close. These and other psychological theories are discussed more fully in Chapter 9.

Some of the basic premises of the psychological approaches have been tested in major sociological theories. Activity theory and disengagement theory are the two major social gerontology theories.

### Sociological Theories

Disengagement theory (Cumming & Henry, 1961) was an ambitious project that sparked both controversy (cf. Maddox, 1964–1970) and refinement. It fulfilled a function of good theories in that it stimulated other work. Disengagement theory emphasized the withdrawal from social interaction that occurs in old age as a natural process and hence universal and inevitable. As people age, the theory goes, their bodies begin a process of disengagement. Their eyes, ears, and other sensory organs become less adept at detecting external information. They therefore begin to look inward. Society pulls away from them at the same time as they turn from it. Disengagement is therefore seen as a mutual process of withdrawal.

According to the theory, withdrawal is a positive experience for the elderly. Old age leads to increased reflection, increased preoccupation with self, and decreased emotional investment in persons and events. Old people therefore experience disengagement as a natural, not as a socially imposed, process.

Support for disengagement theory was mixed. Some researchers liked the theme but found it theoretically unjustified. Researchers such as Maddox (1970) argued that disengagement was probably a process initiated early in life rather than a

*According to disengagement theory, the withdrawal from social interaction that occurs in old age is a natural process.*

*Active adults are typically happier than disengaged adults.*

late-life personality change. In his counterargument, activity theory, Maddox suggested that retired persons need to remain productive and happy. Active adults are typically happier than disengaged adults. Moreover, happiness has been associated with involvement and adjustment. Maddox urged old people to find substitutes for terminated roles if they wanted to achieve successful aging.

In particular, activity theory postulated that old people must make four main role realignments in late adulthood: loss of occupation, related loss of income, declined health status, and changes in family configuration. Maddox argued that role realignments to counter role loss are an integral part of successful aging. He stressed late life as a time for new role opportunites rather than disengagement.

Activity theory too has received criticism from gerontologists. Activity per se does not sustain self-concept; only meaningful activity does. Although there appears to be a relation among morale, ad·ustment, and acvitity levels, activity theory, like disengagement theory, appears to be an oversimplification of the aging process. Neither theory fully explains the phenomenon of successful adjustment to old age. Both must be looked upon as representative only of particular patterns of aging rather than of the definitive pattern all people must follow to age "successfully."

### Conclusions

All the psychosocial theories have faced the difficulty of defining a target class of behaviors that are empirically testable by appropriate methodologies. Although aging is a multidirectional change process, the word *aging* has often been used to describe a steady state. Such misuse of the word has had two potentially damaging consequences for theories of aging. The first effect has been the association of aging with deterioration and decrement. The second has been the conclusion that age is the major determinant of the behavior of those who are old. The common use of such statements as "he died of old age" or "she has a poor memory because she's old" rapidly leads to ageism and gerontophobia.

Kalish (1979) has presented an exposition of the various models psychologists and sociologists have used in their approaches to aging. These models largely reflect the research methodologies used and results of studies conducted with these methodologies. The first model used to describe old age, and the most negative, is termed the *pathology model*. In it old age and the elderly are seen as sick, strange, and falling apart. Old age as a period of the life cycle is seen as a static period with change, if it occurs at all, going in a negative direction.

The decrement model, which followed the pathology model, was based on cross-sectional studies. It stated that old age always brings with it decreases in function, income, and any other variable measured. This was an improvement over the view of old age as pathology, but it still stressed the negative realities of old age. As longitudinal studies began to be used more extensively, the model of choice became the minimal change model. According to this model, although decrement is a reality of old age, it is minimal and can often be compensated for.

The prevailing model today is the normal person model (Kalish, 1979). In this approach, old people are seen as the same as any other age group—they are diverse and their behavior is adaptive to the situations they confront. The cognitive and health changes they manifest may result from isolation or diet but not from aging per se.

Although the normal person model is a fairly optimistic approach to old age, Kalish (1979) suggests yet a fifth model, the personal growth model. According to this view, old people have a unique ability to achieve personal growth. This model

*Old people are diverse;
their behavior may be
seen as adaptive to the
situations they confront.*

may be seen as a reflection of the humanistic views of Erikson and Jung. Kalish (1979) states that old people have reached a point in the life cycle at which earlier responsibilities have been transcended; the children are raised, the boss no longer has to be answered to, and so on. Many old people have worked through their fears of dying and have learned how to set priorities, cope with health problems and loss, and be satisfied with their life circumstances. The acceptance of death and the awareness that one's life is finite, Kalish believes, provide the impetus for a person to use the time that is left constructively and achieve a sense of personal wholeness that is not possible at any other point in the life cycle. According to Kalish, the later years should be seen by psychosocial theorists and researchers as providing opportunities for flexibility, joy, pleasure, growth, and sensuality.

This personal growth model is in direct conflict with some of the more prevalent negative views of aging held by professionals and laypersons alike. It is a model that needs to be tested and validated, but it has great potential for improving the quality of life of the elderly in our society.

Current psychological theories of aging are incomplete and do not tell us much about the aging of individuals. Not a great deal is known about the plasticity and modifiability of aging as a process or of change occurring in behavior over time. We have yet to explicate the nature of assumed age functions in after-maturity-adult behavior; we do not know the extent to which such behavior is stable, shows irreversible decrement, shows reversible decrement or decrement with compensation, or increases (Schaie, 1973).

Psychosocial theories have tended to explain or predict limited aspects of behavior. There has been no push in the field toward a unifying theory of how behavior becomes organized over time. Such a theory would include biological, behavioral, and social variables as well as the interaction of these variables. Erikson (1963) and Riegel (1973b, 1973c) make strides toward such a theory but have neglected the biological spheres. Furthermore, Erikson's stages in interpersonal commitment are difficult to test empirically.

## Summary

Biological and psychological theories of aging have primarily focused on successful aging. The hidden purpose behind these theories has been the design of interventions either to help individuals age successfully or to stop the aging process entirely. Because of methodological difficulties, pre-experimental biases, and lack of multidisciplinary focus, there is no one theory that unifies the biological, psychological, and social perspectives on aging. Aging is a multidirectional process, and few researchers are broadly enough trained to consider all the potential variables. Various theories explain and predict limited aspects of aging, but even these view aging as a static condition rather than as a dynamic process. Theoretical approaches to aging are therefore currently incomplete. They do, however, have the potential for refinement, enhancement, and synthesis.

*Why can't an individual's behavior be explained in terms of either genetic factors alone
or environmental factors alone?*

*Why is it important in experimentation to control for extraneous or confounding
factors?*

*What are the advantages and disadvantages of the classic developmental designs?*

*What do we mean by "individual differences" and "individual change" and how are
these assessed in the classic developmental designs?*

---

P REVIOUS chapters introduced central issues in the psychology of aging, discussed theories of how aging occurs in the biological and psychosocial spheres of a person's life, and considered population trends that may affect the individual's experience of aging. The remainder of this text discusses the available research findings that detail the aging experiences of many persons.

For the student of aging, knowledge of research methodology is an invaluable tool with which to assess the truth of aging processes. Gerontological research is a means of amassing a body of knowledge that will prove or dispel many of our beliefs about aging. It is the main vehicle for determining whether an intervention to improve the quality of life of older persons really works. In short, research and its appropriate methodologies are the sole source of an efficient, verifiable, and accurate psychology of aging.

However, whereas research done well has an infinite capacity to enhance our knowledge of aging, research done poorly serves to propagate illusion, waste, and stereotypes. The prime task of the researcher is to choose the appropriate methodologies with which to answer the questions posed. This chapter considers and offers critiques of the classic developmental designs used in research and discusses alternative methodologies.

**Definitions of Age**

Conducting research on aged persons is extremely difficult. The central focus of developmental research is aging or behavior change over time. The crux of the difficulty lies in the definition of *time*.

Developmental researchers in the past, and many laypeople today, have used age as an index of change (Birren & Renner, 1977). For example, there are often many fairly obvious differences between the average twenty- and the average forty-year-old. The twenty-year-old is apt to wear trendier clothing, maintain a more active life-style, be unmarried, be emotionally less mature, and have different life goals from the forty-year-old. It would be tempting to explain the stability of the forty-year-old by discounting experience and stressing age—"Of course he's more stable. He should be! He's older!" Presumably, however, these differences are not caused by age. They are rather a result of the interaction of complex social, biological, and psychological changes, as well as of differences in amount of experience accumulated (Botwinick, 1973).

Chronological age per se has often been used as an explanatory variable, i.e., as a variable that explains why things occur in a causal fashion. However, age neither causes nor explains anything. Age is rather an index on which sets of explanatory factors (e.g., social influences or biological changes) and a set of consequent attributes (e.g., attitudes or personality processes) interact (Friedrich & Van Horn, 1976). The passage of time, or age, might best be compared to the inches on a ruler. The inches indicate a framework for measuring height, but they do not cause height to be gained. So too is time used to measure certain physical events. Given that chronological age is only an index of the length of time a person has been alive, we know only that age changes or age differences in certain behaviors occur with age, not that they are caused by age (Wohlwill, 1973). Besides using age as an explanatory variable, researchers have often mistakenly assumed that all variables are similarly correlated with age. Old age is often defined socially, biologically, and psychologically as well as chronologically (Neugarten & Datan, 1973). Although these definitions arise from different frames of reference, they are not necessarily independent.

### Chronological Age

Chronological age is measured for each person from the time of birth in a socially determined way. In our culture and historical period, the passage of 365 days is equated with 1 year. Chronological age, however, is only roughly correlated to the other measures of age discussed in this chapter. For example, various longitudinal studies on early- and late-maturing adolescents have suggested that different rates of biological maturation may lead to different patterns of psychological maturation among individuals of the same chronological age. These patterns appear to persist at least into the forties. Consequently it is possible that different psychological ages may exist among elderly individuals of the same chronological age.

Chronological age is a fairly arbitrary metric, given differences in the mean ages of different societies. For example, sixty-five years of age may indeed be "old" in a developing country in which the average life expectancy is only forty-seven years. However, in Abkhasia, Vilcabamba, or Hunza, where a high percentage of persons live into their nineties, sixty-five may be relatively young.

### Social Age

Social age is a system of segregating people into different levels of maturation according to social factors. Social time is marked by life events such as marriage, the birth of a first child, widowhood, and retirement. Transitions from one life event to another are often formalized or ritualized by rites of passage. In our culture such events as graduation, first communion, and bar mitzvah are rites of passage.

Social age, like chronological age, suggests a certain set of behavioral expectations; for example, forty is a little old to go to school, and fourteen is a little young

*Social time is marked by life events such as marriage and widowhood. Transitions from one significant life event to another are often formalized by rites of passage.*

to have a child. Social age is a system of age-based expectancies shared by all members of a given society. However, social age varies widely not only across cultures, but also across ethnic groups within a culture.

### Psychological Age

Psychological age is a system whereby maturity is measured in terms of capabilities, adjustment, and knowledge. Such theorists as Piaget with his cognitive development, Kohlberg with his moral development, and Fowler with his religious thought development have suggested criteria for assessing maturity on the basis of these psychological functions. It is possible in this system for a person to be mature with respect to a particular variable but not to have attained what is considered social or chronological maturity.

### Biological Age

Biological age, a person's rate of biological maturation, is influenced by both heredity and environment. Here again it is possible for a person to be biologically old but chronologically young. A person with the disorder progeria, for example, is physiologically aged but chronologically a child or teenager. "Symptoms" of age in chronologically young persons who are slow and lack muscular strength and coordination may in fact be caused by sedentary living or lack of dietary control.

**Factors Affecting Age**

All measures of age are influenced by both culture and history. Chronological and biological age alone are not good predictors of behavior; the society to which a person belongs is also a factor. Each culture has its own set of psychological and social expectancies for every age level. Moreover, such factors as health status and nutritional status, which vary widely between various cultural groups, influence biological aging.

In addition to culture, history shapes the patterns of aging experienced by members of a group. Historical forces shape social expectancies, psychological adjustments, and biological tendencies. For example, industrialization and Westernization have prolonged adolescence, influenced family styles, and created retirement populations and communities. Famines, droughts, and wars may curtail life expectancies. History may in fact reshape a society's entire age-graded system.

Age is thus a relative and multifaceted concept that should be clearly defined in terms of the society and historical time of the subjects being measured. However, even within this framework considerable individual differences are generally found. In general the correlation among the four indices discussed is very rough. Chronological age describes old age in a social sense, but not all individuals defined as "old" will be old in terms of the other indices of age (Neugarten & Datan, 1973).

Developmental research aims to measure two things: the age structure of people and the age structure of the roles people perform. Both of these age structures are fluid, shifting from culture to culture and historical epoch to historical epoch. These structures are derived from age dynamics and societal dynamics. Age dynamics determine how many people are located in a given age structure at a given time, which is of course affected by such factors as population dynamics. Societal dynamics determine and continually change the age structure of the roles to which people are assigned. There is continuous interaction between these two forces, described developmentally as interaction between the processes of aging and the flow of cohorts (Riley et al., 1968). Figure 4-1 illustrates this concept. At any point in historical time, many cohorts exist simultaneously. Individuals born into those cohorts age from birth to death. They change their attitudes, feelings, and actions. Cohorts also are born, are absorbed into the system, and pass away as their members die.

Biological aging is important to this process of growth. As persons develop, certain physical events occur to them, but progression through the life cycle is only one source of age-related change. A historical time line parallels a person's life line, affecting that individual's progression through the life cycle (Figures 4-2 and 4-3).

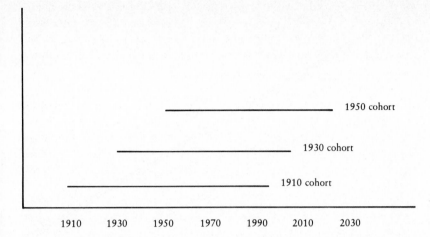

Figure 4-1  The interaction between aging and cohort flow

The cultural and historical experiences individuals are exposed to at various points in their lives have an effect on their attitudes, values, and abilities. For example, the 1960s were filled with turmoil; everyone alive then was exposed to assassinations, student unrest, civil rights conflicts, and the Viet Nam war. However, the influence of those events on a person depended considerably on that person's chronological age. The grade-school child perceived student unrest from a very different perspective from the college student or the college student's parents. The college-age person not in college also experienced these events in a different manner from his student cohort member.

Factors such as those described above suggest that we cannot speak of a unique, highly similar class of people called "the elderly." All age groups comprise highly

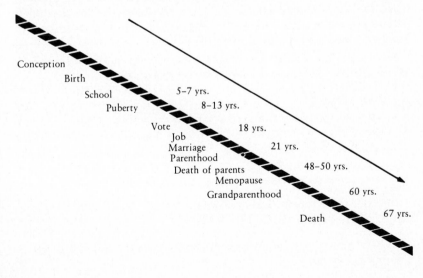

Figure 4-2  Time line illustrating the parallel passage of chronological age and personal developmental events

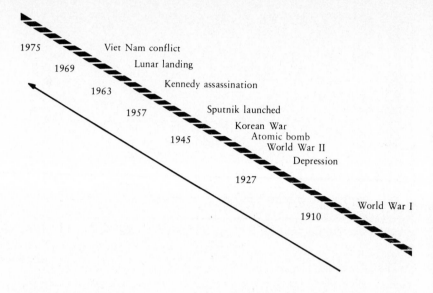

*Figure 4–3    Time line illustrating the historical events that individuals born in different years have been exposed to*

diverse persons. Furthermore, such groups are increasingly heterogeneous the older their members. Age changes and age differences can be accurately measured in research only with careful controls. Experimental design and control are discussed next.

**Methodology**

As stated, using scientific methodology to look at behavior change over time is difficult, and many so-called developmental studies have serious methodological flaws. The student of the psychology of aging needs to understand developmental research methods in order to be able to evaluate the validity of age functions and specific research studies.

Any sort of psychological experimentation begins with the same basic format. The experimental method essentially consists of four steps:

1. Define the problem.
2. Formulate hypotheses as to the suspected causes of the problem.
3. Investigate the hypotheses.
   a. Collect the data.
   b. Analyze the data.
4. Demonstrate the causal relations suggested in the hypotheses.

To illustrate these concepts, a sample developmental study looking at change in a particular behavior over time is presented below.

1. *Define critical behavior* (What is the behavior in question?): Adult health-seeking behavior.

*The cultural and historical experiences to which individuals are exposed at various points in their maturity have an effect on their attitudes, values, and abilities.*

2.  *Formulate hypothesis* (**What affects that behavior? What is your theory as to the cause of increased health-seeking behavior?**): Health-seeking behavior increases when an individual has greater information about health.

3.  *Test your theory* (for this you need an operational definition that allows you to measure your variables): Health behaviors (e.g., number of visits to doctor, participation in exercise programs) or amount of information known about health (e.g., health education course).

4.  *Choose your design variables.*
    a.  Dependent variable (the outcome or effect of the experimenter's manipulation): Health-seeking behavior
    b.  Independent variable (the experimental manipulation): Health education
    c.  Subject variables (variables the experimenter selects for but does not directly control, such as age, sex, race, IQ, eye color, place of birth): Health status

Once the problem is chosen and the hypothesis and experimental variables picked, possible designs to test the hypothesis can be explored.

Two experimental designs that are often used in studies of adult development are the cross-sectional and longitudinal designs (Nesselroade & Harkins, 1980; Wohlwill, 1973). The cross-sectional design tests people of different ages at the same time on a particular measure or set of measures. The longitudinal design tests the same subjects repeatedly over time. Examples of both designs for a study to determine health-seeking behavior are shown below.

In the cross-sectional design, the experimental manipulation, or independent variable, was the giving of a health education course to half of the subjects in each age group. After the course was completed the subjects were measured on the number of health-seeking activities they engaged in over one month. As can be seen, the results indicate that people who take a health education course engage in more health-seeking behavior than those who do not. Another factor that seems to affect health-seeking behavior is age. The older a subject is the more likely that subject is to engage in health-seeking behavior, regardless of exposure to a health education course.

In the past, results such as these might have been interpreted as meaning that people engage in more health-seeking behavior as they age. This statement suggests the occurrrence of change with age. However, cross-sectional studies cannot determine change; they simply measure static behavior, i.e., behavior that different groups of people are found to exhibit in one test session. The only way one can measure change is with a longitudinal design, in which the same subjects are tested at least twice. The design presented below is an example of correlational rather than experimental research.

Because it uses repeated measurements, the longitudinal design allows determination of age change in behavior. In the study of health-seeking behavior, the longitudinal design considers the subject variable of self-assessed health status as the main variable of investigation. The data indicate that middle-aged people in excellent health engage in more health-seeking behaviors than those in good, fair, or poor health as measured by a self-administered health status questionnaire. However, elderly adults in poor to fair health engage in more health-seeking behaviors, and all persons engage in more health-seeking behaviors as they age.

It would be tempting to suggest that this is a pure age change in behavior.

*Cross-sectional design*

| Age group | N | Health education course | N | Number of subjects engaging in health-seeking behavior |
|-----------|-----|------------------------|-----|-----------------------------------|
| 45 | 100 | Yes | 50 | 50 |
|  |  | No | 50 | 50 |
| 65 | 100 | Yes | 50 | 50 |
|  |  | No | 50 | 20 |

*Longitudinal design*

| Age group | N | Year tested | Health status | Number of subjects engaging in health-seeking behavior |
|-----------|---|-------------|---------------|--------------------------------------------------------|
| 45 | 15 | 1983 | Excellent | 7 |
|    |    |      | Good | 5 |
|    |    |      | Fair to poor | 3 |
| 65 | 15 | 2003 | Excellent | 3 |
|    |    |      | Good | 5 |
|    |    |      | Fair to poor | 7 |

However, this cannot be stated definitively on the basis of the data. It is possible, for example, that all members of the cohort tested had been exposed to some natural disaster or historical event that made them more sensitive than usual to the need for health care. It is also possible that the month during which health-seeking behavior was measured was associated with special health needs for the test group.

### Problems with Traditional Developmental Designs
As can be seen from the above discussion, neither design provides clear, unequivocal interpretation of results. These two traditional designs confound several factors:

Age, i.e., actual physical maturation
Cohort, i.e., the generation to which subjects belong as indicated by date of birth
Time of measurement, i.e., idiosyncrasies in behavior associated with the timing of data collection (Friedrich & Van Horn, 1976)

Age per se tends to be a biological measurement, cohort provides a social dimension to the experiment, and time of measurement focuses on historical events occurring in the interval between two or more test times.

Cross-sectional designs generally compare not only two or more age groups, but also two or more cohorts. Suppose the subjects in our cross-sectional example had vast generational differences in addition to their obvious age differences. Suppose the forty-five-year-olds had had extensive training in health education in their formal schooling and had lived through a historical era in which physical fitness was considered important. Suppose in contrast that the sixty-five-year-old subjects had had no formal previous training in health and were too old to get caught up in any physical fitness mania. The behavior of the two groups, could then be attributed not only to biological factors associated with aging but also to the cohorts' particular experiences. Because of this difficulty in data interpretation, cross-sectional designs are said to be *age x cohort confounded.*

The longitudinal design compares not only two different ages but also two times of measurement. Suppose that health-seeking behavior is assessed in the summer for the first test and in the winter for the second test. Health status may vary seasonally, especially in elderly subjects, who are more vulnerable than younger persons to respiratory and viral infections; or in the interval between test times, old and young subjects may be equally affected by cultural emphasis on physical fitness. In this case, the results would not be due to pure age change but might also be a function of historical events occurring between test times. Because of this difficulty in data interpretation, longitudinal designs are said to be *age x time of measurement confounded.*

In summary, the cross-sectional design is economical and may often suggest fruitful hypotheses to be followed up by a more expensive and time-consuming longitudinal design. However, the cross-sectional design does not account for behavioral age differences between two age groups that might be due to sociocultural change. The longitudinal design allows assessment of individual change over time but is plagued by selective sampling errors. The main difficulty with the longitudinal design is that the subjects who volunteer for longitudinal studies tend to be higher in intelligence, health, and socioeconomic status than the general population. Another difficulty with the longitudinal design is the occurrence of selective drop-out and repeated testing effects (Botwinick, 1973; Friedrich & Van Horn, 1976), discussed later in this chapter.

### Sequential Developmental Designs

Many developmental researchers use a design that combines the cross-sectional and longitudinal designs with the time-lag design (Baltes & Nesselroade, 1973; Schaie, 1973). The time-lag design tests different subjects of the same age in different historical times, e.g., eight-year-olds in 1970, 1980, and 1990. In using sequential strategies, the researcher assumes that age, cohort, or time of measurement is not crucial to data interpretation (Friedrich & Van Horn, 1976). An example of this sort of design is the bifactorial model suggested by Baltes and Schaie (1973).

In the bifactorial model the researcher must have at least two cohorts that are sampled across time. Under this model the following assumption is made:

$R = f (A, Co)$ where
$R$ = dependent variable
$A$ = age
$Co$ = cohort

This procedure claims to eliminate the time-of-measurement error by adding parallel cohorts and contrasting their performances. In reality it only assumes that the time-of-measurement error is not an important factor (Botwinick, 1973; Friedrich & Van Horn, 1976).

An example of the bifactorial model is presented in Figure 4-4. As can be seen, the design simultaneously tests subjects using cross-sectional, longitudinal, and time-lag methods. However, sequential designs tend to be very expensive to

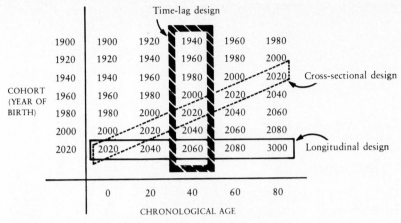

Figure 4–4 The bifactorial design of Baltes

Dates in the middle of the matrix indicate year of testing of the particular cohort.

conduct and are statistically complex. They also are not without flaws (Botwinick, 1977) despite claims to the contrary.

Overall, the consensus among developmental researchers is that some sort of longitudinal or sequential method is by far the best way to assess age change. However, even with such a method researchers must be very cautious in their data interpretation and must try to control subject variables adequately or assess them so as to minimize unexplained variances. The cross-sectional design, though it does not assess age change, presents a quick, efficient method with which to collect data on variables that might be studied more fruitfully in a longitudinal manner. As such, this design may be thought of as a preliminary step in any longitudinal investigation.

### Other Potential Methodological Problems
Aside from the problems with confoundings presented by research designs are other potential methodological problems. These problems may seriously compromise the interpretation of data gained from research. They include the problem of representative sampling, the novelty-of-disruption effect, experimenter effect, the sensitization-retest effect, selective drop-out, and selective mortality (Friedrich & Van Horn, 1976).

Some types of subjects are more available for sampling at one point in development than at another. As people from a particular age group get older and die, the subject sample from that group becomes less representative of the population as young adults; this is the problem of selective mortality. Persons who are healthier, stronger, and more intelligent than normal have a higher probability than normal of surviving to old age. Thus, any subject group of old persons is automatically a

*When comparing young to old subjects, it is more representative to compare community-dwelling members of each group. In general, community dwellers are in better health than their institutionalized peers.*

select sample. This problem demonstrates the difficulty of obtaining a representative sampling, i.e., a subject group with the same characteristics as the population as a whole. Without a representative sampling, the differences and generalizability of the data need to be carefully spelled out as much as possible. An obvious example of these flaws is seen in the tendency of researchers to compare healthy, community-dwelling younger people with institutionalized elderly people. These are clearly different populations as well as different cohorts.

The novelty-of-disruption effect is the effect of experimentation upon a subject's behavior. Especially in studies of institutionalized elderly persons, the experiment itself rather than the experimenter's manipulation often produces the effect of behavior change. The subject's behavior may be atypical because of the individual attention, enthusiasm, or disruption caused by the experiment in an otherwise routine environment. Factorial designs and pre- and postmeasures may be used to compensate for this effect.

In the problem of experimenter effect the behavior of the subject is intentionally or unintentionally influenced by the characteristics or behavior of the experimenter. The experimenter, for example, may unconsciously use body language to cue the subject to make a certain response. The experimenter's biases may also influence the interpretation, recording, or choice of data to be analyzed. Experimenters engaged in research should examine their own values, biases, and behaviors before and while conducting research.

The problem of sensitization retest is simply that a subject's experience on one test may influence that subject's performance on subsequent tests. Similarities between tests in content or format may indirectly cause improvements in sequential performances.

### Conclusions

The classic developmental designs are susceptible to a variety of factors and errors that may influence the validity of experimental results. In particular, each design confounds age with some other variable. The cross-sectional design confuses age-related change with cohort effects, whereas the longitudinal design confuses age-related change with time-of-measurement effects. Various complex developmental research designs, such as sequential procedures, have been suggested by researchers such as Schaie and Baltes as a means of independently analyzing the factors of age, cohort, and time of measurement.

One of the best examples of the way in which the choice of research design may lead to inappropriate interpretations of data is the selective survival and drop-out effects that give rise to the notion of *terminal drop.*

**Research Case Example: Terminal Drop**

Kleemeier (1962) first presented the notion later referred to as the *drop before death* or *terminal drop* when he suggested that

> factors related to the death of an individual cause a decline in intellectual performance and that the onset of this decline may be detected in some instances several years prior to the death of the person. (Kleemeier, 1962, p. 169)

Since the introduction of the notion of terminal drop there have been a number of studies supporting the theory (Baltes & Schaie, 1974; Berkowitz, 1965; Botwinick et al., 1978; Jarvik & Blum, 1971; Lieberman, 1965, 1966; Riegel et al., 1967), but there have also been several studies refuting the theory (Eisdorfer, 1963; Palmore & Cleveland, 1976). Palmore and Cleveland (1976) report that terminal drop studies have a number of methodological and conceptual weaknesses that lessen the credibility of their results and make them somewhat unclear.

In research on the relations between intelligence and terminal drop there are numerous factors that must be accounted for, such as the type of experimental design used, the nature of the subjects and their personal characteristics, methodologies used, and other confounding influences. As discussed, cross-sectional and longitudinal designs have traditionally been used to study the relation between intelligence and age, and each design has its flaws. Cross-sectional studies tend to confuse the effects of age with the effects of cohort. This problem is particularly relevant to research on intellectual aging, since different cohorts often have different educational experiences (Botwinick, 1967). Although longitudinal studies generally avoid this problem by using the same subjects each time, they are somewhat limited by the intervention of uncontrolled factors between test times. Changes between tests may be produced by unique and unintentional sociohistorical influences rather than by the study sample growing older (Friedrich & Van Horn, 1976). By virtue of the deaths of a cohort's least viable members, longitudinal studies on elderly persons tend to show IQ performances higher than would be expected in the general aging population; in contrast, cross-sectional studies tend to show depressed performances by old people because of different cohort experiences. These findings are discussed in more detail in Chapter 8.

Except for a recent prospective study (Botwinick et al., 1978), studies investigating terminal drop have all been retrospective in nature. Retrospective studies generally involve post hoc (after-the-fact) hypotheses, which means that the data have already been collected for one purpose and are now reanalyzed with a new use in mind. Retrospective studies on aging have usually involved the following pattern:

1.  Old subjects were tested for reasons other than prediction of mortality.
2.  Between test times several subjects died.
3.  The idea of comparing the test scores of the survivors and the dead emerged, and statistical comparisons were performed. (Botwinick et al., 1978)

In the prospective design prediction of mortality was the research's main purpose. Despite this procedural difference, however, similar results were found in many of the studies investigating terminal drop.

The importance of subject variables such as age, sex, initial IQ, and type of housing has also been supported by research on terminal drop. As Palmore and Cleveland (1976) indicate, the number of subjects used in the Kleemeier (1962), Berkowitz (1965), and Riegel (1971) studies was very small, for the most part fewer than twenty-eight. Botwinick, West, and Storandt (1978) have reported that many studies used institutionalized subjects or others whose medical problems and custodial care needs bring their representability into question. The ages of subjects in terminal drop studies ranged anywhere from fifty (Berkowitz & Green, 1965; Reimanis & Green, 1971) to eighty (Lieberman, 1965). With such a variety of sample populations it is somewhat suspect whether the results of these studies lend themselves to comparable conclusions.

There are other methodological differences and procedural discrepancies among the various studies. Different subject selection criteria were used. Riegel (1971) suggests that selective survival effects often prevent researchers from obtaining truly homogeneous samples, especially in cross-sectional studies comparing younger with older age groups. A similar consequence is a result of selective participation, in which less able persons are not as likely as more able persons to participate in a study because they have too many problems of their own to contend with. Many studies, such as that of Botwinick, West, and Storandt (1978), required that subjects take a certain number of tests to be included; those who dropped out or died before completing three measurements were not included in the results. Other studies had no such requirements.

The number of testings given and the time interval between tests also differ among the various studies. Berkowitz and Green (1965), for example, administered two examinations with a mean time interval between them of 8.5 years, whereas Lieberman (1965, 1966) tested his subjects every 3 to 4 weeks over a 2 ½-month period. Palmore and Cleveland (1976) contend that at least three measurements are required for detection of terminal drop in accordance with their definition of the phenomenon, i.e., a curvilinear or accelerating drop in intellectual performance before death. Conversely, Jarvik and Falek (1963) assert that in repeated testing situations the risk of "test-wiseness," i.e., the risk that a subject's score increases because of familiarity with the test instrument, is a confounding variable.

Despite these disparities among studies and methodological problems, terminal drop remains an attractive theory. Palmore and Cleveland (1976), who do not support the notion, cite the attractiveness of the theory as one of the main reasons for its widespread acceptance and continued fostering of research. The theory concurs with the patterns of some old people whose functioning remains stable throughout their lives until shortly before death. The theory also helps lessen the conflict between the results of cross-sectional studies, which have found a steady life-cycle decline in functioning, and longitudinal studies, which profess maintenance of or even a possible increase in intellectual functioning throughout the life cycle. Finally the theory is appealing because most people would prefer that their own lives reach a stable plateau and that they experience only a short, quick decline before death (Palmore & Cleveland, 1976; Fries & Crapo, 1982).

In reviewing the literature on terminal drop theory Ilene Siegler (1975) concludes that

> The concept of terminal drop was seen to be useful when partitioned into its component parts: the relationship between the level of cognitive performance with survival and with distance from death, and the relationship between changes in cognitive performance and death. Health status and age at death

emerged as important intervening variables in understanding the terminal drop concept.*

The methodological flaws presented above, coupled with the substantial evidence favoring terminal drop (despite differing subjects, methods, and procedures), suggest that the theory is plausible, at least in Siegler's (1975) context. There is, however, a need for more prospective studies, such as that of Botwinick, West, and Storandt (1978), to offer additional clarification of the relationships between such variables as health status and age.

Research frequently leads to practical applications aimed at improving the quality of life of elderly persons. Terminal drop research, which aims to develop a mortality prediction formula that could be used preventively, has such applicability. Prevention of death might focus on behavioral intervention, stress reduction, assessment of subclinical disease states, and other variables that may affect longevity; potential interventions are discussed in Chapter 6. Efforts have been made to develop such a predictive formula. For example, Palmore (1969) found that actuarial life expectancy at initial testing, physical functioning, work satisfaction, and performance intelligence are the four best predictors of longevity.

The terminal drop literature points out possible linkages betwen psychology and medicine, research and application, and intelligence and health. Although still a controversial area, the terminal drop theory shows what rich possibilities developmental research on late life offers both researchers and practitioners.

**Summary**

In general, research with human subjects aimed at the assessment of developmental functions is not easy to design and conduct. There are invariably problems in the evaluation of the relative contributions of each factor in the results obtained. In natural environments, factors involved in causing certain behaviors are interdependent and may even exert their effects simultaneously. This is especially important to remember in developmental research, which attempts to determine and describe discrete factors and their interactions as they influence the course of the life cycle.

One of the most frequent questions involved in developmental research is that of the relative contributions of heredity and environment in the occurrence of behavior. With regard to aging, this question translates into discussion of the age-dependent nature of behaviors in late life, i.e., the extent to which the behaviors of old people are determined by inevitable processes of aging or by environmental events. The heredity and environmental explanations of such behaviors assert that the behaviors of old age have a single cause. Thus, the developmental researcher's task, regardless of the researcher's position on the

*Siegler, I.C. The terminal drop hypothesis: Fact or artifact? *Experimental Aging Research*, 1975, *1*, 169

*Behaviors of old people
are in part influenced by
environmental events. To
live alone in a large city
entails certain problems
and stresses that influence
the aging process.*

heredity-environment issue, is to find a single factor that provides an index of the causes of age change in behavior.

The most convenient and commonly used index of the cause of developmental change is some version of the variable age—biological, social, psychological, or chronological. Depending on the researcher's theoretical position, age may be interpreted as an index of change that is either fixed or influenced by environmental factors.

Research methodologies are a direct reflection of the assumptions made by the researchers. Contemporary gerontologists and developmentalists generally assume that behavioral change occurs as a result of interaction between heredity and environment. By contrast, the classic research designs were based on the assumption that developmental change is caused by a single factor, either heredity or environment.

The three classic developmental designs—cross-sectional, longitudinal, and time-lag—reflect the traditional single-factor or age-as-cause manner of considering behavioral change. As stated earlier in this chapter, however, these designs are problematic in that they don't measure the effects of age alone. This is not to say that they should be discarded and new methodologies sought; rather, researchers should specify what their data indicate or do not indicate on the basis of the limitations of their research designs.

*Aging is partially influenced by heredity.*

The truth of age-related and age-dependent behaviors will be elucidated only when researchers clearly specify the variables influencing or even potentially influencing their results. This is not an easy or fast task, and in some cases it may be impossible. However, as researchers become more broadly trained in the processes of aging and the multidisciplinary aspects of gerontology, they will at least improve the quality and specificity of the research questions they ask.

*What can each of us expect as part of "normal" aging?*

*Do improvements in today's health-care system mean that we will all be faced with either eventual senility or early death?*

*Are there any differences between the processes of aging and disease processes?*

5

*Physiology of Aging*

Oₙₑ of the most commonly voiced fears about aging is that of entering a long period of disabling physical and mental decline before death.

Many persons see old age as a period of negative growth, i.e., physical change that is deteriorative and irreversible and to be actively avoided. They are afraid that as they get older, they will inevitably get psychologically senile, physically crippled, and behaviorally dependent. "After maturity it's all downhill" has become a prevalent statement among people of all age groups. The historian Lord Toynbee even suggested in *Mankind and Mother Earth* that improved medical care has given us the awkward dilemma of choosing between an early death or eventual senility. To persons who fear death, longevity thus appears at best a mixed blessing.

Our physical and health status as we age is a valid concern. Persons sixty-five years old and older constitute the fastest growing segment of society. From 1960 to 1975, for example, the age group of persons seventy-five years of age and older increased by thirty-six percent. As will be seen in this chapter, the over–seventy-five segment of our population is at especially high risk for health problems. This age group makes up the majority of the over one million persons currently living in long-term care facilities. Fifty to sixty-five percent of the persons living in such institutions have significant orientation, cognitive, and emotional problems. The costs of this long-term care in 1976 were $10 billion, and it is believed that this amount will increase significantly as our population ages (USDHEW, 1977).

As the elderly population increases further, certain issues about our health delivery system will need to be addressed. The risk of emotional and physical problems significantly increases with age, and the health problems of the elderly tend to be chronic disorders requiring palliative rather than curative medical procedures. The manner of health care delivery in the United States will thus have to change, and more health care will need to be made available to serve the increased needs of the aging population. Unfortunately, given increased demand for health care, inflation, and the skyrocketing costs of medical equipment and procedures, it is expected that the costs of medical care will increase radically (Kart et al., 1978).

Given this scenario of the future, society must assess what normal aging is and what the effects of disease processes are. This will allow researchers to design interventions to alleviate or prevent some of the symptoms now viewed as inevitable aspects of aging. It will also allow people to see that the "old age" they fear is really created by disease, not by the mere passage of time.

This chapter deals with aspects of physiological aging that are essential to and

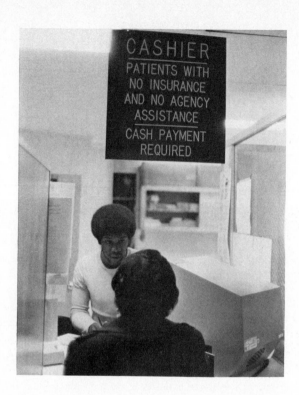

*Given increased demand for health care, inflation, and the skyrocketing cost of medical equipment and procedures, it is expected that the costs of medical care will continue to increase in the next decade.*

characteristic of life. Major physical changes found to occur with advanced age are summarized, and it is shown that these age-related changes are separate from disease-related deterioration and are often successfully adapted to. The major focus is the individual's optimal adjustment to these age changes rather than the inevitability of decline and prolonged senescence before death. Negative age changes are seen in many elderly individuals, but they are not inevitable, need not be prolonged, and are debilitating only when accompanied by disease.

The statement has been made that "nobody has ever died of old age." This is true. Life itself is terminal, and old age, since it is often closest to the end point, has become associated with death merely by contiguity. Death is actually caused by the destructive effects of disease, pollution, stress, and so on acting on the body at any point in the life cycle, not by the elusive specter of "old age."

Only recently have researchers obtained a clear idea of the types of changes that occur as a result of the aging process. Research before the 1950s tended to confuse aging processes with changes due to disease processes (Botwinick, 1977). This is an easy error to make, since the probability of disease increases with age. A greater percentage of old than of young persons are affected by disease. If a great number of diseased individuals are included in a subject sample of old persons, a negative bias against the elderly is created. This error caused early researchers to misrepresent changes caused by the aging process itself and assume that all elderly persons perform at low levels. The results of this methodological flaw have been long-standing; the myths of intellectual decline and senility with age persist. This chapter explores the physical bases for exploding these myths.

Finally, this chapter discusses prevention and intervention as they apply to physical aging and looks at some of the techniques, prostheses, and adaptations that may limit or remove potential physical disabilities associated with advanced age.

Humans have always lived with a conflict between two concepts: the idea of old age as the debilitated end of life, and the idea of longevity or immortality.

**The Historical Context**

The myths of ancient Greece have a very negative view of old age. The Greek goddess Aurora wed a mortal, Tithonus. She was so in love with him that she petitioned Zeus to allow him to live forever. Zeus, touched by her plea, granted her request. As the years passed, however, Aurora watched Tithonus become withered, enfeebled, and decrepit and finally pray for a release from life. Too late she realized that she had asked for immortality but not eternal youth.

The later Greek philosophers Aristotle and Cicero offered the advanced view that aging is not a disease process but rather a natural, universal aspect of life. This is a view we are only now returning to over two thousand years later.

Babylonian and Chinese physicians created death-preventive potions and elixirs of such esoteric compounds as garlic and powdered dog testicles. Throughout the middle ages and into the Renaissance magic, sorcery, and alchemy were used against the feared presence of old age. Even Benjamin Franklin is said to have sought rejuvenation through electricity and chemical potions.

Today we see the battle for eternal youth being waged by scientists such as Ana Aslan of Hungary. Aslan has created a drug called *gerovital,* the ingredients of which include procaine and alcohol. Proponents of the use of gerovital claim that it removes symptoms of aging such as stiffness and slowing. With these ingredients it may very well merely make one "feel no pain." That it halts aging, however, is unlikely. Paul Niehans of Switzerland uses nonhuman embryonic cell therapy to halt aging. His clinic has been visited by many of the rich and famous seeking injections to restore their youth. This therapy is also unlikely to produce the effects its adherents claim. Nonhuman embryonic cells are probably attacked and destroyed by the body's immune system and are thus rendered impotent (Kart et al., 1978).

Thus, whether motivated by a desire for immortality or fear of a protracted period of dependence and disability, philosophers, scientists, and physicians throughout history have been concerned with the reversal or halting of the aging process. The emphasis today is shifting to improvement of the quality rather than the quantity of life. Improved research techniques and methodologies have enabled gerontologists to formulate a more definitive view of the physical changes associated with old age. These changes are neither as disabling nor as damaging as was once believed. It has been found that disease, not age alone, causes the negative symptoms we all fear and hope to avoid.

**Disease Versus Aging**

The distinction between aging and disease processes must be made if fears and prejudice are to be removed from old age and persons who are old. Gerontologists, therefore, want to study aging free of disease. There are two basic ways to do this. One is to use an animal model to simulate what happens as humans age; the other is to control the health status of the individuals to be studied.

### Use of the Animal Model

It is always difficult to use human beings as the subjects of experiments on the nature of physiological aging. Most adult humans have uncertain genetic backgrounds, varying exposures to environmental stressors, different histories of disease processes, and highly idiosyncratic diet and drinking habits. Humans are not amenable to complete life-cycle studies. Moreover, they tend to drop out of any study that becomes too demanding, and this usually occurs just when the experimenter feels things are beginning to get interesting.

Certain animal species, such as the laboratory mouse or rat, make much better subject populations than humans. Others, such as the Galapagos tortoise, which lives for several hundred years, are immeasurably worse. On the whole, animal models must meet several criteria. First, the researcher must be reasonably certain that findings based on the animal model are transferable to humans. Second, the life span of the animal must be short enough to allow study of the whole life cycle. Third, the species must be sufficiently immune to disease to allow the effects of aging to manifest themselves. Finally, the animals used should be small enough to be fed and reared at reasonable expense (Elias et al., 1977).

Given these criteria, many gerontologists have chosen mice as their animal model. Mice have a life span of approximately three years, and they are able to reproduce after twenty-one days. Furthermore, mouse metabolic and endocrine processes lend themselves to human extrapolation. A difficulty with animal models is that psychological variables such as stress that may affect aging in humans are not easily studied in animals; scientists using animal models are therefore limited to studying biological rather than psychological aging processes.

### Controlling for Health Status

As stated, gerontologists generally want to study aging as free of disease processes as possible. The animal model, although workable, largely overlooks the effects of cognition and personality variables on aging. Ideally, then, studies of human aging should use humans as subjects. There are two current methods of doing this. In the first, only healthy subjects are included in the sample. The results of this type of cross-sectional design should reflect true aging processes without the effects of disease. However, as noted in Chapter 4, an age-by-cohort confounding may bias them. For example, today's sixty-five-year-olds grew up before the age of extensive immunization and antibiotics and are thus likely to have had mumps, measles, or even rheumatic fever. The normal physiological aging processes of these individuals may reflect the effects of this past history or serious diseases and thus may be different from the normal aging processes of younger cohorts.

The second way to study human aging with human subjects is to compare optimally healthy old persons (i.e., persons who are totally free of the effects of disease) with normally healthy old persons (i.e., persons with only subclinical manifestations of disease or some trivial illness). In this way researchers can obtain data on aging per se as well as on the interactive effects of disease processes during old age. This method is the better of the two because it lends itself to the study of the overall effects of aging in all types of individuals and eliminates the age-by-cohort confounding of the first method.

Disease and aging interact. Many people over sixty-five are afflicted with atherosclerosis, arteriosclerosis, and so on; these diseases appear to be a result of diet and environmental stressors, which are relatively difficult for most people to escape, especially city dwellers. Therefore, "normal" aging often entails some interaction with disease states.

Methodological improvements were implemented in three major longitudinal projects started in the late 1950s that are now giving us information on normal aging, i.e., aging free of disease. Schaie (1958) investigated age changes in five hundred healthy individuals aged twenty-one to seventy at the onset and living in the community. Birren et al. (1963) and Granick and Patterson (1971), working through the Philadelphia Geriatric Center between 1955 and 1971, collected data on "forty-seven healthy old men," the colloquial name of the study. The subjects were between sixty-five and ninety-one years old at the onset of the study and were free of disease and major psychological disabilities. The final study, conducted by Palmore (1970) between 1955 and 1974 at the Duke University Center for the Study of Aging, was actually two studies. In the first (1955-1973) Palmore studied sixty- to ninety-year-old individuals; in the second (1968-1974) he studied forty-six- to seventy-year-old individuals. The subjects in both studies were normal, healthy community residents from Durham, North Carolina.

The material on physiological aging in the rest of this chapter is largely based on data collected by researchers in these three studies and on more recent studies using similar methodologies (Finch & Hayflick 1977).

Despite different populations, procedures, and measured variables, all the studies of physiological aging show some of the same general changes in physiology with aging (Table 5-1).

Contrary to common misconceptions, physiological changes generally occur

**Generalized Age Changes in Physiology**

*Table 5–1    Generalized age changes in physiology across the adult life span*

Physiological changes are gradual unless disease is present.
Vulnerability to disease increases with age.
Functional decrements are significantly greater in complex than in simple behaviors.
Homeostatic balance becomes increasingly difficult to maintain.
Differences between and changes within individuals are the rule rather than the exception.

gradually throughout adulthood into old age. Therefore, during the greater part of adult life—in the absence of disease—there is a slow decrement in physiological function involving simple, single-organ activities. A greater decrement is observed in complex multiple-organ functions. For example, there is a greater decline with age in maximum breathing capacity than in nerve conduction because nerve conduction involves only the nervous system whereas breathing capacity involves coordinated responses by nerves, muscles, lungs, and so on (Botwinick, 1977).

A common age decrement is seen in ability to resist disease. Older populations have a greater incidence of disease than younger populations owing to increased susceptibility to and inability to combat germs and stress. The immune system, which eliminates foreign substances from the body, appears to lose effectiveness with age and may even begin to turn against the person's own cells (Strehler, 1976). This may lead to an increase in the incidence of such diseases as cancer, stroke, cardiovascular disease, and arthritis. These processes are discussed in greater detail in the next chapter.

Declining physiological function and increased disease with age may be due in part to decreases in the body's homeostatic mechanisms, as discussed in Chapter 3. Homeostasis acts to maintain the chemical and biological equilibrium within the body. This balance is moderately well maintained during old age, but the responses of elderly persons are not as adaptable as those of younger individuals. For example, ability to respond to stress, whether physical or emotional, and then return to prestress levels of bodily functioning is reduced with age. The aged are less able than young persons to cope with blood loss, temperature changes, and infection. In general, they work less time before becoming exhausted and take longer to recover. If their sleep is interrupted, they are less likely to return to deep sleep. Their blood pressure and heart rate at rest are comparable to those of young adults, but when aroused these measures are slower to respond and once they have responded take substantially longer to return to resting levels. All of these changes may be viewed as manifestations of the loss of reserve capacity, that "second wind" that helps us cope with daily crises and stresses (Elias et al., 1977).

For most elderly people some amount of physiological decline is inevitable. When this normal aging is combined with disease processes, the physical and psychological changes are multiplied, as exemplified by the "forty-seven healthy old men" study (Birren et al., 1963). Twenty-seven of the subjects in this study, group I, showed no evidence of major disease or only slight evidence of trivial disease. The remaining twenty men, group II, showed slight evidence of disease

*An example of a "healthy old man."*

with possibly serious implications. (This disease evidence was so slight as to be undetectable in any but the most sophisticated medical examination.) Group II members showed evidence of disease especially in their cerebral circulation and metabolism. However, reduced cerebral blood flow (CBF) and oxygen consumption did not occur among group II subjects with high blood pressure but without arteriosclerosis and did not occur at all in the optimally healthy group I. It therefore appears that reduced CBF and oxygen utilization are due to disease rather than aging (Botwinick, 1977).

Another aging-disease distinction that emerged in the Birren et al. (1963) study relates to the slowing of brain waves with age. Both the optimally healthy and normally healthy old men had slower dominant wave (alpha wave) frequencies than younger subjects. However, the normally healthy subjects showed significantly greater slowing than the optimally healthy subjects. It thus appears that brain-wave changes are age related but are accelerated by disease processes.

Birren et al. (1963) also found that such early manifestations of mental decline as decreased comprehension, memory, attention, and readiness to respond are more closely related to disease processes than to aging. Some group II subjects had early signs of organic brain syndrome (i.e., "senility") without arteriosclerosis, cerebral circulatory and metabolic deficits, or other indications of pathological brain change. This finding indicates that social, psychological, and experimental phenomena, as well as organic disease, may play a role in the symptoms of what is commonly called "senility." The premorbid personalities of these men (i.e., their personalities before the disease manifested itself) often showed depression, a condition that leads to functional deterioration not related to disease. Psychomotor slowing and psychiatric depression may well be caused by negative environmental influences that act to modulate the psychomotor decrement. If disease is added to a poor premorbid personality stance, an overall precipitous decrement occurs. These concepts are discussed further in Chapter 10.

The overall results of the longitudinal studies of physical aging indicate that aging per se is accelerated by depression from environmental loss and disease-related vascular changes such as high blood pressure, arteriosclerosis, and atherosclerosis. In the absence of these factors, little if any behavioral decrement is observed for the greater part of the adult life cycle. Individual differences of course affect the emergence of these age changes. Not only do individuals age at different rates, but different tissues and systems within an individual may age at different rates as well. These differences among and changes within individuals render any statement on general age changes probabilistic. Certain physiological changes tend to occur with age, and everyone who lives long enough will manifest them to some degree. However, the extent, duration, and onset of these behavioral symptoms vary widely enough that there is no time-limited, "typical" pattern of aging.

### Functional Age Changes in Physiology

The organ systems of most persons show a 0.8 to 1 percent decline per year in functional ability after the age of 30 (Hayflick, 1977). Some of this decline is normal, some is disease related, and some is caused by the misuse of our bodies. Health and nutritional status, stress history, occupational status, sex, and many other factors affect a person's pattern of aging, so that individual differences are often the rule rather than the exception. Nonetheless, normal aging processes can be placed in a tentative framework.

*Tissue Changes*   Tissue changes are often the first observed, most noticeable, and least desired indices of a person's age. The tissues that most visibly show the effects of time and contribute most to the images and stereotypes of old age are the skin, hair, and teeth. The skin serves certain functions for the body: it protects our inner organs, eliminates toxins, and provides us with our tactile sense. As we age, the skin changes (Table 5-2). Collagen is a molecule that makes up the bulk of connective tissue. As time passes, the hydrogen bonds between molecules of collagen break

*Table 5-2   Normal changes with age in the skin*

Decreasing number of cells
Decreasing amount of subcutaneous fat
Decreasing number of nerve cells and nerve cell endings
Decreasing amount of blood flow
Decreasing elasticity
Decreasing amount of secretions of sweat and sebaceous glands
Increasing areas of pigmentation
Increasing amounts of dryness and coarsening of nails and hair
Increasing susceptibility to infection and trauma

down, and the molecules of collagen in the skin cross-link. This causes the skin to thicken, harden, and become less elastic.

Normal skin cells in a thirty-year-old live approximately one hundred days; in a seventy-year-old they live only forty-six days. In elderly persons cells die faster and are replaced more slowly than in young persons. Subcutaneous tissue begins to disappear, and the skin over it looks "loose." The number of nerve cells enervating the skin decreases, and the tactile sense becomes less sensitive. The skin loses its ability to retain fluids with age; as a result it becomes dry and brittle and loses its flexibility. Spots of pigmentation occur, and wounds heal less quickly than before. These effects may also be caused by changes in collagen, which tightens and immobilizes skin tissue. Hair also grays and thins because the melanocytes, the cells that normally provide pigment, run out of pigment granules.

Other cosmetic tissues also show age-related changes. By age sixty-five, fifty percent of the population have lost all their teeth, a condition called *edentia*. It is believed that this is a cohort effect and will become less common as younger cohorts who have been exposed to fluoridation and good dental techniques reach old age. In general, bone tissue shows extensive evidence of aging (Table 5-3). The skeleton is fully formed by the early twenties. Bones become increasingly brittle and susceptible to breakage with age. Calcium deposits and diseases of the joints also increase with age. For example, arthritis becomes more common owing to simple wear and tear on the joints and alterations in collagen structure, which act to limit the flexibility of the muscles.

The slight loss of stature generally seen among elderly persons appears to be due to the wearing or shrinkage of disks in the spinal column. The extent of shrinkage

*Table 5-3   Normal changes with age in the human skeleton*

Decreasing hardness of bones
Decreasing elasticity of joints and ligaments
Decreasing mobility of joints
Decreasing activity of bone marrow
Increasing shift of mineral salts from bones to blood
Increasing postural and foot changes

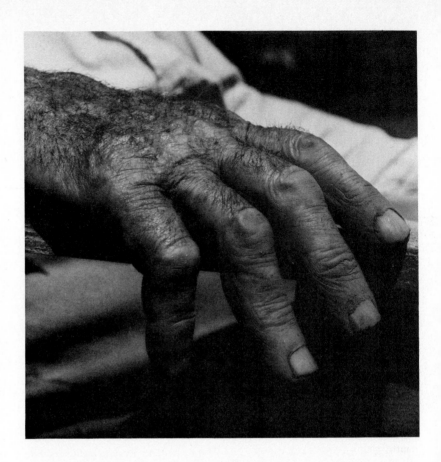

*As people age, the skin loses its ability to retain fluids and becomes dry, brittle, and less flexible.*

may be exaggerated, however, by the greater height of younger generations resulting from such factors as improved nutrition. Whatever the cause, diminished stature may present a psychological problem for elderly individuals who feel that their social roles and prestige are also shrinking.

Muscle tissue decreases in size and strength after peak muscle quality is achieved between age twenty and thirty (Table 5-4). Muscle mass goes through a steady though gradual decline after maturity. Although muscle may be built up to some extent by exercise and diet, muscle tone becomes increasingly difficult to maintain with age because of an increase in fatty substance within the muscle fibers. Muscle strength also declines with age because it requires the coordination of complex groups of muscles, and complex functions deteriorate with age more quickly than simple functions.

The loss of muscle size and strength with age is easily observed, but its causes are not simple. The decline appears to be due to at least three nonmuscular events. First, the lungs are not as efficient as before in oxygen uptake and show a diminished breathing capacity. This causes the overall amount of oxygen available

*Table 5–4   Normal changes with age in muscle tissue*

Decreasing muscle mass
Decreasing amount of stored glycogen
Decreasing blood flow
Increasing variability of nerve conduction and irritability
Increasing amount of waste products retained
Decreasing elasticity of tendons and ligaments
Decreasing endurance and agility
Increasing variability of muscle tonicity
Increasing amount of muscle spasms

---

for metabolism to be decreased. Second, partially because of this diminished uptake and partially because of inadequacies in the circulatory system, not enough oxygen is carried to the muscles to maintain their viability. Finally, as a result of the relatively inactive role they are forced to take in our society, old people do not get enough exercise to maintain muscle tone.

Nerve tissue also shows age-related decrements. There is some slowing in the speed of nerve conduction with age, but this is minor. More important is the irreversible loss of nervous tissue from the time of birth on. The decline in complex-system coordination that occurs with age may be due in part to nerve loss or slowing. Decreases in nerve impulse speed may thus have an indirect effect on participation in exercise and other activities by the elderly (Weg, 1975).

Although tissue decrements occurring with age involve only single sets of cells, their effects are much broader. The loss of height and teeth, balding and graying of the hair, wrinkling of the skin, and lack of physical strength all have a potentially negative effect on an individual's self-concept and confidence, especially in our youth-conscious culture. In the United States there is generally no prestige associated with age; there is only forced retirement and loss of identity. Old age might not be such a haunting specter in a society in which senior citizens were valued for their wisdom and experience.

## Molecular and Cellular Changes with Age

The general changes (see Table 5-1) and the tissue alterations discussed above may well arise from molecular and cellular aging. Since the tissues and organs of the human body are composed of cells, it makes intuitive sense that changes at this "micro" level might well produce larger alterations in the functions of the body.

Cellular aging is a complicated process that gerontological biologists are only now beginning to understand (Finch & Hayflick, 1977). Not all cells in our bodies age in the same way. With a few exceptions—notably nerve cells and certain types of muscle cells—the human organism changes completely every few years (Hayflick, 1977). Our cells are constantly developing, reproducing, and dying within our bodies.

Cells age in three essentially distinct ways. The first class of cells continually

*Physical signs of aging have a potentially negative effect on an individual's self-concept, but for many old people they are irrelevant.*

reproduce, but their regenerative capacity slows. The second class of cells, called *postmitotic cells* by geneticists, lose their reproductive capacity before birth or shortly thereafter. The third class of cells, which make up intercellular connective tissues such as collagen, show altered function and structure over time. The third class is discussed extensively in Chapter 3; the second class of cells is discussed in Chapter 12.

As a person ages, the cells that continue to reproduce do so at a slower rate. The cell repair rate is slower, and the potential for chromosomal errors to occur is thus greater. Chromosomal errors also tend to occur in cells that no longer reproduce. These errors may cause enzymes to be incorrectly produced or utilized. Consequently, organs may begin to misfunction. If the cellular errors in either cell type are sufficiently serious, the immune system may attack the cells as "foreign invaders" and cause further cell dysfunction or necrosis (i.e., cell death). In any case, normal aging at the cellular level may well have systemic, or whole-body, effects.

## Changes in Physical Systems and Their Consequences

As mentioned, age-associated deteriorated functioning is most evident when complex structures or behaviors are involved. The body systems, such as the cardiovascular and pulmonary systems, involve such coordinated responses by diverse tissue groups. Decrements in these systems also have a potentially more lethal effect than decrements in single organs because they may eventually evolve into a whole-body response. For example, hormones, which are produced by the endocrine system (a coordinated system of ductless glands), help control blood volume, excretion of waste, metabolism, blood pressure, growth, and so on. Decreased responsivity of the endocrine system alone could thus lead to a lack of homeostasis throughout the body.

### Respiratory System

The respiratory system, which comprises the airways and lungs, is responsible for breathing and thus for life itself. As can be seen in Table 5-5, the respiratory system undergoes many changes with age. One change is a measurable reduction in breathing efficiency; the lungs of an old person do not expand to take in as much air as the lungs of a young person. Oxygen uptake in the lungs is diminished, so that less oxygen is transported by the blood in old than in young persons. The decreased availablity of oxygen has important health implications because oxygen is necessary for the synthesis of body building blocks such as amino acids, glucose, and fatty acids, as well as for the production of energy. A person who is not getting enough oxygen will be less active, less aware, and less strong than one who is getting enough oxygen. This decline appears to be part of normal aging and is perhaps due to increased collagen in the lung tissue and walls of blood vessels. When disease such as emphysema or arteriosclerosis is present, the decline is more obvious and of course more significant.

### Gastrointestinal System

The gastrointestinal system undergoes considerable changes with age (Table 5-6). The two main changes appear to be the decreased production of digestive juices and a reduction in peristalsis. Peristaltic action, which consists of waves of contraction that force the contents of the digestive system downward, is involved in the metabolism and excretion of food and is therefore essential to overall health. Malnutrition and constipation, which occur increasingly with age, are indicative of digestive system changes. It is unclear, however, whether these system changes are caused by or whether they themselves cause the malnutrition and constipation associated with age.

The food intake of the typical elderly person is low in both amount and quality. This decrease may occur for several reasons. It may be due to ignorance of what constitutes a healthful diet. An adequate diet requires some daily balanced intake of protein and carbohydrate; thus, a person on a balanced diet must consume meat, cheese or other dairy products, fruit, cereal, and vegetables every day. Since the elderly are not able to utilize these foods optimally once they have been consumed,

*Table 5-5  Normal changes with age in the respiratory system*

Decreasing elasticity of alveoli
Decreasing tonicity of intercostal muscles and diaphragm
Decreasing vital capacity
Decreasing blood flow
Increasing dessication of respiratory mucous membranes

*Table 5-6   Normal changes with age in the gastrointestinal system*

Decreasing capacity for biting and chewing
Decreasing capacity for smelling and tasting
Decreasing production of digestive enzymes
Decreasing gastric and intestinal mobility
Decreasing thickness of gastrointestinal lining
Decreasing number of liver cells and liver function
Increasing variability in swallowing reflex
Increasing variability in peristalsis
Increasing variability in amount of bile flow

it is more crucial for them than for young persons to maintain a reasonably well balanced diet. Malnutrition is becoming a serious problem among the elderly. Potassium, calcium, iron, and vitamin $B_{12}$, which are necessary for adequate heart, muscle, bone, and thyroid function, become easily depleted in the elderly, and their depletion can lead to serious health problems. Elderly persons must be especially careful to follow the dictates of nutritional law rather than their stomachs or pocketbooks. Macaroni may be cheaper and more filling than yogurt, but yogurt is much more healthful and nutritious and therefore ultimately cheaper. Problems like these show the utility of programs for the elderly such as nutrition classes, Meals on Wheels, and community dining sites.

Another possible cause of malnutrition and constipation in the elderly is lack of appetite. Since the digestive processes in elderly persons are greatly decreased, the signals indicating hunger are not readily produced. This should not be taken to mean that the body's demand for food is decreased, but merely that the utilization of vitally needed nutrients is lower.

Poor dentition also affects eating habits. Persons who have few or no teeth, do not enjoy eating much, and the types of food they can eat are limited. Poor dentition and decreased appetite may well be related psychologically. Persons who can't eat what they want to eat may well decide not to eat at all. Not being able to afford desirable foods also psychologically affects appetite. Many old persons are on small, fixed incomes and cannot afford to buy the food necessary to maintain a well-balanced diet.

Poor nutrition may be responsible for all the other changes noted with age in digestive system functioning. Even constipation may be due to dietary insufficiency, such as lack of fiber, rather than to biological change. It may also be that the supposed increase in constipation merely reflects age differences in concern with constipation. Old people may have more free time than young persons in which to dwell on changes in their physical processes. Another possible psychological cause of constipation is cohort differences in toilet training. Excessive concern or undue harshness in toilet training may well give rise to later emphasis on changes in urination and defecation. This is a rather Freudian interpretation of constipation, but it does present the notion of interaction between a person's psychological and physical functions.

*It is crucial for the elderly to maintain a reasonably well balanced diet.*

### Cardiovascular System

The cardiovascular system, which includes the heart and the blood vessels throughout the body, tends to show the effects of normal aging relatively slowly (Table 5-7). It also shows several disease-related decrements in old persons that were formerly thought to represent processes of normal aging. For example, a steady increase in blood pressure often occurs with age. However, studies show that optimally healthy old individuals have blood pressures similar to those of young healthy subjects, so such an increase must be due to disease processes. In fact, this blood pressure increase appears to be due to narrowing of the blood vessels caused by two diseases: atherosclerosis, the deposition of fatty substances on arterial walls; and arteriosclerosis, the hardening and thickening of those walls. When the blood pumped from the heart meets with increased resistance in the peripheral constricted

*Table 5-7   Normal changes with age in the cardiovascular system*

Decreasing muscle tonicity
Decreasing elasticity of blood vessels
Decreasing body fluids
Increasing heart size
Increasing time required for heart to return to rest
Decreasing cardiac output
Decreasing venous return
Decreasing blood cell production
Increasing arterial resistance to passage of blood
Increasing variability of neutral conduction and irritability

vessels of the cardiovascular system, increased blood pressure results. High blood pressure is a health hazard because it places strain on the vascular system, heart, kidneys, and body tissues.

Resting heart rate and beat decline with age, as does the heart's response to exercise. These are indices of heart muscle tone. However, when disease is present, blood pressure goes up with exercise because of increased peripheral resistance occurring as a function of the amount of damage or narrowing of the peripheral blood vessels.

In optimally healthy persons, there is generally no change in cerebral blood flow (CBF) with age. CBF is decreased in persons with vascular disease, and until recently this was thought to be due to the lack of flexibility and volume of the vessels. However, it now appears that such CBF changes may be secondary to pathological lesions and changes in brain tissue structure (Bondareff, 1980). This means simply that disease-produced lesions create areas in the brain that call for little or no blood. Therefore, regardless of whether the CBF is reduced or increased, damaged tissues produce local areas of ischemia (blood deprivation).

### Endocrine and Immune Systems

With age, a person generally produces fewer hormones, and the hormones produced are not adequately received by the target organs. This, in turn, produces malfunction of these organs. Glucose tolerance decreases, and the body loses its ability to maintain an adequate fluid balance. The immune system loses its efficiency partially because normal feedback systems in the body no longer function effectively. The immune system also tends to turn against the body in an auto-immune response, as more and more cells become faulty. The total effect of the changes in the endocrine and immune systems is that aging persons show an increasing inability to adapt to stresses from their inner and outer environments, such as infections, temperature change, and psychosocial distress. Normal age-associated changes in these systems are shown in Table 5-8.

### Urinary System

The urinary system includes the kidneys, bladder, and ureters. A variety of normal changes in these organs act to lower the general efficiency of the urinary system in

*Table 5-8   Normal changes with age in the endocrine system*

Decreasing number of cells and size of glands
Decreasing amount of secretions
Decreasing capacity for tissue repair
Decreasing capacity to maintain Na, K, and fluid balance
Increasing variability in adapting to stress
Increasing variability in calcium/glucose metabolism
Increasing variability in inflammatory response
Increasing variability in tolerance to temperature changes

elderly persons (Table 5-9). The number of cells in the kidney decreases, and this causes decreased excretion of wastes and toxins from the body. Furthermore, the bladder becomes less elastic, causing urinary leakage to become more common and in extreme cases leading to urinary incontinence.

These two factors may lead to serious health problems for the elderly. First, the kidney's inability to excrete wastes may affect a person's response to drugs. If drugs are not properly excreted, they may build up in the body and combine with other drugs to produce serious side-effects. This is especially relevant to persons over sixty-five, who take three times as many prescription drugs as all other age groups combined. Second, incontinence is the most frequently cited reason for institutionalizing a failing older person.

## The Brain and Central Nervous System

The aging of the brain and central nervous system (CNS) acts to integrate the diverse realities of aging. The brain of course plays a critical role in the aging of various parts of the body. In turn, aging processes within the body play an important role in determining the functional status of the brain. For example, when the heart becomes less efficient in pumping blood or when cholesterol and lipids block the lumen of blood vessels, CBF is decreased, affecting the health of brain cells. Another example is stress. In a person subject to stress, autonomic nervous system overarousal leads to a massive neurohumoral discharge. The limbic system, hypothalamus, pituitary gland, and other parts of the brain become involved in a "fight-or-flight" response. In a person under continual stress, the CNS response may well lead to fatigue or death. Old people as a group tend to be both more subject to stress and less able physiologically to deal with its effects than young people.

### Central Nervous System Aging: Behavioral Indices
Why is brain aging of psychological concern? Many geropsychologists and gerontological researchers consider the aging of the human brain to be the most crucial effect of senescence. Senescence of the brain and other CNS tissue produces both personal anguish and secondary effects on other organ systems (Terry & Gershon, 1976). The brain is an ideal organ to study in research on CNS aging because the subject can offer personal reports of its functional integrity and various activities.

*Table 5-9   Normal changes with age in the urinary system*

Decreasing number of cells in kidney
Decreasing blood flow to kidney
Decreasing elasticity of bladder
Decreasing muscle tonicity of urethra
Increasing variability in irritability and neural conduction to urethra
Increasing concentration of urine

The CNS is a model system in that it can allow analysis from as low as the molecular-genetic level to as high as the level of psychometric performance.

The progression of CNS senescence is measured by behavioral indices. Aging in the brain results from the postmitotic nature of CNS tissue. The neurons of the brain and CNS tissue are irreplaceable cells, i.e., cells that no longer undergo mitosis or cell division. The mitotic arrest of CNS cell populations has certain psychological advantages; it makes possible intelligence, self-concept, and long-term memory. However, this same cell constancy also prevents indefinite functioning and immortality.

> If the CNS had evolved in such a manner as to be capable of an indefinitely long existence without decrement in function, most if not all other bodily functions could foreseeably be replaced by prosthetic mechanisms at worst or by regenerated tissues at best. But substitutions of new brain cells for old ones would do violence to the continuity of that entity we call the self, the benefactee of that complex of self-preservative reactions we undertake reflexively and through acquired behavior. . . . No other creature is burdened with a knowledge of his own impermanence. Although such knowledge may add to the delight of years each of us has, it also generates an invisible background shroud that most of us can ignore most of the time.*

When it cannot be ignored, the "background shroud" gives rise to the fears and myths of senility discussed earlier.

The CNS shows certain predictable and universal changes as a function of age (Table 5-10). The most definite change is the disproportionate slowing of complex reaction time over simple reaction time. This slowing of responses to external stimuli is at least in part a manifestation of changes in perceptual ability. One measure of perceptual ability is the time it takes to recognize a stimulus. Reaction time tasks used in experiments, however, often involve more than one sensation and reaction, and they frequently also entail interpretation (recognition). Therefore, reaction time, like other perceptual measures, involves some degree of central processing. Reaction time is considered in greater detail in Chapter 7.

Botwinick (1977) states that response slowing is due to age-related changes in central rather than peripheral processes such as decreased sensory organ sensitivity. Evidence provides some support for this view. Apparently, age-related declines are due to changes in several processes rather than in a single CNS process. Some relations found indicate that cogntive functions frequently come under the control of central processes, which thus affect reaction time. For example, there is some correlation between extent of brain damage and reaction time, between reaction time and measures of reasoning ability, and between reaction time and memory. Reaction time also appears to be more closely associated with general intellectual performance among old than among young subjects. All of these factors strongly

*Strehler, B.L. Introduction: Aging in the human brain. In R.B. Terry & S. Gershon (Eds.), *Neurobiology of aging.* New York: Raven Press, 1976, p. 1.

Table 5-10    Normal changes with age in the nervous system

Decreasing number of cells and cell endings
Decreasing irritability and conduction
Decreasing rate of arterial flow
Decreasing rate of venous flow
Increasing variability in perception, equilibrium, and motor coordination
Increasing variability in reception, integration, and response to external and internal stimuli

implicate a deterioration of CNS function in the response slowing that occurs with age (Birren et al., 1980).

Additional age-related changes in the CNS are decreased numbers of cells and cell endings, decreased conduction speed, and overall decreased efficiency. The behavioral effects of these physical age changes include lowered sensory awareness, greater variability in integrative capacities, and an increased pain threshold.

CNS aging is highly variable and difficult to measure because it is intrinsically linked with our intellectual abilities. For example, anxiety, cautiousness, and personality factors, as well as response speed, all influence a person's ability to respond on a given task. Because these factors are often difficult to control or predict, the relation of many facets of CNS aging to behavior may be incorrectly estimated; the extent of CNS aging as determined in the laboratory setting may thus have no observable effect in the real world where the old subject is relaxed, familiar, and supported.

The integrity of the cerebral cortex, the outer surface of the brain, is affected by diseases that result in cell loss, interference with circulation, and ischemia (oxygen deprivation associated with decreased blood flow). Diseases affecting the cerebral cortex are hypertension (Light, 1975; Spieth, 1965), coronary heart disease (Abrahams & Birren, 1973), and cerebrovascular disease (Light, 1978). Even the medications used to treat these disorders may affect the cerebral cortex (Light, 1975, 1978). Researchers believe that the slowing of reaction time found even in healthy old people indicates some level of neurologic damage associated with ischemia (Birren et al., 1980). Many researchers also believe that loss of reaction time speed is the central mediating process in CNS function and cognitive performance in old age (Birren et al., 1980; Salthouse, 1980).

*Sensory Acuity*    As will be discussed in Chapter 7, sensory acuity generally declines in a predictable fashion with age. This decline is at least partially caused by a loss of peripheral nerve fibers. However, the cerebral cortex has also been implicated in the loss of the ability to understand speech patterns that sometimes occurs in advanced old age. Because this loss occurs even when the ability to hear component sound stimuli remains intact, some central processing deficit appears to be responsible.

*Attention and Arousal*    Many elderly persons suffer from short attention spans and are less aroused by changes in their environment than younger persons. This attention deficit is believed to be a central processing phenomenon (Strehler, 1976).

*Altered Brain Wave Activity*   The frequency of alpha rhythms slows in old persons by approximately twenty percent, going from ten to twelve cycles per second to eight to ten cycles per second (Birren et al., 1980; Botwinick, 1967). This decline is believed by researchers to indicate a decrease in the functional ability of the CNS and the existence of some sort of neurologic pathology.

In general the functional capacities of the CNS, like those of other bodily organ systems, are perfectly adequate to carry out responses to everyday challenges and living activities. However, when the brain and CNS of an elderly person are challenged by a demand for large work output or by stress conditions, their reserve capacity is depleted, and the differences between young and old persons become more noticeable. One of the most fundamental manifestations of brain aging is decreased homeostatic adaptation to environmental challenges; old organisms are simply more susceptible to system overload than young organisms

### Brain Aging: Physical Correlates

There are four main structural constituents of the brain: nerve cells (neurons); neuroglia (glial cells, which are the functional supporting cells of the CNS); the

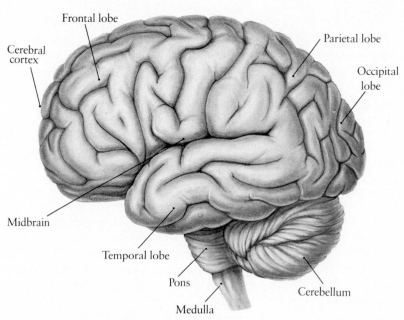

*Figure 5–1   A lateral view of the human brain*

(Source: Carlson, N.R. *Physiology of behavior*, Second edition. Boston, MA: Allyn & Bacon, 1981, p. 112)

vascular system, including the blood-brain barrier; and simple connective tissue. Each of these four structures depends on and affects the others.

*Normal Brain Anatomy*   As shown in Figures 5-1 and 5-2, the brain is an organ composed of various substructures. The brain stem, which is contiguous with the upper portion of the spinal cord, is composed of the medulla oblongata, the pons, and the midbrain. The *medulla* is a direct continuation of the spinal cord into the skull through which all ascending and descending nerve fiber tracts connecting the brain and spinal cord must pass. Within the medulla are the centers for control of respiration, periperal vasoconstriction (blood pressure), heart rate, functioning of the gastrointestinal tract, and the strength of heart muscle contractility. The medulla also plays a fundamental role in attention and arousal.

The *midbrain* merges with the thalamus and hypothalamus, which are impor-

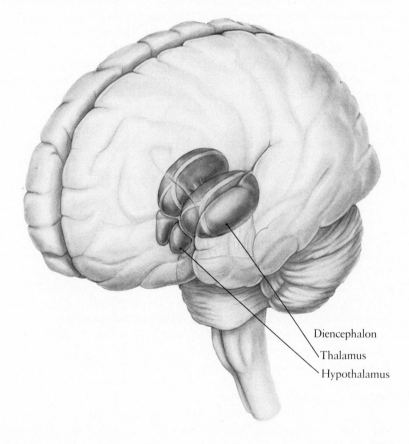

Diencephalon
Thalamus
Hypothalamus

*Figure 5-2   A schematic representation of the human brainstem and diencephalon*

(Source: Carlson, N.R. *Physiology of behavior*, Second edition. Boston, MA: Allyn & Bacon, 1981, p. 117)

tant centers in the endocrine control of behavior. The midbrain contains relay structures that control vision and hearing and is involved in the control of eye movements and muscle coordination.

Above the brainstem and below the cerebral cortex, buried between the right and left hemispheres of the cortex, is a part of the brain called the *diencephalon* or *old brain*. In an evolutionary sense this is the oldest portion of the human brain. It is important in the elicitation of many primitive behavioral responses and is integrally involved in the function of another series of brain structures referred to as the *limbic system*. The diencephalon has two major components, the thalamus and hypothalamus.

The *thalamus*, a group of many small structures, acts as a relay station between the brain stem and the cerebral cortex. Some areas of the thalamus receive specific projections from specific sense organs that are then relayed to specific areas of the cerebal cortex called the *sensory association areas*. The thalamus does not receive information directly from sense organs but integrates sensory information and relays it to the appropriate cortical association area. The *subthalamus* is involved in the extrapyramidal system of motor responses, e.g., the control and coordination of motor activity. In patients with Parkinson's disease (discussed in Chap. 6) the neurotransmitter dopamine is absent from the terminals of the axons that originated from cell bodies in the substantia nigra, a subthalamic structure.

The *hypothalamus* contains centers for the control of vegetative functions such as eating, drinking, sleeping and the regulation of body temperature, sexual behavior, water balance, and so on. The hypothalamus also closely controls the pituitary gland, a key component of the endocrine system. These two glands are involved in the modulation of emotion as well as in the moderation of approach and avoidance behaviors.

The *limbic system* is a series of structures the main components of which are the amygdala and hippocampus. This system interacts with the hypothalamus in controlling emotions and emotional expression and in the "fight-or-flight" response. It has also been implicated in determining learning and memory. The functions of the *amygdala,* which lies deep in the base of the temporal lobe, are unclear. However, this portion of the limbic system is believed to play a role in territoriality, interference with avoidance learning, social dominance, and emotions. Removal of the amygdala causes a behavioral syndrome characterized by compulsive oral responses (i.e., putting all possible objects into the mouth), loss of fear, aggressiveness, hypersexuality, and increased psychomotor activity. The *hippocampus* is evolutionarily the oldest portion of the brain. It is thought to be involved in memory (especially immediate memory), emotion, visceral activity, and behavioral suppression.

The last area of the brain implicated in changes associated with aging is the *cerebral cortex*, in humans the largest portion of the brain. The cerebral cortex is separated into two hemispheres that are connected by numerous fiber tracts above the thalamus. The two hemispheres of the brain are believed to have distinct yet complementary functions. The left hemisphere, which controls the right side of the body, is believed to control language production, analytical ability, and sequential processing. The right side of the brain, which controls the left side of the body, is believed to control language reception, spatial ability, and certain types of reasoning. The cortex as a whole contains centers for vision, hearing, speech, sensory perception, emotions, and other skills believed to be unique to human beings.

Besides being separated into two hemispheres, the cerebral cortex is divided into four lobes: frontal, temporal, parietal, and occipital. The area in which the frontal and temporal lobes are contiguous appears to be implicated in some of the behavioral indices of brain aging.

*Changes in Brain Structure with Aging*    Various neuronal alterations have been associated with aging (Bartus et al., 1982; Coyle et al., 1982). These include changes in subcellular level, the accumulation of lipofuscin in nerve and glial cells, the neurofibrillary changes of Alzheimer, granulovacuolar changes, the development of senile plaques, the development of angiopathies and amyloid bodies, and the development of capillary fibrosis.

Brain neurons generally decrease in size with age and lose Nissl bodies, and their cell nuclei also decrease in size. The amount of lipofuscin in the cells increases, and metallic elements—especially copper and iron—begin to accumulate in the cell body. Essential synthetic processes within neurons are thus gradually impaired.

Alzheimer's neurofibrillary tangles, named after the man who first described them in 1907, are ofen found in the nerve cells of old people. These tangles, believed to reflect abnormal protein metabolism and to eventually lead to neuronal death, are skeins and whorls of microtubules that proliferate and form parallel bundles within the cell's cytoplasm. As they fill out the inner part of the cell, they displace the nucleus. It has been reported that after the cell's death the wicker-basket-like strands may persist for a time after the rest of the cell has disappeared.

Neurofibrillary tangles are usually seen in both the hippocampus and amygdala of mentally well preserved old people. Up to one hundred percent of centenarians have shown tangle formation in these areas upon autopsy (Strehler, 1976). However, heavy tangle formation throughout the neocortex, often compounded by a large number of senile plaques, has been found to be restricted to persons with dementia.

In combination with senile plaques and neurofibrillary tangles researchers often find granulovacuolar degenerations in the cell bodies of normal and demented old persons. Granulovacuolar degenerations are dense granules surrounded by vacuoles. They are often found in cell cytoplasm, especially in the hippocampus neurons of the left frontotemporal cortex. These areas displace the Nissl substance of the cell and cause its outline to become irregular. Granulovacuolar degenerations increase with age, but there is no proof that they constitute a stage of neuronal degeneration. Their origin is unknown (Adams, 1980; Strehler, 1976).

As mentioned, senile plaques are often found in conjunction with Alzheimer's tangles and granulovacuolar degenerations. These plaques are amorphous structures of unknown origin believed to be formed of one or several degenerated neurons. Their center often contains amyloid, a by-product of immune system activity.

Researchers found small numbers of senile plaques in fifteen percent of autopsied fifty-year-olds, fifty percent of autopsied persons in their seventies, and seventy-five percent of autopsied persons in their nineties. (These figures are based on a clinically unassessed population dying in an acute general hospital [Tomlinson & Henderson, 1976]). The majority of old people in whom large numbers of plaques in their cortex were found on autopsy were demented, and the majority of old people with few senile plaques found on autopsy were those with well-retained intellectual ability. Although the general rule was that the larger the number of plaques present the greater the degree of dementia, there were exceptions.

Senile plaques in demented subjects seem most densely compacted in the frontotemporal cortex, specifically the amygdala and hippocampus. When numerous, however, they generally occur at all levels of the cortex. The cells in which senile plaques occur also show axonal abnormalities.

Researchers involved in age-related brain morphological changes generally indicate that the difference between the brains of normal and the brains of demented subjects is one of degree rather than kind (Adams, 1980; Tomlinson & Henderson, 1976). In old subjects showing considerable dementia, heavy cell loss has been found in areas of the brain simultaneously affected by senile plaques, neurofibrillary tangles, and cell loss. This is usually the frontotemporal cortex, the part of the brain that seems to be involved in immediate memory, emotions, inhibition, and aggression. It is interesting to compare the physiological correlates of dementia with the behavioral symptoms. As will be seen in Chapter 10, the behavioral symptoms that would be predicted on the basis of the areas of the brain showing the most critical cell destruction are in fact often seen in various sorts of dementia. In demented persons in whom tissue destruction is not massive but rather approaches the amount found in nondemented old subjects, the distribution of lesions is probably critical (Tomlinson & Henderson, 1976).

## Environmental Intervention in Brain Aging

The patterns of physiological aging in the brain and the body are as varied as the individuals who age. A person's life history as well as genetics affects the aging pattern (Fries & Crapo, 1981). Poor diet, overeating, smoking, excessive drinking, misuse of drugs, accidents, and stress all affect health. Since each person has a unique experience with these factors, there is great diversity in the physical manifestations of aging. The Roman philosopher Seneca stated that "Man does not die, he kills himself"; it might be added that some people do it more effectively and quickly than others. However, there are interventions that might be suggested to prevent disability or deal with its effects in old persons who have undergone extensive functional deterioration because of life-style or disease.

From the above discussion it appears that the only thing that separates normal from demented old people is number of shared physical pathologies. However, this is only a partial picture. The causes of dementia are still unknown. Recent studies have supported the conclusions of the researchers cited in this chapter. Cohen and Eisdorfer (1982) have reported that serum immunoglobulins are present in far higher concentrations than normal in the blood of patients with senile dementia. They found that impaired persons with low total circulating antibody levels had significantly lower cognitive test scores than impaired persons with higher serum levels. Results in this area thus remain unclear, and research should therefore continue.

Animal researchers have increasingly suggested interventions to improve cognitive functioning and slow the processes of brain aging. Interestingly, their results are now being substantiated by research on human aging populations.

Diamond, Rosenzweig, Bennett, Lindner, and Lyon (1972) studied the effects of the external environment on the cerebral cortex of the male rat. They separated littermates, who are genetically similar, into three environments: standard (three rats to a cage), enriched (twelve rates to a "super cage"), and impoverished (one rat to a cage). Rats raised in the enriched environment showed thicker cerebral cortices, more glial cells, more dendritic branching, and a greater RNA: DNA ratio than the other rats. The effects of environment varied depending on the age at which the rats were placed in the environment. However, in rats of all ages the enriched environment produced the same positive effects, the only variance being in degree of response.

Corso (1976) reported that the effects of aging are less deleterious than normal in intelligent, highly educated, active people. Recent studies on individual differences in intellectual ability suggest that old people who maintain an openness to the environment, are willing to take risks, and maintain a high level of activity are more likely than normal to preserve their cognitive performance as they age (Fozard, 1980).

As discussed, many of our society's myths about aging are based on misinformation, prejudice, or poor methodology. Many of the early studies on human aging were carried out on hospital or mental patients, not on normally functioning elderly persons who led active lives. It has become increasingly obvious that researchers interested in the psychology of aging need to establish which observed changes are due to the aging process itself and which are due to environmental factors such as disease, diet, and lack of exercise.

Current research on individual differences using healthy elderly persons as subjects offers hope for the development of interventions to improve the quality of life and function of all old people. Preliminary evidence suggests that in the absence of disease, an impoverished environment, and poor nutrition, the CNS has the potential to combat any marked deterioration with aging. Of course, stress of any sort places a tremendous workload on the CNS. Stress acts to accelerate aging by increasing the organism's vulnerability to disease, by quickening age-related physiological changes, and by lowering the organism's total ability to respond. However, in an environment in which stress is controlled and stimulation is present, both old and young people will flourish.

**Environmental Intervention in Physiological Aging**

For most of their adult lives, most individuals are free of any serious consequences of aging. Neugarten makes the distinction between the "young-old" and the "old-old." As a group, the "young-old" (aged 55–75) are considered old by society but for the most part manifest none of the stereotypic changes associated with this label. In fact they have many benefits of maturity; they are often retired and have much leisure time and the good health to enjoy it, should they so desire. In contrast, the "old-old" (aged 75 and up) as a group suffer from more extensive functional loss, health problems, and the stereotypic age changes discussed in earlier chapters. There are of course exceptions to these age norms. These exceptions are the focus of the remainder of this chapter.

### Dealing with Minor Age Changes
Change is a fact of life. However, minimal physical age-related changes often produce disability when some simple environmental adaptations could compensate for them. Homeostatic imbalance makes it difficult for old people to maintain body temperature; reaction time slows with age; stiffness and lack of muscle coordination or flexibility frequently accompany old age; and sense of balance is often affected. Nevertheless, none of these functional changes need be disabling unless the environment or disease increases these symptoms out of all proportion to their reality.

It is important that family members, members of the helping professions, and the aged themselves understand that the physical changes that occur with age produce real needs and that elderly persons are not merely "making demands." It is of the utmost importance to their dignity that aged persons remain as active and independent as possible. No one likes to be helpless or even to be perceived as helpless. Helplessness can lead to low self-esteem, health problems, depression, and even death. Preservation of a sense of personal control and utility is thus a health intervention.

Encouraging independence involves creating a safe, nonrestrictive living space. Whether the elderly person lives alone, with family members, in a senior citizen's high-rise, or in an institutional setting, certain environmental needs should be met. Some of these needs are safety related, and some are dictated by comfort, but all will improve the quality of life of the elderly person.

Since temperature control is difficult for the elderly to maintain, they should have individual heating and cooling controls. For example, elderly persons living with family members could have a portable electric heater and air conditioner installed in their living quarters, thereby minimizing discomfort to the rest of the family.

*Frequently stiffness, lack of muscle coordination, and a decreased sense of balance accompany old age. These physical factors cause old people to move more cautiously.*

The slow reaction time of the elderly can be accommodated to by slow elevator doors in apartment buildings where many elderly persons live. Family members and other people coming in contact with the aged can walk, talk, and move more slowly than usual to accommodate the actions of their elderly companions. It is extremely disconcerting to any aged person to feel rushed by others; this in itself increases anxiety and cautiousness and might thus eventually decrease mobility.

Certain constructions must be avoided in the elderly person's home. For example, hidden stairwells or changes in floor level or slope can cause persons with balance problems to fall. Undue exposure to heat, cold, or weather can produce health problems such as hypothermia or heat stroke. Slippery surfaces or unanchored rugs can lead to falls. Stairways should be well lighted, and nightlights should be used in high-traffic areas. Handrails should also be provided on stairs.

Furniture is often not designed for the aged. For example, low, densely cushioned sofas or chairs may be difficult for the elderly to get out of. Seats are now available that lift and tilt persons with muscle weakness or stiffness. Chairs with arms are also easier to get up from.

Often windows, elevators, faucets, heat controls, and so on are difficult for aged joints or stiff fingers to manipulate. Oversized knobs help in these areas (as does a little soap on the window jam).

All of these are simple interventions. To become old does not necessarily mean to become disabled. Compensatory and prosthetic devices used sensibly, early, and effectively can allow old persons to function well despite deficits.

### Nutritional Intervention

Many of the physical changes discussed earlier in the chapter are believed by some researchers to be related to poor nutrition (Weg, 1975). The typical diet in the United States tends to be high in cholesterol, fats, sugar, and refined grains; recent research suggests that the diet of the average adult in our society is composed of twenty percent refined sugar and forty-five percent fat (Barrow & Smith, 1979). The diets of old persons are also believed to be low in calcium, iron, magnesium, vitamins A and C, thiamine, niacin, and folic acid, all of which are necessary for optimal metabolism, homeostasis, nerve transmission, bone viability, and good heart function. It is obvious how these dietary insufficiencies could relate to, cause, or increase age-associated physiological changes.

Research has found that a diet high in saturated fats and cholesterol leads to atherosclerosis. A lack of fiber in the diet has been linked to the development of cancer of the colon or large intestine, a high-fat diet has been associated with breast cancer, and a diet deficient in vegetable fiber has been linked to diverticulitis. Many researchers believe that up to eighty percent of cases of diabetes mellitus may be controlled by diet alone (Barrow & Smith, 1979).

Whether an old person has these diseases is irrelevant. What is important is the effect of diet on normal function. As discussed, peristalsis and digestive processes generally slow with age while constipation increases. A high-fiber diet may well lower the degree of slowing (Weg, 1975) and decrease or prevent age-related constipation. Furthermore, increased protein and decreased fat and sugar intake may increase overall energy and physical functioning.

The social factor plays an important role in malnutrition in the elderly. The social aspect of meals is frequently more important than their nutritional content. Many isolated and lonely elderly persons are simply not motivated to eat. They avoid meals, or they forget them because the normal physical cues signaling hunger are changed and the social cues are absent.

Social service agencies have made an extensive effort to reach the isolated or "invisible" elderly. The federal government's nutritional programs, including Meals on Wheels and community dining sites, are designed to provide adequate nutrition, social interaction, and nutrition education. Such nutritional intervention appears effective for those it reaches. However, evaluation studies need to be conducted to determine the actual health benefits of such programs as well as the effects of improved nutrition on the aging process.

### Drug Intervention

Our culture is drug oriented. From youth on, people rely on drugs to cure headaches, relieve constipation, and change emotional moods. The elderly tend to be the greatest users of both prescription and over-the-counter (OTC) drugs.

*The elderly are the greatest users of both prescription and over-the-counter drugs.*

The elderly take OTC drugs for many reasons. People who are short of money may self-prescribe to save doctor's fees or because they feel OTC drugs may be cheaper than prescription drugs. Persons may choose OTC drugs because they value their independence or fear physicians. Regardless of why they are used, however, OTC drugs are potentially harmful and may contribute to or quicken the processes of physical aging.

Aspirin taken in large quantities acts as a stomach irritant and decreases blood coagulation. Laxatives impair normal bowel function and may become psychologically addictive. Often additional water, a more fibrous diet, or exercise relieves constipation far better than OTC laxatives; furthermore, these measures do not produce side-effects. Many laxatives contain stool softeners, which can increase the effects of "normal" age changes in the lower gastrointestinal tract.

Old persons often undergo changes in their sleep patterns for which they take OTC sleeping aids. However, such drugs may actually cause insomnia. Natural interventions such as drinking a glass of warm milk or wine, taking a walk in the evening, or keeping a daily diary assessing how much one actually sleeps are all better methods of dealing with sleeplessness or altered sleep cycles. Even counting sheep occasionally works.

Another potentially dangerous class of OTC drugs are the antacids, used to deal with indigestion and nausea. One problem is that symptoms such as indigestion often indicate more serious difficulties such as ulcers, infections, or structural disorders. By removing minimal symptoms, antacids may allow such disorders to become more firmly established before professional treatment is sought. The primary ingredient of antacids is sodium bicarbonate, which can lead to serious health problems. In large doses sodium bicarbonate leads to alkalinization of body fluids, which disrupts homeostasis and causes kidney stones, recurrent kidney infections, and diminished kidney function. Sodium bicarbonate can also be harmful to persons with hypertension or congestive heart failure (Kart et al., 1978).

Thus, the effectiveness of many OTC drugs has been seriously exaggerated. In many cases these drugs are not only a waste of money but may also provide no relief of the problems for which people take them. For example, researchers have found that because of their high alcohol content mouthwashes may not eliminate bad breath in the elderly but only serve to dry the mouth's mucous tissues (Kart et al., 1978). OTC drugs taken in high doses by elderly persons may also compound the aging process and lead to serious health problems.

### Exercise Intervention

For persons of any age physical fitness improves circulation and respiration, diminishes stress, helps preserve a sense of balance, promotes bodily flexibility, and induces better sleeping patterns. Interestingly, the reverse effects are considered symptoms of normal physical aging. There is thus a clear relationship between the loss of physical function called *aging* and decreased physical fitness.

It has been well documented that old people don't get the exercise they need. In a national adult physical fitness survey, for example, Conrad (1976) found that thirty-nine percent of those sampled who were older than sixty received no systematic exercise; only one percent jogged, three percent bicycled, four percent swam, and six percent engaged in calisthenics. Members of our culture tend to be highly sedentary at any age, but the effects of this "spectator" life-style become increasingly serious with age.

Overall functional capacities are improved through physical conditioning, good nutrition, and relaxation, all of which tend to decrease as we grow older. Some researchers believe that the results of all studies on normal aging are suspect because these studies have not taken into account the possible effects of habitual physical activity on aging (DeVries, 1975).

DeVries (1975) has stated that the physically based changes in human performance discussed earlier in this chapter are more closely related to decreased physical activity than to age itself. He and other researchers (Weg, 1975) believe that three processes are involved in the changes in functional capacity referred to as *aging*: the first is unrecognized incipient disease, such as arteriosclerosis; the second is age-related shifts in physical status; and the third is the long-term results of physical deconditioning associated with a sedentary lifestyle. "Aging" due to this third cause is essentially a disuse phenomenon. Given the relatively quick muscle atrophy

*For persons of any age, physical fitness helps maintain good health, improves circulation and respiration, and diminishes stress.*

and weakness that result from bed rest, for example, this posited third cause appears to make sense. It also offers the possibility of intervention, such as physical conditioning programs tailored to old persons.

As stated, exercise increases cardiovascular and respiratory function, improves muscle strength and body composition (i.e., decreases the amount of fat in the body tissues), and helps relaxation. DeVries (1975) and others have found that a fifteen-minute walk at a moderate rate (by definition a pace that raises the heart rate to 100 beats per minute) has a tranquilizing effect on the body lasting up to one hour after the walk. Regular exercise also decreases the risk of stress-related diseases.

The type of exercise one does is important. Walking, jogging, running, and swimming, which rhythmically exercise large segments of the body's musculature, appear to be best suited to the conditioning needs of sedentary persons. Isometric exercises, which focus on the contraction and relaxation of small muscle masses, are not effective in producing the full-body effects detailed above. In all cases exercise programs of any type for a person of any age should not be undertaken without a medical examination, and group exercise should be conducted under well-trained professional leadership. Exercise programs conducted along these basic parameters greatly enhance physical health and vitality. All old persons, regardless of their previous histories of physical conditioning, can benefit from a program of vigorous physical exercise designed to meet their particular health and skill needs. The type of decreased human performance that is caused by disuse may in fact be the only sort of age-associated deterioration in which intervention can be truly effective.

### Psychological Intervention

Psychological factors are associated with the processes of physical aging. In general these psychological correlates extend from the social realm (e.g., ageism as it affects the elderly person's ability to stay in good health) to the idiosyncratic (e.g., the "excess disability" created by a person's symbolic investment in a particular skill or body locus). For most aging persons the physical changes described in this chapter need not be disabling. However, for some persons these losses are overwhelming.

Diverse psychological interventions can be used to help old persons cope with loss in general and physical disability in particular. Psychotherapy following rehabilitation counseling is often used in combination with a general strengthening of traditional support networks, such as the family and service agencies. The overall goal of such procedures is to encourge or help maintain the disabled elderly person's sense of personal competence and independence. Strengthening support networks often entails increasing meaningful interpersonal contacts. Family members and significant others are frequently included in the treatment program so that the client will not become dependent on the therapist. They are also involved in the treatment program so that they may become aware of the anxiety that often accompanies a threat to physical integrity, including the changes associated with aging.

It is important for family members and other involved persons to be aware of the fears associated with functional loss. These fears may be realistic or irrational, but they should not be taken lightly. The disabled elderly person is likely to be afraid of degenerating steadily and eventually becoming helpless and dependent. The disabled person is usually also worried about social disapproval, avoidance by others, and loss of prestige. If they are not dealt with, these concerns, themselves may creating additional disability.

## Summary

This chapter has discussed the nature of functional changes over time. Such changes vary widely among individuals. Past history, genetics, diet, exercise, and coping mechanisms (Fries & Crapo, 1981) all affect the aging process. Common symptoms of brain aging include impaired memory and decreased sensation, balance, coordination, and arousal. These disabilities and complaints lead to up to ninety percent of the serious dependency of persons over sixty-five (Busse & Blazer, 1980). However, "loss" of function does not necessarily lead to disability. Various sorts of intervention can change the pattern of normal aging, making it easier for elderly persons to adjust to functional loss. In the absence of disease, the view of aging as an inevitable, debilitating decline is just a myth.

To what extent does disease in the brain and the rest of the body act to exaggerate normal aging processes? Aging need not be malignant or destructive. Numerous cases have been reported of persons who, despite tremendous physical losses, functioned well with appropriate support from the environment.

The postmitotic cell population of the human brain partially is responsible for our death but also for the fullness of our life. The constancy of cells makes possible the sense of self; similarly, the loss of cells may obscure self-concept. For most persons the redundancy of the system, i.e., the fact that different physiological pathways lead to the same behavior, prevents any truly malignant cognitive loss; however, each person's reality is different, and all science ultimately deals in is probability statements.

## 6

## Aging
## and Health

*Why in the past did people assume that aging and disease were inevitably linked?*
*Why may chronic disease become more prevalent with age?*
*What sorts of factors affect survivorship?*
*In what way do social factors affect longevity?*

*T*HE confusion of the processes of normal aging with those of disease has been one of the prime causes of ageism in our society. As discussed in Chapter 4, changes in physical function occur over time. These changes may or may not be disabling. Persons who escape the hazards of youth from age sixty on grow increasingly vulnerable to stress, disease, and complications of the aging process. It is important that these age changes be recognized if health care for the elderly is to be improved.

Health status of the elderly may be broken down into three general areas: mortality and morbidity, discussed in Chapter 2; normal effects of aging in the body, presented in Chapter 4; and types of health problems the elderly confront and modes of prevention for these problems, discussed in this chapter.

**Introduction to Aging and Disease**

An understanding of the principles of health in the elderly is essential for any meaningful consideration of the health status of the elderly as a group (Table 6-1).

The first principle is that average life expectancy (ALE) is increasing overall but not for persons sixty-five and older. Since 1650 in the United States ALE at birth has increased over thirty-five years; in this century alone it has increased approximately twenty-five years (Table 6-2) (Cutler & Harootyan, 1975). However, ALE at age sixty-five has increased less than four years since 1900 (see Table 2-1).

This differential between ALE at birth and ALE at age 65 is attributable to several factors. The biggest increase in life expectancy at birth comes from medical science's defeat of life-threatening childhood diseases such as smallpox, diphtheria, and whooping cough. No commensurate breakthrough has occurred in life-threatening diseases of middle and late adulthood. Diseases such as arteriosclerosis, cancer, and diabetes are still largely incurable. There is thus a continued need for research into diagnosis, treatment, and intervention for the chronic diseases commonly found late in the life cycle.

The second general principle of health gerontology is that the elderly as a group are more likely to suffer from chronic than acute conditions. Medical science has developed various techniques, such as vaccines and antibiotics, for combatting acute disease. However, efforts directed at chronic diseases have been palliative rather than preventive. Acute diseases usually are brief, have a known cause with a particular mode of treatment, and produce reversible pathologic changes in function. In contrast, chronic diseases begin insidiously and often produce irreversible pathologic effects before they are detected. Chronic diseases are usually progressive, irreversible, and amenable only to control, not to cure (Kart et al., 1978).

Table 6-1   *Introductory principles of health gerontology*

Average life expectancy at birth is increasing, but life expectancy at age 65 has not increased significantly.
The elderly as a group are more likely to suffer from chronic rather than acute conditions.
The elderly as a group are more likely than other age groups to suffer from multiple chronic conditions. However, these need not be disabling.
Disease in the elderly may manifest itself differently from disease in younger persons.
Physical disorders in the very old are more likely to have psychological symptoms than physical disorders in the young.

Given the natural history of chronic illness, it is not surprising that such disorders are seen more frequently in old than in young persons. Frequently the agents for such disease are nonliving; rather than being due to viruses or bacteria, they are often caused by long-term exposure to substances in the environment such as carcinogens or radiation.

Chronic illness in late life may also be due to the interaction of such normal aging processes as decreased homeostatic ability and system integration with disease processes. Old people may be physiologically more vulnerable than young people to the effects of the agents of chronic illness.

Regardless of the reason, the incidence of chronic illness increases sharply at about age forty-five and begins to be very high from age seventy onward. The conditions involved are frequently degenerative, involving the cardiovascular and cerebrovascular systems, renal or vascular insufficiency, or locomotor disorders, all of which appear to be related to decreases in central nervous system (CNS), endocrine, and immune system efficiency. Mental and physical infirmity and

Table 6-2   *Life expectancies of humans from prehistory to 1971*

| Time period | Average life span in years |
|---|---|
| Prehistory (3500 B.C. to 1000 B.C.) | 18 |
| Ancient Greece (500 B.C. to 300 A.D.) | 21 |
| Middle Ages (600 A.D. to 1300 A.D.) | 33 |
| Colonial America (1650 A.D. to 1700 A.D.) | 35 |
| 19th Century, Western Europe | 41 |
| 1900, U.S. | 47.3 |
| 1939, U.S. | 63.7 |
| 1971, U.S. | 71 |

(Adapted from: Hendricks, J., & Hendricks, C.D. *Aging in mass society.* Cambridge: Winthrop Publishers, 1977, p. 32; Cutler, N.E., & Harootyan, R.A. Demography of the aged. In D.S. Woodruff and J.E. Birren (Eds.), *Aging.* New York: Van Nostrand Reinhold, 1975, p. 32)

residual disability often persist after such an illness, especially in very old persons (Adams, 1978).

The third principle of health gerontology is that the elderly as a group are more likely than other age groups to suffer from multiple chronic conditions. As discussed earlier, medical science usually focuses on the diagnosis of single dysfunctions and their subsequent treatment and cure. Among elderly persons single problems are generally the exceptions rather than the rule. Old people frequently suffer from the degenerative changes of senescence compounding one or more chronic diseases. These multiple physical conditions become superimposed on each other, rendering treatment and diagnosis difficult. For example, chest pain in an elderly person may be due to heart disease, a potential heart attack, gastrointestinal disorders, esophageal problems, or nervousness. Old people with multiple conditions may overlook important symptoms of a new disorder, confusing them with

*The elderly as a group are more likely than young persons to suffer from multiple chronic conditions, but these need not be disabling.*

the symptoms of already existing conditions; chest pain may thus be assumed to be indigestion, bone pain due to a fracture may be attributed to rheumatism, or the rectal bleeding of cancer may be mistaken for hemorrhoids (Adams, 1978; Kart et al., 1978).

Despite the difficulties of multiple pathology, an old person may be afflicted with a number of chronic conditions but not be severely limited by any of them. Many old people function effectively with mild arthritis and diabetes, mild visual and hearing impairments, few or no teeth, and a mild heart condition. Conversely, there are also people, young and old, who are bedridden by one chronic illness (Barrow & Smith, 1979).

The fourth general principle of health in the aged is that disease in the elderly may manifest itself differently from disease in younger persons. Diagnosis of disease in old persons is difficult because age-related changes alter the traditional clinical picture associated with particular diseases. For example, pain sensitivity is decreased and pain localization is often capricious in the elderly. Angina pectoris and appendicitis are frequently devoid of pain in old persons. When pain does occur, it may not be severe or may be forgotten in persons who are mentally confused. Furthermore, health professionals and the aged alike may dismiss pain as a burden of old age one must learn to live with, despite the fact that pain is not inevitable with age (Kart et al., 1978). The effects of drugs differ in old and young persons; a therapeutic dosage in a young person may have an iatrogenic effect in an old person. Pyrexia (fever) is not always present in severe infections.

Other factors also influence the expression of disease symptoms in the elderly. With age there is increased vulnerability to infection associated with degenerative changes and disease. For example, the muscular strength of the bladder decreases with age, and this may lead to incomplete emptying of the bladder. The increased residual urine creates an environment in which disease-causing microorganisms may multiply, leading to infection. Age-associated circulatory dysfunction is also associated with an increased incidence of infection. If tissues are not adequately nourished by blood vessels, necessary blood-borne components of the immune system will not reach them in time to prevent infection. Finally, the immune system weakens with age, placing the elderly at high risk for many diseases (Adams, 1978; Kart et al., 1978).

Elderly persons recover slowly from disease owing to homeostatic imbalance. The healthy adult organism is in equilibrium with its environment and maintains cell function and repair. Once senescence is reached, maintenence and repair functions become less effective, cells die, and organs become less efficient. Subclinical dietary deficiencies produce metabolic changes that may compound this process. Senescence combined with illness, deprivation, trauma, and other stresses reduces the physiological reserve capacity. This reduced capacity is usually concealed until some new stress upsets the fragile balance. Homeostatic inefficiency renders old people particularly susceptible to plasma or blood loss, dehydration, potassium depletion, and metabolic disruption. At rest, the aged can maintain a constant, balanced internal environment. However, stress reactions and even responsiveness to daily activities may decline, and equilibrium may not be restored after responses because coordination between bodily systems is disrupted by differential rates of aging.

The altered response of the elderly to disease may have life-threatening consequences. The following hypothetical case material illustrates the interaction of disease and aging as they affect diagnosis and treatment in the elderly.

A middle-aged person who developed pneumonia would have a cough, maybe some chest pain, some fever, perhaps some shortness of breath. This person would go to a doctor, who would hopefully do a number of diagnostic studies. This would include a history and physical examination and certain laboratory studies, including a sputum examination. The physician would stain and culture the sputum to identify the type of bacteria and the antibiotics to which they might be susceptible. He/she would also do a blood count, since an elevated white blood count would also be a sign of bacterial infection. Because in pneumonia there is a significant incidence of bacteremia (bacteria in the blood), the doctor would also take a blood culture. A chest x-ray would presumably show a cloudiness, indicating the infiltrate — the site of pneumonia or pneumonitis. The physician would start the patient on an appropriate antibiotic, and after twenty-four to thirty-six hours the patient would be feeling better. The temperature would have decreased, as would the coughing and the chest pain. The patient would then have what has been called a "walking pneumonia." The physician, however, would keep the patient on the antibiotic for seven to ten days, and have the patient come back for a check-up. At this time the physician would preferably supplement the physical examination with another x-ray, which would probably show virtually complete resolution of the pneumonia. There might be a little shadow, a little soft infiltrate left, but the physician would not worry about that. The physician would stop the antibiotic, and the patient would be fine. The physician would have the patient return in another week or two for another check-up; perhaps he/she would take another x-ray to show complete resolution of the pneumonia. At this time the radiographic shadow would be completely gone.

An eighty-year-old who developed pneumonia would hopefully receive at least as careful an examination. The doctor would take an electrocardiogram (ECG) because there are frequently cardiac complications in pneumonia, especially in older people. The doctor would identify the infecting organism by sputum smear, culture, and sensitivities; do blood counts, cultures, and other indicated tests; and start the patient on the appropriate antibiotic.

Unfortunately, it is often the case that older people frequently get fewer diagnostic studies. There is a tendency not to look as carefully, or to do as much evaluation of older people.

*Diagnosis can be difficult in the elderly.*

Instead of feeling better within twenty-four to thirty-six hours after institution of antibiotics, the eighty-year-old person may not feel much better until forty-eight to seventy-two hours have elapsed. The doctor would keep up the antibiotic, usually for the same amount of time as for a younger person (seven to ten days) and then have the patient return for another follow-up; at that time, the physician would check the chest and take another x-ray, which would show a virtually complete resolution of pneumonia — perhaps just a slight shadow remaining. The doctor would stop the antibiotic, and the patient would be fine for a day.

If the patient were in a nursing home, the caring situation might be the same. For some reason, however, antibiotics frequently seem to be stopped on Friday night in nursing homes. The patient is fine on Saturday, but on Sunday morning, the nurses notice that the patient has a little temperature, maybe 100° F (37.8° C). The patient does not eat as well, and the staff says, "We'll wait to see how the patient is tomorrow. The doctor's away golfing today, or he's at the lake for the weekend, and it's hard to get hold of him." When Monday morning arrives, the patient is moribund. He/she may be comatose, in shock, and virtually at death's door.

What has happened? The older person had that little bit of residual infiltrate at the end of the antibiotic treatment. It takes approximately a day after discontinuation for the drug to be excreted or metabolized, or both. Then, without the residual antibiotic in the system, the older person's decreased immunocompetence isn't sufficient to bring about resolution of the little bit of residual pneumonia. What happens is that when the antibiotic is eliminated, the pneumonia reactivates, spreads, and becomes lethal.

In other words the decreased immunocompetence of the older person requires different and more assiduous treatment and follow-up. This same problem is seen not only in pneumonia, but in urinary tract infections; it is seen in septicemia, bloodstream infections, and infections in all parts of the body. The special problems presented by health care management of older people are largely unrecognized.

It is still unclear how long the older person needs treatment. Some older people appear to have fairly good immunocompetence and may do as well with the standard antibiotic treatment. Some may require considerably longer. The judgment has to be based on the clinical findings: Older people generally should be treated until there is complete resolution of infection, because they may be immunologically compromised.*

The final general principle of health gerontology is that physical disorders in the elderly are more likely to have psychological symptoms than physical disorders in the young. The long-term effects of drug therapy for chronic disorders may have mental manifestations. Transient dizziness, giddiness, confusion, and psychotic symptoms have been found to result from various medications taken frequently by the elderly. Drug effects are discussed later in this chapter.

Irreversible and long-term chronic disease may lead to mental depression. Reduced cerebral blood flow (which may be reversible) may stimulate mental changes, such as disorientation, memory deficits, sudden mood shifts, and impaired intellectual functioning (Kart et al., 1978). Hearing loss may perpetrate paranoia (Corso, 1977). Unfortunately, mental confusion and "senility" are often considered normal accompaniments of aging. Therefore, there is often no search for the cause of deterioration of functioning in elderly patients. Ageism itself thus creates disability or "senility" with age in a self-fulfilling prophecy.

These general principles of health gerontology have serious implications for the delivery of health care to old persons. Health care in the United States is aimed at cure, not disease prevention. This is exemplified by our health insurance plans; insurance generally covers crisis, i.e., diagnosis and treatment, but not preventive measures such as physical examinations. Nursing homes, hospitals, and physicians are reimbursed for sick care, not for prevention or rehabilitation.

*Reiff, T.R. Biomedical aspects of aging and their relation to geriatric care. In G. Lesnoff-Caravaglia (Ed.), *Health care of the elderly*. New York: Human Sciences Press, 1980, pp. 41-43. Copyright © 1980 by Human Sciences Press, 72 Fifth Avenue, New York, NY 10011

Chronic disease is the key health problem of the elderly. The lack of cures for chronic disorders frustrates physicians and leads them to avoid elderly patients. Many health care professionals, as well as the elderly and their families, expect that to be old means to be sick and therefore spend little effort on restoring function or health in the old. Finally, few doctors are interested in treating geriatric patients (Kart et al., 1978). In England geriatricians are even referred to as "clinical undertakers" (Adams, 1978), whereas in the United States nursing homes have been referred to as "warehouses for the dying" (Butler & Lewis, 1977).

Despite the bias against the aged, many health professionals find many rewards — expected and unexpected — in their work with elderly patients. The definition of geriatrics, "the branch of general medicine concerned with the clinical, preventive, remedial and social aspects of illness in the elderly" (Adams, 1978, p. vii) cannot explain its rewards.

> It cannot explain the absorbing range of diagnostic and remedial opportunities in medical work with old people. It cannot describe the rewards of involvement in their unexpected recoveries after critical illness, in devising successful management of their protracted disabilities, or in assuring them of comfort and dignity in their last hours. Nor can it reveal the attractions of their personalities as patients; their wisdom, often concealed behind an outward facade of reticence; their humour; their courage in adversity; and their dislike of insincerity or bogus attitudes (especially in professional advisors).*

## The High-Risk Elderly

As mentioned, although susceptibility to disease increases with age, disease is not an inevitable companion of old age. Stressful life events or other occurrences may lead to illness and death at any age. The elderly as a group, however, have a cohort liability for certain degenerative changes, diseases, and stresses. Furthermore, they are exposed to these noxious events when their reserve capacities and support networks are at their lowest levels.

When people are ill or distressed, they usually depend on support from friends, relatives, and social service agencies. This support is not always available to the elderly. Frequently elderly people, especially elderly women, outlive their friends and relatives and become recluses who are essentially lost to society's view. The support network has also been affected by the high proportion of women working in our society. In the past daughters were the main care providers for ill parents. However, women working outside the home do not have the time housewives once did to take care of ailing parents. Unfortunately the unavailability of daughters as care givers and other complex factors have forced the care of frail elderly persons into society's hands or, in many cases, into no one's hands at all (Adams, 1978).

Community surveys of health status have found a high incidence of disability

*Adams, G.F. *Essentials of geriatric medicine.* Oxford: Oxford University Press, 1978, p. vii

*In the past, daughters were the main care providers for ill parents.*

among old people living outside of institutions. A profile of the high-risk elderly suggests that the old person most likely to need health care is older than seventy years of age, lives alone, is recently bereaved, is disabled by locomotor disorders, and has recently been discharged from a hospital (Adams, 1978). Persons fitting this profile are more likely than normal to be disabled by their diseases and to have a seriously deprived quality of life.

Of course, not all elderly persons fit this profile. Although national health surveys indicate that the incidence of various chronic ailments increases with age (Fig. 6-1), these ailments are not necessarily disabling. As can be seen in Table 6-3, almost sixty percent of all elderly persons with some chronic condition report no limitation to their activity as a result of that disorder. Only thirty-seven percent report limitation of their major activity. This number is higher than the percentage for the total population but in no way reflects that all old persons are disabled by their infirmities (USDHEW, 1978).

**Disease Incidence in Old Age**

The risk of death for certain diseases, including cardiovascular disease, hypertension, cancer, and respiratory disorders, increases with age. These diseases are broken down into three categories in the sections that follow: diseases that are present to

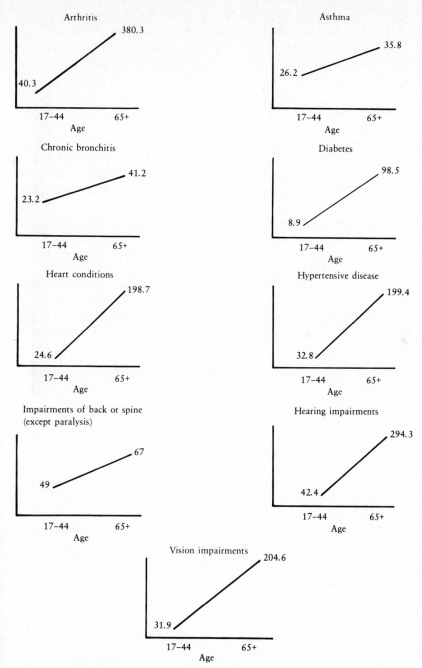

Figure 6–1  *Age and various chronic conditions in the United States: 1969–1973*

Data are based on household interviews of samples of the noninstitutionalized civilian population. Numbers are per thousand population.
(Source: USDHEW, *Health United States 1978*. Washington, D.C.: Public Health Service, 1978)

some extent in all aging individuals (age-dependent diseases); diseases the incidences of which increase with age but which are not universal in the population (age-related diseases); and diseases that are not causally related to aging but have more serious consequences in old than in young persons (age-traumatic diseases) (Upton, 1977).

### Age-Dependent Disease

Most gerontologists agree on only one age-dependent disorder: arteriosclerosis. Arteriosclerosis in mammals is universal, progressive, and irreversible and inevitably proves fatal if other causes of death do not intervene first (Upton, 1977). Arteriosclerosis is thought to arise spontaneously and is the leading cause of death in the elderly if one considers its involvement in cardiovascular, cerebrovascular, and other diseases.

In arteriosclerosis degenerative changes occur in the elastin and collagen of blood vessel walls. These changes take two forms: arteriosclerosis, which involves lesions of the vessel walls themselves, and atherosclerosis, which involves fatty deposits within the lumen of the blood vessels. Arteriosclerotic changes are influenced to some extent by heredity and environment but are essentially a universal accompaniment of aging.

Depending upon the anatomical distribution of arteriosclerotic changes, functional impairment and degeneration can occur in virtually any organ of the body.

Table 6–3   *Persons in the United States with activity limitation caused by chronic conditions: 1969–1970*

|  | Total population (%) | Elderly (65+) population (%) |
|---|---|---|
| *All persons* | 100.0 | 100.0 |
|  | (203,212,000) | (20,066,000) |
| With no activity limitation | 88.3 | 57.7 |
| With activity limitation | 11.7 | 42.3 |
| With activity limitation in major activity | 9.1 | 37.0 |
| *Persons with activity limitation* | 100.0 | 100.0 |
|  | ( 23,237,000) | ( 7,958,000) |
| Heart conditions | 15.5 | 20.5 |
| Arthritis and rheumatism | 14.1 | 21.2 |
| Visual impairments | 4.8 | 7.0 |
| Hypertension without heart involvement | 4.6 | 6.4 |
| Mental and nervous conditions | 4.5 | 3.0 |
| Other | 56.5 | 41.9 |

(Source: U.S. Department of Commerce, Bureau of the Census. *The American almanac: The statistical abstract of the United States,* 1974, Table 125)

These changes steadily progress throughout life, complicate senescent processes, and are largely unopposed by mechanisms of biological repair (Upton, 1977).

### Age-Related Disorders

The occurrence of age-related disorders is dependent on age but also on other factors such as susceptibility, exposure to carcinogens, and the dying-off of susceptible populations. Disorders fitting this rubric include bone disease, cancer, cardiovascular disease, cerebrovascular disease, late-onset diabetes mellitus, and parkinsonism. All of these diseases require time for the induction and/or evolution of their pathologic processes, but they occur only in certain populations (Upton, 1977). These diseases in no way represent all the disorders of old age, nor do they occur only in old age. They are, however, the main causes of disease and death in late life.

*Bone Disease*    Age-related metabolic bone diseases include osteoporosis, bone loss from the entire skeleton; osteomalacia, deficient calcification of bone osteoid in the whole skeleton; and Paget's Disease, patchy asymmetry of diverse skeletal areas (Adams, 1978). The first two disorders are most common in persons of advanced age.

The symptoms of osteoporosis are difficult to separate from normal aging. Everyone loses bone with age, although there are sex differences in the timing of peak loss. Women have rapid loss from approximately age forty-five to about age sixty; men have bone loss beginning at about age seventy and increasing through the eighties (Adams, 1978). Osteoporosis is thought to be caused by immobility (because of sedentary living, fracture, or stroke), corticosteroid excess (caused by stress and anti-inflammatory drugs), alcoholism, rheumatoid arthritis, hypogonadism (low levels of gonadal hormones), and nutritional factors (Adams, 1978). The diagnosis is usually made on the basis of a major structural change such as collapse of vertebral bodies or the development of a dowager's hump or back pain.

Osteomalacia is caused by a loss of vitamin D. It is associated with lack of nutrition and sunshine. Not surprisingly it occurs frequently in reclusive women over seventy years of age. This disorder is often confused with osteoporosis. However, it has additional symptoms, including muscle weakness and/or stiffness, a waddling gait, and skeletal deformities (Adams, 1978).

The incidence of Paget's disease increases after age fifty. Approximately ten percent of persons ninety years old and older are believed to have this disease, the cause of which is unknown. Paget's disease appears to differentially affect skeletal bones in the following descending order: pelvis, femur, skull, tibia, lumbosacral spine, dorsal spine, clavicles, and ribs (Adams, 1978). There is an imbalanced sequence of increased bone resorption accompanied by increased bone formation. Symptoms include bone pain, headache, deafness, paraplegia, and heart failure. Calcitonin given twice a day relieves some of these effects (Adams, 1978; Kart et al., 1978).

Another bone and joint disease is arthritis, inflammation or degeneration of a joint. Normally articulating surfaces where bones join (as in the knee joint) make movement possible. The ends of articulating bones are covered by cartilage, which is encased in a capsule with a highly vascular membrane liner called the *synovial membrane*. This membrane also produces fluid for smooth articulation (Kart et al., 1978).

In osteoarthritis, an age-related degenerative disorder, the articulating cartilage wears away, exposing the rough underlying bone. Wear and tear cause bony outgrowths called *osteophytes* to form. Osteoarthritis usually is not accompanied by inflammation, in contrast to other types of arthritis.

There is no cure for osteoarthritis. Aspirin and acetominophen (Tylenol) decrease the pain accompanying the disorder, and if inflammation occurs, anti-inflammatory drugs are also used. The symptoms of osteoarthritis are insidious, and the disorder is often asymptomatic. However, it is also often associated with pain and eventual disability. The disability occurs because of joint instability, muscle wasting, difficulty walking, and a tendency to fall (Kart et al., 1978).

Rheumatoid arthritis, a more serious disorder, has a greater potential for pain, disfigurement, and crippling. Rheumatoid arthritis is not a disease of old age per se,

*For those who suffer from arthritis, simple actions such as buckling boots may become nearly impossible owing to pain.*

though many old persons have it. First symptoms generally occur in persons between twenty and fifty years of age. The disease is a chronic inflammatory disorder beginning in the synovial membrane, which swells, thickens, and becomes persistently inflamed. During healing, scar tissue and granulation tissue form a pannus structure. This structure overrides and destroys the articular cartilage and may cause deformity (Kart et al., 1978).

The cause of rheumatoid arthritis is unknown, but the disorder is thought to be due to either an immune system inefficiency or an autoimmune response. Emotional upset has also been found to trigger episodes of inflammation. For this reason rheumatoid arthritis is often considered a psychosomatic ailment.

Treatment involves a balance of bed rest and exercise. Bed rest combined with splinting of the joints during flare-ups seems the best preventive therapy against permanent joint stiffening. Aspirin is a mainstay of people with rheumatoid arthritis, but long-term aspirin therapy also has serious side-effects, as mentioned in Chapter 4. Surgery (arthroplasty) also has good effects in cases in which it is possible to remove the diseased bone head and replace it with a prosthetic device (Kart et al., 1978).

*Cancer*   Cancer is a group of diseases of unknown and probably multiple origins that arise in tissues that are composed of potentially dividing cells. Pathologic changes in these tissues permanantly impair the normal growth control mechanism and cause progressive growth. Cancer may arise following many sorts of stimuli (viral, physical, or chemical), but it usually manifests itself only after a long latent period. Cancer cells can arise in any body tissue in persons of any age. As infectious diseases are brought under control, increasing the longevity of a population, the incidence of cancer in that population increases (Upton, 1977). Currently 50 percent of all cancer deaths are in persons older than 65, and the mean age of death from cancer is 67.5 years. In addition the incidence of certain types of cancer increases significantly with age, in particular those of lung and stomach cancer. However, as demonstrated by Wilms' tumor, which occurs predominantly among children and adolescents, advanced age alone does not "cause" cancer.

There are several possible explanations for cancer: cancer occurs when a critical number of cells become altered and rapidly reproduce; cancer is the end result of a succession of mutational changes; cancer is due to prolonged exposure to carcinogenic stimuli; cancer is the result of an age-dependent decline in immunocompetence allowing faulty cells to reproduce; cancer is due to the activation of latent oncogenic (cancer-causing) viruses; and cancer results from disturbances in hormonal regulation (Upton, 1977). Latent tumor viruses have received particular scrutiny in the study of cancers of old age because of the discovery that they cause certain types of organic brain syndrome.

Oncologic research carried out on aging mammals presents many benefits not available to researchers of human aging, as discussed in Chapter 4. One advantage is the possibility of rearing animals in germ-free environments. Even in germ-free states, animals develop many of the neoplasms and arteriosclerotic lesions that are characteristic of senescence, suggesting that microorganisms contaminating the external environment do not play a critical role in the pathogenesis of these diseases (Upton, 1977).

It is felt by researchers that the activation of latent oncogenic viruses may be an important mechanism of neoplasms in old age. These viruses were only recently discovered because they do not follow the usual pattern of viruses, that of causing rapid onset of disease and being rapidly detectable thereafter (Upton, 1977). It is believed that tumor viruses require specific interactions of heredity (i.e., susceptible populations) and environment. The neoplasms developing from these viruses develop after a long period of latency, may appear in few of the infected organisms, and are themselves noninfectious.

It appears that the viral genes are integrated into the genes of the host cell, where they interact with the RNA and DNA to produce cell misspecifications. The mechanisms by which these cells become activated are unknown, but it is suspected that the viruses are released by radiation, chemical carcinogens, and chemical mutagens (Upton, 1977).

Old persons are more likely than young persons to develop viral tumors; cells from patients with chromosomal abnormalities show greater susceptibility than normal to viral transformations, and old people are more likely than young people to have chromosomal aberrations. Cancer research has confirmed the possibility that viruses are involved in the chronic and degenerative diseases of aging through a slow, progressive viral infection.

The slow viruses have certain characteristics in common. They have a long incubation period, insidious onset, protracted clinical course, and fatal outcome. Disorders due to slow viruses also show pathologic changes unlike the changes of typical viral diseases but more like those of senescence. For example, scrapie in sheep brain and kuru in the human brain are caused by slow viruses, as is Creutzfeldt-Jakob disease. Both kuru and Creutzfeldt-Jakob disease produce brain cell lesions leading to intellectual and physical deterioration.

Other diseases are assumed to result from the latent effect of other viruses. A type of parkinsonism, for example, is due to latent effects of the 1918 pandemic of encephalitis (Adams, 1978), and epidemiologists have found a relation between mumps virus and juvenile diabetes. Pathobiologists are now theorizing that cancer and degenerative diseases of old age are the result of a multigene susceptibility and slow virus combination (Upton, 1977). Since this interaction is most likely to occur in old age, the incidence of cancer in old age should continue to increase.

*Cardiovascular Disease*   Cardiovascular disorders, the most debilitating health problems, are the major cause in the aging population. These disorders comprise the following subclassifications: arteriosclerosis, atherosclerosis, hypertension, coronary heart disease, angina pectoris, and congestive heart failure. Three disease processes may override or precipitate the occurrence of the other disorders listed above: arteriosclerosis, atherosclerosis, and amyloidosis.

*Arteriosclerosis.*    Arteriosclerosis is a group of processes that have in common thickening and loss of elasticity of the arterial walls. This disorder is implicated in the increase in peripheral vascular resistance that is correlated with age-related high blood pressure.

*Atherosclerosis.*    Atherosclerosis is a type of arteriosclerosis. Although atherosclerosis is not inevitable, all human probably show some degree of it with age. There is, however, marked variation in the degree of arterial involvement in people of every age, depending on the presence of the following risk factors: obesity, high serum lipids, hypertension, diabetes, male gender, stressful life-style, and prolonged hemodialysis (Kohn, 1977). Death occurs when circulation to vital organs is diminished or obliterated by atheromas (fatty tumors within the blood vessel walls) or thrombi (clots) forming on the atherosclerotic plaques.

*Amyloidosis.*    Amyloidosis is the increased accumulation of amyloid (immunobody or antibody fragments) in extracellular masses causing atrophy of the adjacent cells. When amyloid accumulates in the heart and vessels, heart failure can result. It is not clear whether deposits of amyloid are part of the normal aging process or whether they occur only in certain population subgroups. Some researchers feel that amyloid may be a normal component of connective tissue and that persons with amyloidosis simply have excessive amounts of it (Kohn, 1977). Whatever the cause, excessive amyloid can lead to serious heart or vessel disease.

*Hypertension.*    Hypertension results from functional and/or structural abnormalities of the arterioles produced by pressor mechanisms or stress. There are two types of arterial blood pressure: systolic, the pressure generated by cardiac contraction; and diastolic, the pressure exerted in the resting heart by outflow resistance against the arterioles. Generally blood pressure increases with age, and an increase per decade of 10 mm Hg systolic and 5 mm Hg diastolic is considered by many researchers to be normal; thus if 120/80 mm Hg is normal for a twenty-year-old, 160/100 mm Hg would be within the normal limits for a person of sixty-five (Kart et al., 1978). However, other researchers point out that although such an increase in blood pressure may be adaptive, it indicates the occurrence of pathologic changes in the cardiovascular system (Elias et al., 1977). The pathologic pressor mechanisms implicated in the increase of hypertension with age include the following:

The lowering of cerebral blood flow (the cerebral ischemic response) and increase in blood pressure in response to high intracranial pressure due to cerebrovascular disease.

Lesions of the arterial baroreceptor afferent fibers, i.e., the nerve fibers registering intravenous pressure to the autonomic nervous system.

Oversecretion of renin or aldosterone leading to renal hypertension.

Reduction of renal capacity for excreting sodium and water leading to high blood pressure in chronic renal failure.*

*The reduction of renal capacity for excreting sodium and water is the cause of high blood pressure in chronic renal failure. The progression begins with fluid retention, which increases cardiac output. Fluid retention then increases peripheral vascular resistance and systemic arterial blood pressure.

Baroreceptor resetting (beginning as an adaptive response to prolonged high blood pressure) leading to chronic high blood pressure (Eisdorfer & Wilkie, 1977; Kohn, 1977).

The increased incidence of high blood pressure with age is therefore not a normal aging process but rather is due to disease processes.

Hypertension has been found to have many detrimental effects on intellectual and affective functioning. Mild judgmental and memory defects, insomnia, loss of energy, anxiety symptoms, and impaired intelligence have all been considered consequences of essential hypertension. Using the Rorschach test, IQ, and the Reitan-Halstead Impairment Index, Reitan (1955) found that hypertensives are anxious, depressed, and show hysterical tendencies similar to those found in patients with organic brain syndrome. Others (Elias et al., 1977) have found similar results and feel that these cognitive and affective changes may be due to impaired cerebral function. Many persons show symptoms of altered cerebral vascular function, including headache, tinnitus (ringing in the ears), dizziness, irritability, fatigue, and weakness, even before permanent hypertension is established (Kohn, 1977).

Untreated hypertension progresses to acute hypertensive encephalopathy, which forms cerebral lesions. In the terminal phase death results from massive brain damage following cerebral hemorrhage or thrombosis or from acute cerebral softening due to failure of intracranial circulation (Kohn, 1977).

*Coronary Artery Disease.*   Coronary artery disease is a symptomless subcategory of coronary heart disease characterized by thickening and deterioration of the blood vessels of the heart. The thickening probably begins in the first few years of life owing to twisting of the coronary arteries. This twisting causes tiny wounds and tears, which the arteries try to patch with new cells, which thicken the vessel walls. Scar tissue has also been implicated in this process. Frequently this cellular patch accumulates large amounts of lipids and cholesterol in the form of tumors. The tumors in turn expand to encroach on the vessel lumen, which blocks blood flow.

The process is irreversible when the arterial cells become infiltrated with arterial plaque. If the plaques remain dormant, even if half of the artery is obstructed, the person appears normal. However, the plaque is living tissue with its own microvascular system to nourish it. If there is not enough blood to nourish the cells or if fat or cholesterol interferes with the plaque nutrition, the inner portion of the cells dies (undergoes necrosis). The dead cells are then replaced by a bone-like material called *coronary bone* or a pool of grease-laden debris. This may cause future health problems but is still not noticeable by electrocardiography (ECG) (Rosenman & Friedman, 1974). Essentially the rupture of the plaques changes the basically benign coronary artery disease into the potentially lethal coronary heart disease. Only in three percent of afflicted persons does coronary artery disease progress to coronary heart disease, and this occurs only when the arteries become so constricted that they cannot supply blood to the heart. Coronary artery disease is detectable through coronary arteriography or through an exercise ECG (Kohn, 1977; Rosenman & Friedman, 1974).

*Angina Pectoris.*   Angina pectoris is a pain that arises at the moment at which the heart muscle suffers from a lack of oxygen (ischemia) because of inadequate blood supply. This ischemia is caused by a sudden change in long-standing coronary artery disease and usually occurs when the afflicted person requires more of the heart muscle than it can provide without running out of oxygen, such as running, overeating, or becoming emotionally upset. Angina is not a heart attack; no permanent or significant damage is done. It is rather a warning signal of exacerbated coronary artery disease (Kohn, 1977; Rosenman & Friedman, 1974).

*Myocardial Infarction.*   If a large thrombus forms over the arterial plaque, thus entirely obstructing the artery's lumen, the blood flow through the artery becomes completely cut off. This ischemia causes an area of heart muscle (usually in the left ventricle) to die because of failure to get oxygen for too long a time. If the infarct involves some portion of the conduction system, arrhythmias may arise, and if the damage is severe enough, death may occur (Kart et al., 1978; Kohn, 1977; Rosenman & Friedman, 1974).

*Congestive Heart Failure.*   For congestive heart failure to occur, one of the three main arteries to the heart must be totally occluded. When this occurs, the heart muscles gradually weaken and fail to contract sufficiently to circulate the blood flow. The already weakened left ventricle does not pump blood, which therefore accumulates in the lungs. The right ventricle continues to pump additional blood into the lungs, which causes shortness of breath. If this continues, the air spaces of the lungs may flood with fluid seeping from the distended blood vessels, a condition called *pulmonary edema.* If the right ventricle weakens further, the liver enlarges and ankles, legs, and abdomen swell. Drugs may be given to make the left ventricle work harder or make the kidneys excrete the excess fluids (Kohn, 1977; Rosenman & Friedman, 1974).

*Risk Factors in Coronary Heart Disease.*   Stress has been implicated in the development of coronary heart disease, especially stress due to an uncertain outcome or to the need to maintain vigilance until an outcome is reached. Certain coronary-prone behaviors have been labeled *type A personality* (Rosenman & Friedman, 1974). Type As are characterized by work overload, time pressure, well-controlled aggression, compulsiveness, and rigidity. Type Bs, in contrast, although equally ambitious, strive toward goals in a relaxed, time-irrelevant manner; they rarely take on multiple projects and are more likely than type As to focus their attention on a finite set of goals. In the absence of clinical coronary heart disease type As have significantly longer reaction times in choice reaction time tasks than type Bs, even when the effects of age are controlled for (Abrahams & Birren, 1973).

Researchers (Elias et al., 1977) have found similar slowing in persons with arteriosclerotic coronary heart disease, essential hypertension, and recovered myocardial infarctions. The slowing appears to occur in the decision phase of the response, mimicking the slowing of reaction time observed in old persons.

Abrahams and Birren (1973) hypothesized that type As show the reaction time slowing characteristic of a disease state prior to disease onset. By virtue of their behavioral predisposition to coronary heart disease, type As may already have central nervous system circulatory insufficiency due to early, subclinical cardiovascular pathology. These physiological concomitants of type A behavior have been labeled *geromimetic* (i.e., similar to old age) and are believed to be related to stress.

The increased incidence of high blood pressure and atherosclerosis seen in old age is also believed to be linked to stress. The simplest explanation of increased coronary heart disease in old age is that normal age changes relating to stiffening of the heart and blood vessels compound the original poor design of the system. Continual stress and primary intrinsic cell aging then add to the progressive movement into heart disease.

*Cerebrovascular Disease*   Like cardiovascular disease, cerebrovascular disease involves arterio- and atherosclerotic lesions in the blood vessels nourishing the brain. These lesions lead to cerebral vascular insufficiency, blood clots, and hemorrhage culminating in a cerebrovascular accident (CVA) or stroke. According to Adams (1978, p. 30), "a stroke is an acute disturbance of cerebral function of presumed vascular origin with disability lasting more than twenty-four hours." However, CVAs are only one manifestation of cerebrovascular disease and are not necessarily the most important.

Other cerebrovascular disorders include transient ischemic attacks (TIAs) or ministrokes, postural fixation and balance disorders, and dementia. Dementia and arteriosclerotic brain disease are discussed in Chapter 10. Postural difficulties include simple faints (in response to stress, heat, pain, or anemia), postural hypotension (because of cardiac or cerebrovascular insufficiency) leading to dizziness on standing up too quickly, and falls. It appears that approximately twenty-five percent of the falls of old persons are *drop attacks*, in which the knees suddenly fail owing to muscular collapse. It is not known what causes drop attacks, but the condition is aggravated by arthritis, trauma, and peripheral vascular disease (Adams, 1978).

The most visible cerebrovascular disorder is stroke. Depending upon the locus of the lesions in the brain, strokes show a characteristic pattern of symptoms. The left side of the brain controls the right side of the body and is the main locus of language production. Strokes of the left hemisphere therefore result in right-side paralysis and certain cognitive defects including speech and language production deficits, rigidity and cautiousness, and word memory deficits. The right side of the brain contols the left side of the body and receptive speech. Right-side lesions therefore lead to left-side paralysis and spatial-perceptual defects, performance memory loss, and decreased language comprehension. An understanding of this hemisphericity is crucial to the interactions of staff and family members with a stroke patient. It does not follow that a person who cannot produce speech also cannot understand it. It is not unusual to see the families of speechless stroke

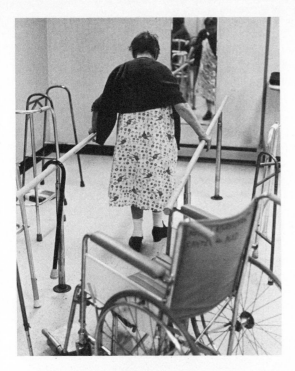

*With special care, old people may be rehabilitated from strokes as successfully as younger people.*

patients discussing the patients in their presence as though they lacked comprehension. This is both demeaning and frustrating to the stroke victims, who may fully understand both explicit and implicit communication.

Strokes are often life-threatening events. Patients who survive the first forty-eight hours frequently progress toward recovery. The mean survival time post-stroke is three and a half years. Fifty percent of stroke victims die early, ten percent need care for total disability, thirty percent have moderate to severe handicaps, and ten percent are slightly disabled (Adams, 1978).

Persons afflicted with cerebral lesions often have cognitive deficits that may halt their recovery. Clouded consciousness, aphasia (speech defects), and memory defects may decrease the person's ability to learn. Body perceptions may be disturbed because of paralysis. The afflicted person may have loss of postural fixation, including *apraxia*, loss of the ability to initiate a familiar movement; *agnosia*, failure to recognize people, objects, etc.; *perseveration*, continued response to stimuli no longer present; and *synkinesia*, associated movements of parts of the body where one set of movements is voluntary and the corresponding movement is involuntary. Strokes are also accompanied by fear, depression, loss of confidence, and other emotional responses to loss. Frequently the stroke patient is unaware of these symptoms and therefore does not complain about them. Family and hospital staff members must recognize these symptoms when they occur; if they are not recognized and dealt with, they will hamper successful rehabilitation (Adams, 1978: Kart et al., 1978).

*Late-Onset Diabetes Mellitus*   Age and obesity are the main predisposing factors for diabetes mellitus. The incidence of diabetes increases every decade, especially in persons over the age of fifty. Diabetes essentially involves elevated blood glucose levels or decreased glucose tolerance, although individual measures of these responses vary widely. These two disagnostic measures also show age-related variance, i.e., low levels in young people and high levels in old persons (Jarrett, 1973). On the basis of glycosuria (sugar in the urine) and glucose tolerance tests, it is suspected that at least as many undiagnosed diabetics live in the community as are already known to exist, especially old and obese diabetics. Furthermore, borderline abnormality in glucose tolerance has been found to lead to asymptomatic diabetes and later to symptomatic diabetes and blindness (Sharp et al., 1964).

The onset of diabetes in old persons is sometimes as sudden and severe as in young persons but is more often gradual and less dramatic. Late-onset hyperglycemia is believed to result from insulin inactivation or impaired tissue response to insulin, in contrast to juvenile diabetes, which is due to insulin deficiency.

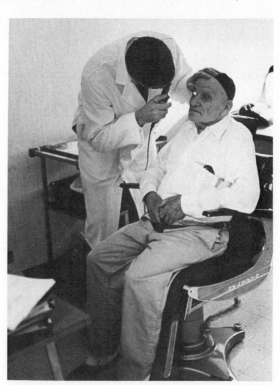

*Late-onset diabetes is often detected during visits to an eye specialist.*

Side-effects of diabetes can lead to disability in elderly diabetics. Diabetic retinopathy, accelerated aging and deterioration of the retinal blood vessels, is one such complication. Asymptomatic diabetes in middle-aged persons is often detected during visits to eye specialists because of decreasing vision. Visual impairment caused by diabetes consists of macular edema, vitreous hemorrhage, retinal detachment, and neuromuscular glaucoma. These symptoms occur to some extent in eighty-five percent of all patients who have diabetes longer than twenty-five years (Fozard et al., 1977).

Diabetics also often have vascular problems associated with metabolic disturbances. They develop atheromas more frequently and earlier than unafflicted persons the same age. Diabetics are at higher than normal risk for ischemic heart disease, CVAs, and peripheral vascular occlusion leading to gangrene. The microvascular degeneration found in the retina also occurs in the kidneys, leading to high blood pressure and renal failure in long-term diabetics. It is not unusual for old diabetics to require hemodialysis.

Diabetic polyneuritis, the loss of myelin in peripheral nerves, is another common complication of diabetes. The symptoms of this syndrome include sensory ataxia (decreased postural sensitivity), pain, weakness, abnormal sweating and gut motility, loss of bladder tone, impotence, and postural hypertension (Adams, 1978).

The management of diabetes in the elderly is difficult. Late-onset diabetes is frequently controlled by diet and oral insulin and sometimes by injections. Diet is difficult to control because of the confusion and isolation of many elderly diabetics and the expense of the food required. Insulin injections carried out by the patient are difficult because of the decreased coordination, excessive tremor, loss of sensitivity, and confusion of elderly persons. The use of oral drugs is not only susceptible to the confusion of elderly persons but is also potentially harmful over long periods of time; the risk of hypoglycemia and cardiovascular disease increases dramatically with some oral antidiabetic drugs (Jarrett, 1973).

*Parkinsonism    Parkinsonism* is a general term referring to certain disorders with the following common characteristics: tremor, muscular rigidity and slowing, weakness, and poverty of movement. There are three types of parkinsonism: idiopathic, the disease per se; postencephalitic, present in the survivors of the 1916-1918 pandemic of encephalitis lethargica; and sympathetic, caused by cerebrovascular disease, phenothiazine poisoning, or tardive dyskinesia (Adams, 1978).

The symptoms of parkinsonism involve the movements and appearance of afflicted persons. Parkinson patients are stiff and have immobile facial expressions and flexed limbs; their voluntary movements are uncoordinated and impoverished; they are slow; their eyes have poor convergence ability; they show mastication and swallowing movements; and their synergic movements are impaired. Consequently these patients cannot coordinate gestures with speech, swing their arms while walking, or perform other associated behaviors. They experience tremors that begin unilaterally then spread. The tremors are increased by emotional upset and decreased or halted by voluntary movement, conscious effort, or sleep. Parkinson patients have overactive autonomic nervous systems, indicated by flushing, sweating, excessive salivation, and temperature imbalance. They also experience emotional changes, such as irritability, depression, delirium, and dementia (Adams, 1978). In idiopathic parkinsonism, which is incurable, progressive deterioration of function eventually leads to total dependency. Old persons often complain of slowing and a sense of weakness, tremor, or stiffness. Physicians could easily dismiss early parkinsonism for "old age."

The causes of parkinsonism have only recently been uncovered. The basal ganglia of the brain are involved in the control of posture and movement. The messages between neurons are transmitted by chemical substances called *synaptic transmitters*. Acetylcholine, an excitatory transmitter, and dopamine, an inhibitory transmitter, are usually in balance in the substantia nigra, caudate nucleus, and putamen, those parts of the basal ganglia that are involved in movement. An imbalance in the ratio of these two transmitters in these parts of the brain leads to movement disorders. For example,

> dopamine overreaction induces muscular hypotonia and the hyperkinetic movements of Huntington's chorea or tardive dyskinesia whereas deficiency produces the clinical features of Parkinson's disease. (Adams, 1978, pp. 46–47)

It is not clear what causes the dopamine deficiency of Parkinson's disease, but it is clear that the brain compensates for the dopamine loss for a long time. However, eventually symptoms occur. The drug levodopa or L-dopa, a precursor of dopamine, withdraws the patient from a decompensation state to compensation, but it does not cure the disorder (Hornykiewicz, 1975).

Parkinsonism patients are treated according to one of the following three pharmacological formats: drugs that enhance dopaminergic activity; anticholinergic drugs, i.e., drugs that inactivate acetylcholine; or a mixture of dopaminergic-enhancing and anticholinergic drugs. Levodopa is effective in all but sympathetic parkinsonism, for which only anticholinergic drugs work; these drugs include trihexyphenidyl (Artane), benztropine (Cogentin), procyclidine (Kemedrin), and orphenadrine (Disipal). Anticholinergic drugs are frequently given to psychiatric patients long-term in combination with phenothiazines. Unfortunately they produce certain bizarre side-effects: blurred vision, agitation, hallucinations, confusion, and urinary incontinence, all of which together resemble the constellation frequently seen in psychosis. This constellation of symptoms is called the *central anticholinergic syndrome*. If it is not recognized, it can produce permanent organic damage in elderly patients, who are especially susceptible to it.

The relation between physiological and cognitive functioning is complex. Intellectual and sensory impairment often do not manifest themselves in elderly persons unless some stress such as illness intervenes. A principle called the *discontinuity hypothesis* (Birren, 1964) states that intellectual functioning may remain fairly autonomous of physical function until some limit is reached. When such a limit is reached, probably as a result of disease or stress, a new relationship between cognition and physical functioning is established.

Stress has two major effects. It permanently disrupts the physiological state, and it potentially accelerates aging. Stress, disease, aging, and behavior are clearly related. An understanding of their interactions may help lead to intervention in the health status of old persons at both the behavioral and somatic levels.

**Stress, Disease, and Behavior**

In the past decade the fields of psychosomatic medicine, crisis intervention, and epidemiology have jointly approached the study of diseases and their causes. The physical and social environments have been found to significantly affect the development of such diseases as diabetes mellitus, rheumatoid arthritis, peptic ulcer, and cancer. Psychosocial factors have also been found to influence the course and outcome of disease, as well as the patient's response to treatment, utilization of medical care, and compliance with treatment (Moos & Tsu, 1977). When physiological homeostasis becomes compromised, as in old age, the relations among physical, social, and psychosocial factors become even more significant.

The psychosocial environment includes cognitive factors in addition to relationships with people. Cognitive appraisal, the perception of threats, and the importance of self-regulation have all been found to affect health and illness in people of all ages. People's health behaviors reflect their perceptions of their health status as well as personal concerns over health. Three types of behavior have been found to influence the health status of individuals: illness behavior, sick-role behavior, and at-risk behavior (Baric, 1969; Kasl, 1974). Of particular concern to the elderly is at-risk behavior, which is a factor when chronic illness is present. Certain aspects of the at-risk role can create stress in an elderly person. The at-risk person is not institutionalized but is institutionalizable. The at-risk role has obligations but no privileges attached to it, and it may last indefinitely. The at-risk person does not receive adequate reinforcement from family, friends, or health professionals. Finally, the at-risk person does not receive continual treatment and therefore lacks the feedback that changes in symptomatology or in treatment procedures would provide (Hickey, 1980). As can be seen, this role is normless. The person is sick but not helpless or disabled; the person is also unable to get well, which the sick role per se demands. Support from family and friends is at best ambivalent because of the protracted time course of chronic illness. Even the health care system is directed at curing acute disorders. An elderly person already suffering from normlessness and

**Causes of Illness**

loss may be pushed by chronic illness toward cognitive, emotional, and perceptual decompensation.

**Chronic Illness as Crisis**   Since the advent of community psychology in the 1960s, crisis theory has become an important basis of discussions of preventive psychiatry and intervention techniques. One basic assumption of this theory is that the human organism needs homeostasis in all spheres of its existence, physical, psychological, and social. People have characteristic patterns of behavior. When something upsets them, they use habitual problem-solving mechanisms to restore balance in the affected sphere. A crisis is a situation so novel or major that the person's usual responses are inadequate. This leads to a state of psychic disorganization accompanied by fear, anxiety, guilt, and other powerful emotions. These emotions in turn lead to further disorganization and, unless balance is restored, to decompensation and death.

It is impossible for a person to remain in severe disequilibrium indefinitely. Therefore, a crisis is by definition limited; within a few days or weeks some new equilibrium must be established. The new balance may be either a healthy adaptation or a maladaptive response that works for a while because it temporarily removes anxiety. Maladaptive responses are short-run answers obtained at the expense of long-term solutions.

Figure 6-2 depicts the crisis resolution choices of a person facing a diagnosis of cancer. In the adaptive pattern the person seeks appropriate treatment, which places the symptoms in remission or at least puts the patient in a supportive environment (ideally). In the maladaptive pattern the person removes anxiety by

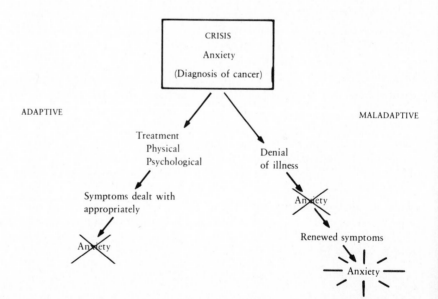

Figure 6-2   Crisis resolution in illness

denying the illness. However, the symptoms continue, anxiety returns, and the person is again in a crisis situation.

Any crisis situation must be seen as a turning point that has implications for the way the person will handle crises in the future. In the case presented, both paths are a shift from usual behaviors and the person's future life course will be affected by the choice made.

Serious illness almost always represents a crisis. When people are ill, their normal supports are distorted. If seriously ill, they are separated from family and friends. Frequently key roles are lost. Self-image and self-esteem are assaulted by permanent shifts in appearance or body function. Anxiety, anger, guilt, and helplessness in the face of an unpredictable future may be overwhelming (Moos & Tsu, 1977). If the person who is ill is also elderly, additional stresses compound the crisis. Perhaps the afflicted person sees this illness as the last step before death or a slide into debilitated dependency. Perhaps the person is alone and has no confidant with whom to share fears and other feelings. Perhaps even the person is offered no support by those who could provide it — the physician, nurse, or spouse.

Nevertheless, crises have a positive thrust. According to crisis theory, an individual in crisis is more receptive than usual to intervention by trained or sensitive care givers. The tentative nature of chronic illness in the elderly — with its multiple crises — increases the opportunity for caregivers to have a strong impact on successful crisis resolution. This possibility underscores the necessity for workers with the frail or ill elderly to learn appropriate crisis intervention and psychosocial counseling techniques. A conceptual framework for coping with physical illness is discussed in the next section.

### Coping with Physical Illness
We all may face serious illness or injury in our own lives or in the life of someone close to us. Each person facing a crisis decides upon adaptive tasks to resolve it. These adaptive tasks may require certain coping skills. The person's cognitive appraisal of the situation, perception of the tasks involved in relieving the crisis, and selection of coping skills are all influenced by three general factors: the background and personal characteristics of the individual; the presence of illness; and the psychosocial environment (Moos & Tsu, 1977).

The relationship between physical changes and social environmental stimuli may be similar to a reciprocal feedback loop (Fig. 6-3). In the case of the elderly, this cycle can rapidly have negative effects. For example, the relative ageism of the perceived social environment of old persons causes them to act slowly and with caution. This may lead to inappropriate coping strategies, which lower physical reserves and increase stress. This weakness and stress is in turn met by a nonsupportive environment.

Age, intelligence, cognitive and emotional development, philosophical beliefs, and previous coping experience all influence crisis response. These factors also influence ego strength and self-esteem, both of which affect prognosis. The timing of the illness in the life cycle partially determines the coping skills chosen. A child

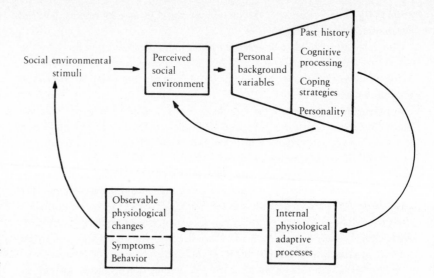

*Figure 6–3 Conceptual
model of the relationship
between social environ-
mental stimuli and observable physiological changes*

with diabetes has different concerns from an elderly adult with diabetes. Greater
maturity and more extensive coping experiences may provide the elderly with
greater personal resources on which to rely. Conversely, some elderly patients
already have a degree of organic damage or cognitive deterioration that seriously
hampers their coping skills.

Illness-related factors influencing coping skills include type and location of
symptoms (e.g., symptoms affecting body areas vested with importance versus
body areas low in ego involvement), symptom sequelae (e.g., disease-related
confusion or imbalance), and rate of disease onset and progression. The physical
and social environments also affect coping skills. Is the ill person in the hospital or
at home? Does the person have adequate privacy, personal space, and sensory
stimulation to adapt? Are social supports from family, friends, similarly afflicted
persons, and the community accessible and available? It is assumed that persons
lose physiological adaptability with age and that old persons are therefore less able
than young persons to cope with stress or environmental change (Eisdorfer &
Wilkie, 1977). If stress and environmental change occur simultaneously, the old
person whose homeostasis is already fragile may well become confused and
experience crisis.

### Adaptive Tasks

To resolve a crisis a person must adapt, usually by performing fairly discrete tasks
toward which particular coping skills may be applied. Adaptive tasks have been
divided by researchers into tasks that pertain to any crisis and tasks that pertain
solely to the crisis of illness (Moos & Tsu, 1977). The general adaptive tasks a
person must carry out in any crisis include preserving a reasonable emotional

balance, preserving a satisfactory self-image, preserving relationships with family and friends, and preparing for an uncertain future.

These tasks still hold but present a subtly different problem for the elderly. A crisis is potentially more traumatic for the elderly, because aging per se and social reactions to it render emotional balance and self-image difficult to preserve. Old age has been called a "season of loss," and many old people experience multiple losses in addition to illness. Family and friends may be unavailable, and the future is more uncertain for old than for young people. It would thus appear that old people are potentially more handicapped than young people in resolving crises; however, as mentioned, old people have had more extensive experience successfully coping with crises and thus may have an easier time of it than young people. Individual differences strongly affect how a person handles crisis situations.

Adaptive tasks that pertain solely to illness include dealing with pain and incapacitation and dealing with the hospital environment and special treatment procedures. Symptoms such as dizziness, weakness, incontinence, paralysis, loss of autonomy, and permanent disfigurement, which often accompany serious illness, are difficult for persons of any age to handle. What makes them especially difficult for old people is that they are frequently associated with "senility" and are

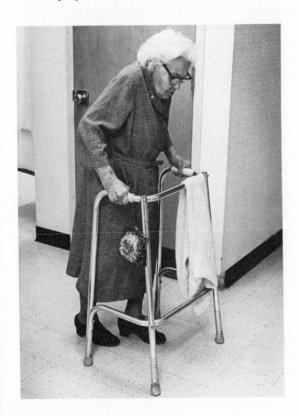

*Dealing with incapacitation is one of many illness-related adaptive tasks.*

therefore seen as irreversible. Health professionals may hesitate to deal with these symptoms because of the underlying belief that their efforts will be wasted. Many persons believe that permanent disfigurement should not affect old persons because they are sexually inactive and not "attractive" according to most of our biases and stereotypes.

The hospital environment and procedures themselves may be stressful. Colostomies, chemotherapy, radiation, arteriograms, and other procedures are frightening and often painful. In some cases the treatment may produce symptoms that are more painful than the illness. The hospital staff may exacerbate an illness simply by not providing any emotional support, or they may even avoid seriously ill old persons because of the ageist association linking age and illness to death. Finally, an old person with significant sensory deterioration and latent cerebral arteriosclerosis may be confused by being placed in a sterile, unfamiliar environment. All usual stimuli are removed; the patient is moved around by brusque, efficient people; treatment is difficult and often painful; and the person just doesn't feel well. Unless treated promptly, confusion can progress to chronic brain syndrome.

### Major Types of Coping Skills

Almost anything a person does to handle a crisis can be a coping skill if it involves an adaptive task. The seven skills presented in Table 6-4 are commonly used in dealing with physical illness. Coping skills are rarely used singly or exclusively. It is not uncommon for an old person to minimize the seriousness of his or her illness while simultaneously seeking information and emotional support. Any crisis situation is multifaceted and therefore demands a combination or sequence of coping skills (Moos & Tsu, 1977). Coping skills are also inherently neither adaptive nor maladaptive. Our own biases may judge them to be maladaptive, but in practice they are so only when they are used indiscriminately in every situation regardless of appropriateness or when they become life threatening. The fact that such skills exist indicates that coping with physical illness can be taught.

Minimization of the seriousness of or denial of the existence of the crisis is manifested clinically by detachment and lack of emotion when speaking of the symptoms. The ability to become emotionally detached in a crisis often provides the time necessary for acceptance of a situation's realities. It prevents a person from

*Table 6–4   Major types of coping skills*

Denying or minimizing the seriousness of crisis
Seeking relevant information
Requesting reassurance and emotional support
Learning specific illness-related procedures
Setting concrete, limited goals
Rehearsing alternative outcomes
Finding a general purpose or pattern of meaning in the course of events

being overpowered and allows that person to mobilize other personal coping resources. The negative aspect of this coping mechanism is that if a person persists in denying illness, especially serious illness, death may result.

Seeking relevant information is a good coping skill in that adequate information and familiarity with procedures relieves anxiety caused by uncertainty or misconceptions. It also provides "busy-work," which may help give the ill person a sense of control. A negative aspect of this coping mechanism is that not all persons find it anxiety-reducing; rather, they become more anxious when apprised of the reality or possible course of their illness.

Reassurance and emotional support from concerned family, friends, and hospital staff may provide strength during a crisis and help the person understand that he or she is not alone in illness but has access to concerned others. However, some people do not seek this sort of emotional support, looking upon it as a sign of weakness.

Learning specific illness-related procedures may be an excellent way for a person to regain a sense of control. This coping mechanism provides confirmation of personal ability and effectiveness at a time when opportunities for meaningful action are scarce. Generally the more control is allowed a person in a crisis, the better is the adaptation of that person. However, as discussed, confused elderly persons or elderly persons suffering from organic brain dysfunction may not be able to use this coping skill. In their case supervised personal care may be an alternative approach.

Setting concrete, limited goals perhaps has the greatest impact on prognosis. The skill is to break seemingly overwhelming problems into smaller, more manageable chunks. This is vitally important in preventing depression in elderly patients. Frequently old persons expect a quick, complete recovery from illness, which is especially unlikely in illnesses with recurring severe phases, such as emphysema and diabetes, and in illnesses in which relapses or new attacks are likely, such as stroke. Each subsequent phase or attack in such an illness may further sap the elderly person's reserve capacity. In this coping skill, the patient and care provider set up simple competencies to be gained, each building upon the previous one so that successes rather than failures accumulate.

Rehearsing alternative outcomes is a difficult skill, particularly for concerned family members. This coping mechanism consists of mental preparation for and rehearsal of outcomes with friends, family, and care providers. Outcome rehearsal allows patients to analyze procedures, remind themselves of previous successes, and perhaps undergo anticipatory grief over losses to come. This planning, inherently difficult, is hardest when the outcome being considered is death or severe disability. Nonetheless, such planning allows patients eventually to come to peace with expected outcomes.

The final coping skill relating to physical illness is finding a general purpose or pattern of meaning in the course of events. This is difficult to do, especially if events seem capricious or uncontrolled. Many persons find solace in religion or in a personal philosophy that allows them to view their experience in a long-term perspective. Other persons find the process of rationalizing their illnesses very stressful. However, when this skill is mastered, much psychological pain and uncertainty is allayed.

**Psychosocial Counseling**

Health care providers may help elderly people master crisis coping skills by increasing meaningful contact with them. Significant others are included in the treatment so that the old patient does not become dependent on the counselor. In the elderly normal physical changes are associated with an awareness of loss of prestige, lovability, and sexual potency. These changes are also often linked with attempts to deny the loss of integrity of body and mind and with fear of rejection. Some of these attempts at denial are mistakenly perceived by family, friends, and hospital staff as personal attacks.

Research has shown that the openly aggressive patient is often a better rehabilitation risk than the unaggressive patient; being demanding is a sign of a sense of personal integrity and the will to work for something better (Kir-Stimon, 1977). In contrast, patients whose whole lives are spent passively waiting for disability and death may respond with extreme negativism to rehabilitation and may even move toward their own destruction.

Psychosocial counseling begins with the careful assessment of how much function is lost and what residual skills are left, what the person's cognitive appraisal of the situation is and what coping skills he or she is using, and where the person is in relation to time and goals in the life cycle. Once these assessments are made, certain

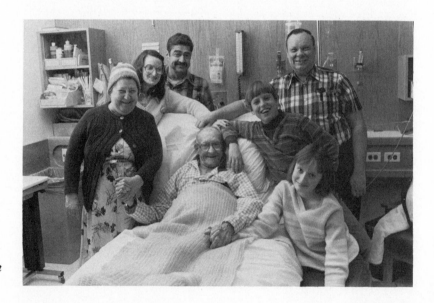

*The inclusion of significant others in the treatment of elderly patients can help prevent patients from becoming dependent on the therapist.*

fallacies about disability must be dealt with. Patients must realize that they will not be absolved of responsibility for their lives simply because they are ill or disabled. Patients must also come to grips with who they are and what the future holds for them.

Counselors of elderly patients must realize that they are not responsible for getting their patients well — the patients must do this. Counselors must not treat their patients as "sick"; that merely creates dependency. They should not help patients accept future physical limitations; rather, they should help patients learn to accept the present more fully. Finally, counselors must not deprive elderly patients of illusions or dreams, because each person — young or old — must create his own reality and live in it (Kir-Stimon, 1977).

If these fallacies are laid to rest, the emotional rehabilitation process may proceed as a paradigm in which the patient says to himself:

Who am I?
I am different than I was.
I don't like me.
Nobody likes me.
I am not worthwhile.
Perhaps I was never worthwhile.
Who was I?
I have no real identity anymore.
I have changed. Nothing is the same as before.
My friends, my family, the world about me has changed.
I am lost.

From here he might go on as follows:

I am the same as I was before.
I have not really changed and the world is the same.
If it's a mess of a world now, the world was actually the same before.
Only I didn't see it.
I was a fool, an immature child.
It's all pretty absurd and in a sense amusing.
Let me confront reality as it is, was, and will be.
Let me confront myself as I was, am, and will be.
It's all right that I am what I am.
It doesn't really matter who I am—I may never know anyway.
Life keeps changing and so do I.
What matters is where am I now? what am I doing? how can I live? where do I go from here?*

*Kir-Stimon, W. Counseling with the severely handicapped: Encounter and commitment. In R.P. Martinelli, A. E. Dell Orto (Eds.), *The psychological and social impact of physical disability.* New York: Springer, 1977, p. 364

Such a pattern of analysis may allow the crisis of physical illness to be a turning point or time for reassessment. It may be a time for personal discovery, ego integrity, and life review as envisioned by Erik Erikson. Finally,

> when the individual is able to recognize again his own self-worth in the scheme of things and realizes also the worth of the scheme of things in himself, he is in effect no longer disabled.*

**Summary**

Health status is a basic indicator of personal aging. The specter of disease raises various concerns in the elderly: fear of loss of personal autonomy, fear of the economic costs of prolonged health care, and a dread of health care itself. Elderly persons are generally considered at risk for serious illness because of the physiological processes of senescence they are undergoing and the prevalence among them of multiple chronic conditions.

This chapter considered the specific course of several diseases with a particularly high incidence among old persons. Though chronic illnesses are not always debilitating, they do make life difficult and lower resistance to other diseases. However, coping skills and adaptive tasks can be used to minimize their disabling effects.

---

*Kir-Stimon, W. Counseling with the severely handicapped: Encounter and commitment. In R.P. Martinelli, A. E. Dell Orto (Eds.), *The psychological and social impact of physical disability*. New York: Springer, 1977, p. 364

7

*Sensory Processes and Psychomotor Responses*

THE past three chapters discussed the nature and consequences of physiological changes in relation to aging and disease processes. This chapter deals with the senses as they act to link the central nervous system (CNS), the outside world, and the behavior of aging individuals. The CNS controls and integrates voluntary body functions as well as reflex or autonomic (i.e., involuntary) actions. The CNS also receives, processes, and stores information about the internal and external contacts a person makes with the environment. The senses shape the relationship among the environment, our mental constructions of it, and the way we react to its demands.

The sense organs change as a function of age. The changes associated with sensory aging in turn produce perceptual changes, which are manifested by behaviors. Thus, persons may perform more slowly as they get older because they no longer receive adequate information about their environment. Alternatively, old people may respond more slowly not because of decreased input but because the social stereotypes of age say that old people are "failures," making them want to perform correctly even at the expense of speed. A third interpretation is that sensory decrement has no disabling effect on performance and that the factor causing slowing is disuse. Regardless of the explanation researchers offer for this phenomenon, speed of response does decline with age. However, the degree of sensory decrement and response slowing varies depending on life-style, overall health, and extent of environmental contact.

This chapter discusses age-related changes in sensation and some of the effects aging has on perception and psychomotor response. Information on sensory and perceptual aging has not come from a particularly well integrated body of research (Elias et al., 1977). Research has been largely atheoretical, and findings have been made in isolation, often with no application to behavior or intervention. Nonetheless it is clear that with advancing age there is a decrease in the function of all sensory systems. It must be inferred that the behaviors observed are caused by these sensory decrements. Although the exact nature of the central processes intervening between sensory stimulus and behavioral response is unknown, the sorts of factors that influence behavior in old persons are generally agreed upon by researchers.

Many neurological functions show the effects of age; vision fails, eye movement and pupil size abnormalities become more common, hearing loss occurs, vibration and touch sensation as well as two-point discrimination decline, weakness of

**General Age Changes in Sensation**

muscles increases, and gait, posture, and coordination decline (Murray et al., 1980). However, there is no consistent pattern of loss across the aging population, and many aspects of neurological function are affected only slightly.

Sensory changes occur slowly throughout adulthood and are often not noticed until they interfere with daily life. The perception of simple stimuli changes only mildly until a person reaches sixty or seventy, when it may show a steep decline. However, complex perceptual abilities, such as speaking, reading, and operating machines, show functional decreases early in adult life (Marsh, 1980).

There are cerain general changes in sensation and perception that occur with age. First, higher intensities of stimulation are required for perception to occur, i.e., sensory thresholds increase (Botwinick, 1973; Woodruff, 1975). This appears to be due to the decreased efficiency of sense organ receptors with age. Second, sensory function appears to decline. The loss of visual and auditory acuity is particularly important in that it may create sensory deprivation and social isolation, both of which have profound social and psychological consequences. For example, elderly persons who live in a world where environmental stimuli are largely unseen and unheard may become paranoid. They may feel people are whispering about them when in reality they are talking in normal tones. They may fail at tasks because of difficulty in perceiving incoming stimuli, and such failure may lead to discouragement and damage their self-concept.

Changes in particular sense organs, like the changes in tissues discussed in Chapter 5, may thus be more profound than they appear at first glance. Deteriorated sensory function has ramifications for psychopathology and intellectual functioning as well. However, it is also possible for old people to maintain function through various compensatory mechanisms. For example, an eighty-year-old pianist regarded the loss of the use of her legs as a minor inconvenience as long as she could continue to play the piano.

## The Visual System

For most people in our culture, vision is the dominant sensory modality through which to gain environmental information and social intercourse. Various age-related structural changes may hinder the flow of information from the eye inward to the CNS. Figure 7-1 depicts the various parts of the eye.

With age the eye sinks in its orbit because of the loss of surrounding fat, the lacrimal gland decreases its output, and the eye muscles lose tone, strength, and control. Except for the decreased muscle tonus, these changes have little effect on function. The latter change causes the arc in which the eye moves to become constricted, especially in the upward course (Marsh, 1980).

The most important changes in the structure of the eye that occur with age are in the tissues and substances passing light to the retina, i.e., the cornea, lens, iris, and aqueous and vitreous humors.

*At age seventy poor vision is the rule rather than the exception.*

## Cornea

The cornea is the major refracting surface of the eye; any corneal changes therefore have a serious effect on the eye's image-forming ability. The cornea flattens, thickens, and increases its horizontal diameter relative to its vertical diameter with age. These changes predispose old persons to problems of astigmatism (Marsh, 1980).

Arcus senilis, the accummulation of lipids or fats in a gray ring along the outer edge of the cornea's membrane, is a condition seen in approximately forty percent of people sixty years of age and older. It has no functional effect but causes the eyes to look less lustrous (Marsh, 1980).

## Crystalline Lens

The crystalline lens is a pale yellow, oval, spheroidal collection of fibers enveloped in a membrane called the *capsule*. Three major sets of changes occur in the lens as a result of age (Marsh, 1980).

First, the lens becomes less resilient after the age of forty, and the ciliary muscle that holds it in place loses strength. The fibers within the capsule become cross-linked, and the inner cells harden. These changes cause the lens to have decreased transparency and a greater refractive index. The shift to less resiliency leads to perceptual change and loss of accommodation.

Second, the lens loses transparency and becomes more yellow. This makes the eye less sensitive to certain colors of the spectrum and changes the perception of hue (Botwinick, 1973; Marsh, 1980).

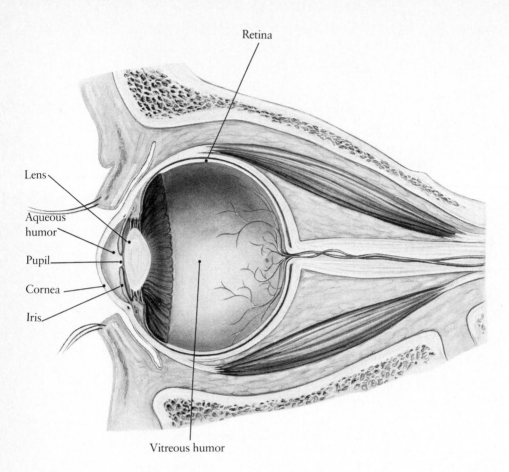

Retina

Lens

Aqueous
humor

Pupil

Cornea

Iris

Vitreous humor

(Source: Carlson, N.R. *Physiology of behavior.* Boston: Allyn & Bacon, 1981, p. 188)

*Figure 7-1*    *The eye*

Third, the lens is prone to the development of cataracts, especially in persons over sixty. Cataracts are the most common visual disability of old persons, and many researchers feel we would all develop them to some degree if we lived long enough (Kart et al., 1978). A cataract is an opaqueness of the lens of the eye that prevents light from entering the eye and scatters or diffuses whatever light does enter. There are two major classes of cataract: *nuclear,* in which the lens core darkens; and *cortical,* which is caused by stress, especially high blood sugar levels (Marsh, 1980). Depending on the extent of the cataract, the afflicted person may develop blurring and dimming of vision.

### Iris

The iris is the pigmented portion of the eye. It is the muscle that determines the size of the pupil. Light passes through the iris to the lens lying immediately behind. The iris contracts to reduce light flow to the lens when light is bright and when the eyes converge to see objects that are near. With age the iris loses flexibility and produces a small, fixed opening at the pupil under all lighting conditions. As Marsh (1980) has reported, in well-lighted conditions the old eye screens fifty percent more light than the young eye, and this percentage increases in lower light levels.

## Aqueous Humor

The aqueous humor fills the area between the cornea and the lens of the eye. The cornea has no blood supply of its own and therefore obtains nutriment from the aqueous humor. The aqueous humor is continuously secreted and absorbed and is thus completely renewed every four hours (Gregory, 1967). It shrinks with age as the lens grows larger, especially at its outflow point between the sclera and the iris. This increases the potential for outflow blockage with age (Marsh, 1980).

## Vitreous Humor

The vitreous humor lies between the retina and the lens. With age this fluid tends to aggregate, leading to other changes. For example, there is an increase in the number of inclusionary bodies found in its substance, and this increases the amount of light scatter. The color of the humor tends to darken with age, and there may be local discoloration from small hemorrhages in the retina (Marsh, 1980).

## Retina

The retina is a thin sheet of interconnected nerve cells interspersed with blood vessels. The nerve cells are light-sensitive rod and cone cells, which convert light stimulation into electrical impulses that are channeled into the CNS (Gregory, 1967). There is little documented change caused by normal aging in the retina. However, forty-five percent of vision problems in the elderly are caused by the deterioration of macular elements of the retina (Fozard et al., 1977). Senile macular degeneration is the leading cause of blindness in the elderly. It often begins insidiously by destroying the ability to discriminate detail such as fine print. Macular degeneration never affects peripheral vision, so in the absence of other defects it need not be disabling. The cause of senile macular degeneration is unknown, but disease processes such as diabetes mellitus, arteriosclerosis, and hypertension have been found to aggravate the condition in some persons (Kart et al., 1978).

Table 7-1 presents a list of the major changes that occur in the visual system with age. As stated, these changes need not be disabling.

## Changes in Visual Perception

Our perception of the world is mediated by our sense organs but is not just a series of sensory events. Learning, thinking, and motivation, as well as physiology, play a role in central processes.

The major age-related changes that occur in perceptual functioning are mediated

*Table 7-1   Normal changes in the eye*
Decreasing eye muscle tonicity
Decreasing peripheral vision
Decreasing elasticity of lens
Decreasing ability of pupil to change size
Decreasing ability to adapt to dark
Decreasing depth and color perception
Decreasing moisture on cornea and conjunctiva
Increasing changes in blood vessels of eye
Increasing time required for fluid to drain from eye chambers
Increasing eyelid droop
Increasing tearing
Increasing vulnerability to disease

---

by two types of alterations in the eye's structure. The first, which occurs between thirty-five and forty-five years of age, consists of changes in the transmissiveness and accommodative power of the eye. These changes affect distance vision, sensitivity to glare, binocular depth perception, and color sensitivity. The second, which begins to occur between fifty-five and sixty-five years of age, involves the retina and CNS. Circulation and metabolic changes in these areas lead to a decrease in the size of the visual field, in adaptation to the dark, and in sensitivity to flicker (Fozard et al., 1977). These sensory and perceptual changes may have a serious effect on vision.

*Acuity and Accommodation*   Most seventy-year-olds have poor vision (USD-HEW, 1978). This is due to a decline in acuity, i.e., the ability to see objects clearly at a distance. Acuity peaks in the teens, is constant until age forty-five to fifty, and declines gradually thereafter. There is a sharp drop in acuity beginning at about age sixty, but it causes no distress until age seventy or seventy-five. Acuity decreases for various reasons. Light input to the retina is decreased, and there is more light scattering. The crystalline lens becomes less efficient, and macular elements in the retina are lost (Marsh, 1980).

Accompanying the change in visual acuity is the decreased ability of the eye to accommodate, or focus on near objects. The loss of accommodative ability, which occurs earlier than the loss of acuity, is manifested by a decreased ability to accommodate to moving targets (Fozard et al., 1977). Decreased accommodation is mainly due to a loss of elasticity in the crystalline lens of the eye, which gradually occurs from age five to age sixty. The loss of lens elasticity causes presbyopia, or farsightedness, as a result of which most people need reading glasses by the time they reach middle age (Kart et al., 1978). CNS difficulties in calculating range and controlling the increasingly slow accommodation process compound the effects of the increased stiffness of the lens (Marsh, 1980).

*Visual Threshold*   The minimum amount of light that can be detected, i.e., the visual threshold, increases with age (Elias et al., 1977). This increase is probably influenced by the smaller pupil size and lower transmittance of the ocular media that occur with age. It may also be due to metabolic changes and cell loss, which cause the retina to need more light to function. The ability to adapt to decreased illumination (dark adaptation) and the ability to make brightness discriminations decline with age. The eyes of old persons are also more susceptible to glare than the eyes of young persons because of the physiological changes discussed earlier and the presence of cataracts.

Because of a decrease in the size of their pupils (a phenomenon called *senile miosis*) and the passage of less light to the retina, old individuals generally need more light for reading than young persons. The decrease in dark adaptation that occurs with age means that old people may have difficulty driving at night or getting around safely in the dark. Ways to compensate for these difficulties are discussed later in this chapter.

*Color Perception*   Color vision changes with age because of the yellowing of the lens of the eye. The yellowed lens filters out the shorter wavelengths (i.e., blues and violets) without affecting longer wavelengths (i.e., yellows and reds). The spectrum of affected colors is depicted in Figure 7-2. It is especially difficult for old persons to discriminate among blues, blue-greens, and violets. The perception of color brightness also declines in persons beyond their twenties, although less so in women than in men. Research shows that the eyes of old persons with the lens removed still show color discrimination deficiencies, suggesting that the decreased color perception of the aged may not be due entirely to the yellowing of the lens. The exact nature of this decrement is therefore unknown (Marsh, 1980).

*Other Changes*   Older people have other decrements in vision that may affect function. Their depth perception decreases. They also experience longer visual after-effects or image persistence than younger people; this indicates that they need more time to process stimuli, although it does not indicate at what level of the CNS this slowing occurs (Marsh, 1980).

Critical flicker fusion (CFF) also slows with age. CFF has as its response measure the frequency at which a flickering light appears to fuse into one light source. CFF is a valuable indicator of CNS and sensory processing efficiency. However, the

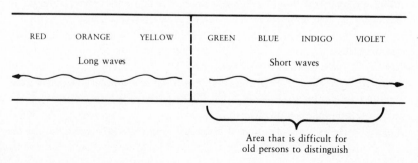

Area that is difficult for
old persons to distinguish

*Figure 7-2   Color spectrum*

exact nature of what CFF indicates about neurological function is not clear. CFF may be due to peripheral factors relating to the pupil and lens rather than to central factors; when a large amount of light reaches the retina, CFF does not show as much decline as when only a small amount of light reaches the retina. However, the effects of peripheral and central involvement in CFF slowing vary depending on the level of illumination, a factor that makes definitive statements about CFF difficult.

The same sorts of circumstances might well exist for the other perceptual measures discussed. In a review of the literature Elias, Elias, and Elias (1977) made the following summary statement:

> If nothing else, they illustrate the kinds of difficulties involved in perceptual research with different age groups of adults and the dangers involved in assuming that age changes or age differences in CFF are centrally mediated or somehow reflect structurally based intellectual changes with age. (Elias et al., 1977, p. 184)

## The Auditory System

Like vision, hearing shows decreased function with age. It is difficult to separate the effects of noise trauma from normal aging in the ear, although much progress has been made in this regard (Corso, 1977).

*Outer Ear*   The human auditory system includes the ear and its associated neural pathways (Fig. 7-3). The parts of this system that are readily visible are the pinna (outer ear) and the external auditory meatus (ear canal). The pinna becomes longer, wider, and less flexible with age, but the functional effects of this change are probably negligible. The ear canal frequently becomes impacted with an excessive buildup of cerumen (ear wax). This buildup frequently leads to conductive hearing loss, which is remedied by removal of the wax (Corso, 1977; Marsh, 1980).

*Middle Ear*   The middle ear often shows characteristic structural change with age. The tympanic membrane (eardrum) stiffens. The ossicular chain, which is composed of the malleus (hammer), incus (anvil), and stapes (stirrup) and which is involved in sound transmission, is frequently afflicted with arthritic changes. The ossicles tend to have difficulty transmitting higher frequencies with age (Marsh, 1980), although this difficulty does not appear to be due to the arthritis (Etholm & Belal, 1974). The eustachian tube, which connects the middle ear with the nasopharyngeal passage, frequently becomes blocked with age, causing decreased hearing ability.

*Inner Ear*   The age-related changes that have the most profound effect on hearing loss are found in the inner ear and the auditory pathway of the CNS. The main structure of the inner ear involved in audition is the *cochlea*, a coiled organ divided longitudinally by a combination of bony shelf and the *basilar membrane* upon which the endings of the auditory nerve are located. These nerve endings are in contact with epithelial hair cells collectively called the *organ of Corti*. Movement of these hair cells is believed to stimulate the auditory nerve endings to fire and begin the neural process by which we perceive sound (Geldard, 1966). Figure 7-4 presents a cross section of the cochlea showing the organ of Corti and the basilar membrane.

With age the cochlea shows loss of elasticity in the basilar membrane, atrophy of the stria vascularis, loss of auditory neurons, and loss of sensory receptors (i.e., hair cells) in the organ of Corti (Marsh, 1980). These losses are summarized in Table 7-2.

### Changes in Auditory Perception

The age-related changes in physiology of the auditory system have perceptual

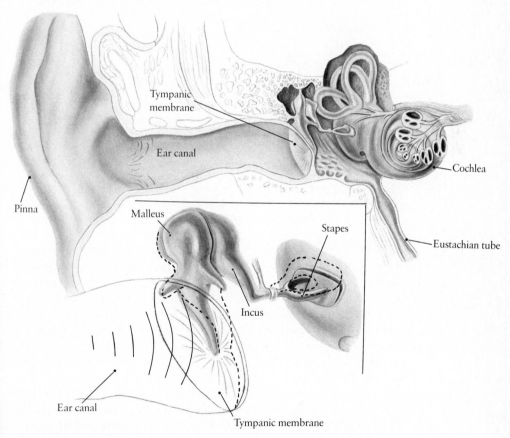

(Source: Carlson, N.R. *Physiology of behavior*. Boston: Allyn & Bacon, 1981, p. 188)

*Figure 7-3   The auditory apparatus*

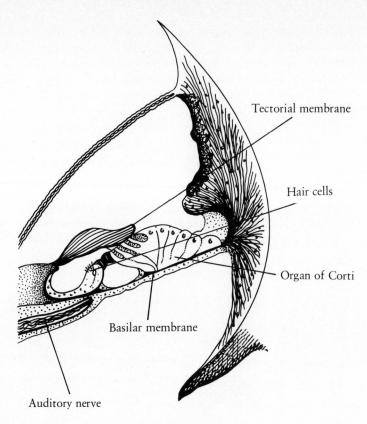

Tectorial membrane

Hair cells

Organ of Corti

Basilar membrane

Auditory nerve

*Figure 7-4    The inner ear*

consequences. In particular the cochlear changes discussed above have been associated with marked loss in the perception of high-pitched tone frequencies, a
characteristic disorder called *presbycusis.*

*Presbycusis*    Presbycusis begins as a gradual loss of hearing at the highest frequencies at approximately twenty-five years of age. Women hear high frequencies better
than men but normal speech tones more poorly (Botwinick, 1973). This hearing
loss is due partially to environmental noise pollution and partially to age-related
changes in the cochlea and auditory pathway.

As can be seen in Figure 7-5, the mechanisms of the ear are only the first step in
the process of hearing. The stimulus (sound) is received by the ear and its
mechanisms and is then transformed into electrical impulses in the inner ear. From
the cochlea the impulses travel up the auditory nerve into the auditory nuclei of the
brain stem. The path from the brain stem is up the ascending tracts to the primary
auditory area of the temporal lobe and from there into the cortical association
subsystem, where they interface with other stimulus memories and with appropriate emotional overtones through the thalamus and its associated systems. If the
individual hearing the sound wishes to offer a spoken response, the effector

*Table 7-2   Normal aging changes of the ear*
Decreasing flexibility of pinna
Decreasing elasticity of eardrum (tympanic membrane)
Decreasing number of neurons and fibers in auditory tracts and cortical areas
Decreasing number of sensitive cells in middle ear
Increasing rigidity of small bones in middle ear
Increasing accumulation of cerumen
Increasing rate of time for passage of impulses in auditory nerve

subsystems become involved and another auditory stimulus — a word — is
emitted.

The process of audition and reciprocal communication is very complex. Given
that emotional and cognitive functioning as well as physiological functioning play
a role in hearing, much of the etiology of hearing disorders is still uncertain.

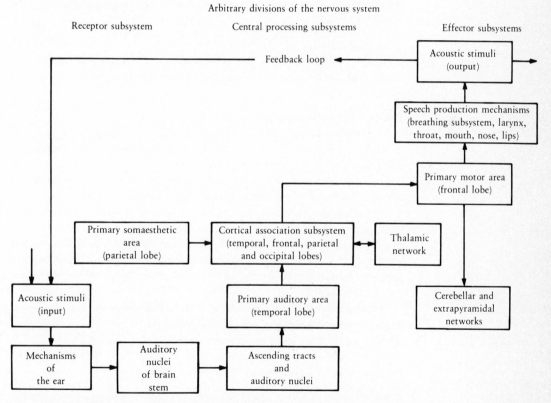

(Source: Corso, J.F. Auditory perception and communication. In J.E. Birren & K.W. Schaie (Eds.), *Handbook of the psychology of aging.*
New York: Van Nostrand Reinhold Company, 1977, p. 537. Copyright © 1977 by Van Nostrand Reinhold Company. Reprinted by
permission of the publisher)

*Figure 7-5   Schematic diagram of the functional aspects of the human nervous system in voice communication*

Presbycusis has at least four separate causes, each of which is manifested by a slightly different pattern of symptomatic hearing loss.

First, the loss of elasticity of the basilar membrane makes it difficult for the CNS to discern particular stimuli. This is due to the high-frequency sense receptors being more closely packed on the short, thick, narrow section of the basilar membrane than the low-frequency receptors; as a result, the high-frequency receptors receive proportionally less stimulation when the basilar membrane flexibility decreases. The atrophy of these structures associated with vibration is called *mechanical presbycusis* (Corso, 1977; Marsh, 1980). It is manifested perceptually by increasing hearing loss values from low to high frequencies (Corso, 1977).

Second, atrophy of the stria vascularis of the cochlea leads to associated deficiencies in the bioelectric and biochemical properties of the fluids bathing the cochlea. Changes in these metabolic properties cause hearing loss for all frequencies and often for loudness recruitment as well (Corso, 1977; Marsh, 1980). Loudness recruitment is seen in

a person reporting relatively normal loudness for low intensity sounds, but reporting relatively high loudness for moderate intensities; and painful or distorted loudness for only moderately high intensities. (Marsh, 1980, p. 156)

This type of presbycusis is referred to as *metabolic presbycusis.*

Third, the loss of auditory neurons produces a disorder called *neural presbycusis,* the major symptom of which is loss of high-frequency–discrimination but not of pure tone thresholds (Corso, 1977; Marsh, 1980). This disorder is believed to be genetic, and it is often associated with growth of the temporal bone and its subsequent pressure on the auditory nerve (Marsh, 1980).

The fourth type of presbycusis is *sensory presbycusis,* which is caused by atrophy and degeneration of hair cells and their supporting cells in the organ of Corti. This type of deterioration causes loss of hearing for high-frequency pure tones but not for speech frequencies (Corso, 1977; Marsh, 1980). It appears to be either a response to trauma or due to a genetically caused metabolic problem in the hair cells (Marsh, 1980).

Other perceptual age differences have also been linked to physiological events or disease. Loss and atrophy of cells in the auditory portion of the CNS lead to impairment of directional hearing and decreased speech discrimination while perception of pure tone thresholds stays normal (Kirikae, 1969). The loss of neurons and nerve fibers appears to accelerate after age sixty.

It is estimated that from 2 to 26 years there are on the average 32,500 acoustic nerve fibers; but from 44 to 60 years, only 30,300 fibers. By 80 to 90 years the channels for the nerve bundles are almost completely closed by osteoid and contain few, if any, fibers. (Krmpotic-Nemanic, 1969)

*Like vision, hearing
shows decreased function
with age.*

*Pitch Discrimination*   Pitch discrimination declines with age. There is a gradual decline in pitch discrimination from ages twenty-five to fifty-five and a more rapid decline thereafter. As with auditory thresholds, the greatest age decline appears to occur in discrimination ability at the highest frequencies (Marsh, 1980). This may be a function of noise pollution. However, speech comprehension, which involves communication, also decreases steadily with age. This implies that some loss of auditory perception is related to changes in CNS processing and not merely to sensory (or peripheral) decline.

*Sound Localization*   With age there is a loss of sensitivity to sound localization, especially in the high frequencies. The localization mechanism depends on intensity differences between the two ears, and the mechanism for high frequencies weakens in both ears with age. Furthermore, the ability to localize sounds depends on quick analysis, which also declines from age thirty on (Marsh, 1980).

*Auditory Masking*   Many psychologists believe that audiograms are conservative in their estimates of hearing loss in the elderly because they are performed in quiet conditions. Experimental test conditions usually pair simple stimuli with low background noise. Old people show a severely diminished ability to disentangle signals from background noise. When the signals are complex, as in speech, their ability is even more hampered (Marsh, 1980). This problem may be complicated by *tinnitus* (ringing in the ears), which further blocks signal detection (Kart et al., 1978). This disorder is estimated to occur in up to ten percent of old persons. It is not only annoying, it also blocks desired stimuli.

*Speech Comprehension*    A decrease in speech comprehension is potentially the most damaging consequence of sensory loss with age. Consonants are the differentiating aspect of most words, and they are usually recognized by their high-pitched components. In presbycusis, the hearing of high-frequency sounds and thus speech discrimination is lost. Furthermore, consonants are low in power and are therefore easy to mask (Corso, 1977).

The psychological consequences of poor audition can be debilitating for an elderly person, and many elderly suffer from hearing loss. It has been estimated that thirty percent of persons over sixty-five suffer a significant loss of auditory capability. Hearing loss is potentially the most problematical of all perceptual impairments. It can lead to greater social isolation than blindness and may produce suspiciousness, paranoia, or depression because of its concomitant lack of communication. Elderly who are hard of hearing are often excluded or ignored at social functions. It is easy to mistake them for senile or mentally subnormal because either they don't hear and therefore don't respond or they repeat things. Hearing loss receives little social sympathy because it is not a visible handicap. The loud speech of many hard-of-hearing individuals and their frustration at their inability to communicate may cause people to avoid them altogether. These factors combine to severely restrict social and environmental interaction.

Hearing losses may be exaggerated among the elderly because of their cautiousness and inability to remain attentive to tasks that are repetitive and relatively meaningless. Given that many standard test to measure hearing loss are dull, anxiety-producing, or meaningless, such confounding is a possibility. The hearing loss observed in elderly persons may also be in part due to cognitive factors; as stated, the elderly process information more slowly than young persons.

**The Other Senses**

Most research on sensory processes has focused on vision and audition. These two senses are the main channels for communication and interpersonal relations and, it would also appear, the most necessary for survival. However, in the elderly the other senses of taste, smell, and somesthesis are also vital to both the quantity and quality of life.

### Taste and Smell

Persons are motivated to act on the basis of the taste and smell of things. They seek "pleasant" smells or tastes and avoid "unpleasant" smells or tastes. Researchers of these sense modalities are calling for research into hedonic changes with age rather

*Decrease in taste and smell, when they occur, may **have a debilitating** effect on a person's overall function and health, partly by leading to poor eating habits. Positive eating environments may do much to counter these perceptual changes.*

than studies of mere acuity (Engen, 1977; Schiffman, 1977; Schiffman & Pasternak, 1979).

The sense of taste follows vision and audition in declining with age. Sensitivity to the four primary taste qualities — sweetness, sourness, saltiness, and bitterness — generally decreases with age, though there is some evidence that sensitivity to bitter tastes increases with age instead (Engen, 1977). In general elderly persons are less able to recognize food tastes than younger persons (Schiffman, 1977). It is believed that this is due to the atrophy or loss of gustatory cells and their nerve fibers. Diet also has an important effect on taste; vitamin B deficiency, for example, has been associated with a decrease in taste sensitivity (Kart et al., 1978). Taste preferences also show changes with age. The preference for bitter foods decreases and the preference for sweet foods increases. It is generally assumed but not established that this also is due to physiological changes (Engen, 1977).

The number of taste buds decreases with age beginning at about age forty to forty-five in women and age fifty to sixty in men. It has been suggested that this decrease is related to levels of gonadal (sex) hormones. By age seventy-five, approximately two thirds of all papillae have atrophied (Marsh, 1980). Other physiological factors, including fissuring of the tongue and the decreased production of saliva with a high mucus content, are also assumed to affect taste and smell (Marsh, 1980).

In the past the sense of smell was believed to decline with age, but this is suspect. It appears that normal old people in a physically superior state show little if any deficit in sense of smell (Engen, 1977; Marsh, 1980). However, elderly persons not in optimal health show a considerable decline in sense of smell. Elderly persons with chronic disorders in one study could not smell the stimulus even when it was directly under their noses (Schiffman & Pasternak, 1979). The loss of smell discrimination is assumed to be due to various causes, including decreased number of olfactory nerve fibers, atrophy or loss of neurons in the olfactory tract, and chronic catarrhal conditions.

A recent explanation of age-related loss of smell as a function of impairment of the neural code for individual odors (Schiffman & Pasternak, 1979) is based on the work of Erickson (1963), who posited that individual neural units are not specific to any chemical stimulus. Erickson believed that the neural code consists of a pattern of firing across many neural units.

> A general loss in the olfactory system could decrease the amount of information in an across-fiber pattern making it more difficult for the elderly to discriminate patterns of different chemical stimuli. (Schiffman & Pasternak, 1979)

The theory is tied to the health of the sensing person. Research has shown that the memory of elderly demented subjects is so impaired that these subjects cannot hold two stimuli in their memory long enough to compare them (Craik, 1977). Such memory loss has been correlated with cellular loss and atrophy in the hippocampus and amygdala regions of the brain (Tomlinson & Henderson, 1976). Diseases such as cerebral arteriosclerosis and hypertension may be involved in lesions in these areas of the brain, and loss of smell may thus reflect a decreased ability to make comparisons rather than sensory loss per se. Table 7-3 gives a synopsis of normal aging changes in taste and smell.

Factors other than physiology may be involved in the loss of taste and smell discrimination with age. Improved oral hygiene has been found to increase taste sensitivity, in part by removing oral inflammation. Dentures may block some gustatory nerve endings (Marsh, 1980), and smoking may also have a detrimental effect on taste (Engen, 1977; Schiffman, 1977; Marsh, 1980). Decreases in taste and smell sensitivity may lead a person to develop poor eating habits and thereby have a debilitating effect on that person's overall function and health.

*Table 7–3　Normal age changes in the senses of taste and smell*

*Taste*
  Decreasing number of taste buds
  Decreasing production of saliva
  Decreasing number of neurons and nerve fibers
  Increasing fissuring of tongue
*Smell*
  Changes observed appear due to health status rather than age

## Somesthesis

Touch, vibration, temperature, kinesthesis, and pain sensitivity are all included in the category of *somesthesis*. "Somesthesis includes those sensations that arise from normal and intensive stimulation of the skin, the viscera, and kinesthesis — the muscle and joint sense" (Kenshalo, 1977, p. 562). Some changes in somesthetic quality are a direct consequence of growing old. Other changes result from injury or disease affecting the skin, receptors, or sensory tracts of the CNS. For example, peripheral neuropathies have been associated with such disorders as diabetes and arteriosclerosis.

In general the somesthetic properties — tactile sensitivity, temperature and pain sensitivity, the vibratory and vestibular senses, and kinesthesis — decrease with age, affecting the quality of contact elderly persons have with the external environment. However, use of cutaneous sensitivity to determine the mean thresholds for the somesthetic senses may be misleading; different parts of the body vary in sensitivity, and different ages and sexes show different patterns (Kenshalo, 1977).

The tactile sense (touch) is housed in the skin. The skin is highly complex, with many specialized neurological structures, including bare nerve endings, which are responsible for the perception of pain; Meissner's corpuscles, which respond to heat; and Vater-Pacini corpuscles, which are sensitive to pressure.

The anatomy of the skin shows changes with age that affect perception. The epidermis thins, the amount of the connective tissue collagen decreases, and there is a decrease in the elastin fibers in the upper layers of the dermis. It is unclear whether the dermis and epidermis thin with age. In many old people such thinning is readily seen in the hands, where the symptoms include prominent blue veins and yellow tendons. However, these effects are not found in all aged persons (Kenshalo, 1977).

Structural changes in the skin lead to morphological changes. The skin is relatively easy to deform in old persons, and this leads to an increased number of spots sensitive to touch and pain. However, there is also a decrease in the number of Meissner's corpuscles, which are responsible for refined sensitivity to light touch. Perceptually, old people require more time and higher levels of stimulus intensity to register stimulation (Kenshalo, 1977).

Temperature and touch sensitivity also varies across parts of the body. Little change occurs until age fifty to sixty; then a rise in touch threshold occurs, i.e., the force of tactile stimulation must be greater for that stimulation to be perceived. This rise in touch threshold may also be responsible for the decrease in pain perception that appears to occur with age.

There is little empirical data on age change in pain perception. One reason for this is that it is methodologically difficult to measure pain, the most subjective of all senses. What a person reports as painful may be influenced by that person's feelings, tolerance for pain, experience with pain, and upbringing (i.e., cultural, generational, and gender expectancies). Body sensitivity to pain also varies across locations; for example, the ear lobe is relatively insensitive to pain whereas the fingertips are highly sensitive.

There appears to be a decline in sensitivity to pain with age. Illnesses and minor operations are reported as less painful by old than by younger subjects. The time required to perceive pain and the pain threshold show a gradual increase until the age of sixty, when a dramatic increase occurs. This is possibly a manifestation of lack of CNS integration with age, but it probably also reflects age differences in attention, caution, and experience (cohort differences) (Botwinick, 1973; Kenshalo, 1977).

A decrease in vibratory sensitivity occurs with age as measured by a tuning fork placed against the skin. This sensory ability has diagnostic value in the assessment of CNS disorders. A large number of old subjects who are free of disease or detectable neuropathy appear to lose this sense. The loss appears to start at about age fifty and is more severe in the lower than in the upper extremities (Kenshalo, 1977). The anatomical causes of decreased vibratory sensitivity include the following factors, though in what combination is unknown (Kenshalo, 1977): decreased numbers and changed morphology of Meissner's and Vater-Pacini corpuscles, decreased numbers of spinal root nerves, diminished circulation, changes in nerve conduction velocity, and dietary insufficiencies (especially thiamine deficiency).

Kinesthetic insensitivity is another important change of old age. Kinesthesis is an internally stimulated sense rather than an externally stimulated sense like vision, audition, taste, smell, and touch. Kinesthesis is the mass of sensations generated by the movements of the body itself, including the continuous, and often unconscious, sensations originating in the muscles, tendons, and joints (Geldard, 1966). Kinesthesis originates in the muscle afferents of the CNS and joint receptors. Stimulation of this sense comes from the relative positions of the body parts during active and passive movements as well as from the strain that is felt with resistance to limb movements (Kenshalo, 1977).

Decreased kinesthetic sensitivity increases susceptibility to falls (Kart et al., 1978).

> Such falls may be occasioned by dizziness, muscular weakness, or a decreased input from the muscle and joint receptors. Disturbed gait due to cerebral vascular problems . . . [and] decreased or outright failure of input from kinesthetic receptors may be a contributing factor. (Kenshalo, 1977, p. 572)

Table 7-4 summarizes the normal changes found in somesthesis with age. The loss of general somesthetic sensitivity in old persons seems to be related to disease, injury, or circulatory insufficiency rather than to age per se. The loss of touch sensitivity occurs in only about twenty-five percent of all persons older than sixty-five. Similarly, the loss of vibratory sensitivity is not universal among the elderly. Old persons are less able than young persons to overcome the stress of thermal extremes (Kenshalo, 1977). Finally, sensitivity to pain appears to decrease with age, though this statement is subject to the qualification of methodological

*Old people are more susceptible to falls than young persons, but compensation is possible.*

problems. The consensus of researchers about somesthesis is that changes in sensory thresholds and quality do not have a significant impact on function unless disease or trauma is simultaneously present (Kart et al., 1978; Kenshalo, 1977; Marsh, 1980).

As mentioned earlier in this chapter, our perception of the world is mediated by our sense organs but is also influenced by learning, motivation, and thought. Psychomotor response and reaction time also play a role in perception.

Reaction time has achieved great popularity as an index of sensorimotor performance. However, it is a better description of relations between variables than an explanation of their causal relations (Elias et al., 1977). Reaction time has been used as a measure of the functional capacity of the CNS, but it has also been found to be strongly affected by such cognitive factors as motivation, response strategies and style, cautiousness, and anxiety (Botwinick, 1973; Elias et al., 1977; Welford,

**Psychomotor Response and Reaction Time**

*Table 7–4   Normal aging changes of the somesthetic system*
Decreasing number of cells in dermis and epidermis
Decreasing amounts of collagen and elastin
Decreasing number of Meissner's corpuscles
Decreasing number of Vater-Pacini corpuscles
Decreasing number and efficiency of sensory afferent fibers
Decreasing nerve conduction velocity
Increasing circulatory and dietary insufficiencies negatively affecting somesthesis

1977). Diseases, life-style, and sensory changes in vision and audition have also been found to influence reaction time.

Exercise is clearly associated with reaction time among young subjects. In fact, young adults who don't exercise have been found to be no faster than normal elderly adults in reaction time tasks (DeVries, 1975). Individual differences play an important role in determining how much reaction time slowing occurs with age. These differences in reaction time are at their greatest among old persons. Many elderly adults continue to have faster reaction times than the majority of young adults (Botwinick, 1973). Practice improves reaction time for virtually everyone. However, it disproportionately aids old subjects and therefore acts to reduce age differences (Botwinick, 1973; Welford, 1977). Motivation is also involved in reaction time slowing with age. High motivation may disproportionately aid old subjects in regular interval reaction time tasks and thereby lower age differences. For example, old persons are more motivated than young persons to decrease their reaction time when they receive a mild shock to the wrist for slower than average reponses. This technique may even improve CNS function and integrative capacities (Botwinick, 1973). Finally, personality characteristics have been associated with response slowing. Persons exhibiting coronary-prone behavior (Type A personalities) have been found to have slower reaction times than persons not exhibiting such behavior (Abrahams & Birren, 1973).

### The Causes of Slowing
Age-related slowing down of perceptual, motor, cognitive, and physiological processes in response to external stimulation has been well documented. This section considers how research in this area was carried out and what the implications of its results are for the behavior of elderly persons.

Response slowing was initially thought to be caused by peripheral processes of the CNS such as reduced receptor efficiency and reduced nerve conduction velocity. Botwinick (1973) disputed this assumption, hpothesizing instead that response slowing is due to age-related changes in central processes. Botwinick and his colleagues proceeded to test this hypothesis and two other explanations of response slowing: slowing is due to sensory and perceptual loss causing difficulty in discriminating stimuli; and slowing is caused by decreased nerve conduction velocity (Botwinick, 1973).

The first tests were conducted to rule out sensory-perceptual factors in stimulus discrimination as the main cause of slowing. In a series of three studies it was found that reaction time slowed as stimulus discrimination became more difficult, that age differences were greatest for the harder discriminations, and that old subjects were slower than young subjects at every level of difficulty (Birren & Botwinick, 1951; Botwinick, 1970; Botwinick & Storandt, 1974). These results led to the conclusion that slowing is not entirely due to perceptual factors, since it occurred even when discriminability was controlled for. Equating age levels for stimulus intensity failed to eliminate age-related response slowing; therefore, sense organs are not responsible for most reaction time slowing occurring with age.

The second set of studies was aimed at ruling out nerve conduction speed as the main factor in slowing (Birren & Botwinick, 1951; Botwinick, 1973). Researchers had reasoned that the longer the neural pathway stimulated is, the longer the reaction time should be. On the basis of this hypothesis the greatest age differences would be expected to occur in the longest neural pathways. The studies carried out by Botwinick and colleagues found no support for conduction speed as the cause of response slowing.

Third was the investigation of the role of CNS mechanisms in response slowing. Slowing appeared in all behaviors mediated by the CNS. In these studies reaction time was separated into two components, motor time and premotor time:

$$RT = (Motor\ time) + (Premotor\ time)$$

*Motor time* is the time from firing of the muscle to completion of the response. *Premotor time* is the time from stimulus onset until firing of the muscle. Premotor time involves three distinct processes — sensory transmission, central interpretation, and response decision — and was found to take up eighty-four percent of the total reaction time. Motor factors were thus essentially eliminated, leading to the conclusion that reaction time is slowed by central, interpretive factors involved in decision processes. Botwinick had effectively proved his hypothesis.

The central mediation hypothesis was supported and enhanced by Surwillo (1963) and Woodruff (1972) in studies on electroencephalogram (EEG) slowing with age. Surwillo correlated increased reaction time with EEG slowing. His assumption that the alpha component of brain waves is the master timing mechanism in behavior led to one of few supported causal hypotheses in the psychology of aging (Birren & Renner, 1977): the hypothesis that EEG slowing leads to diffuse slowing in information and specifically to increased reaction time.

Woodruff (1972) tested the Surwillo hypothesis through biofeedback procedures. She trained subjects to increase or decrease their alpha waves in response to stimulus presentation, thereby allowing each subject to act as his or her own control. The results were that faster reaction times occurred when alpha speed increased.

EEG slowing was subsequently related to survival (Muller et al., 1975). Differences in alpha waves were contrasted in survivors and nonsurvivors over a five-year period. Slow alpha waves were more marked in subjects who died during this period. These findings lead to intriguing speculations about longevity, e.g., could individuals increase their alpha waves and decrease their reaction times and thereby extend their lives? Clarification is still needed on the degree to which slowing of response and EEG with age is a consequence of disease, aging, or some "phylogenetic pattern to some extent modifiable by experimental manipulation" (Birren & Renner, 1977, pp. 29–30).

### Age Changes in Reaction Time

The sensorimotor system can be diagrammed in a way similar to the auditory system. As can be seen in Figure 7-6, a large portion of sensorimotor response falls in the category of central processes. In simple reaction time tasks in which subjects are asked to respond to a single stimulus, there are insignificant increases in reaction time with age. However, increases in reaction time become significant if the tasks involve any of the following protocols:

A discrimination involving withholding of response.
A discrimination in which one response is made while another is withheld.
A series of responses.
Matching stimuli to determine a correct response. (Elias et al., 1977, p. 189)

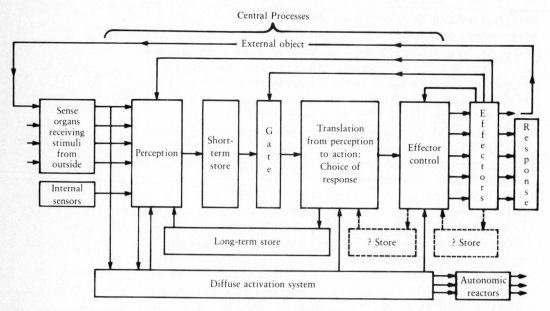

(Source: Welford, A.T. Motor performance. In J.E. Birren & K.W. Schaie (Eds.), *Handbook of the psychology of aging*. Van Nostrand Reinhold Company, 1977, p. 451. Copyright © 1977 by Van Nostrand Reinhold Company. Reprinted by permission of the publisher)

*Figure 7–6    Block diagram of the human sensorimotor system*

In short, in any task involving choice old persons show a disproportionate slowing when compared to young adults.

Older persons show slowing as a result of various cognitive factors in addition to the reasons discussed above. Old persons rely more on expectations than young persons; in paradigms in which the length of time between warning signal and stimulus is first short, then long, they are seriously handicapped by their frequently mistaken expectancies of what the warning interval will be (Welford, 1977). Old persons are less prepared to respond than young persons, as manifested by heart rate slowing during waiting time; heart rate acceleration is associated with information processing (Welford, 1977). Old persons are also either over- or underaroused in performance situations, although research suggests that arousal is unlikely to play a significant role in their slow reaction times (Welford, 1977).

Sensory after-effects may in part explain the slow reaction time of elderly persons in choice tasks. In repeated-signals tests it may be that the after-effect of each signal acts as "noise" for the next. The most likely explanation is that when a new signal follows very shortly after the previous signal, the translator mechanism is still monitoring either the previous response or data from the warning. The data of the new signal is thus delayed, and monitoring takes longer (Welford, 1977).

Response slowing is an important phenomenon in age-related performance decrements. The crucial portion of reaction time is not the speed with which an entire task is performed; this involves experience, special skills, and specific learning, all of which are amenable to intervention (Birren, 1964; Welford, 1977). Rather, the greatest amount of reaction time slowing in elderly persons appears to be in the premotor time segment between the presentation of a stimulus and the initiation of the response. The slowing of reaction time with age is only weakly associated with intellectual ability. However, response slowing is also independent of culture and modality and is found even among animals and young adults who do not exercise. It apparently reflects age-associated changes in central processes and is related to increased caution and rigidity. The problem of slowing among the elderly can be counteracted to some degree through exercise, practice (i.e., learning), and motivation; many elderly at optimal levels of function in these three areas may even have a quicker reaction time than the majority of young adults.

## Intervention

Sensory, perceptual, and sensorimotor slowing may have important effects on the functioning of old individuals. If these sensory changes are sudden or severe, as they may be when disease processes intervene, or if they involve the deterioration of abilities vitally important to the affected person, serious disability may occur. This section considers the factors leading to disability and explores interventions that may alleviate or prevent disability.

Functional loss is a highly subjective experience. The specific nature of the loss determined objectively does not predict disability; the manner in which the loss affects the afflicted person's relationship to self and the world is a more effective predictor. The symbolic meaning of the disturbance thus has great implications and may create an excess disability, i.e., a disability disproportionate to the actual functional loss. Excess disability may result from sensory loss or change but is more likely to result from response slowing because of the value our culture places on youth, productivity, and quickness. An elderly person who believes the cultural stereotype that old age is the negation of these qualities may unconsciously conform to the caricature in a self-fulfilling prophecy. The person may move more cautiously, respond more slowly, and think more rigidly than dictated by physical condition alone, i.e., show excess disability.

Anxiety accompanies any threat to physical integrity. Loss of vision, audition, and somesthetic sensitivity may be perceived as such a threat. Affected individuals may be afraid of becoming completely helpless and dependent on others. Their self-esteem may be lowered because of the cultural value placed on environmental mastery and self-assertion. They may even feel anxious about losing prestige or social approval. Once they have lost control of their anxiety, they develop defensive responses. They may withdraw from other people and activities. Their behavior may change; for example, they may become more orderly or compulsive. Many people cope positively by concentrating on limited activities. Some overcompensate for or deny their limitations. Some develop defenses such as dependency, depression, or demanding, irritable aggressiveness in an attempt to restore a sense of personal value.

Disability is difficult for persons of any age, but for the elderly it is potentially more destructive. Disability in old persons may lead to social isolation and from there to emotional distress. It is important for family, friends, and professionals dealing with the elderly to recognize the damage that sensory deprivation and social isolation can do and to carry out interventions to halt this damage.

### Visual Intervention

Poor vision has various critical consequences in the elderly. Given that many of our "survival stimuli" are visual in nature (e.g., stop signs, stop lights, street signs, flashing warning lights), decreased vision hinders adaptation to the social environment. Poor vision also increases isolation and immobilization. It contributes to a sense of poor orientation and confusion, and it may even cause frightening visual impressions resembling hallucinations. Poor vision may also decrease the number of pastimes open to the elderly. Knitting or carpentry becomes difficult, as does anything that requires a shift from close work to distance perception. Finally, lack of vision may make the elderly more prone to crime or injury.

An empirical demonstration of the above effects of poor vision was provided by Palmore's (1971) Duke longitudinal study reports. As vision declines, elderly individuals tend to show low participation in group activities, low levels of emotional security, and low feelings of status. It thus appears that vision is important to the mental and physical health of the elderly.

At a practical level little has been done to use existing research to improve the visual functioning of old people. Specifically lacking are age-specific lighting requirements, medical intervention for such disorders as macular degeneration, and surgical procedures to reduce opacities in the vitreous humor (Fozard et al., 1977). However, certain environmental features may help improve the functioning of persons with poor vision; for example, large typefaces may be used in books to improve reading ability, and bright nonglare lights may be used. Objects that contrast with their background are also easier to see. Certain types of visual disorders may make it difficult for old persons to recognize other people at a distance. This limitation should be understood and not mistaken for unfriendliness or forgetfulness.

Environments designed to include optimum lighting, color, and contrast encourage continued ambulation. Family and hospital staff should verbally help visually impaired people become oriented to new rooms. Furniture should not be moved unnecessarily. Hallways should be kept clear of clutter, and handrails should be installed.

Blind or visually disabled persons should be helped to make maximum use of their residual skills. Their remaining vision should be used, but verbal communication should also be used as much as possible. The sense of touch can be utilized to guide and reassure the disabled person. Persons dealing with the newly visually handicapped must be sensitive to the fact that the adaptive capacities of the disabled person are at their lowest level.

### Auditory Intervention

Despite our knowledge of the relations between changes in the auditory system and performance, hearing prostheses are still needed for the aged.

> Hearing aids which merely amplify auditory input are obviously of limited usefulness in noisy auditory environments because they amplify both signal and noise. With high amplification, such aids may even result in further deterioration of speech intelligibility. (Warren et al., 1978, p. 735)

Impaired communication is a personal and social problem, not just a statistical one. Impairment of speech, language, or auditory processes may significantly alter an old person's adjustment to the environment. Familiar sounds are absent. There are no audible warning signals, so personal security is compromised. Social skills and their concomitants are decreased. Deafness has even been found to lead to paranoia in persons with a predisposition to it (Corso, 1977).

Elderly persons with hearing disorders may be successfully rehabilitated. However, there are two problems. First, many old people need professional assistance but claim they have no time, money, or motivation to obtain it. Second, many who do seek professional medical help are treated so passively that they feel they can't handle their own lives. Many professionals and family members confuse hearing loss with senile deterioration (Corso, 1977); the person who is hard of hearing may demand repetition (which is seen as memory loss), respond inappropriately (which is seen as confusion), become withdrawn, and possibly exhibit other signs of psychopathology.

Environmental compensations may improve the functioning of old hearing-impaired adults. Persons with hearing loss cannot compensate for themselves and must depend on others to speak so they can hear. People speaking to old persons should speak slowly and clearly and avoid abrupt topic changes. Facial expressions should be used, and the face should be well lighted to allow for lip reading. Since hearing loss is greatest for high frequencies, voices should be lowered when speaking, and sound systems should be adjusted so that base and low tones are predominant. Background noise should also be controlled as much as possible. Finally, alternative sensory modalities should be stimulated. Writing as a means of communication should not be overlooked, and opportunities for enjoyable activities requiring little speech should be provided.

### Taste and Smell Intervention

Old people rely on the appearance of food for its identification and for motivation to eat. Texture, temperature, and color are all important for the identification and enjoyment of food. A pleasant mealtime atmosphere in a social setting enhances gustatory enjoyment. Condiments, spices, and foods with strong flavors may help maintain interest in food and eating. Finally, since a poor sense of smell and taste may make it difficult to recognize spoiled foods and the smell of gas, old persons who live alone should be encouraged to check the age of their food and the pilot lights of their stoves regularly.

### Somesthetic and Sensorimotor Intervention

Murrell (1978) found that long term-practice speeds up reaction time whereas disuse slows it down. Spirduso (1975) found that old active sports enthusiasts show less reaction time slowing than sedentary persons. Although it is not clear whether this association is caused by personality, physiology, or motivation, the relation between exercise and decreased reaction time clearly exists and should be used in rehabilitation programs.

**Summary**

This chapter discussed age-associated sensory and perceptual changes and their relation to response slowing. The role of central mechanisms is clearly implicated in the perceptual and speed loss frequently observed in old age. There is no clear evidence that somesthetic decline occurs with age, but it can be precipitated by some environmental factors. There are interventions than can be used to maintain optimal functioning in and utilize the residual skills of the sensory-impaired elderly.

Changes in sensory function and motor response do not necessarily lead to disability. Many of these changes are gradual and may be ameliorated or reversed by prosthetic devices such as eyeglasses or hearing aids. Others, such as changes in color vision or the loss of high-tone perception, may have minimal impact on the

*Many changes in sensory function are gradual and may be ameliorated by prosthetic devices such as hearing aids.*

elderly person's daily life. Even changes that have a significant impact on function, such as response slowing or severe presbycusis, may be compensated for by a carefully structured environment.

The sorts of sensory changes and motor slowing that occur in late life do not occur in isolation. The affected person's perception of these changes may lead to depression or anxiety, which in turn may affect performance on intellectual measures or tasks of daily living. The person may become distressed, maladjusted, or, in extreme cases, subject to psychiatric disability. However, these risks are not unique to the elderly population. They apply to persons of any age adjusting to changes in bodily function.

# 8
# Cognitive Processes

*Is intellectual decrement inevitable with age?*

*What factors lead to intellectual decrement?*

*Can factors other than intelligence per se affect performance on an IQ test?*

*Why are the processes of learning and memory so intrinsically related?*

*How does motivation affect learning ability?*

*What does Krech's statement, "He who lives with his wits dies with his wits" mean?*

*Why do so many people believe that "the worst old age is that of the mind"?*

O N E of the most controversial issues in the psychology of aging has been that of intellectual decrement with age. Arguments about the truth of the statement "intellectual ability inevitably declines with age" have been extremely heated. Both the supporters and opponents of this statement have presented well-based arguments for their relative positions. Researchers on both sides have also been well intentioned in their belief that the lot of the aged could be improved by an awareness of the decrement or its lack. If intellectual decrement does occur with age, cognitive interventions could be designed to address the areas of decline, or older people could be excused from intellectual tasks that are too demanding. If intellectual decrement does not occur with age, the false belief that it does must be strenuously removed from the minds of both young and old; the danger of myths is that they easily become reality if people internalize them. The often-heard comment by older people that "I must be getting senile" attests to the pervasiveness of this myth as well as to its potential destructiveness.

For persons interested in the psychological aspects of aging, the area of cognitive processes is much broader than the issue of intellectual decline. Memory, learning, and problem-solving ability are also of interest. The definition of intelligence is crucial, as is the way in which intelligence is measured. Procedural and methodological artifacts of testing must be considered. The functional implications of health status and its impact on memory, learning, and cognitive ability are also of interest. Finally, the role of generational or cohort differences in the cognitive function of the elderly must be considered. This chapter is concerned with research on and current thinking about cognitive change occuring with age. Cognitive abilities have a serious impact on basic adaptability and personal survivorship, to be discussed in the chapters that follow.

Developmentalists such as Piaget consider intelligence a measure of adaptation. The notion is that people must learn to adapt to the demands of their environment. These demands change, sometimes increasing and other times decreasing. Persons who make their way successfully in life do so in part because of their adaptive intelligence (Nash, 1978). Many elderly people are well adapted to the demands of their environment because they remove themselves from situations to which they cannot adapt. When placed in a more demanding environment (e.g., an experimental learning study or intelligence test), they may show less "intelligent" behaviors than younger persons for whom such a demanding environment is normal.

An example of this is that of the frail elderly person who functions fairly well in the home environment but becomes disoriented and helpless in any novel situation.

> Mrs. Black, aged eighty-six, lived with her husband in the home they had owned for fifty years. With his help she was able to cook, clean, and keep house fairly well. He often covered for her memory loss in conversations by filling in comments where appropriate. However, the extent of her cognitive impairment became obvious when she entered the hospital for minor surgery. She immediately became disoriented, could not remember how to dress herself, and began talking about visits from her parents, who had been dead for thirty years. These symptoms vanished when she returned home to her normal, structured environment.

One of the key characteristics that distinguishes human beings from other animals is the ability to solve problems and to reason. Man has emerged as a viable species through long evolutionary processes favoring learning and plasticity of behavior. Learning, the ability to modify behavior through experience, helps people adapt to changing environmental conditions. Without such adaptability people would soon succumb to environmental stress. Cognitive ability is therefore crucial at all stages of the life cycle but especially late in life, when stresses tend to be cumulative.

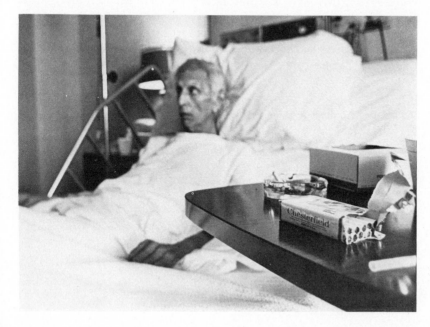

*Hospital stays can be lonely and disorienting.*

**The Nature of Intelligence**

One of the keys to determining the nature of intellectual change with age is an adequate definition of intelligence. The problem of the lack of one agreed upon definition of intelligence among researchers has been compounded by methodological difficulties in separating generational effects from the effects of aging per se. The nature of the tests themselves has also been a detriment, with different tests tapping different aspects of cognitive function. In addition, many professionals and laypersons have considered performance on a particular intelligence test an index of full intellectual capacity. This is not a valid assumption. Table 8-1 illustrates the factors preventing researchers from having a full understanding of the nature of intellectual change with age.

### The Problem of Definition

A standard opening question used by professors in class discussions of intelligence is what intelligence is and how it is measured. The definitions often cover an entire blackboard and range from "the ability to 'reason'" (whatever that is!) to "the IQ score computed from intelligence test performance." The discussions often become heated when the professor asks the students to defend their statements against rival definitions. It soon becomes obvious that consensus is not easy.

Intelligence has been described as a genetic capacity quantifiable by psychometric measures such as IQ tests; according to this view, IQ scores reflect intellectual capacity, i.e., the upper limit of cognitive function. Alternatively, intelligence has been thought to arise from experience; according to this view, IQ tests reflect only limited intellectual ability, or performance on a particular test at a particular time. In the latter model intellectual capacity may be inferred but not measured directly (Botwinick, 1977). It has also been suggested that intelligence is a combination of genetic attributes (fluid intelligence) and experientially based skills (crystallized intelligence) (Horn, 1970). Theories state that the relative contribution of each

*Table 8-1   Difficulties in assessing the nature of age changes in intellectual ability*

There is no single definition of intelligence.

The lack of an accepted definition leads to a circular definition: "Intelligence is what intelligence tests measure."

There is a tendency to believe that intellectual capacity is represented by IQ test performance.

"Intelligence" tests reflect varying aspects of intellectual ability.

Generational effects confound the influence of normal aging processes.

Tests may have theoretical or predictive utility. What does the researcher want to do with the test? Predict what people will do in the future or what they will do on related measures?

factor may be measured by the appropriate test instruments or experimental methodology (Schaie, 1974).

These arguments, which continue to persist (Horn & Donaldson, 1976, 1980; Schaie, 1974) have had a profound impact on our understanding of cognitive processes in old age. In general three major concepts have emerged from controversy:

It is important to differentiate between performance and capacity.
It is not nature or nurture that determines intelligence but nature and nurture.
Performance may be influenced by genetic capacity (nature).

These issues are discussed in detail later in this chapter.

The results of the above argument have led researchers to understand that psychometric measures of intelligence vary in content. Some, like the Army Alpha Test, consist mainly of verbal measures such as analogies and definitions. Others involve perceptual motor performance measures; in the block design subtest of the Wechsler Adult Intelligence Scale (WAIS), for example, subjects are asked to match colored blocks to two-dimensional pictures or designs. Still others, such as the full WAIS, attempt to measure a balanced combination of verbal and performance skills. Some intelligence tests stress speed, which, as discussed in Chapter 7, may penalize the elderly. Some psychometric measures stress power, i.e., how well a subject does when given unlimited time to complete test items. Some tests use practical concrete information; others, such as the Ravens Progressive Matrices, use abstract designs to measure reasoning ability. In the Ravens test, the subject is asked to determine which sample design from several options completes the missing portion of a larger stimulus design.

The following test scenario shows how such tests might be utilized in an elderly person:

Mrs. Adams, aged eighty, had been complaining of the loss of her recent memory. Her physician asked for a cognitive evaluation by a psychologist, Dr. Baker. Mrs. A was tested with the Ravens Progressive Matrices on a timed basis. The results indicated that her performance was considerably below the norm.

Dr. B discussed the results with a colleague who had been trained in gerontology. He then gave Mrs. A the WAIS and found that her performance IQ was considerably below her verbal IQ. Her best performance seemed to be on the vocabulary and information subtests. When he compared her performance to the age norms for old people, he found that she was at the low end of the normal range. A check of her memory function on the Wechsler Memory Scale indicated normal function there also.

Dr. B made his report to Mrs. A's physician, who told her that her memory and intellectual function were normal for her age and that everyone suffered from occasional memory loss.

This case report is ideal in many ways; given professional rivalries and ageism, a physician might never consult a psychologist, or a geriatrician might not be handy to explain the existence of age norms for old people on the WAIS or the negative impact of abstract, timed measures on the performance of old persons. A person like Mrs. A might easily be given a series of tests that he or she would be destined to do poorly on. The case report also raises several considerations:

Old people tend to perform best on verbal, concrete tests of power. Conversely, they do poorly on measures with a performance focus, on abstract measures, and on timed tests.

Until recently there were no age norms for the elderly for many psychometric measures. This led to low scores for old people, who have significantly different educational backgrounds from young people.

There is often little correlation between complaints of memory loss by old people and actual performance. Often these complaints are more indicative of depression than of organic brain dysfunction, which would be the expected diagnosis.

Although many types of intelligence measures are related, each subject manifests considerable variation across these measures. For example, some people do well at math and badly at verbal tests regardless of their age.

Given these qualifications of old people's intelligence test performance, determinations should be made of intellectual functioning levels for each measure for every age rather than of changes in some global measure of intelligence. Results of full-scale IQ scores are compared with subtest performance on the Primary Mental Abilities Test and WAIS later in this chapter.

### Performance versus Capacity

Even if multiple measures were used to compute a profile of the intellectual performance of old people, there would still be the issue of performance versus capacity, i.e., how well does a subject's performance on particular IQ measure reflect intellectual capacity? A variety of factors in addition to capacity influence performance; health, education, familiarity with testing or the test materials, personality (e.g., cautiousness), and motivation all influence cognitive performance (Botwinick, 1977; Hartley et al., 1980). Any or all of these factors may systematically vary with age and thereby exert a corresponding effect on intelligence. For example, elderly people as a group tend to be cautious (Okun, 1976). Cautiousness tends to slow them down, and slowing leads to errors of omission and thus overall poor performance on timed measures, which make up the bulk of diagnostic psychometric instruments. Furthermore, elderly persons may maintain their intellectual ability but not be motivated to perform in situations such as intelligence tests because of lack of energy or of interest in "proving themselves."

*Old people who remain mentally active often score better than younger people on tests requiring experience.*

The content of many standard IQ measures may seem meaningless or irrelevant to or provoke anxiety in old people. The content of many intelligence tests is also unfamiliar to old people, who have different educational and historical backgrounds from young people, for whom the tests are designed. For example, the vocabulary subtest of the WAIS asks for definitions for such words as *Koran* and *apochrypha*, which may not be in the normal vocabulary of persons in their seventies and eighties. The Cohort IQ Test presented in Figure 8-1 was developed by Robbie Iadeluca, at the time a fifty-six-year-old doctoral student in psychology at Syracuse University. This test mimics the information and comprehension subtests of the WAIS but is biased in favor of the testees over sixty-five. Another test in which old people tend to excel is the Test of Obscure Knowledge (source unknown) presented in Figure 8-2. This instrument is actually a measure of Figure test-taking ability. When the purpose of this test is revealed, old people tend to do better on it than young people, especially if they have kept mentally active. Older people respond to it as a challenge, whereas college students tend to respond to it with hostility, particularly if it is presented as a "pop quiz." This instrument readily attests to the influence of generational differences in educational experience on the differential performance of young and old.

Contrary to popular myth, intelligence is not an all-or-none thing but rather a dispositional concept. Related terms, such as *ability, capacity,* and *brightness,* are also dispositional concepts. A disposition is a tendency or likelihood. One never "sees" dispositional concepts; they are simply a shorthand way of saying that under certain conditions a certain sort of behavior or response can be expected. For

Prior to 1933, when was Presidential Inauguration Day?
What is the date of V-E Day?        V-J Day?
What is a common use for lampblack?
What is the full name of the A&P Store?
From what field did Lindbergh leave for Paris?
Who was "Wrong-Way Corrigan"?
What were Alben Barkley's last words before dying?
Who was Paul Siple?
What is a grammar school?
Which is larger, pea or nut, and by what weight is it ordered?
What is toxin antitoxin?
What special feature does a Morris chair have?
Who was Henry Ward Beecher?
What famous book was written by his daughter?
How did Little Black Sambo win over the tigers?

*Figure 8–1   Cohort
IQ Test*

example, to say that an old person is "senile" is a rough prediction that the person fails to solve problems, gets into difficulties, is forgetful, and so on; "Senility" is not a thing but an implied prediction of a class of behavior.

Dispositional terms are involved in the description and measurement of intelligence. Four such terms are identified below:

*Ability* is the disposition or tendency to solve problems or complete tasks. To say that someone has an ability is merely to state that the person is likely to perform a given class of behavior in the future.

*Capacity* is the disposition or tendency to acquire ability, given suitable antecedents such as training, maturation, or motivation. To say that someone has a capacity is to state that the person is likely to profit from future instruction or experience, not that the person can perform the activity in question now. For example, the capacity to play the piano exists or does not exist before the first lesson, although it's of course impossible to know in advance. There is always uncertainty in any prediction, regardless of the age of the person being studied.

*Intelligence* is an arbitrary pattern of cognitive abilities that a given culture decides define its intellectual tendencies. There is some generality across cultures, but intelligence is largely based on whatever aspects of behavior a given society prizes and holds valuable.

*Brightness* is a similar concept; however, it refers not to ability but to the capacity to acquire intellectual traits in the future, given appropriate training or practice and motivation. The distinction between present brightness and intelligence is the same as the distinction between present estimated abilities and future capacity.

1. Medaclopis was a
   a. Omniverious dinosaur
   b. Early pagan god
   c. Ancient herbal medicine
   d. Mongol warrior

2. *Deliticulate* means
   a. Humble
   b. Disturb
   c. Bother
   d. Faze

3. Which country has the largest deposits of marl?
   a. Lisbon
   b. Bulgaria
   c. Calcutta
   d. Bangkok

4. The Quadreci Arch used extensively in Etruscan architecture was
   a. Restricted exclusively to the construction of temples
   b. Used only to connect transverse pillars
   c. Never used in conjunction with alternate arch designs
   d. Able to support a great deal of weight

5. *Medacloptic* is an adjective referring to
   a. A fierce and totally ruthless warrior
   b. A defect in night vision
   c. An insurmountable obstacle
   d. An extremely large and powerful body

6. The Greek writer Antigoras was noted for his
   a. Geometric proofs
   b. Political influence
   c. Philosophical paradoxes
   d. Literary accomplishments

*Figure 8–2    Test of Obscure Knowledge*

It is clear that generalizations about a person's intellectual capacity made from that person's performance on intelligence test measures may be illogical. Such a generalization is warranted only if the following two qualifications are met:

If the sample of items or performance is appropriate, unbiased, and representative of the area of interest, and if previous experience is irrelevant, equally absent for all, or present in the subject, then it may properly be inferred ( 1 ) that the subject possesses the *ability* to do the particular items demanded by the test, and (2) that the subject could, if presented with them, do other items of the same sort.

If all of the above are true, and if in addition performance in other types of behavior has been systematically linked to the abilities in question and motivation and opportunity exist at the proper time, then the subject's current performance may properly be used to estimate that subjects potential or *capacity* to acquire the behavior in question.

Although the logic of these requirements is straightforward, meeting them is difficult and inferences about ability and capacity are seldom completely justified. The only data we actually have is what a person does; everything else rests on inference. This statement is true whether the subject is eight years old or eighty years old. Without considering and testing these factors, one cannot make any valid statements about or comparisons of the data collected by various researchers on the intelligence of elderly persons. Any discussion of age-related changes in intelligence should take into account the following questions:

What test is involved?
What skills or abilities is the test tapping?
What are the motivational, educational, personal, and experiential characteristics of the person being examined?

## Intelligence Measures

Psychologists, psychometricians, and educators have been studying the intellectual performance of large subject samples on standard intelligence tests for most of this century.

### Classic Cross-Sectional Studies

In cross-sectional studies, many people of different ages are tested at the same time. One of the earliest such studies purporting to investigate intellectual change with age was that of Jones and Conrad (1933). These researchers tested residents from ten to sixty years of age in rural towns in New England during the Great Depression. They used an interesting method to obtain subjects: they offered a free movie in the town hall. The Army Alpha Test was then administered to the entire group halfway through the movie. Jones and Conrad also made an effort to test all the townspeople who did not attend the movie. They therefore distinguished in their results between "hall-tested" and "home-tested" subjects. The results of the study were that adults from forty-five to fifty-nine years of age did more poorly than adults from seventeen to twenty-one years of age; there was a gradual decrease in IQ test performance after the age of twenty-one (Fig. 8-3). However, when the researchers charted the results of the home- and hall-tested subjects separately, different trends emerged (Fig. 8-4). The postmaturity decline was far more significant in the home-tested subjects; the hall-tested adults showed only a minimal decline through adulthood. Given the assumption that during the Depression most townspeople who were able would have gladly attended a free movie, it appears likely that the home-tested subjects were abnormal in health or mental functioning.

Another body of early cross-sectional research is the WAIS normalization data

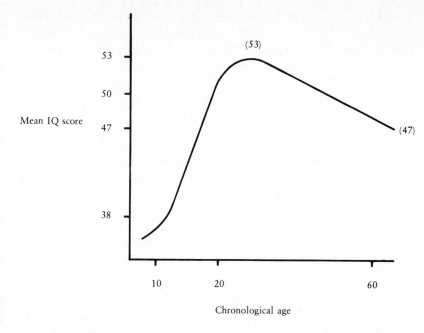

*Figure 8–3 Relationship between age and IQ score on the Army Alpha Test in cross-sectional design*

(Doppelt & Wallace, 1955) and the earlier normalization data of the Wechsler-Bellevue Intelligence Test (Wechsler, 1939). The WAIS is one of the best and most commonly used measures of adult intelligence. The test has been in use since 1939, and in 1955 age norms for groups older than fifty-five to sixty-four were developed.

The WAIS consists of six verbal subtests for which one can obtain a verbal IQ:

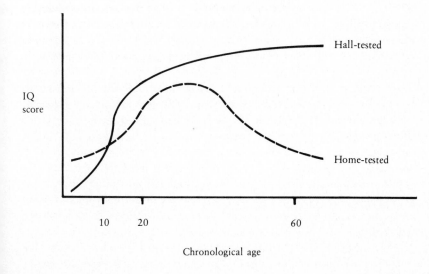

*Figure 8–4 Relationship between chronological age and IQ score for hall- and home-tested subjects in cross-sectional design*

information, designed to tap a person's general awareness of historical, governmental, and daily routine items; comprehension, which focuses on the person's understanding of cliches, morality, and so on; arithmetic, a timed mental mathematics section in which the problems get progressively harder; similarities, which involve the individual's explanation of the similarity between two related words; digit span, forward and backward recall of from three to nine numbers; and vocabulary, in which the person is asked to give the meanings of forty words.

A performance IQ may also be computed. This is composed of the scores on the following five subtests: digit-symbol substitution, a timed test in which the subject is asked to replace numbers with symbols in a particular sequence; picture completion, in which the testee is asked what critical part of a picture is missing; block design, a timed test in which the subject is asked to replicate ten two-dimensional pictures with blocks; picture arrangement, a timed test in which the individual puts picture cards together in a way that tells a story; and object assembly, a timed puzzle completion test. The WAIS allows the tester to formulate subtest scores, verbal IQ, performance IQ, or full-scale IQ. A profile may also be created of comparative performance on the subtests. The WAIS is often used as a diagnostic tool by psychologists; various diagnostic entities, such as organic brain dysfunction, depression, and schizophrenia, offer particular subtest profiles.

The results of the cross-sectional normalization data led Wechsler (1939) to conclude that most human abilities decline progressively after the age of eighteen to twenty-five. In the 1955 normalization data (Doppelt & Wallace, 1955) IQ scores peaked at about age thirty and declined slowly thereafter. However, there was no sharp drop in full-scale IQ until after the age of seventy. Moreover, the rate of decline in old people on the verbal IQ was not a full standard deviation below that of the younger subjects.

Performance scores on the WAIS tend to decrease steadily after age eighteen, whereas verbal scores do not show significant decline; the performance tests are therefore believed to be age-sensitive (Botwinick, 1967) and the verbal tests to be age-insensitive. It is thus probable that a decrease in verbal scores in an old person reflects the effects of disease processes rather than of aging per se (Botwinick, 1967, 1977).

As stated, the full-scale and verbal IQ scores hold fairly steady across all age groups. The only appreciable decline occurring with age is in similarities and digit span (Botwinick, 1977). Results of the vocabulary subtest are also similar for different cohorts, correlating 0.95 with the full-scale IQ. In addition, the vocabulary subtest shows little deterioration with any sort of pathology and is therefore often used by clinicians as a measure of premorbid intellectual function. The performance subtests, in contrast, show a one-standard deviation decrease by age sixty and even more of a decline by age seventy-five. Digit symbol, picture completion, and picture arrangements show an even greater decrease, whereas object assembly is lower only in the over-seventy-five year sample (Harwood & Naylor, 1969).

Many psychologists believe that the age-related decline seen in performance on these subtests results mainly from the speed factor; if the tests were not timed, subjects would not be as negatively affected by them. Moreover, it is difficult to assess what these subtests really measure. Digit symbol, for example, is often described as a measure of the ability to perform quickly. However, it also involves the perceptual abilities of searching and matching, coordination of these behaviors, translation into writing, and perhaps also memorization of the number/symbol associations (Botwinick, 1967).

> Does this mean that the subtest measures functions which have relevance to the complex needs of everyday life which involve speed of response, perception, memory and motor skills? Does it mean that low ability in these areas excludes significant intellectual contribution? On the other hand, is the test a measure of the limited, circumscribed ability of eye-hand coordination which is hardly more than a child's game?*

This suggests that neither the real-world significance of deteriorating age-sensitive functions nor the maintenance of age-insensitive functions is easily determined.

A final cross-sectional study of interest was conducted by Schaie (1958), who used the Primary Mental Abilities (PMA) Test. Schaie tested five hundred people, fifty in each of ten five-year periods. The PMA test consists of five subtests: verbal meaning, space, reasoning, number, and word fluency. In plotting the composite scores for these functions Schaie (1958) found no appreciable decline from age twenty to age fifty. After ages forty-six to fifty the decline is clear, but it is not until after age sixty that scores are more than one standard deviation lower than peak performance at ages thirty-one to thirty-five (Botwinick, 1977).

The classic cross-sectional studies of intelligence found that most verbal skills are well maintained by healthy old people. There are declines on performance measures, however, even among optimally healthy elderly persons. These same patterns were seen in numerous cross-sectional studies carried out from 1932 to 1959.

It now remained for researchers to determine whether the group results of cross-sectional designs held for individuals of the same age tested repeatedly as they aged. Such a design would eliminate the effects of generational differences from the analysis of data results. These longitudinal studies, also called *panel* or *repeated measures* studies, were conducted to determine age change rather than age differences in intellectual function.

### Classic Longitudinal Studies

Longitudinal designs, by virtue of the fact that they test the same subjects over time, minimize cohort differences and allow consideration of age change in a less contaminated way than cross-sectional studies. Longitudinal studies also have methodological flaws, such as survivor effects, selective drop-out, and familiarity

*Botwinick, J. *Cognitive processes in maturity and old age*. New York: Springer, 1967, p. 13

effects from repeated testing. However, they present a different view of age-related intellectual function from cross-sectional data, and the two together provide a relatively comprehensive picture of intellectual change with age.

In 1919 363 people took the exam for admission to Iowa State University. This exam was the Army Alpha Intelligence Test. Owens (1953, 1966) retested 127 of these people in 1950 (the others were dead or missing or refused to participate) and 96 of the original group in 1960. In 1976 Cunningham and Birren retested the group as its members approached sixty years of age. These studies tested an educationally homogeneous group as they moved through adulthood. The results created a trajectory for, though they did not measure directly, the intellectual functioning of this group in old age.

Between the 1919 and 1950 testings, the full-scale IQ of the surviving group members increased by 5.5 IQ points. There were no significant changes between 1950 and 1960, nor were there significant changes in the 1973 testing. This longitudinal study thus found no evidence of a decrease in full-scale IQ, in contrast to the cross-sectional studies of Army Alpha Test performance (Jones & Conrad, 1933).

Cunningham and Birren (1976) used a varimax rotation to examine the factor structure of the Army Alpha Test. They matched results from a sample of people who were twenty in 1973 with results from a sample of twenty-year-olds from 1919. Factor analyses of cognitive variables showed more similar patterns for the two groups of twenty-year-olds than for members of each group tested subsequently as they aged. These results suggest two conclusions: first, that educationally heterogeneous samples increase the extent of cohort differences found in cross-sectional studies; and second, that cognitive variables change as a function of age, especially variables that involve speed. Cunningham and Birren's (1976) main conclusion was that the use of educationally homogeneous samples would help isolate ontogenetic (individual development) differences and thus make measurements of change in intellectual ability more accurate.

Bayley and Oden (1955) reported the results of a longitudinal study of Terman's group of gifted individuals. Terman's group consisted of 422 men and 346 women born between 1903 and 1920. The subjects ranged between ten and twenty-seven years of age at the study's inception. Selection for follow-up was based on the subjects' attaining an initial IQ on the Stanford-Binet of 140 or above, which placed each person studied in the ninety-ninth percentile of Terman's group test for that age group. Initial IQs ranged from 140 to 200.

The subjects were tested initially in 1930 and then followed up in 1940, when their average age was thirty, and again in 1952, when their average age was forty-two. Two equivalent forms of the Concept Mastery Test, a test of verbal and reasoning skills, were used in the 1940 and 1952 testings. It was hoped that the use of different forms and the twelve-year interval between tests would reduce practice effects, which might otherwise inflate performance. Every subject tested improved significantly on the retest.

There are certain problems with this study. The Concept Mastery Test concentrates on verbal skills and therefore minimizes performance skills, which tend to peak early in adulthood and decline steadily thereafter. The Terman study tested highly motivated volunteers who were test-wise, having been extensively tested in many cases since the age of ten. There was undoubtedly some practice effect because of the similarity in format between the two equivalent forms of the test given. Furthermore, it has generally been found that subjects with high IQs used in Terman's study, peak later in their general intelligence scores and show a more gradual decline in their scores than subjects with low IQs. Finally, the subjects of this study did not even approach the age of seventy or eighty, which is when declines in speed become especially critical.

The Berkeley Growth Study was a longitudinal test of IQ that tested individuals from soon after birth to adulthood (Bayley & Oden, 1955; Maas & Kuypers, 1974). The 130 initial subjects in the study, volunteers taken from a cross-section of community dwellers in Berkeley, California, were given the WAIS. The results showed a continuous increase in verbal IQ until the mid-thirties. A measurable decline in performance measures occurred after the mid-twenties, even in this positively biased sample, in which the average IQ score was 122. However, because the subjects were young adults, these results cannot be generalized to old age. Furthermore, because the subjects were retested frequently, there was undoubtedly practice effect, and the results therefore cannot even be applied to the population in general.

## Conclusions

As indicated above, longitudinal studies tend to be performed with nonrepresentative samples. Their subjects tend to be "healthier, wealthier, and wiser" than the general population (Botwinick, 1967, 1977) or than the populations tested in cross-sectional designs. Persons who continue with longitudinal studies into old age without dropping out or dying are not representative of the total adult population. In general longitudinal studies present the "best" view of old age, since their subjects tend to be survivors. Cross-sectional studies examine a broader range of subject health, income, and ability.

The effects of impending death on intelligence test performance have been described in Kleemeier's concept (1962) of *terminal drop* or *drop before death*. Terminal drop is the assumed decline in intellectual performance that occurs several years before death in old persons. The lower intellectual performance of old cohorts may be partially due to terminal drop among some subjects. Alternatively, the decrease in intellectual performance seen with age may be due to cohort effects, with older cohorts who have had little formal education performing more poorly than younger cohorts whose educational experience has been more extensive.

Either explanation is important for any interpretation of the performance of an individual. However, on a group level old people generally do less well on standard intellectual measures than young people because of impending death, decreased health and income, and different educational levels. The initial level of ability of the subjects of any group, whether young or old, is important in that it predicts the pattern of intellectual change during adulthood and old age.

The question of initial level of ability and its effect on age changes in intelligence is controversial. Some research projects have found correlations between age and IQ scores, specifically between the subjects' scores when young and old (Birren & Morrison, 1961), whereas others have found an association between initial ability and age (Foulds & Ravens, 1948). These discrepancies may be partially explained by the use of different methodologies and procedures.

Birren and Morrison (1961) did not specifically use initial IQ as a measure of initial ability; rather they chose to consider educational level as an index of ability, i.e., less than eight years, eight to twelve years, and thirteen or more years of formal education. Their subjects were from the WAIS standardization sample. In contrast, Foulds and Ravens (1948) gave subjects fifteen to sixty-four years of age two tests, the Ravens Progressive Matrices and the Mill-Hill Vocabulary Test, the latter of which is similar to the WAIS vocabulary subtest. Neither group of researchers analyzed age or ability statistically, although inferences about these factors may be made from their data. Moreover, these cross-sectional studies did not consider the interaction among ability levels, age changes, and types of task involved (Botwinick, 1967). The effects of initial level of ability on life-span intellectual performance require additional attention and research (Kausler, 1982).

The overall results of cross-sectional and longitudinal studies suggest that

> people who perform relatively well when young will also perform relatively well when old. However, the performance level when young is no yardstick of whether age decline will be great, small or neither. (Botwinick, 1977, p. 603)

Despite this caveat, experimenters should determine the initial ability level of their subjects, since this may significantly affect the pattern of IQ test performance. For example, the heterogeneous subject samples used in most cross-sectional studies probably show a greater range of initial ability level than the relatively selective subject samples used in longitudinal studies. It is even possible that the discrepancy in performance between these two classic designs is strongly influenced by the initial ability level of their subjects.

Both cross-sectional and longitudinal studies of adult intellectual performance are subject to procedural and methodological flaws. Longitudinal designs tend to have the problems of nonrepresentative samples, selective mortality, and retest familiarization effects. They also tend to separate the effects of aging from the effects of historical events that intervene between test times (Schaie, 1980). Subject performance as seen in longitudinal studies in all likelihood is somewhat inflated over what one could expect to find in the general population. These studies tend to negate the cultural and educational bias one finds in cross-sectional studies, which test not only different ages but also different cohorts. Practice effects may occur in longitudinal studies. Cross-sectional studies, in contrast, confuse age-related performance with cohort or health-related changes such as terminal drop. Cross-sectional studies measure static performance, i.e., age differences in performance, not age change.

Generally the changes seen in IQ with age are neither as decremental as the cross-sectional designs indicate nor as minimal or incremental as the longitudinal designs suggest. The truth of age functions appears to be somewhere in the middle. Age-related declines in intelligence are probably less exaggerated and occur later in life than indicated by cross-sectional research (Botwinick, 1967). Any change in IQ or problem-solving ability before the late fifties is generally pathological. From the early sixties to the middle seventies there is clearly a decrease in some but not all abilities. Decline after eighty is the rule for most people (Schaie, 1980). The timing and cause of these changes, however, are neither simple nor universal. For example, speed abilities decrease after the midfifties owing to changes in the central nervous system (CNS). Most intellectual abilities requiring speed decrease in people with cardiovascular disease or a socially deprived environment from the late fifties to early sixties. Fast social change leads to obsolescence effects for persons older than fifty-five, decreasing the performance of these people relative to that of younger people, even if their current function is adequate (Botwinick, 1977; Schaie, 1980).

It is difficult to assess the causal effects of change in intellectual function over time. It is mentally seductive to see age per se as the cause of the differences that exist between the average forty- and seventy-year-olds, but these differences are not caused by age. Rather, they are a result of the interaction of social, biological, and psychological changes in addition to length of life and accumulation of experience. Age is an index of change, but it neither causes nor explains events itself.

The task for the clinician or geropsychologist remains to distinguish between the effects of individual cognitive loss, which may require therapy, and those of obsolescence, which may require remedial education (Schaie, 1980). In either case the adequate differentiation of these factors requires more longitudinal studies in problem-solving to suggest age trends in skills and the development of age-appropriate instruments (Monge & Gardner, 1972) or age simulations.

## Learning and Memory

The first part of this chapter has emphasized quantitative aspects of cognition, e.g., intelligence test performance and IQ scores. There is no doubt that intelligence tests utilize skills of learning and memory, but their basic emphasis is more integrative than discriminative; in other words, learning and memory are micro levels of overall intellectual and cognitive ability. Our knowledge of cognitive processes has been limited by their very nature. Cognition is a defining characteristic of human beings, yet it is incorporeal, i.e., without physical substance and therefore subjective and idiosyncratic.

From early in infancy on we perceive "images." As our language skills improve, we use images less and less. However, we do depend on memory, without which language, personality, art, and self-concept are nothing. A person's sense of self depends on that person's perception of his or her own history, which is essentially obtained through memory, the storage and retrieval of information. Learning and memory are also inevitably linked. Learning is the way in which information gets into our cognitive information processing system; memory is the mechanism by which information gets filed and retrieved. It is easier to distinguish these terms conceptually than operationally, since in many laboratory experiments learning is determined by recall, a memory operation. Despite this operational difficulty, however, learning has traditionally been thought of as the short-term acquisition of knowledge, whereas memory has been considered a more stable, long-term change in cognitive performance (Kausler, 1982).

### Information Processing

Learning is the formation of new associations as well as the acquisition of general rules and knowledge about the world (Craik, 1977). It has been the traditional, popular view that learning performance tends to be poorer in late than early adulthood. This belief is manifested by statements such as "You can't teach an old dog new tricks."

Three questions may be asked to elucidate the truth of this belief:

Do specific conditions affect the learning of old people?
Is the magnitude of age differences affected by specific conditions?
Does the nature of learning change with age? (Arenberg & Robertson-Tchabo, 1977).

To answer this set of questions, researchers must methodologically distinguish between the internal process of learning and the external action of performance. The ability to learn may be relatively unchanged in old persons, but noncognitive factors such as poor motivation, lack of confidence, cautiousness, and test anxiety (Arenberg & Robertson-Tchabo, 1977; Botwinick, 1967; Kausler, 1982; Okun et al., 1978; Rabbitt, 1977) may make elderly persons unable to demonstrate what they have learned. If this is true, then the learning deficit seen in old people is actually an inability to express learned information, not a deficient internal acquisition process (Botwinick, 1967).

Associated with this hypothesis is the view that the deficit in verbal learning, problem-solving ability, and skill performance seen in late adulthood may be a result of decreased short-term memory (Arenberg & Robertson-Tchabo, 1977). According to this view, the information processing view, old persons may improve their learning by modifying their use of control processes such as mnemonics and mediational aids. The three-stage memory model of the information processing view is depicted in Figure 8-5.

Information in the environment is first detected by the senses and placed in sensory store for specific modalities. If the person attends to this input, it may move into short-term memory; if it is then rehearsed, it is displaced into long-term memory. Items in short-term or primary memory are in conscious awareness and

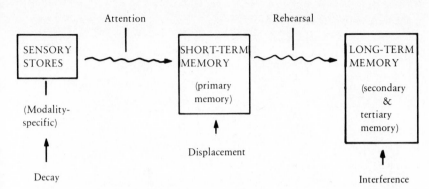

*Figure 8–5    A three-stage memory model*

(Adapted from: Craik, F.I.M. Age differences in human memory. In J. Birren & K.W. Schaie (Eds.), *Handbook of the psychology of aging.* New York: Van Nostrand Reinhold Company, 1977, p. 386)

may be maintained in primary memory by rehearsal, a process that also transfers information to the larger and more permanent secondary memory. Primary memory is generally a temporary holding and organizing process, not a structured memory store (Craik, 1977). The durability of a memory depends on how deeply the information is processed. Craik (1977) states that this "depth of processing" is related to the number and qualitative nature of perceptual processes carried out on the input. This idea is explored in more detail later in this chapter.

The information processing view uses three particular terms that are relevant to learning and memory: *encoding,* the symbolic representation of one thing by another; *storage,* the persistence of information over time; and *retrieval,* the recovery and utilization of stored information (Arenberg & Robertson-Tchabo, 1977). Research has suggested that pronounced age decrements occur in the capacity to remember newly acquired information; there is thus a defect in either encoding or retrieval (Fozard, 1980). In contrast, other studies have found that the capacity of old people to remember information in short-term or long-term memory is not decreased but merely takes longer to occur. There is considerable support for the view that old people are more efficient in searching their long-term memory than are young people (Fozard, 1980).

### Primary Memory

In early research on the capacity of hypothesized memory stores it was assumed that long-term memory was limitless. Consequently attention was focused on determining the limits of short-term memory (Hartley et al., 1980). Craik (1977) suggested that it might be better to distinguish among primary memory, a short-term store from which information is lost if not rehearsed; secondary memory, the repository for newly learned information; and tertiary memory, the storage site for old memories. For something to be transferred into tertiary or secondary memory it must be actively processed or worked on through "working

*Rules of complex games such as chess or Mah-Jongg may never be forgotten because of practice.*

memory," i.e., knowledge of a set of conventions for a particular cognitive task (Fozard, 1980).

The most recent evidence supports the idea that old people, despite their frequent complaints of memory loss, show little if any loss of tertiary memory. Age differences in primary memory capacity are also minimal. However, in any task that requires data manipulation or organization; i.e., secondary memory aspects, the old individual appears at a disadvantage.

> To the extent that attention cannot be focused exclusively on performance of the memory span task, or that organization of the material is required or encouraged by the task, older people perform at a lower level than younger people. (Hartley et al., 1980, p. 240)

Evidence suggests that old people have a particularly difficult time in situations in which they must divide their attention. Craik (1977) suggests that the capacity of old persons may be largely taken up in programming the division of attention, leaving relatively little capacity to process the stimuli. Thus, in a situation demanding reorganizing or restructuring, the primary memory capacity of old persons decreases, leading to reduced secondary memory strategies (Hartley et al., 1980).

### Secondary Memory
As stated, secondary memory involves the use of encoding or control processes, e.g., remembering the first names of people at a cocktail party or grouping nonsense syllables by sound. The primary memory of old people is not as great as that of

young people, and this may contribute to age-related deficits in secondary memory. Although the age deficit is easily demonstrable, however, it is not known whether the focus of the deficit is in acquisition, encoding, or retrieval. (Storage has been proved to be minimally affected by age [Hartley et al., 1980; Kausler, 1982]). If encoding is the focal point of the loss, information simply does not get into secondary memory. Current research focuses on encoding versus retrieval deficiencies as the basis of decreased learning ability and memory in old people.

Information processing research strategies generally use three paradigms: divided attention tasks, such as dichotic listening or bisensory paired associates (the pairing of visual and auditory stimuli); primary memory tasks focusing on free recall of learned items; and secondary memory tasks using structured or serial recall. The following findings have been made about short-term memory retention in old people:

Short-term memory retention is higher when stimuli are presented auditorily rather than visually for all age groups. However, old people do not appear to benefit disproportionately from auditory presentation unless they must divide their attention among various control processes. (Craik, 1977)

There is a significant decrease with age in ability to recall sequences of nonsense syllables, words, and symbols. (Botwinick, 1967)

There is an age-related decrease in ability to recall incidental aspects of the learning situation. This indicates a degree of attentional rigidity. (Botwinick, 1967)

Despite the use of different paradigms, which leads to difficulty in generalizing results, aging appears to have a greater detrimental effect on recall performance than on recognition. (Craik, 1977)

Retrieval failure appears to account for the bulk of the age decrement in short-term memory, but certain modalities and data also reveal encoding deficits relating to acquisition (Hartley et al., 1980). Additionally, storage deficits may be involved. (Kausler, 1982)

The speed of recall also decreases in old people. (Birren et al., 1980)

Old people do not spontaneously use mnemonic mediators to organize the information they acquire. They are capable of performing these mediational processes, but they fail to carry them out spontaneously. They thus do not process information deeply enough to have it be retrievable later. However, this mnemonic production deficiency is neither inevitable nor irreversible.

### Experimental Evidence on Memory

Using a paired-associates task that combined a nonsense syllable with a familiar word, e.g., *tl + insane*, Gilbert (1941) found that paired associate tasks were especially difficult for old people. In a cross-sectional study she found lower paired associate performance for old people than for young people. This study was used as support for the claim that learning ability declines with age, but in reality the study did not show this. The experiment used fast-paced stimuli, though speed is not usually relevant to normal verbal learning responses outside a laboratory setting; moreover, its cross-sectional design cannot accurately determine learning ability.

Canestrari (1963) improved on Gilbert's fast-paced format by placing his old and young subjects into one of three different stimulus pacing schedules: fast, in which a stimulus occurred every 1.5 seconds; medium, in which a stimulus occurred every 3 seconds; and self-paced. There was no difference in correct performance between young and old subjects in the self-paced condition; however, there were significant age differences in the other two conditions. Canestrari concluded that it takes longer for old people than for young people to express newly learned information. He also found that old subjects made certain types of errors, e.g., errors of omission. Old subjects appear to prefer not to respond rather than to respond incorrectly, a phenomenon called *cautiousness*.

Monge and Hultsch (1971) varied both the inspection interval (the length of time a subject examines the stimulus) and the anticipation interval (the time before the subject must respond) in a serial learning paradigm. They found that old subjects took longer to learn and were generally more cautious than young subjects. Both young and old subjects appeared to benefit when the inspection interval was longer. The longer inspection interval increased rehearsal of the response and optimal encoding of the material. However, the long anticipation interval appeared to be of greatest benefit to the old people, allowing them to take longer to retrieve the correct response and thereby reducing their anxiety.

Eisdorfer, Nowlin, and Wilkie (1970) also implicated central cognitive processes in the production deficiency of old people. These researchers gave propranolol, a drug that suppresses autonomic nervous system activity, to old subjects about to perform a serial learning task. Old subjects on the drug performed significantly better than control subjects and made fewer errors. Eisdorfer et al. concluded that the control subjects were overaroused in the learning situation and that this overarousal (as measured by free fatty acid levels in the blood) negatively influenced their learning performance. This conclusion must be viewed somewhat critically. The study had certain methodological weaknesses; it used no young comparison group and no placebo control group, and the injection (even without its drug content) may well have led to overarousal. Despite these criticisms, however, it appears from these studies that cautiousness and fear of failure made old subjects anxious, which suppresses their use of mediators.

*Cautiousness* is broadly defined as discomfort with new and uncertain events leading to a loss of self-confidence and the expectation of failure. Cautiousness tends to inhibit risk-taking behavior even if the venture is considered to be of low risk. Individuals who are cautious value accuracy highly, try to avoid making mistakes at all cost, and have a great need to be certain of the answer before they respond to a question or problem. Old people often lack self-confidence in their responses (Botwinick, 1967; Okun et al., 1978).

Lachman and Lachman (1980) offered support for the role of cognitive processes in errors of omission by elderly subjects. Their research involved tertiary memory of test material, including movies, sports, and current events. Subjects were asked to write the answers to questions such as "What was the former name of Muhammad Ali?" and indicate the degree of certainty of their responses. These sureness measures ranged from "Do not know" to "Could remember if given more time." Items not recalled were then presented in a multiple-choice format (recognition memory), and subjects were asked to indicate the sureness of their responses on these items on a scale ranging from "Definitely sure" to "Wild guess."

The Lachmans found that total knowledge increased with age and that subjects of all ages were equally accurate in estimating the degree of confidence of their knowledge. There were also minimal differences in recall behavior among the three age groups tested, with the category indicated by "Could remember if given more time" taking the longest time for recall and response. It is clear that when old subjects are given a way around a totally incorrect response, as with sureness measures, they perform better. Good long-term memory retention appears to be the rule rather than the exception among old persons when they feel no anxiety over a possible judgment error (Fozard, 1980). As can be seen in Figure 8-6, the

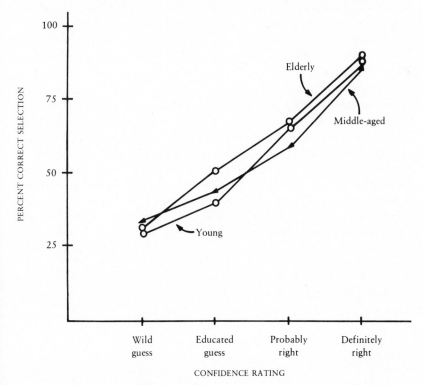

Figure 8–6 *Confidence ratings in correctness of response from Lachman and Lachman*

(Source: Fozard, J.L. The time for remembering. In Poon, L.C. (Ed.), *Aging in the 1980s: Psychological issues*. Washington, D.C.: American Psychological Association, 1980, p. 276. Copyright © 1980 by the American Psychological Association. Reprinted by permission)

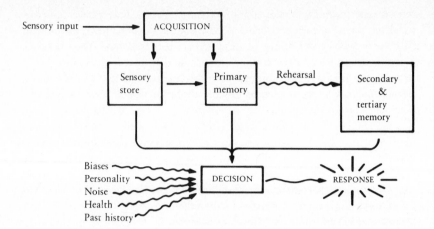

*Figure 8-7   Influences on decision-making by old persons*

efficiency of memory in the Lachmans' study remained constant across age, and all age groups were equally accurate in estimating the confidence of their knowledge.

Memory research thus indicates that old people suffer from age-related decreases in secondary memory. The deficit appears to be caused by the old person's failure to use control processes in organizing incoming data, i.e., failure to organize information into temporal groups, semantic clusters, or hierarchies, as well as failure to use mnemonic devices. In addition, old people need more time than young people to deeply process incoming cognitive material. Stimuli presented at a fast pace therefore cause anxiety to increase and performance to decline.

As can be seen in Figure 8-7, the memory process is quite complicated. Acquired sensory and verbal information goes into either an iconic sensory store or primary memory. If rehearsed, it may be processed more deeply and placed into either secondary or tertiary memory storage (Table 8-2). When a person is asked to make a decision regarding knowledge about or learning of an event, many factors impinge, such as biases, personality, and expectation of success; health status; and environmental noise distracting attention from the task at hand.

When left to their own mnemonic devices, old people do not process informa-

*Table 8-2   Examples of remembering from different hypothetical memory stores at a party*

| Sensory | Primary | Secondary | Working | Tertiary |
|---|---|---|---|---|
| Shortest time required to identify letters of new name | Recall new name just after hearing it | Recall new name after meeting 10 other people | Recall rule to use only first names at party | Recall own name |

(Source: Fozard, J.L. The time for remembering. In L.C. Poon (Ed.), *Aging in the 1980s: Psychological issues.* Washington, D.C.: American Psychological Association, 1980, p. 274. Copyright © 1980 by the American Psychological Association. Reprinted by permission)

tion as deeply as young people. Age differences in memory are minimal when direct recall of short-term memory data is involved, but if information is held in short-term memory and must be manipulated some way (e.g., reversal of digits in the digits-backward section of the WAIS) or if two tasks have to be performed simultaneously, old persons perform less well than young persons. In addition, the amount of time required to search for information held in short-term memory increases during adulthood even when the number of items recalled remains stable (Lachman & Lachman, 1980).

It is obvious that the short-term memory deficit of old persons is in reality a processing deficit (Botwinick, 1977; Craik, 1977; Fozard, 1980; Hartley et al., 1980). The evidence for age-related decline in memory capacity is presented in Table 8-3. As can be seen, the bulk of the deficit lies in secondary memory. The main exception is in anecdotal reports from primary and tertiary memory, i.e., people's statements about their memories.

## Learning

Mnemonics and control processes require initial training to instill their use and then practice to maintain their availability. If old persons are trained to organize material, they may remember more; or, "if we train them to be selective in material they commit to memory, they may *have* to remember less (Rabbitt, 1977, p. 609)." There is a strong dependency between memory load and the capacity to organize material efficiently and selectively. This is where learning and strategies to learn material effectively enter the picture.

Arenberg and Robertson-Tchabo (1977) have argued that all adult learning is transfer of training—the effect of the learning of one task on the acquisition of a second task. Transfer effects may be positive or negative, i.e., they may enhance or hinder the acquisition of data. Interference with or inhibition of the acquisition of

Table 8–3   *Evidence for age-related declines in memory capacity*

| Type of study and type of evidence | Memory store | | | | |
|---|---|---|---|---|---|
| | Sensory | Primary | Secondary | Working | Tertiary |
| *Cross-sectional studies* | | | | | |
| Anecdotal | — | Positive | Positive | Positive | Positive |
| Psychometric | — | Negative | Positive | — | Negative |
| Experimental | Positive | Negative | Positive | Positive | Negative |
| *Longitudinal studies* | | | | | |
| Anecdotal | — | — | — | — | — |
| Psychometric | — | Negative | Positive | — | Negative |
| Experimental | — | — | Positive | — | — |

data inhibit understanding of a task's structure and retention. Interference is of two types:

Retroactive interference, effects on retention generated by information obtained after the to-be-remembered material

Proactive interference, the effect on retention of information presented before the to-be-remembered material (Arenberg & Robertson-Tchabo, 1977)

Proactive interference would appear to be a special problem for old people, who have long years of previous information gathering and experience to cloud current cognitive efforts. However, it is not yet possible to evaluate whether old people are more susceptible to interference than young people; it is methodologically difficult to equate individuals of different chronological ages for rate of learning (Arenberg, 1977). As Rabbit (1977) has pointed out,

> The greater the memory load, the greater the time for each operation. The greater the time, the greater the probability of memory inaccuracies. The greater the probability of memory inaccuracies, the greater the probability of incorrect decisions which have to be modified by extra operations. The greater the number of extra operations, the greater the elapsed time and interference by this extra activity and the greater the probability of memory inaccuracies, etc., etc.*

Research needs to be done to explore how much of the age differences in memory result from a processing deficit that could be overcome by teaching old people correct encoding strategies (Hartley et al., 1980). It is also likely that such mnemonic manipulations would not eliminate age differences because the processing deficit alone does not explain the whole age difference. Researchers have suggested that the memory deficit seen in old people is caused by a general decrease in speed of behavior due to changes in the CNS (Birren et al., 1980; Salthouse, 1980; Waugh & Barr, 1980). Thus, a decrease in the rate at which operations are accomplished by the CNS limits memory, a phenomenon implicated by Rabbitt (1977) as a factor in decreased problem-solving ability by old people.

The area of speed requires additional research. The sensory factors involved in response slowing were discussed in Chapter 7 and the physiological correlates of brain aging were explored in Chapter 5. Slowing is undoubtedly involved in the memory and the learning performance decrement of old people, but its contribution to this phenomenon still needs clarification.

**Intervention**

Both acquisition and retrieval seem to be implicated in the age-related decrease in information processing ability. Strategies for acquisition and retrieval might help

---

*Rabbitt, P. Changes in problem solving ability in old age. In J.E. Birren & K.W. Schaie (Eds.), *The handbook of the psychology of aging*. New York: Van Nostrand Reinhold Company, 1977, p. 619. Copyright © 1977 by Van Nostrand Reinhold Company. Reprinted by permission of the publisher

old people improve their secondary memory ability. Since old people are less likely than young people to use these facilitating aids, they may need to be taught their use. It is also possible that the research paradigms used to measure information processing ability may need to be redesigned.

Fozard (1980) has presented three types of intervention designed to diminish age differences in memory by focusing on memory capacity and speed:

*Task redesign* may be accomplished by either the experimenter or the subject. It consists of operations that simplify either the display of information or the achievement of a response. For example, giving feedback on stimulus groupings may increase memory capacity, and decreasing the number of items to be memorized may increase speed of memory (Fozard, 1980). Aural presentation of materials may also help increase capacity and speed, as may decreasing anxiety by using familiar procedures.

*Training* involves increasing secondary memory capacity by increasing the number of items acquired. This may be accomplished by the use of imagery or relatively task-specific cognitive skills training. For example, the subject may simplify paired associate tasks by creating a visual image of the aural pair. Task-specific cognitive skills may involve hierarchical ordering, grouping techniques, and so on.

*Individual differences* involves intervention in such cognitive or personality factors as cautiousness, health, and risk-taking behavior. Fozard (1980) and others have suggested that such individual difference variables may be preferable to chronological age as subject or independent variables in study design. Chronological age is a relatively poor classification schema for stable psychological function such as memory or intelligence.

The projected success of such interventions is presented in Table 8-4. The results of task redesign on memory capacity are generally minimal. Secondary memory speed may be helped by training, but individual differences in speed may reflect physiological variables that are at best minimally affected by any intervention.

## Individual Differences

Factors such as health, anxiety, and education — variables on which people tend to show a considerable degree of individual difference —influence performance on cognitive tasks. The role of health and exercise, especially their influence on response time, has been discussed in earlier chapters. Abrahams and Birren (1973), for example, found that persons with Type A coronary-prone behavior are more likely than persons with Type B personality structures to show response slowing in reaction time tasks.

Robertson-Tchabo, Arenberg, and Costa (1979) looked at the relationship over six years between scores on the Benton Visual Retention Test and traits found on the Guilford-Zimmerman Temperament Survey. They found that the men whose performance was stable were more active, energetic, productive, responsible,

Table 8–4   *Interventions to diminish age differences in memory*

| Type of intervention | Primary | Secondary | Working | Tertiary |
|---|---|---|---|---|
| *Capacity* | | | | |
| Task redesign | — | Poor | Good | Slight |
| Training | — | Good | Fair | Slight |
| Individual differences | — | Good | — | Fair |
| | | | | |
| *Speed* | | | | |
| Task redesign | Good | Slight | — | Slight |
| Training | Slight | Good | — | Slight |
| Individual differences | Fair | Fair | — | Fair |

self-restrained, and task-oriented and less impulsive than the men whose perform-ance declined.

Fozard and Costa (in press) examined the correlation between results on the Cattell 16 PF Questionnaire and results on tests of speed of memory retrieval. Good secondary memory performance in old subjects was associated with greater impulsiveness, lower control, greater arousal, and greater openness than poor performance. High speed of retrieval from primary memory and tertiary memory was associated with impulsiveness, whereas slow recall speed was associated with imaginativeness. These trends held for primary and tertiary memory in all age groups tested (Fozard, 1980).

All of the traits cited above are ways of dealing with and responding to the environment that are favorable to the cognitive processing skills of older people. These traits reflect an active involvement with the world and a readiness to interact with it. Memory and learning are selective, constructive cognitive processes that are strongly affected by personality, expectations, and past experience.

### Depression

Memory impairment, especially if severe, is often a behavioral symptom of depression or senile dementia. Given the common social stereotype that "senility" is inevitable, many old people believe that any change in memory indicates the presence of "senility." Old people typically complain about their memory, even though research indicates that such complaints are often not accompanied by any decrease in memory function (LaRue, 1978). A partial explanation of this phenome-non is that affective status and memory are interrelated and that there is a relation between depression and memory performance (Kahn & Miller, 1978). Old persons who suffer from depression may complain that they are losing their memory when in reality they only perceive they are losing it because of their negative affect and self-concept.

Depression is commonly associated with some degree of cognitive impairment, although this is usually minimal unless the depression is severe. Research indicates that twenty-one percent of depressed patients show impaired recent memory and fourteen percent show poor remote memory. Some depressed patients perform poorly on standard psychometric measures in a way that parallels the symptoms of organic brain dysfunction. This is further discussed in Chapter 10.

Depressed patients tend to see themselves as helpless and report difficulties doing tests of any sort. However, actual impaired memory tends to be associated with organic brain dysfunction, whereas complaints about memory loss are generally a symptom of depression (Zarit et al., 1975). Depressed persons are pessimistic in predicting their ability and have a negative self-image. They also often suffer from sleeplessness or anorexia. Depressed persons tend to think stereotypically, tend to use cliches, and have a generally low level of intellectual ability. In contrast, old persons with organic brain dysfunction tend to complain less about memory loss than depressives, either because they use denial extensively as a defense or because they are unaware of the extent of their cognitive loss (Kahn & Zarit, 1975). In any case, complaints about memory in old persons are generally a sign of pathology rather than of normal age-related changes in intellectual functioning.

### Why Intervene?

As stated, intervention in the cognitive performance of old people may be carried out by three different channels: task redesign, training, and therapy dealing with individual traits that may be harmful to cognitive function. Fozard (1980) suggests that intervention is both practically and scientifically useful:

Intervention will help set limits for age-related changes in normal memory and cognitive function as well as determine the impact of pathology.
Intervention will provide a rapid, self-correcting approach to dealing with noncognitive factors related to age differences in cognitive function, such as motivation, anxiety, and depression.
Intervention will help determine the validity of current memory theories about changes in memory and cognition through the life span.

Successful intervention will also increase the positive expectancies of old people about their own cognitive performance and will decrease stereotypes concerning the inevitability of cognitive decline in old age.

**Summary**

As Rabbitt (1977) has stated, old people are not the passive victims of cognitive degeneration. They conserve and explore their intellectual reserves. When a task's complexity exceeds these reserves, they try to avoid unnecessary blunders and thereby make some errors of omission. It is important for psychologists interested

*Some cohort differences may be due to an emphasis in one generation on manual skills as opposed to "formal," book-based education.*

in old age to study not only age-related decrements that occur in intellectual performance but also adaptations to these decrements.

The nature of cognitive task performance changes with age. This is seen in IQ tests and standard laboratory procedures such as paired associate and serial learning tests, but its effect on real-world performance is not clear. Research seems to suggest that old people have a retrieval deficit. Old persons are particularly disadvantaged when given only a short time to respond to a question or problem, but even under self-paced conditions, when speed is not a consideration, age differences in performance are found. Rate of response is not the only factor limiting the performance of old persons. Also implicated are the amount of information encoded (if information is not encoded, it is unavailable for retrieval), and the type of encoding strategy used. Because of individual differences, some seventy-year-olds will perform like some thirty- or forty-year-olds, thereby perhaps rendering "age changes" as described by researchers ontogenetic rather than universal (Arenberg & Robertson-Tchabo, 1977).

Cohort effects also influence cognitive task performance. As can be seen in Table 8–5, the different educational experiences of different cohorts color performance in old age. Cohort differences must be distinguished from true age changes (Schaie & Labouvie-Vief, 1974). Unlike childhood cognitive changes, which presumably stem from biomaturational growth processes, adult cognitive changes appear to be strongly based on experience (Flavell, 1970). They are more quantitative than qualitative until late old age, and they are not universal. The cognitive develop-

*Table 8–5   Comparison of inferences drawn from cross-sectional and longi-
tudinal studies of intellectual ability*

| Variable | Cross-sectional | Longitudinal |
|---|---|---|
| Verbal meaning | Sharp decrement from middle adulthood to old age | Modest gain throughout life from young adult plateau |
| Space | Sharp decrement from young adult peak to old age | Modest decrement from adult plateau |
| Reasoning | Sharp decrement from young adult peak to old age | Modest gain from young adult plateau till old age |
| Number | Modest gain and loss before and after midlife plateau | Modest gain from early adulthood to plateau at old age |
| Word fluency | Moderate decrement from plateau extending over major portion of adulthood | Moderate gains from young adult levels |

(Source: Schaie, K.W. A reinterpretation of age-related changes in cognitive structure
and functioning. In L.R. Goulet & P.B. Baltes (Eds.), *Life-span developmental psychology: Research and theory.* New York: Academic Press, 1970, p. 499)

mental changes of adulthood and old age are better seen in judgments, attitudes,
and beliefs than in skills on psychometric tasks (Flavell, 1970; Kohlberg, 1973).
These changes may be as momentous as the developmental changes of childhood;
awareness of death for example, may significantly affect one's life-style and
radically change one's thinking. They are also highly individual in nature.

The endlessly reductionistic approach to information processing currently popular in gerontological research may be missing the mark in its search for universal age
changes. A more fruitful approach to cognitive change may be to consider the
impact of individual difference variables on performance and then design interventions appropriate to counter the negative impact of such variables.

Students of aging should ask not how much cognitive deficit exists in the typical
seventy-year-old and why he or she performs so poorly, but rather how, in the face
of growing disabilities, the typical seventy-year-old performs so well (Rabbitt,
1977). This sort of approach may dramatically undercut some of the negative
stereotypes about cognitive impairment mentioned in this chapter.

# 9

# Personality and Adjustment

*What is personality and how much does it change in adult life?*

*Do the images of aging presented by the media tend to idealize or caricature old persons?*

*What images tend to prevail?*

*What is self-concept and how does it affect psychological functioning?*

*Are the developmental tasks of late life the most difficult tasks of the life cycle?*

*Why should we study personality change with age?*

*Are there fundamental differences between the processes that shape personality in youth, maturity, and old age?*

*Why is successful aging so difficult to define?*

---

*T*HERE is a diversity of ways in which one can perceive the process of growing old. Some persons stress the overall mental and physical decline and deterioration that often occur in old age; others focus on various patterns of growth that occur even to the moment of death. Personality changes during senescence have frequently been portrayed by novelists, poets, and dramatists. Depending on the writer's outlook or purpose, experience, and philosophy, elderly characters are either caricatured or idealized.

Psychologists treat the elderly the same way as writers. Some stress personality closure in childhood, others see a decline in personality with age, and still others assert that personality in old age grows and transcends the levels reached during early maturity. Their manner of perceiving personality and adjustment in late life is largely dependent on their own expectancies of and attitudes toward aging. In contrast to novelists, however, psychologists also base their views of aging on systematic study and empirical testing.

Three broad areas of personality research relate to old age:

The principal developmental tasks of late life
Theoretical approaches to late-life personality dynamics
The measurement of psychological well-being, adjustment, and successful aging among elderly persons.

This chapter focuses on the developmental tasks associated with late life and adjustment. Normal personality structures and dynamics as well as positive ways of coping or adjusting are discussed. The pathological aspects of personality and psychiatric distress are considered extensively in Chapter 10. For most elderly persons the issues of psychopathology are never of concern. The vast majority of old persons, like the majority of young persons, are never disabled by mental illness, although many persons of all ages occasionally show various symptoms of mental disorder, usually in times of crisis or stress. Many old persons are merely practiced versions of their younger selves.

Humans have always been interested in themselves, especially when things go wrong! The study of personality grew out of an attempt to explain pathology; for example, Sigmund Freud's approach to personality dynamics was derived from his work with hysterical neurotics, and Harry Stack Sullivan's theory grew from his work with schizophrenics. Increasingly, however, the emphasis in the field of aging has been on normal aspects of personality and social development.

Personality is a combination of traits, talents, roles, and coping styles integrated in a recognizable way (Newman & Newman, 1980). Personality involves both stability and change throughout the life cycle. Concepts of personality, like aging, are culture and time bound (Neugarten, 1977). The person described by Eastern psychology is far different from the person of the West; so too does the person of the medieval philosophers differ from the individual envisioned by twentieth century existentialists.

### How to Study Personality
Scientific methods to study personality have been difficult at least partially because of the broad disparity in theoretical views of what personality is. The behaviorism

**What Is Personality?**

*Personality is a combination of traits, talents, roles, and coping styles that are integrated in a recognizable way.*

of B.F. Skinner, for example, says that personality per se does not exist and that the main focus of research should be behavior. Behavior in turn is described in terms of environmental manipulations and the observable responses made to them. Attempts are made to avoid any subjective component that cannot be directly measured. The psychoanalytic tradition of Freud, in contrast, focuses on inner dynamics, which are largely inferred.

Lack of consensus in such theoretical approaches is not necessarily negative; it gives rise to further research aimed at resolving the conflicts. Disagreement among findings in personality research should lead to critical consideration of the different subject variables, methods, and instruments used to test premises. The research questions being asked should be considered and contrasted. Finally it should be realized that researchers often test situation-specific aspects of personality; it may be that some combination of multiple research approaches and results would give us a fuller portrait of personality change and stability in old age.

The life-span developmental approach has been increasingly applied to the study of adult and late-life personality development. This perspective focuses on "those changes that can be demonstrated to vary with age regardless of the direction of the change" (Neugarten, 1977, p. 630). The developmental perspective therefore attempts to determine continuities and discontinuities in personality both across and within individuals as they age. It focuses particularly on changes caused by the adaptation of persons to their environment.

This chapter considers some of the important issues that have emerged from life-span and personality research. The questions crucial to late-life personality development include the following:

How do life events shape personality or determine the conflicts a person must resolve?

What is the relationship between personality and life satisfaction or adjustment?

Does personality change or is it stable across the adult life span into old age?

What sorts of changes occur in masculinity, femininity, interiority, and passivity in late life? Are these changes culture specific?

### Personality Assessment

A first step in the study of personality is measurement of it and its various components. Methods used to assess personality structure and function include case studies, subjective measures, questionnaires or scales, observation, and experimentation.

*Case Studies*    Case studies have been long used to provide anecdotal reports of the processes of aging. They are useful chronicles of the passage of individuals through their lives, but they often lack reliability or methodological rigor. Case studies also often rely on personal report, which is always subject to personal bias, focal memory loss, or reconstruction of events to prevent cognitive dissonance. Nevertheless, case studies often provide fairly quick information on personality issues, and the merits of this information can then be examined by more trustworthy and reliable methods.

*Subjective Measures*    Subjective measures of personality include projective tests such as the Thematic Apperception Test (TAT) or the Rorschach Inkblot Test, in which the subject is asked to respond to purposefully ambiguous stimuli. In the TAT persons are shown a standard set of pictures and asked to describe what is happening and to speculate on what will happen next. The Rorschach Test presents the subject with a standard set of inkblots, some in color and some in black and white. Subjects are asked to tell what they see in the inkblots.

The essence of subjective tests is the stimulus ambiguities, which allow the person to make individual, idiosyncratic interpretations. The principle underlying such subjective measures is that personality conflicts are often unconscious and will thus not be elucidated by direct questioning. Projective measures rely on the interpretation of standard stimuli by trained professionals as a means of bypassing such unconscious or deliberate concealment of conflict (Newman & Newman, 1980). Although the Rorschach Test and TAT have been used with elderly populations, however, they have not been a principal focus of research in gerontology.

*Questionnaires*    Questionnaires involve structured approaches to aspects of the personality usually involving an individual's self-report. The self-concept scale (Dusek et al., 1979; Monge, 1973), illustrated in Figure 9-1, is a questionnaire involving a series of bipolar adjectives used to tap various aspects of personality structure. Another sort of questionnaire may be seen in Figure 9-2. The Rosenberg self-esteem scale involves varying degrees of agreement in response to several statements. Other scales involve open-ended sentence completion or

| | |
|---|---|
| smart-dumb | good-bad |
| success-failure | happy-sad |
| leader-follower | relaxed-nervous |
| sharp-dull | steady-shaky |
| superior-inferior | refreshed-tired |
| valuable-worthless | satisfied-dissatisfied |
| confident-unsure | stable-unstable |
| kind-cruel | rugged-delicate |
| friendly-unfriendly | hard-soft |
| nice-awful | strong-weak |
| healthy __ : __ : __ : __ : __ : __ : __ sick | |

*Figure 9-1   Bipolar adjectives used to assess self-concept*

(Source: Dusek, J.B., Kermis, M.D., & Monge, R.H. The hierarchy of adolescent interests: A social-cognitive approach. *Genetic Psychology Monographs*, 1979)

1. On the whole I am satisfied with myself.
2. At times I think I am no good at all.
3. I feel that I have a number of good qualities.
4. I am able to do things as well as most other people.
5. I feel that I do not have much to be proud of.
6. I certainly feel useless at times.
7. I feel that I am a person of worth, at least on an equal plane with others.
8. I wish I could have more respect for myself.
9. All in all, I am inclined to feel that I am a failure.
10. I take a positive attitude toward myself.

Subjects rate each item on the scale below:

Strongly agree        Agree              Disagree           Strongly disagree

*Figure 9–2   Rosenberg self-esteem scale*

(Source: Rosenberg, M. *Society and the adolescent self-image.* Princeton: Princeton University Press, 1965, p. 8. Copyright © 1965. Reprinted by permission of Princeton University Press)

carefully structured broad-based surveys of total functioning. Measures such as the Duke Longitudinal Study's multidimensional functional assessment, the Older Americans' Resource Survey (OARS) methodology, and scales of life satisfaction have been used extensively in the study of personality development in late life (Kausler, 1982).

*Observation*    An individual's behavior has often been observed to determine the discrepancies between verbal reports and what the person actually does. Observation is subject to the same criticisms as the other methods of personality assessment, any of which alone presents an incomplete portrait of personality. However, experimentation has provided some more comprehensive views of total personality structure and function.

### Conclusions

Psychometric measures such as questionnaires and psychological tests are generally preferable to case studies. They are fairly quick and convenient, offer a greater range of observation, and are more objective and quantifiable than the more psychodynamic approaches. Both methodologies, however, measure only indirect or inferential aspects of personality structure (Bromley, 1974). Researchers must therefore be cautious about drawing conclusions.

Self-health reports are frequently used to assess an individual's perceived health status. Subjects are asked to rate their current health and function and arrive at an overall assessment of their health as excellent, good, fair, or poor (Shanas & Maddox, 1976; USDHEW, 1980). Such self-health ratings appear to be better predictors of a person's daily activities and functions than are a physician's objective diagnoses (Adams, 1980; Hickey, 1980). This is not surprising when one considers the role of attitude and expectancy in overall health (Fries & Crapo, 1981). However, questionnaires and self-report responses are not necessarily accurate indications of behavior; they need corroboration. Persons may rate their health as very good because they do not want to burden others or because they feel they are doing well given their problems. This response should be interpreted as indicating not good diagnostic health but merely the individual's perception of his or her health.

Old people as a group tend to use extreme response categories on attitude scales because they prefer simple, unambiguous situations (Bromley, 1974; Kausler, 1982). They are more likely than young persons to use "Don't know" responses and omit answers because they are cautious, afraid of making mistakes, or unable to think of satisfactory solutions (Bromley, 1974; Okun et al., 1978). All of these factors tend to influence their performance on any subjective or objective ambiguous measure.

As stated, personality is the core part of human beings. It is difficult to define because of its subjectivity, especially over time. Theorists generally agree that personality comprises a stable core and temporary adaptations to situational demands. Personality is determined and preserved by social interactions in the context of the groups most important to the individual (Back, 1976; Monte, 1980). Some of these groups affect personality through time, such as family and ethnic groups from which a person draws a racial and personal history; other groups, such as friends and co-workers, affect personality through space, moving the person beyond the immediate family setting (Back, 1976). However, all the social groups and settings in which persons exist offer opportunities for positive or negative growth because of the functional adaptations they require throughout the life cycle.

**Personality Dynamics**

Changes in functional behavior required by aging may be seen in the individual's interaction with the family. The family offers a link between past and future. In childhood the family is the person's primary social group. Intense emotional attachments are formed between the child and the nuclear and extended family. The child is dependent on the family for all needs and wants. However, as the child moves toward adolescence and youth, total dependency begins to be replaced by independence and less intense emotional involvement with family members.

In young and middle adulthood the familial focus turns from the family in which a person was born to the family of procreation. Recent research (Neugarten, 1977) has suggested that with increased longevity the middle generation often has its loyalties, resources, and care divided between its adolescent children and aging parents. Such polarization can lead to significant stress and guilt at a time in the life cycle when one is pointed toward retirement and one's own health and financial needs.

*The family provides a link between a person's past and future.*

In late life the individual faces many losses requiring difficult adaptation, e.g., the loss of one's spouse and one's health. These losses may cause the old adult to become dependent on middle-aged children. Such dependency may be extremely difficult for all involved.

Throughout these changes the family relationship is generally a focus of continuity and intensity. The individual's personality and its characteristics are shaped in part by the changing family context and the individual's adaptation to it. A person who does not adapt to changing social demands in a positive way assumes negative qualities; a person who adapts positively integrates mature qualities (Back, 1976; Erikson, 1963; Monte, 1980).

### The Ego Psychologists

Ego psychology is a contemporary modification of psychoanalytic theory that emphasizes the creative action of the self or ego. Ego psychologists include Charlotte Bühler, Else Frenkel-Brunswik, Carl Jung, Alfred Adler, and Erik Erikson.

*Charlotte Bühler*    Charlotte Bühler started her therapeutic work with children in Vienna using a modified psychoanalytic technique. She gradually moved to a life-span humanistic perspective emphasizing the person as the constructor of his or her own reality. Bühler's theory emphasized shifts in needs and motives as typical of progress through the life cycle. She believed the central human motives to be self-actualization, intentionality in behavior (as opposed to unconscious forces), goal seeking, and goal restructuring (Neugarten, 1977).

Bühler believed that these basic human motives all act to some extent at every age but have periods of dominance at different times that determine life-style. The life tasks of aging persons, for example, include need satisfaction, adaptive self-limitation (i.e., adjustment), creative expansion, establishment of an inner order, and self-fulfillment (Bühler, 1962). This is a positive interpretation of late-life personality development, in contrast to the Freudian view presented in Chapter 3. According to Bühler, the old adult is still vitally involved in determining his or her own personhood. Bühler's approach lends itself to discussion of the psychological work and developmental tasks performed by old persons.

*Else Frenkel-Brunswik*  Else Frenkel-Brunswik, a colleague of Bühler's who moved from Vienna to Berkeley, California, in the 1930s, studied the social adjustment of men in their sixties and older. Her research was later published by Reichard, Livson, and Peterson (1962). This was the first systematic study of the personality of men of retirement age.

Like other ego psychologists, Frenkel-Brunswik stressed the impact of social factors on one's self-concept and construction of reality. She believed that retirement, decreasing health, and death all require considerable adjustment and adaptation. With age persons increasingly reflect on their past lives, oncoming death, and

*Old persons faced with physical, social, and psychological changes need not be forced into rigidity or senility. They may instead develop unique, creative patterns of continued personal closure and ego integrity.*

loneliness. Frenkel-Brunswik found that the conflicts and frustrations of this period of transition were often resolved by the construction of a "balance sheet" of life, typified by memoirs or autobiographies. This approach is predictive of Butler's (1963) later finding of the value of life review and reminiscence presented by Erikson (1963).

*Carl Jung*   Carl Jung was originally a disciple of Freud who disagreed with Freud over his emphasis on sexuality and determinism. Like Buhler and Frenkel-Brunswik, Jung believed that human beings are motivated by the achievement of selfhood. As persons move into middle and late life, they show an increase in introversion and a reorganization of values toward the inner self. This movement toward interiority has been extensively documented by many psychologists, including Gutmann (1964, 1971) and Neugarten, Havighurst, and Tobin (1961).

*Alfred Adler*   Alfred Adler was originally a part of Freud's inner circle, the Vienna Psychoanalytic Society, but like Jung, he split from orthodox Freudianism over the meaning of the unconscious and the emphasis on sexuality. Much of Adler's theory is applicable to human aging, although he emphasized the first half of the life cycle.

Adler's own sickly childhood led him to make "inferiority" a key component of his theory. He believed that striving to master feelings of inferiority is an inherent characteristic of human beings. Inferiority arises from the individual's perceptions of his or her physical, psychological, and social abilities. Persons who feel themselves to be inferior compensate for their inferiority with self-expansion, growth, and competence. According to Adler's theory, the old person encountering physical and social changes would first feel inferior and then counteract that inferiority with attempts at creativity and self-perfection.

Death had an important position in the theories of Freud, Jung, and Adler. Jung focused on the spiritual, mystical aspect of death; Freud was awed by its inevitability; and Adler worked to overcome helplessness in the face of it.

> For Freud, death was a biological process he struggled to comprehend *intellectually, theoretically*, perhaps in an effort to master his own uneasiness. For Jung, death was but another aspect of an already paradoxical existence, inviting one to explore its spiritual and psychological reality. For Adler, death was the ultimate enemy, the supreme obstacle to self-fulfillment, the paramount state of helplessness against which one must struggle at all costs.[*]

The ego psychologists present a positive view of the psychological work of late life. The old person faced with physical, social, and psychological changes need not be forced into rigidity or senility. The aged person may instead develop unique, creative patterns of continued personal closure and ego integrity.

[*]Monte, C. *Beneath the mask: An introduction to theories of personality.* New York: Holt, Rinehart & Winston, 1980, p. 315

*Erik Erikson*    Erikson has had the greatest impact of all the ego psychologists on the field of gerontology. His theory derives from Freud's but focuses on healthy maturation and adjustment, whereas psychoanalytic theory emphasizes neurotic and conflicted maladjustment. According to Erikson's psychosocial conflict theory, personality development goes through a series of eight crises or stages in which ego development takes place. At each stage a crisis is either successfully resolved or fails to be resolved. Failure to resolve a crisis leads to incomplete or inappropriate development of some aspect of the personality. This negative resolution does not prevent later personality development, but it does make later development more difficult.

Erikson's stages of psychosocial crisis correlate with Freud's psychosexual stages (Table 9-1). The crisis stages reflect interaction between the maturing person and constantly changing environmental demands. Like Freud, Erikson stresses the hierarchical organization of these stages and their reliance on each other for skill development. For Erikson, however, the human personality develops in stages predetermined by the person's readiness to respond to, perceive, and interact with a widening social radius. Society in turn is structured to meet and encourage the succession of social interaction types manifesting the psychosocial stages. Society also acts to assure and encourage the timing and sequence of their unfolding by social norms and stratification. This formulation is similar to the notion of disengagement which was also believed to reflect a mutual process of withdrawal by society and the aged person. Disengagement is discussed later in this chapter.

According to Erikson, adults must resolve two crises before they reach old age: intimacy versus isolation for young adults, and generativity versus stagnation for middle-aged persons. The young adult with a newly fused sense of identity is willing to risk that identity by fusing with the identities of others. The healthy

Table 9-1    *Life-cycle ego crises of Erikson as contrasted with psychoanalytic stages of development*

| Life stage | Psychosocial crisis | Psychoanalytic stage |
|---|---|---|
| Infancy (birth–2 years) | Trust vs. mistrust | Oral stage |
| Toddlerhood (2–4 years) | Autonomy vs. shame or doubt | Anal stage |
| Early childhood (5–7 years) | Initiative vs. guilt | Phallic stage |
| Middle childhood (8–12 years) | Industry vs. inferiority | Latency stage |
| Adolescence (13-22 years) | Identity vs. role confusion | Early genital stage |
| Young adulthood (23-35 years) | Intimacy vs. isolation | Genital stage |
| Middle adulthood (35-60 years) | Generativity vs. stagnation | |
| Late adulthood (60 years and older) | Integrity vs. despair | |

young adult becomes open to intimate social contacts, which may demand self-sacrifice and love of another. Erikson believes that a person can truly know himself or herself only through mutual verification with a partner or confidant (Monte, 1980).

Middle-aged maturity follows this intimacy through to love for the next generation, as exemplified by offspring. Concern with the next generation need not be directed only toward one's children. It may be manifested by a concern for the future and for the continuation of mankind's works. The middle-aged adult who resolves this stage negatively is unable to find value in aiding future generations. Such a person has a pervasive sense of boredom and stagnation in the performance of life tasks. This results in an unsatisfying life. As Erikson stated, "mature man needs to be needed, and maturity needs guidance as well as encouragement from what has been produced and must be taken care of (Erikson, 1950, p. 267)." The stagnating adult has not mastered the virtue of care and therefore does not receive it from others.

The final stage in Erikson's theory is that of ego integrity versus despair. According to Erikson, the key to harmonious personality development in late years is the ability to resolve this psychosocial crisis. Ego integrity is a full unification of personality that enables individuals to view their lives with satisfaction and contentment. Social relations and a productive life promote this sense of purposiveness.

Although aware of the relativity of all the various life styles which have given meaning to human striving, the possessor of integrity is ready to defend the

*Contributions to colleges and universities are one way in which elderly people can show concern for the future and for the continuation of mankind's created works.*

dignity of his own life style against all physical and economic threats. For he knows that an individual life is the accidental coincidence of but one life cycle with but one segment of history; and that for him all human integrity stands or falls with the one style of integrity which he partakes. The style of integrity developed by his culture or civilization thus becomes the . . . seal of his moral paternity of himself. . . . In such final consolidation, death loses its sting.*

The lack of accrued ego integration is frequently signaled by fear of death and the feeling that life is too short. Individuals experiencing despair feel that time is running out and that it is too late to start another life or try alternative paths to fulfillment. Consequently such persons view their lives with regret and disappointment. Many persons in despair verbalize the wish that they had used their potential to gain goals established earlier in their lives but never attained. Such persons are often avoided by others who do not know how to relate to their despair. As will be seen in the next chapter, loneliness and isolation are often predictors of psychopathology in late life.

This final psychosocial crisis is precipitated by the awareness of personal mortality caused by retirement, the death of spouse or peers, and the changing social roles associated with late life. Increased introspection and reminiscence leading to the achievement of final ego integrity are most productively carried out with a confidant, close family member, or significant other person in the individual's life.

The dependence of Erikson's stages upon each other is well illustrated in the strong relationship between the stagnated and the despairing person. Persons who did not develop the virtue of caring in middle age often find themselves alone when facing this final life task in old age. These persons risk dwelling on emotionally laden, negative, or unresolved events of early life. With no one to reflect on these events with them, they often fixate on them and end up giving themselves up to despair.

## Social Learning Theory

Learning theory as a paradigm for viewing human behavior is far different from the other theories discussed. For most behaviorists personality is the same as behavior, i.e., one is what one does. To understand personality the behavioral psychologist must investigate and control the stimulus conditions that precede and determine behavior. The emphasis of this approach is therefore not on unconscious mechanisms but on observable behaviors, which are the consequences of reward and punishment.

In 1950 John Dollard and Neal Miller developed a social learning theory many aspects of which are applicable to the field of aging. At the outset of their 1950 statement they set out the goals of their new theory:

*Erikson, E.H. *Childhood and society*. New York: W.W. Norton, 1963, p. 268

Human behavior is learned; precisely that behavior which is widely felt to characterize man as a rational being, or as a member of a particular nation or social class, is acquired rather than innate. To understand thoroughly any item of human behavior — either in the social group or in the individual life — one must know the psychological principles involved in its learning and the social conditions under which this learning took place. It is not enough to know either principles or conditions of learning; in order to predict behavior both must be known.*

Learning and personality as envisioned by Dollard and Miller include elements borrowed from Freudian, cognitive, and other intrapsychic concepts. These elements were combined with key terms from other paradigms into an objective learning theory (Table 9-2).

Unlike more orthodox behaviorists such as Skinner, Dollard and Miller define a response as both the objective behavioral response and the implicit internal response. For example, fear for Dollard and Miller is an avoidance response plus internal cognition plus a physiological response. Reinforcement is any event that tends to increase the probability of a response being repeated.

For the social learning theorists personality is the sum of socialization experience and social roles. This framework is compatible with certain sociological or social psychological views of old age. It is also congruent with the notion of adaptation and learned helplessness advanced by Seligman (1975). In the social learning framework the old adult facing a crisis with a reduced adaptive capacity may feel fear, misery, stupidity, and helplessness, as suggested by Dollard and Miller. If this crisis persists or if additional crises are added, the person may begin to show confusion, memory loss, and health problems. This pattern of stress response is discussed further in Chapter 10.

Table 9-2  *Dollard and Miller's translation of psychoanalytic terms into behavioral learning theory*

| Psychoanalytic terms | Behavioral learning theory terms |
| --- | --- |
| Homeostasis | Need or tension reduction |
| Pleasure principle | Reinforcement |
| Primary process notion | Classical conditioning |
| Secondary process | Instrumental conditioning |
| Conflict | Experimental neurosis |
| Anxiety | Learned fear |
| Transference | Generalization gradients |
| Repression | Learned inhibition of cue-producing responses |
| Ego strength | Ability of learned drives to compete with primary drives |

*Dollard, J., & Miller, N.E. *Personality and psychotherapy.* New York: McGraw Hill, 1950, p. 25

Learning theory has difficulties in developing a coherent theory of personality change in adulthood and old age. However, it presents a useful framework in which to consider behaviors that occur in old age. Aside from Dollard and Miller's theory, behavior theory is not really a theory of personality. It borrows its concepts from other sources, is concerned with processes rather than structures, and emphasizes "pieces" of discrete behavior rather than the whole fabric of personality. Nevertheless, notions such as situational demands, internalized reinforcers, and the impact of environment remain vital to our understanding of behavioral continuity and change in late life.

### Cognitive Psychologists

The cognitive view of personality is relatively new. Although all personality theorists seek to predict and understand behavior, the cognitive theorists do not see physical stimuli as the main determiners of behavior. According to them, reality is determined by the perceptions and expectations of events. Cognitive theorists claim that each person constructs reality in an idiosyncratic manner based on past experiences and association with present circumstances (Kelly, 1955). Reinforcement per se does not determine behavior, nor do purely unconscious mechanisms (Maddi, 1980; Monte, 1980).

Much of cognitive psychology theory has great applicability to aging. For example, according to this model anxiety occurs when the individual's cognitive construct system provides no way of dealing with an event. Anxiety is positive in that it may result in a change or broadening of the system. Threat occurs when a fundamental change in a person's constructs is about to occur, and guilt is the result of the conflict between a person's behavior and the person's ideal self (Kelly, 1955).

These notions may be readily observed in the behavior of old persons, as in the following case:

> Mr. Jones, aged eighty-two, had been placed in a skilled nursing facility following a cerebrovascular accident. His mental faculties were unimpaired, but he was left with a fairly severe paralysis of his right side. Nursing home placement was required, since his eighty-three-year-old wife was unable to care for him at home.
>
> In the first few weeks in the nursing facility Mr. Jones alternated between abusive and compliant behavior. His guilt and anxiety over his seeming inability to control his behavior were apparent. He verbalized fears of being abandoned to his son and often accused the staff of trying to keep him an invalid. As his stay continued and his physical therapy progressed, his interest in patient activities increased and his moods stabilized. He and his family began to enjoy their time together and make plans for his return home.

The above case presents the relation between a person's expectancies or perceptions of a situation and behavior in it. Old people confronted with a novel or ambiguous situation frequently feel anxious or threatened. As they gradually adapt to the situation their anxiety subsides. The cognitive psychologist believes that this occurs because of re-evaluation of the situation as nonthreatening.

The cognitive personality view is particularly useful in any consideration of the behaviors relating to mental and physical health in old age. Human beings' continual attempts to predict and control the events of experience are nowhere better tested than in the diverse crises of autonomy encountered in old age. A person who is unable to change or adjust to such crises as altered physical function may start on a fairly rapid path to decompensation. The stability and coherence of the well-adjusted person, regardless of that person's age, arise from within and without — from the person's own strengths and from the supportive environment in which the person lives. The biggest predictor of adjustment is often the way in which the person is able to construct reality and reconstruct his or her role in it after a crisis has occurred.

Illness is an example of such a crisis. To a large degree prognosis, timing, and duration of illness are affected by the afflicted person's perception of the sort of illness he or she has and past experience or encounters with such an illness. The cases of sudden death one sees in old people who have recently lost a spouse may well reflect feelings of helplessness and inability to construct an alternative reality alone.

Another example of the impact of cognition on personality and adjustment may be seen in the notion of competence or mastery as developed by Robert White (1959). White's view was that human beings are motivated by a need to produce an effect on the environment and that the main reward people seek is the pleasure of a successful act.

This model of effectance motivation or drive for mastery is illustrated in Figure 9-3. Effectance motivation drives a person to make mastery attempts, which are cognitive, social, or physical in nature. Persons who receive positive rewards for these attempts at independent mastery and are not reinforced for dependence in a particular situation are likely to have positive expectations of success in that situation in the future. This perceived competence leads to expectancy of success in other situations and a positive self-image. These persons see themselves as powerful, in control of their own life paths, and in control of situations they find themselves in (Newman & Newman, 1980). Feelings of self-control, self-determination, and autonomy are important aspects of mental health, particularly in the frail elderly, who may least have access to them.

## Conclusions

There is considerable diversity in theories on personality structure in late life; there is also no general theory that attempts to explain the continuities and discontinuities of late-life personality. Each theory presented in this section has applicability to our understanding of late-life personality structure. The ego psychologists see personality growth and integration as life-cycle processes. They feel that ego integrity and self-fulfillment are necessary for adequate mental health at any age.

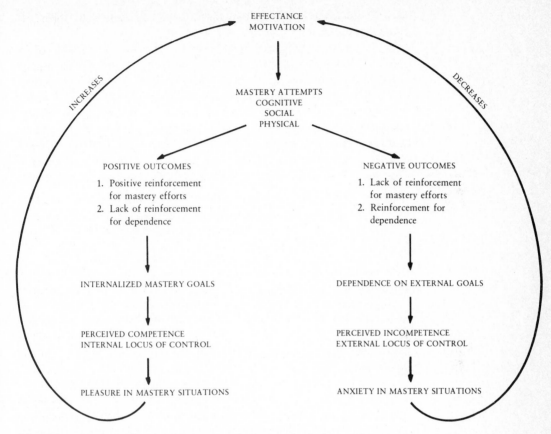

(Adapted from: Harter, S. Effective motivation reconsidered: Toward a developmental model. *Human Development*, 1978, *21*(1), 34–64.)

*Figure 9–3   Developmental model of effectance motivation*

The learning theorists stress the situational determinants of behavior in an individual's response to events and persons in the environment. A more comprehensive approach to understanding a person's behavior in late life can be formulated through a combination of these two approaches.

It may be that much of personality remains stable throughout life. Basic ways of dealing with familiar events, situations, and people may not significantly change because they reflect the individual's self-concept. When faced with stressful or novel situations, however, a person may exhibit discontinuities. These discontinuities may become integrated into the personality if they are effective in helping the person adapt to the unfamiliar situation (Butler & Lewis, 1977; Lowenthal, 1977; Neugarten, 1977). The manner in which the personality of each person has developed, its stability or lack thereof, and the responses the person makes to stress are unique but coherent.

Gerontologists and life-span developmental psychologists have focused on the need to determine what sorts of factors guide the personal development of individuals as they age. Riegel (1977) has presented the notion of *dialectic processes* to explain this development. According to this approach, there is constant interaction between the person and the environment in which "performance dialogues" develop (Riegel, 1977). These "dialogues" are patterns of experience and action that are co-determined by inner biological and sociological-cultural changes. Riegel's theory

> focuses on concrete human beings and the gradual modifications (neurological and psychological) or sudden shifts (accident, disease) in their biological make-up that force them to change constructively their individual psychological operations and, thereby, also the social conditions under which they live. (Riegel, 1977, p. 87)

The theory, a fairly new one, may prove fruitful in describing and predicting behavioral patterns emerging in late life.

An alternative theory explores the nature of interpersonal commitments as determinants of late-life behavior. Some researchers believe that the need for competence or mastery becomes a commitment to survival in advanced old age (Lowenthal, 1977). Areas of commitment may thus offer a promising theoretical framework.

Lowenthal (1977) argues that researchers building unifying theories must consider fluid constructs flowing from such commitments to survival. She has suggested hope and self-concept as two such crucial constructs. Hope is seen as a sense of time projection of the life span. Any person seized with temporal anxiety finds the freedom to live numbed. Humans of all ages are beings in process, and if that process is halted, depression, despair, and death result. Self-concept involves personal knowledge and control. There is no definitive work assessing change in self-concept across the life span. It may be that an earlier self is the main referent for old people and that they project their former selves through their reminiscences to reduce the conflict between the real and the ideal. It has been found, for example, that old persons asked what age they feel themselves to be either give the age of the asker or say they feel middle-aged (Lowenthal, 1977).

Both hope and self-concept are involved in autonomy and adaptation at any age. A big part of adaptive capacity is determined by the degree to which one feels in control of one's life.

## Successful Aging

As said earlier, personality comprises a permanent core, the self, and temporary adaptations necessitated by environmental stresses. Personality is largely determined by social interactions; each person's individuality is determined and pre-

*Groups of friends expand the individual's contacts beyond the home space of the family.*

served in the context of family and ethnic groups and societal, friendship, and work groups (Back, 1976). Ironically, although these groups offer the person continuity, they are also the cause of those stresses that may lead to discontinuity and crisis.

Successful aging is difficult to define because it reflects the values of the person doing the labeling as well as of the society. Most gerontologists agree, however, that successful aging has two important facets: an inner criterion (i.e., life satisfaction) and an outer criterion (i.e., social roles and interpersonal responsibilities). Like personality, patterns of aging reflect the person and the responses of the significant groups in which the person affirms him or herself.

Havighurst (1973) and Peck (1968) have suggested developmental tasks the completion of which acts as life span markers and signposts of adjustment. These developmental tasks combine a drive toward growth with the demands, constraints, and opportunities of the social environment. Some of the tasks are biologically precipitated, whereas others reflect the demands of social role changes. However, each task combines aspects of the biological, psychological, and social environment of the person. It is important to the person's overall adjustment that the tasks for middle age and old age as described by Peck be resolved (Table 9-3).

The tasks of middle age involve resolving the issue of socializing versus sexualizing in human relations, valuing wisdom over physical powers, retaining mental flexibility over mental rigidity, and retaining cathetic flexibility versus cathetic

Table 9-3    *Peck's developmental tasks of middle and old age*

| Life stage | Developmental tasks |
|---|---|
| Middle age | Socializing vs. sexualizing in human relations |
| | Valuing wisdom over physical powers |
| | Mental flexibility vs. mental rigidity |
| | Cathetic flexibility vs. cathetic impoverishment |
| Old age | Ego differentiation vs. work role preoccupation |
| | Body transcendence vs. body preoccupation |
| | Ego transcendence vs. ego preoccupation |

impoverishment. These tasks reflect the individual's realization that his or her physical abilities and social world are changing. What society values — power, youth, attractiveness, quickness — is often no longer in the possession of middle-aged persons. Their children have left home, and spouses often died, and they must reinvest their emotions in other objects or persons. They must maintain a positive mental outlook in coping with these changes. Persons who are unable to complete the positive aspects of these tasks and instead internalize the negative components are often maladjusted or troubled when they enter late life.

The developmental tasks of late life as envisioned by Peck include three normative crises: ego differentiation versus work role preoccupation, body transcendence versus body preoccupation, and ego transcendence versus ego preoccupation. These tasks provide the elderly person with the opportunity for psychological growth and continued adjustment.

The first task, ego differentiation versus work role preoccupation, has as its central issue vocational retirement, which presents a crucial shift in the individual's value system. The person must reappraise his or her personal worth in terms other than career. The individual must establish an interest in living rather than despair over the loss of an important social role. Successful aging often depends on the establishment of a variety of valued self-attributes so that any of several potential alternatives may be pursued with equal satisfaction.

The problem of body transcendence versus preoccupation must also be resolved in old age. As stated in previous chapters, old age often brings with it decreased physical abilities, reduced adaptability, increased susceptibility to illness, and increased bodily aches and pains. Persons who have been concerned with the beauty and function of the body throughout adulthood may deem these changes the gravest of insults. Such persons may become so preoccupied with these physical changes that they turn away from social activities and even constructive psychological work. In contrast, people who transcend their bodily selves may experience declining health, but they enjoy life greatly, emphasizing satisfying personal relationships and active mental work. Only sheer physical destruction can remove the self-esteem and self-fulfillment of such persons.

The final task, ego transcendence versus preoccupation, is essentially that of coming to terms with the reality of one's own death. This reality is often confronted for the first time in the later years, when the death of a spouse and peers indicate one's own mortality. Persons who transcend the fear of death live life fully because they realize that they do in fact extend themselves in time through their children, their friends, and their contributions to culture. They realize that these relationships have an impact that goes beyond their own mortal reality. Persons who do not achieve this realization in old age suffer from a sense of profound loss and depression. Ironically, it is the acceptance of death rather than the fear of death that frees the elderly from time.

These developmental tasks occur in roughly the same sequence for all old people, even those from different cultures. They are not sequentially invariant or necessarily hierarchical, and they do not indicate actual structural changes in personality (Neugarten, 1977). They do, however, indicate an optimum point of encounter with the social environment, and the resolution of this encounter directs the course of each subsequent encounter.

Various longitudinal studies have looked at patterns of successful and unsuccessful aging. In the 1960s there was a series of studies looking at changes in personality in late life. These research efforts were largely multidimensional, i.e., they looked at many aspects of psychological, social, and biological functioning. They used large representative samples, combined interrelated studies, and used multiple convergent measures to assess personality (e.g., objective and subjective instruments, interviews) (Neugarten, 1977). Despite the diversity of measures and methodologies used, certain broad commonalities emerged from these investigations (Neugarten et al., 1964; Oden, 1968; Reichard et al., 1962; Riley et al., 1968):

The personalities of old persons were generally found to be more rigid than the personalities of young persons, i.e., old persons were less disposed than young adults to adapt to changing stimuli.

The attitudes of old persons were found to be more dogmatic than those of younger persons, i.e., old persons were more likely than young persons to hold to rules without exception.

Older people were found to manifest a greater tolerance for ambiguity and to show less susceptibility to social pressure than young adults.

Old people were found to be more passive and conforming in their behavior than young adults.

Old people were found to be more preoccupied with their own emotions and physical functions and generally to be more introverted and concerned with their inner world than young adults.

Some of these changes (e.g., the increased conservatism and dogmatism) were believed by the researchers to be due to cultural factors or cohort effects, whereas others appeared to be a function of the loss of quality of physical contact with the outside world. It was also speculated that some of these changes were due to a decline in intellectual functioning (Neugarten, 1977).

Earlier studies of single dimensions of personality had not found such consistency. The extent of egocentrism, dependency, dogmatism, rigidity, cautiousness, conformity, hope, and creativity showed considerable variation across studies. Only introversion was consistent across all studies, uniformly increasing in middle age. In general, however, these single-dimensional studies also suffered from a lack of consistency in definitions, measures, types of samples, and use of controls. Another common flaw of many of these studies was their use of time or age as a dependent or independent variable. Time cannot be such a variable because it causes nothing to occur; it is merely an index of the relations between causes and effects or behaviors and their consequences (Bromley, 1970; Neugarten, 1977).

In general these longitudinal studies looked at personality and adaptation in late life. Although these are not the same concept, when they are separated personality predicts adaptation. The particular traits that predict adaptation, however, vary as a function of time in the life cycle, environmental and cultural factors, and salient developmental tasks.

### Reichard, Livson, and Peterson

The longitudinal study of Reichard, Livson, and Peterson (1962) grew out of the theoretical formulations of Else Frenkel-Brunswik described earlier in this chapter. This was a study of eighty-seven men from fifty-five to eighty-four years of age at the onset of the study. Half of these men were retired; the other half were not. They were all volunteers, a fact that may have had a serious impact on the outcome of the study in that volunteers are generally healthier, more intelligent, and wealthier than the general population. This was a study of the effects of retirement in addition to an investigation of personality change with age.

Reichard et al. (1962) found that retired men engaged in different patterns of activity than did workers of the same age. They were less active in their recreational pursuits and more active in domestic work, household upkeep, social visiting, and productive hobbies. They showed increased political interest, especially in pension and earnings-related areas. Retired men tended to stress the disadvantages of retirement, whereas those who were still working tended to stress the positive aspects of retirement. The main complaint of the retired men was their reduced financial circumstances.

Retired men were more likely than working men to show fatigue and physical weakness, although they claimed to be in better health and were not excessively concerned with health problems. Retired men were less anxious than working men and tended to see age as an achievement in its own right. They also tended to show considerably less anxiety about death than younger men or working men. The retired group were less defensive, less suspicious, less erratic, and more open and trusting in their social interactions. The men nearing retirement tended to have negative personality traits such as feelings of inadequacy, resentment, depression, and pessimism, and they were often apathetic or contemptuous of themselves.

Reichard et al. (1962) concluded from their research that the time immediately before retirement is a critical adjustment period for most men. Retirement appeared to act as a social marker for old age. The researchers stated that the problem with retirement was "not so much 'being old' as 'becoming old' " (Reichard et al., 1962).

Reichard et al. (1962) determined that there are five major strategies or patterns of adjustment to old age. The well-adapted men had three types of personalities: the *mature* personality, marked by constructive coping efforts; the *rocking chair* personality, marked by dependency on the wife, who was dominant in the relationship; and the *armored* personality, marked by defensiveness. The armored personalities were emotionally overcontrolled as a carryover from earlier neuroticism. They stayed actively engaged in society and social relationships for defensive reasons. They kept busy to avoid death and old age. To the extent that the armored

*Maintaining political interests and making the political voice of senior citizens heard can help people adjust to retirement.*

men were able to keep up their activities, they appeared to adapt successfully to their retirement years.

Two patterns of poor adaptation to old age emerged from these studies. *Angry* men were marked by excessive hostility. They were not depressed, but they tended to blame others for their failures. They were often prejudiced against minority groups, were habit bound, and held unrealistic notions about themselves and the world. They often had unstable occupational histories and were downwardly mobile. They maintained high activity levels to avoid dealing with aging and death and were often envious of and hostile toward persons younger than themselves. The most negative pattern of aging was found in the *self-haters*, who turned their hostility inward. The socioeconomic status of these men was low. The self-haters were passive, depressed, unable to accept responsibility, and often deficient in their interpersonal relations. They often saw themselves as victims of circumstance and in their late years were filled with regret and self-recrimination. They tended to see death as a release from a highly unsatisfactory existence.

Degree of life satisfaction generally declined through these five categories. The least adaptive personality also showed the least satisfaction with life. However, these personality patterns did not develop suddenly upon retirement; they mostly reflected earlier life patterns carried over into late life (Bromley, 1974; Neugarten, 1977).

### The Kansas City Studies

Beginning in the late 1950s a group of researchers from the University of Chicago's Committee on Human Development began a series of studies in Kansas City. The researchers, who included Cumming, Henry, Neugarten, Lieberman, Tobin, and Gutmann, studied over seven hundred community-dwelling adults who were between forty and ninety years of age at the onset of the research. These subjects were followed for five years. They were assumed to be in good health, although no physiological or health data were ever gathered.

Cumming and Henry (1961), who studied 275 community residents for 5 years, found a common pattern of *disengagement* in all very old subjects. They defined this disengagement as a process of mutual withdrawal between aging persons and the social system to which they belong. When the process is complete, the balance between the person and society has shifted, and the person's relations with other people show increased psychological distancing and decreased social interaction. Cumming and Henry looked upon this process as a positive rather than negative experience for the elderly. According to them, since old age is a time of decreased sensory input, increased introversion, and increased nearness to death, decreased emotional investment in people and events is adaptive. Cumming and Henry saw disengagement as a universal, biologically based process.

*Disengagement theory*, as it was called, sparked considerable controversy among gerontologists. Many liked the theory but found it unjustified. The consensus today is that disengagement is a process initiated earlier in life and that it is

*Activity theorists suggest that the retired person needs to remain active and productive and that such involvement leads to increased life satisfaction.*

probably not the best pattern of adjustment to old age. Research has found that old adults who remain active are typically happier than those who have withdrawn. In addition, many of the past societal conditions that forced adults into restricted environments have changed; early retirement, improved health care, increased social security benefits, and higher education levels have opened new avenues of pursuit for retired old persons. Because of these social factors disengagement may be discouraged and more active lives encouraged than in the past. The current view is that disengagement is one of many patterns of aging; its widespread acceptance by most old people (if it existed independent of the research design that discovered it) is a thing of the past.

Despite its weaknesses, disengagement theory sparked new efforts at understanding successful aging. George Maddox and his colleagues at Duke University countered with their *activity theory*, which suggested that the retired person needs to remain active and productive and that such involvement leads to increased life satisfaction. These researchers felt that happiness and adaptation originate from involvement and change to meet life events in addition to the finding of substitutes for terminated roles.

Activity theory presented a needed balance to the concept of disengagement, but it too had its problems. For example, not all activities sustain self-concept, and it is not known how a person's sense of control or competence affects activity. Activity theory had limited empirical support, perhaps in part because it represented an oversimplification of the questions involved. Despite these criticisms, however, there appears to be a correlation among morale, adjustment, and activity levels.

*Neugarten, Havighurst, and Tobin* (1968) determined that four general personality patterns exist across the life span and are carried into old age. These four patterns are the *integrated* and *armored* personalities, both of whom are high in life satisfaction; the *passive-dependent* personalities, who show moderate life satisfaction; and the *unintegrated* personalities, who have low life satisfaction.

Integrated personalities, according to the researchers, have a complex inner life and are relaxed and highly accepting of their own impulses. They rearrange their behavior patterns to meet situational changes and are therefore highly adaptable. Integrated personalities may be of three types: "reorganizers," "focused," or "disengaged." The reorganizers are the optimum agers of our culture. They reorganize their lives as they age so as to find new activities to replace old or lost activities. Those who follow the focused pattern limit their activities somewhat as they age. They choose to focus their energy and attention only on activities they really enjoy. Finally, the disengaged persons fit the classic Cumming and Henry pattern. They have chosen voluntarily to move away from social roles but are still interested in the world. They are high in self-direction and high in self-esteem. These three patterns are called *integrated personalities* because the persons themselves set the patterns of their activity and adaptability. They are healthy, strong personality types.

Armored or defended personalities maintain tight control over their impulses in an effort to build strong defenses against their anxiety over aging. They are an achievement-oriented group and maintain high life satisfaction to the extent that they remain active and deny aging. There are two patterns of armored personality: "holding on" and "constricted." Persons engaged in holding on persist in the patterns of middle age. They try to hold onto their looks, jobs, clothes, and anything else that marks them as younger. They perceive aging as a threat to their self-esteem. Constricted persons are even more anxious over aging. They suffer from feelings of impending doom and channel all their energies into feeling, looking, and acting young. When the defenses they have erected to prevent the reality of aging from setting in collapse, the life satisfaction and life-styles they have created may also be destroyed.

Passive-dependent personalities may be of two sorts: "succorance seeking" and "apathetic." Persons in both of these patterns have medium to low life satisfaction. Succorance-seeking persons need to lean on others and persist in medium levels of activity as long as others direct them. Apathetic persons, in contrast, need to lean on others to successfully complete anything but don't seek others out. These are strikingly passive people whose role activity is low because of their extreme apathy.

The unintegrated or disorganized personality suffers from gross defects in psychological functioning. These persons show poor thought processes and poor ego functioning. Many have functioned only marginally throughout life and have traditionally been close to institutionalization. Their life satisfaction is medium at best.

Neugarten et al. (1968) found that these personality differences, which exist at all ages, are magnified in old age because of experience and practice time. Neugarten concluded that with age people become increasingly "like themselves," both their negative and their positive traits becoming amplified.

## Oden

Oden (1968), whose studies were considered in some detail in Chapter 8, studied persons who had graduated from Ohio State University around 1921. Oden found that persons who were very intelligent were in old age physically healthier, richer, better adjusted, and less likely to need psychological care or commit suicide than the general population. These old persons were more likely to have retained their capacity for original thinking and ingenuity. They had also stayed involved with others in matters of mutual interest. However, they were also more restless, obsessive, and inclined to complain about family members. Oden believed that this apparently negative trait may actually have indicated full engagement in the lives of others.

Oden also reported that subjects with fairly obvious intellectual impairment (though still within the normal range) were more likely to have histories of disease and poor health in their later years than the intellectually superior persons. These moderately impaired persons complained little about their work or finances but were also less articulate. They tended to feel greater satisfaction that they had attained old age than did the intellectually superior old persons.

## Maas and Kuypers

The longitudinal study of Maas and Kuypers (1974) focused on thirty- to seventy-year-olds as they aged. Like other longitudinal studies, this study found that its subjects were generally superior to the general population in socioeconomic status, health, and education. The data collected in this study comprised interviews, diaries, and questionnaires investigating four dimensions: contexts (current health and environmental conditions, socioeconomic status, health of spouse, place of residence); life-style (the major activities of the person's life); personality pattern; and antecedents (early adulthood characteristics such as economics and social activities).

Maas and Kuypers distinguished four major life-styles among their aging subjects: the family-centered person, the hobbyist, the remotely sociable person, and the unwell or disorganized person. The first two patterns are the most adaptive in that they bring continued life satisfaction and personal fulfillment. The remotely sociable person is moderately adaptable, and the unwell person may be uninvolved with others because of mental or physical health problems.

The study concluded that health is the most salient factor influencing both

*Keeping up old interests or finding new ones can provide a continued sense of purpose and personal fulfillment.*

life-style and personality. For example, an old person who is withdrawn or disengaged has often become so because of a decline in health. Health problems early in life were found to cut across social, economic, and physical spheres of life. Later health problems were often found to have been foreshadowed by earlier ones. At least part of a person's personality pattern and life-style may arise out of attempts to adapt to the changes precipitated by such health difficulties.

Most of the elderly persons Maas and Kuypers (1974) studied seemed to be enjoying a personally fulfilling old age without any significant decline, depression, or disengagement. They had many different life-styles, indicating that there is no one way of successfully aging and that old age per se does not determine life-style or personality. Maas and Kuypers state that many of the problems of old age have their roots in early adulthood; this conclusion is strong support for the life-span perspective. Diversity in activities and involvements helps most old people overcome the hardships associated with any single loss. It is only when stresses and losses accumulate that the burden becomes overwhelming.

### Conclusions

If the results of various studies considering personality, intellectual ability, and health status with age were combined, five general patterns of aging would emerge: The *elite* aging, or centenarians; the *survivors* of longitudinal studies as presented in our discussion of intellectual ability; the *normal* agers; the *institutionalized* aged; and the *impaired* aged who are not institutionalized. In each of these patterns there would be still wider ranges of individual differences.

In general anxiety increases with age, especially in women, who are more often alone than men. Cautiousness also increases, and confidence tends to decrease. Persons who are effective at overcoming frustration, resolving conflicts, and achieving some socially acceptable means of satisfaction maintain a high level of personal adjustment. These well-adjusted people, the successful agers, are happy, confident, sociable, and high in self-esteem and productive activity. The opposite is of course true for persons who adjust poorly; they are hostile, unhappy, fearful, guilty, and helpless (Bromley, 1974).

It has often been suggested that illness or poor health is accompanied by maladjustment. Because of this view many professionals and laypeople have viewed old age as a time of inevitable psychopathology. However, persons may be ill or disabled and still make an adequate adjustment to the new demands of the environment. They may manifest fortitude in the face of ill health, reconciliation with people, and growth in self-knowledge even until the time of death.

Life-style and personality depend on the complex interaction of such factors as

The person at the beginning of the process
Recent changes in the person's physical abilities
Recent changes in the person's social system
The person's socioeconomic status and residential situation
Whether the person's cognitive abilities show consistency or change
Whether the person shows consistency or change in activity, interests, moods, creativity, adjustment, or sense of control
The factors impinging on the person's life space
The person's life satisfaction
The person's capacity for restoring balance in the face of stress by coping actively
The social competence demonstrated by the person (Thomae, 1980).

Persons who age successfully are often socially competent, in control of relevant portions of their lives, mentally active, and flexible in their methods of coping with change. These traits are not found only in the young; they are found in persons of all ages, and given the proper circumstances, they may be developed at any age. Aging persons, like young persons, create the patterns of life that give them the greatest ego involvement and satisfaction.

**Adjustment**

"Successful" aging varies from person to person, being largely dependent on the sort of personality the individual has always manifested. Similarly, patterns of adjustment depend on the person's resources, health, and experiences. Adjustment, or positive mental health, also reflects the values of society and culture-specific indices of appropriate behavior.

Jahoda (1958) was one of the first persons to discuss positive criteria for mental health. Her six positive criteria were

A positive self-attitude
Growth and self-actualization

Integration of the personality
Autonomy
Reality perception
Environmental mastery.

Jahoda (1958) and other theorists have regarded these traits as fairly enduring attributes, not merely situational functions that change with environmental demands. According to Jahoda's view, mentally healthy persons basically like themselves, continue to grow and integrate experiences, are realistic in their assessment of self and environment, are self-determining, and master the environment in which they live. Autonomy and personal choice are also crucial aspects of adjustment in late life (Fries & Crapo, 1981; Seligman, 1975; Thomae, 1980). Any factor that acts to limit either of these factors may threaten psychological stability or adjustment.

### Comparative Psychology: David Gutmann

Gutmann's work (1964, 1971, 1975, 1977) is a unique combination of anthropological and psychoanalytic traditions directed at explaining cross-cultural continuities in aging. Gutmann has contrasted the differential patterns of aging for men and women in various cultural systems. His research has supported others (Cumming & Henry, 1961; Neugarten et al., 1964) in the description of broad patterns of adjustment emerging in late life: a move from active to passive mastery of environmental situations, and a trend beginning in midlife toward increasing interiority.

In his work with Asian, Middle Eastern, African, and American Indian social systems, Gutmann (1964, 1971, 1975, 1977) described universal age differences in behavior between young and old men. In general, young men deal actively with physical threats and push to achieve worldly success. Old men shift the focus of their concern to the next world and deal with threats from and communicate with supernatural powers.

> Young men are expected, through their *own* energies, to wrest resource and power from physical nature, from enemy or from both; older men are expected, through rituals or through postures of accommodation, to coax power — whether for good or malign purposes — from the supernaturals. (Gutmann, 1977, p. 305)

Gutmann has also described other cultural universals that occur in old age, including feminization of traits and increased intellectual activity and introversion. He sees old men becoming power brokers in their societies because of their ability to negotiate with the gods.

The role of old women described by Gutmann (1977) is not as positive as that of men. Women are often seen as witches in primitive cultures. The lethal nature of women is chronicled in a folk parable from Morocco (Gutmann, 1977):

> At birth a boy is surrounded by one hundred devils, a girl by one hundred angels. With each passing year one is exchanged, so that the woman ends up surrounded by devils and the man by angels.

Gutmann ascribes these negative attributions to the increase in aggression seen as "bad power," that occurs in women as they age.

Gutmann has provided research support for Jung's stance that introversion and femininity increase with age; he has also generalized certain criteria of good mental health from Western to other cultures.

> Societies that sponsor an egocentric, self-seeking spirit in the population will be lethal to old and young alike. But societies which sponsor altruism and the formation of internalized objects provide security to these vulnerable cohorts. (Gutmann, 1977, p 315)

In cultures such as the latter, old people serve as links to an enduring tradition. They relate the past to the present for younger cohorts. Old persons' behaviors such as reminiscences are therefore not seen as intrusive but rather as instrumental to the preservation of traditional values. Such societies view the aged as valuable members. Such societies also judge the mental health of the aged as positive because of their valid societal role, environmental mastery, and self-determination. Although these attributes are manifested differently in old and young people, they differ in kind, not quality.

### Accommodating Old People to Society: John Lozier

Lozier (1975), like Gutmann, defines the successful ager as someone who fits into the social framework in a way that ensures security and influence. He presents examples of accommodation by old people to aging in the rural Appalachian community of Laurel Creek and the urban setting of New Orleans.

In Laurel Creek, the prime social value is justice; it is incumbent on citizens to give what they properly owe and get what they rightfully claim. In this community young people must pay attention to the legitimate claims of old people. Such a social value will work only in social systems in which people pay attention to what their neighbors do and require. According to Lozier, such social enforcement will not work in anonymous city life.

In Laurel Creek old men who realize they are failing "retire to the porch" (Lozier, 1975). In this society men's major obligation is to secure steady employment. Since economics make this difficult, the nonworking man must display his skill and energy by either looking for a job or working in his house and yard. If a man is seen in repose on his porch too often, he is labeled *bad*.

About age sixty-five, when a man is no longer able to find steady work, he retires to the porch. As he moves into incapacity, others help him maintain his house and yard, just as he had earlier helped others. The old man who has retired to the porch ceases to amass social credit and must now draw on what was accumulated by earlier labor. When illness decreases the frequency of his appearances on the porch, the neighborhood network responds in kind with increased attention and availability. At this stage the person is what Lozier calls *socially terminal*. Ideally death follows with little delay, since the resources required by the dying person cannot be sustained indefinitely without extreme cost to neighbors and family.

In Laurel Creek aged persons feel a commitment to continue with normal activities until death approaches. When death nears, they feel an obligation to die so as not to overburden others. Individuals frequently make a final (carefully orchestrated) appearance on the porch, withdraw into the house, and die soon thereafter (Lozier, 1975).

In the urban setting the pattern is quite different. Although there is no porch, there are areas of high visibility where old people tend to gather, such as the lobbies of high-rises, park benches, churches, and senior centers. In the city, however, there is great mobility, and the "service record" of people to their neighbors is frequently lost; thus no repayment occurs in old age. Lozier concludes that one may be accommodated *to* only by accommodating and that a record of such accommodation must be preserved either by word of mouth or in a contract. This is less likely to occur in urban settings than in tight-knit rural communities.

### Conclusions

Both Gutmann and Lozier stress the need to study not only people who are old but also the social environments in which old people live. To merely describe behavior

*In urban settings people tend to gather in apartment lobbies, parks, churches, and senior centers.*

without considering the environment in which it occurs produces only a partial picture of personality and adjustment in old age. Lozier's and Gutmann's work provides a criticism of the apparently implicit assumption of geropsychologists that the problems of old people can best be understood by the study of old people. This view tends to support the premise that the only solutions to the problems of old age are to be found in old people, not the societies in which they live. Increasingly sociologists, anthropologists, and psychologists interested in aging are seeing social change as a key to improving the quality of life of old people.

Adjustment is not just a function of the person. It is also a function of the expectations, values, and traditions of the society in which the person lives. Old people who live in a society in which they are valued will inevitably be labeled with more positive descriptions than old people who live in a society in which they are viewed as burdensome and expendable.

**Summary**

Personality at any age is a function of internal factors, such as temperament and biology, and external factors, such as culture and environment. The social structure in which a person lives also has a significant impact on that person's patterns of behavior. The social definitions of age and aging, the person's place in the social structure, and the historical epoch in which the person exists all affect personality (Bengtson et al., 1977). Research such as Gutmann's and Lozier's has illustrated the ways in which shared expectations affect group members' patterns of aging.

Despite their various theoretical perspectives, researchers seem to agree that successful aging entails well-being, success, and emotional health. Successful agers score high in certain broad areas related to life satisfaction (Neugarten et al., 1968): they show continued zest for life, not apathy; they show resolution and fortitude; there is a congruence between their desired and achieved goals; they show an optimistic, hopeful outlook; and overall they maintain a positive self-concept. Researchers have also correlated this high level of life satisfaction and mental health with physical health, high activity levels, and financial security, though these correlations may reflect the confounding nature of the variables and instruments used and may not be independent of each other.

A variety of human studies have suggested an association between good health and autonomy, environmental control, and feelings of self-worth (Moos & Tsu, 1977). Some researchers have argued that people have positive feelings because they are healthy, not that people are healthy because of their feelings of self-worth. However, research increasingly suggests that the exercise of personal choice and the experience of the consequences of choice are important to physical and emotional well-being (Seligman, 1975; Fries & Crapo, 1981).

Certain universals have emerged from research comparing personality structure in young and old. First, as people age they move from active to passive mastery of environmental events. Second, as people age they tend to show a higher incidence of feminine traits. Finally, as people age they generally show decreased or focused levels and patterns of activity (Cumming & Henry; 1961; Gutmann, 1971, 1977; Neugarten et al., 1964).

These findings have been replicated and supported by various major studies. Using the Guilford-Zimmerman Temperament Survey, Douglas and Arenberg (1978) found age effects only in general activity and masculinity. Men were more likely than women to show a shift from active to passive mastery and to decreased activity with age. That these were the only age effects found is surprising, given the scope of the Guilford-Zimmerman Survey. This instrument provides scores on ten personality traits: general activity, restraint, ascendance or leadership, emotional stability, objectivity, friendliness, thoughtfulness or introversion, personal relations, masculinity, and sociability (Kausler, 1982). Using this same instrument, Costa and his colleagues (1980) found no major maturational changes on three overall factors: general neuroticism, social activity, and thinking-introversion. Their results showed a slight tendency toward increased introversion and decreased activity.

Perhaps the best summary of personality change with age is that suggested by Bernice Neugarten: "As we become older, we become more like ourselves." Aging persons for the most part continue to be the persons they were in young adulthood. Stressful life events such as illness, trauma, and loss may precipitate changes in personality that can become permanent if they are perceived as successful adaptations. However, although they may be more thoughtful and less active than they used to be, old persons are still the same people they always were.

*Why is "abnormality" so difficult to assess, especially in the elderly?*
*Contrast the medical model with the psychosocial model of psychodiagnosis and treat-*
*ment. How are elderly patients perceived in each model?*
*Why does the medical model create problems for dealing with the old-old person?*
*What are the life-cycle continuities and discontinuities in the ways in which psychiatric*
*disorders manifest themselves?*

10

*Psychiatric*

*Disorders*

O NE of the most persistent and damaging myths of old age is that each of us —should we live long enough — will eventually become quite hopelessly and irreversibly "senile," losing our memories, our minds, and our self-control. This belief is ingrained in most persons who have ever seen an organically impaired old person. The specter of loss of self and loss of autonomy can be haunting, causing aging persons to be overwhelmed by fear as they experience transient forgetfulness and depression. This myth is personally and socially destructive, all the more so because it is so blatantly untrue.

This chapter considers the question of how closely age and mental illness are correlated. The nature of psychiatric disorders in late life as well as their prevalence and suspected causes are probed. Also discussed is the age specificity of symptom patterns for the disorders covered and the lack of age-specific or age-exclusive symptoms and disorders.

Like research on sensation and perception, the investigation of mental health difficulties of the elderly is a fairly new endeavor. Despite a sudden surge in knowledge of the biological, social, and psychological processes of aging, knowledge of the positive and negative aspects of mental health in the elderly remains diffuse and uncoordinated. This lack of knowledge has led to the relative neglect of the interior lives of old people.

Until 1972, for example, there was no real "clinical psychology of aging" because many of the standard clinical assessment tools were not normed for persons older than sixty-five. The Wechsler Adult Intelligence Scale (WAIS), a standard measure of intellectual functioning, as well as the Rorschach Test and the Thematic Apperception Test (TAT), both of which are standard personality measures, all fell into this category.

Another area of relative neglect of the elderly has been in psychotherapy. There has been no personality theory in gerontology, and Freud himself rejected the elderly as patients, a tendency still followed by psychoanalysts today. However, the lack of specific therapies for old clients may be a mixed blessing. On the negative side, therapists may assume that old clients are untreatable with psychological techniques and may therefore treat them with other modalities such as drug therapy, electroconvulsive therapy, or institutionalization. On the positive side, sensitive therapists are likely to try alternative measures if their first treatment choice is ineffective, since there are no specific therapies designed for the elderly.

*Our knowledge of the positive and negative aspects of mental health in the elderly remains diffuse. This lack of knowledge has led to a relative neglect of the interior lives of old people.*

The nature of psychotherapy as it is currently conducted with old persons is discussed in Chapter 11.

Geropsychology has tended to be community-based in its treatment methods and procedures. To a certain extent this has been caused by the hesitancy of many psychologists to conduct psychotherapy with old persons. The most desirable patient for many therapists is one who fits the "YAVIS syndrome" pattern, i.e., who is *y*oung, *a*ttractive, *v*erbal, *i*ntelligent, and *s*uccessful. Since elderly people tend to be stereotyped as not possessing these qualities, they are often avoided by therapists. Mental health treatment for the elderly has therefore tended to consist of group programs in income maintenance, enriched housing, retirement and leisure planning, and so on, as opposed to traditional one-on-one psychotherapy. This applied focus has served to hinder a rapid increase in psychological knowledge of mental health in the elderly (Kastenbaum, 1978).

Despite these drawbacks, the past ten years have seen a rapid increase in our knowledge of the psychological life of old people. This chapter covers the current state of information and concepts about the mental health status of old people.

The notions of "normality" and "abnormality" are difficult to define for persons of any age; they are particularly hazy when applied to a group of people of whom our main source of knowledge is stereotypes. The decision as to whether a minority or ethnic group member is normal is inevitably linked to our understanding and acceptance of that person's cultural uniqueness. The same might be said for the elderly; we do not know enough about what is truly "normal" for the elderly to decide whether an old person is abnormal. For example, the myth of intellectual decline and memory loss in old age is so imbued in our culture that any symptom of such decline is looked upon as indicating "senility." This is true only in old persons; the same symptoms in someone young are seen as "reactive" or caused by "nerves."

The definition of psychopathology is culturally and socially bound. Abnormality is not a discrete entity but rather a continuum of judgments ranging from behavioral qualities all would agree are pathological (e.g., confusion or incontinence) to those veiwed as pathological by a minority (e.g., bereavement). Abnormality is therefore seen as a continuum of performance rather than as one behavior.

Old people are generally judged to be acting abnormally when they simultaneously express distress, disturb others, are incompetent, and show change from a previous state (Eisdorfer & Lawton, 1973). This assessment is especially apt to be made when the old person also meets the following criteria: the person differs from same-aged peers (prevalence); the causes of the person's behavior are internal rather

## The Difficulty with Diagnosis

*We must look at the whole person— symptoms, environment, and supports—to assess and diagnose abnormality accurately. If this woman is poor and alone, her behavior is understandable, not abnormal.*

than environmental (etiology); the acts the person performs are judged to be maladaptive or harmful to the person or others (maladaption); and a treatment exists to slow or reverse the progress of the behavior (treatment) (Butler & Lewis, 1977).

It is the sum of these criteria that defines psychopathology. The lack of any single criterion is enough to exclude that diagnosis. The whole person, including that person's environment and supports, must be examined for abnormality to be assessed and diagnosed accurately. An old person may experience distress because of bereavement or loss. An old person's causing a disturbance may be due to the insensitivity, lack of understanding, or change in the life-style of a family member. Nursing home intake units report that the immediate cause of an old parent's being institutionalized is often not a change in the person's functioning but rather a change in the lives of the care-providing relatives (e.g., a daughter who wants to return to work or who is having marital difficulties). Persons of any age may be judged incompetent if harsh demands are made of them or they are treated as though they are expected to fail. Furthermore, change in function may occur in a positive direction; it need not be negative even in old people.

The definition of psychopathology suggested above is thus not designed to be a fixed rule. It is rather meant to provide a framework for diagnosis. However, there is as much danger in allowing surface use of this definition as there is in having no definition or a definition based on misinformation. In all cases of diagnosis and assessment it is essential that careful case histories be taken and that the environmental and support systems the person lives in be analyzed.

> Mr. P., a white seventy-six-year-old man, had been admitted to the geriatric unit of a local psychiatric hospital by family members with whom he lived. When seen by the psychology interns, he had been there for approximately three months. His symptoms consisted of profuse crying, pacing, and hand-wringing. His speech was unintelligible and was believed to be associated with the residual effects of an earlier stroke, although no other symptoms were present. Upon careful listening, one of the interns, an ethnic Italian, discovered that Mr. P. was speaking fluent Italian. A teary conversation followed in which Mr. P. revealed that his daughter had wanted to return to work and considered him in the way. She had tried to place him in a nursing home but found none available, so she had brought him to the psychiatric hospital with complaints of his wandering, depression, and confusion. After this conversation Mr. P.'s depression cleared, and he was shortly thereafter transferred into foster home care and normal function.

The above case points to the special difficulty of working with minority and ethnic group members as well as the difficulty involved in making an accurate psychodiagnosis of elderly persons.

### Prevalence of Behaviors

One of the most usual ways of assessing the normalcy of a behavior is to look at the extent of its occurrence in a particular group or society. *Prevalence*, a term taken from the field of public health, refers to the number of new cases and continuing cases of a disorder that exist at a particular point in time. Put more simply, the more uncommon a behavior is and the less likely it is to be seen, the more likely it is to be classified as abnormal. The physical changes described in Chapters 5 and 6 are considered normal because they are common in certain age groups. The same changes occurring in someone with progeria would be classified as abnormal because they are rare in the first and second decades of the life span.

The notion of prevalence as a criterion for normalcy breaks down in old age, however, because certain common behavioral features that are not conducive to optimal function occur in significant proportions among the aged populace. Old people as a group show a high frequency of depression because of loss. Nightmares, obsessions, hypochondria, suspiciousness, psychosomatic symptoms, and anxiety are also seen in many elderly persons — as well as in other age groups — but this does not make them normal. Prevalence alone is not a good criterion for normalcy because it overlooks the psychological pain and discomfort that certain prevalent conditions generate.

### Cause of Symptoms

Psychological symptoms are generally considered abnormal if no apparent event precipitates them. This notion of cause speaks to the distinction between functional and organic disorders. Organic disorders are patterns of symptoms caused by some discernible physical event, such as a stroke, infection, or disease. In contrast, functional disorders are caused by a person's symbolic interpretation and internalization of events; they are not caused by physical events but are purely psychological in nature.

The causal relations of many late-life psychiatric disorders are not clearly discernible. In fact, many psychological problems of old people often have a dual cause and simultaneous occurence. For example, it is not uncommon for a person in the early stages of dementia, an organic disorder, to also be depressed. This depression is often caused both by the awareness of cognitive loss and by the altered brain chemistry due to the physical changes in the brain.

A difficulty with the functional versus organic distinction is that it carries over into the sorts of treatment offered to a person diagnosed as fitting either pattern. Organic disorders are often treated with the medical model, in which psychological symptoms are seen as diseases and are treated by physical interventions such as drugs. Implicit in this view is the assumption that organic disorders are not treatable by psychological intervention because of their physical cause. In contrast, functional disorders are often treated with the psychosocial model. According to this view, psychological disorders arise from altered relationships in or perceptions of the environment and as such are to be treated by such psychological techniques as individual or group therapy and supportive environments. The distinctions between the medical and psychosocial models are summarized in Table 10-1.

These models of course cannot be applied indiscriminately. It has been demonstrated, for example, that supportive environments often improve the function of

*Table 10–1   Psychosocial model vs. medical model of mental health*

*Emphasis of psychosocial model*

Prevention
Intervention at the community level
The environment as a prime cause of disorder
Procedures to foster skills and competencies
Disorders or deficits rather than disease
Patient's role in treatment

*Emphasis of medical model*

Treatment
Intervention at the individual level
Internal deficits as a prime cause of disorder
Procedures to remedy deficits or disability
Disease rather than disorder
Professional's role in treatment

organically impaired persons whereas drugs often depress it (Sloane, 1980). Moreover, the distinction between the symptoms associated with functional and organic disorders is not always clear. Psychological disorders in the elderly must thus be assessed carefully and the full role of both psychosocial and biological causes determined. Mixed cause is the rule rather than the exception (Butler & Lewis, 1977; Sloane, 1980).

## Maladaption

Behaviors that are bizarre, harmful to the person's ability to function in society, or harmful to the person's safety are considered maladaptive. It is possible, however, for a behavior to be judged maladaptive by society but serve a useful purpose to the person performing it. It is also possible for a behavior to be maladaptive at one time in the life cycle but adaptive at another. Even life-long pathology may become adaptive in the elderly. For example, obsessive-compulsive mechanisms may become helpful in enforced retirement or isolation. Schizoid detachment may be adaptive to the inevitable losses of old age. Even hallucinations or delusions may be adaptive in lonely persons (Eisdorfer & Lawton, 1973).

Mrs. A., a seventy-six-year-old white woman had been widowed for three years. Each day the Meals-on-Wheels worker who came to deliver her meals found two places set at the table. When questioned about her company she explained that her husband always dined with her, as he had throughout their married life. This was a persistent but harmless delusion that served two purposes: it kept her eating, and it provided company during her otherwise lonely meals.

*Loneliness, a phenomenon that affects both physical and mental health, may lead to decreased interest in eating and other activities.*

## Treatment

It seems paradoxical to suggest that a behavior may be considered normal until a treatment exists to slow or halt its progress, yet this is true (Eisdorfer & Lawton, 1973). Before the discovery of antidepressant medications, for example, depression was simply something people learned to live with. Today drugs are used to treat even such minor symptoms of depression as sleeplessness and fatigue. Anxiety also became treatable with the discovery of tranquilizers. However, conditions for which there is no cure may still be dismissed as part of normal aging.

Patient:    Doctor, my right leg hurts.

Doctor:    You'll just have to get used to it. After all, you are eighty-two years old.

Patient:    But my left leg is as old, and it doesn't hurt!

Many symptoms exhibited by old people (e.g., early morning rising, constipation, memory loss) are assumed to be "caused" by age, but they may in fact be symptoms of psychological disorder. They are often considered symptoms of normal aging simply because of our biases and the lack of available treatment.

### The Issue of Mental Health

What then is mental health in the elderly, and what is psychopathology?

*Pathology*   Pathological behavioral changes and precipitating situations occurring with age may be categorized under the following five rubrics:

*Cognitive impairment*, especially when it occurs as a precipitate decline, is pathological. Loss of memory, judgment, and problem-solving ability is generally indicative of mental disorder. These symptoms do not indicate whether the cause of the difficulty is organic or reactive, but they do point to an underlying psychological difficulty (Sloane, 1980).

*Depression* and its symptoms should never be treated casually. Some transient depressions arise from normal aging changes in brain physiology, but for the most part depression in old people is associated with psychic distress. Given the high frequency of suicide in old age, depression should be considered a life-threatening disorder and treated accordingly (Stenback, 1980). The nature of treatment for depression is discussed in Chapter 11.

*Diminished energy* is often attributed to normal aging, but this may be because it has no treatment or cure (Eisdorfer & Lawton, 1973). Lethargy is often a physical sign of depression, and its causes should be thoroughly investigated to ensure that no physical or mental disorder exists.

*Social isolation* often precipitates psychopathology (Butler & Lewis, 1977; Pfeiffer, 1977). Whether it is a cause or an effect of mental disorder is unresolved, but it is nonetheless believed to be a significant risk factor in mental disorder in the elderly. Especially in sensory-impaired persons, isolation leads to paranoid ideation and delusional thinking (Post, 1980).

*Institutionalization* is the final risk factor associated with mental dysfunction in the elderly. Although the rate of institutionalization increases with age, community-based studies of psychopathology have found that people living in the community have the same patterns of symptoms as persons in institutions (Blazer, 1980; Butler & Lewis, 1977). It appears that the supports that maintain independent function (e.g., neighborhood, family, friends) are the final key to the decision to place a person in institutional care. Institutionalization is thus a result of extreme physical or cerebral disorders plus poor social supports rather than chronological age. Eighty to ninety-five percent of old persons are maintained in their own homes without being an overwhelming burden, even those who are disabled (Butler & Lewis, 1977).

Institutionalization may exacerbate already existing pathology, precipitate new disorders, or lead to institutional neurosis (Pfeiffer, 1977). Many old people

*People who live isolated lives are prone to symptoms of paranoia, fear, or depression.*

with mental disorders are placed in long-term-care institutions such as nursing homes, where they receive no psychological treatment for these disorders (Butler & Lewis, 1977). Institutionalization thus has a negative effect on the mental health of persons subjected to it.

*Positive Mental Health*   It is ironic that mental health, like physical health, is often described negatively i.e., as the absence of disease. Our culture has certain negative biases about what mental health is in the elderly. These biases focus for the most part on incremental disabilities and decremental abilities. As stated earlier, people of all ages age at different rates, even within their own bodies. It is possible for a person to be old in body but young in spirit, and vice versa. Charlie Smith, for example, in 1981 was 121 years old and the oldest living person in the United States. When asked what the future held for him, he stated that he hoped to marry for the fourth time in a year or so because at his age he didn't want to "rush into" anything.

Mental health and the way one copes with stress are important determinants of life satisfaction and success in aging. There are four components to current concepts of mental health for persons of any age (Birren & Renner, 1977):

The presence or absence of mental disorder.

The presence or absence of behavioral deficits or limitations that prevent optimal function.

Life satisfaction, i.e., a sense of contentment derived from one's current and past life experiences.

Approximation to cultural and personal constructions of the "ideal person."

Given the flexibility of these criteria, it is possible for any person to be mentally healthy. The "ideal person," for example, varies considerably from person to person, from culture to culture, and even at different points in the life cycle. The above definition allows persons with a mental or physical disability to evaluate that disability, cope with it, and live fully within its constraints. On the basis of these criteria, such persons would be considered mentally healthy despite their handicaps. It is important that persons dealing with the elderly recognize these positive aspects of mental health and always look for residual skills and capacities even in those aged persons who are severely disabled.

## The Epidemiology of Mental Disorder in the Elderly

Epidemiology is the study of the determinants and distribution of diseases, injuries, and disorders in the human population (Mausner & Bahn, 1974). Epidemiology, like health, is often defined operationally in terms of measurement of disease, but this should not obscure its basic purpose, the prevention of disease through the discovery of its patterns and causes. The epidemiology of mental health in the elderly is concerned with the following:

The identification of cases to provide information on the incidence or first occurrence of mental disorder.

The prevalence of mental dysfunction in elderly populations.

The historical trends of prevalence of mental disorder.

The causes of mental dysfunction.

The utilization of mental health services by old people.

The planning of new services based on projections of future patterns of disorder.

The design of mental health intervention programs and evaluation of their success or failure (Blazer, 1980).

The utilization of epidemiologic principles and methods will thus significantly increase our knowledge of the mental and physical health of old people and help the development of data-based intervention and evaluation programs.

People over sixty-five years of age currently make up approximately eleven percent of our population. This same age group constitutes almost twenty-two percent of first admittances to mental hospitals and only two percent of persons treated in outpatient services. It is estimated that fifty to sixty percent of all residents of long-term–care institutions have some diagnosable mental disorder (Butler & Lewis, 1977). These statistics point to the at-risk status of the elderly with respect to mental dysfunction. They also show that care for elderly persons with psychological problems is often just custodial.

As shown in Tables 10-2 and 10-3, the patterns of hospital admission and diagnosis of elderly persons are complex. From Table 10-2 it appears that the most common mental health service used by sixty-five to seventy-four-year-old men is inpatient care of various sorts. Outpatient care is used by approximately one fourth of this group. The use of mental health services among men seventy-five years old and older is decreased, as is the rate of utilization. However, this decrease occurs at a time when research would lead us to expect an increase in episodes of psychiatric crisis.

Old women tend to use mental health services as would be expected, given their high numbers. However, their patterns of usage vary considerably, as can be seen in the lower part of Table 10-2. Women make far greater use of outpatient psychiatric services than do men. This may be at least partially explained by the status of many women as widows and the psychiatric risk associated with that status.

Table 10-3 shows the breakdown of admissions to various sorts of mental health services by primary diagnosis. As can be seen, organic brain syndromes are significantly more likely to be diagnosed and treated in a state or county mental hospital than in a private psychiatric hospital or a general hospital. State and county hospitals more often deal with long-standing psychopathology than do the other mental health services. Depressive disorders are most likely to be treated in private or acute-care–hospital psychiatric inpatient services. Transient disorders, neuroses, and miscellaneous disorders except alcohol abuse are likely to be treated in an acute-care facility, but they are also significantly less likely to be the primary diagnoses in old than in young persons.

Table 10-4 shows chronic psychiatric care placements for the elderly in a way that enhances the trends shown in Table 10-3. As can be seen, from 1969 to 1973 the number of old persons with chronic mental disorders under any sort of hospital care decreased by approximately forty percent. During that same time the number of chronically disordered patients in nursing homes doubled (Redick & Taube, 1980). This suggests an attitude of custodialism, i.e., care and maintenance but no psychological treatment, toward most old persons with mental health problems. Unfortunately, this pattern persists today.

In a review of a series of studies, Blazer (1980) has demonstrated that old people with significant psychiatric impairment are most likely to be found in long-term-care settings. Blazer (1980) demonstrated that institutional placement is clearly different for different sorts of psychiatric disorders. Organic mental disorders are treated in long-term–care facilities, whereas schizophrenia, paranoia, and other psychoses, relatively uncommon diagnoses in the elderly, tend to be treated in more traditional mental hospitals.

Community-dwelling elderly persons are also not free of pathology, although the nature of the dominant diagnoses for this group varies. Neuroses and psychophysiological symptoms account for the highest rates of disorder in community-dwelling elderly (Blazer, 1980). Similar statistics hold for community dwellers of

Table 10–2  Admission per 100,000 persons over 65 to selected mental health services, United States, 1975*

| | Males | | Females | |
|---|---|---|---|---|
| Type of service | 65-74 years | 75 & over | 65-74 years | 75 & over |
| State & county mental hospital (inpatient) | 168.8 | 74.4 | 72.4 | 44.0 |
| Private psychiatric hospital (inpatient) | 52.9 | 45.2 | 71.3 | 50.3 |
| General hospital psychiatric inpatient unit | 150.1 | 155.8 | 196.4 | 163.2 |
| Outpatient psychiatric services | 135.1 | 114.1 | 289.6 | 346.3 |

*Base population used to compute rate was U.S. civilian population as of July 1, 1975.
(Source: Redick, R.W. & Taube, C.A. Demography and mental health care of the aged. In J.E. Birren & R.B. Sloane (Eds.), *Handbook of mental health and aging.* Englewood Cliffs, NJ: Prentice-Hall, © 1980, p. 65)

Table 10-3  Percent distribution of admissions 65 years of age and older to selected mental health services by primary diagnosis, United States, 1975

| Primary diagnosis | State & county mental hospital (Inpt.) | Private psychiatric hospital (Inpt.) | General hospital psychiatric inpatient unit | Outpatient psychiatric services |
|---|---|---|---|---|
| All mental disorders—number | 20,559 | 12,917 | 38,140 | 53,087 |
| All mental disorders—percent | 100.0 | 100.0 | 100.0 | 100.0 |
| Alcohol disorders | 16.2 | 7.5 | 6.0 | * |
| Organic brain syndromes (excl. alcohol & drug) | 47.1 | 25.1 | 28.9 | 23.8 |
| Depressive disorders | 18.3 | 51.1 | 46.1 | 38.4 |
| Schizophrenia | 10.1 | 4.6 | 3.3 | 6.2 |
| Psychoneuroses | * | 2.7 | 5.1 | * |
| Transient situational disorders | * | 1.8 | * | 11.4 |
| All other | 6.5 | 7.2 | 8.8 | 16.3 |

*Based on 5 or fewer sample cases, data do not meet standards of reliability.
(Source: Redick, R.W. & Taube, C.A. Demography and mental health care of the aged. In J.E. Birren & R.B. Sloane (Eds.), *Handbook of mental health and aging.* Englewood Cliffs, NJ: Prentice-Hall, © 1980, p. 65)

*Table 10–4   Number of resident patients 65 years of age and over in psychiatric hospitals by type of hospital, and number of residents 65 years of age and over with chronic mental disorder\* in nursing homes, United States, 1969 and 1973*

| Type of facility | 1969 | 1973 | Percent change 1969-1973 |
|---|---|---|---|
| State and county mental hospitals | 111,420 [S] | 70,615 [#] | –36.6 |
| Private mental hospitals | 2,460 [S] | 1,534 [#] | –37.6 |
| VA hospitals[†] | 9,675 [S] | 5,819 [#] | –39.9 |
| Nursing homes[‡] | 96,415 [‖] | 193,900 [**] | 101 |

[*]Includes mental illness (psychiatric or emotional problems) and mental retardation, but excludes senility.

[†]Includes VA neuropsychiatric hospitals and general hospital inpatient psychiatric services.

[‡]Data on residents with chronic condition of mental disorder used rather than data on residents with primary diagnosis of mental disorder at last examination, since latter data were not available by age in 1969.

[S]Selected publications of Division of Biometry and Epidemiology, National Institute of Mental Health.

[‖]National Center for Health Statistics. *Chronic conditions and impairments of nursing home residents: United States—1969.* DHEW Publication No. (HRA) 74-1707. Washington, D.C.: U.S. Government Printing Office.

[#]Unpublished data, Division of Biometry and Epidemiology. NIMH.

[**]National Center for Health Statistics. *Profile of chronic illness in nursing homes. United States: National nursing home survey August 1973–April 1974.* Vital and Health Statistics Series 13, No. 19. DHEW Publication No. (PHS) 78-1780. Washington, D.C.: U.S. Government Printing Office.

(Source: Redick. R.W. & Taube, C.A. Demography and mental health care of the aged. In J.E. Birren & R.B. Sloane (Eds.), *Handbook of mental health and aging.* Englewood Cliffs, NJ: Prentice-Hall, © 1980, p. 63)

all ages. Most community mental health surveys report a fifty to sixty percent prevalance of diagnosable psychiatric disorders in community-dwelling adults (MacMahon & Pugh, 1970; Mausner & Bahn, 1974). Blazer (1980) found similar ranges of function in community-dwelling, medical outpatient, and long-term-care elderly. Function ranged from normal to severely impaired in all three settings, but severe impairment was found preponderately in the long-term-care settings (Blazer, 1980).

### Historical and Future Trends

There has been an increase in the incidence of organic brain syndromes in the elderly in this century. There are several reasons for this. First, increasing numbers of people are surviving to be very old, and the risk of dementia increases with age because of the time dependence of many disease processes. Second, medical advances have contributed to the increased incidence of organic brain syndromes by halting deaths due to secondary infection. Third, the rapid upsurge in the incidence of Alzheimer's senile dementia is at least partially due to improved neurological diagnostic techniques. Alzheimer's senile dementia is now considered the fourth or fifth most common cause of death in the elderly in the United States (Blazer, 1980).

There has also been an upsurge in the number of diagnosed cases of depression in the past twenty-five years. A change in societal preoccupation from quantity of life to quality of life has led to an increasing interest in depressive symptomatology. Furthermore, as mentioned earlier, the advent of antidepressant medications has led to changes in diagnosis and treatment, so that dysphoric symptoms once considered normal are now considered pathological.

Life expectancy calculations for mentally ill persons have also shown some improvement as diagnostic and medical treatments have improved. Schizophrenics and paranoid psychotics have had an increase in life expectancy since the advent of phenothiazine drugs such as chlorpromazine. Conversely, it appears that the average life expectancy of diagnosed Alzheimer's patients is significantly lower than that of normal same-aged peers. Once diagnosed, a demented male has a life expectancy of 2.6 years; a nondemented male of the same age, in contrast, has a life expectancy of 8.7 years. A demented female has a life expectancy of 2.3 years, as opposed to 10.9 years for a normal female of the same age (Blazer, 1980).

Given these trends, the number of organically and functionally impaired elderly persons can be expected to increase. Our mental health system will have to change to meet these needs. Staffs of long-term–care facilities will need to be trained in psychiatric principles and behavioral management techniques. Outpatient care will need to better serve the mental health difficulties of old people. As stated, old people make up only two percent of psychiatric care outpatients and nine percent of psychiatric care inpatients. For the quality of life of these mentally impaired elderly persons to improve, there must be an improvement in the psychiatric care delivery potential of long-term–care facilities or in the ability of these patients to interact with the current mental health system.

### Causes of Mental Disorder

The causes of mental disorder are complex, differing from person to person and diagnosis to diagnosis. Historically, individual factors have been suggested as primary causative agents of late-life disorders. These include genetic and biochemical abnormalities, psychosocial stress, loss of social supports, maladaptive personality development, and previous history of physical and mental illness (Blazer, 1980). Recent approaches have focused on the epidemiological triangle as illustrated in Figure 10-1. This triangle consists of three components: host, environment, and agent. According to this model, each component must be analyzed and understood for a prediction of a disorder's pattern of occurrence to be made. A change in any of the components will alter the balance and thus affect the frequency of disorder. The emphasis used to be on the agent, or direct cause, of the disorder. Current focus is on the multiplicity of interactions between host and environment as typified by the "web of causation" model (Blazer, 1980; Mausner & Bahn, 1974).

According to the web of causation model, disorders never depend on single, isolated causes but rather develop as a result of complex chains of events in which each link has multiple causes. This model thus discourages the labeling of any individual factor as *the* cause of depression. A consequence of the complex of causal chains is that it is theoretically possible to interrupt the production of disorder by cutting the chain at different points. Furthermore, a complete understanding of causal mechanisms is not necessary for the development of effective measures for prevention and control (MacMahon & Pugh, 1970; Mausner & Bahn, 1974). For example, social stresses such as loss often precipitate decreased function in old persons, but it is possible to intervene successfully in the social support network without understanding the biological substrate of depression.

In summary, the problems of mental health and disorder in the elderly will be with us for some time in the future. For these mentally impaired individuals to have a high quality of life, we need a better knowledge and understanding of the causes and patterns of disorder. It is only through such awareness that there can be meaningful intervention in pathological behavior patterns and prevention of their potentially lethal effects.

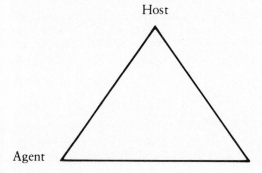

Host

Agent                          Environment    *Figure 10-1    The epidemiological triangle*

**The Psychopathology of Late Life**

What then is the characteristic psychopathology of late life, and how does it differ from normal function? As discussed in Chapter 9, specific adaptive challenges confront older people. These challenges revolve around three focal areas: personal losses, physical disabilities, and cultural prejudices against old age. Often these areas overlap and elderly persons find themselves dealing concurrently with elements of all three. An example of such multidimensional stress and its causes may be seen in the decreased sexual interest experienced by some old people.

It is not unusual for old persons to report decreased sexual interest. The causes of this decrease may be physical, e.g., decreased hormonal levels or increased pain in intercourse. They may be related to boredom with a partner or psychological stress caused by role loss or depression. It is also possible that a major cause of decreased sexual interest is the societal belief that sex in the elderly is humorous or even abnormal, as indicated by allusions to "dirty old men" or "dirty old ladies." This

*Coping with physical disabilities is one of many stresses the elderly may face and handle successfully.*

multiple or complex causation demonstrates that physical and psychological phenomena are intrinsically linked in old age.

It is normally necessary for old persons, especially those seventy-five years of age and older, to adapt both physically and psychologically to impaired physical function and chronic disease. These physical changes lead to changes in self-image. Persons who cannot integrate these changes into their sense of self may experience a decrease in self-esteem and find themselves in a stressful situation.

People of any age under stress mobilize a wide variety of defenses to cope with this threat. Some people insist nothing is wrong but look discomfited. Some persons insist that their symptoms of physical aging are only "nerves," whereas others verbalize an endless stream of complaints. Some persons develop physical illnesses because even a serious physical insult is preferable to an acknowledgment that they are growing old; after all, diseases are "curable," whereas old age is not.

Mr. C., a seventy-year-old white man, came to the hospital complaining of severe pain that radiated from the center of his chest down his left arm. Careful examination revealed no physical basis for his complaint. When he was questioned further, it emerged that he had been a pallbearer in the funerals of three close friends within the previous two months and had strained his muscles. He was also experiencing depression, with no emotional symptoms but severe physical equivalents.

Normally as people move into late life, they are faced with changes in their interpersonal relations. Their sphere of interaction decreases, as do the number of roles they play. People react to these losses in different ways, but certain patterns seem fairly prevalent in old age. Interpersonal relations are needed to sustain emotional life. A person's ability to maintain these relations and the quality of their form are strongly influenced by previous personality patterns, the presence of organic difficulties, and current self-perceptions (Verwoerdt, 1975). When these factors play a negative role, certain characteristic methods of maintaining relations begin to emerge.

As their dependency increases, old people often try to reinstitute earlier patterns of behavior. They frequently treat staff, physicians, and their adult children as parent surrogates. This is difficult for all concerned. Old persons using this defense often expect or demand that others sometimes nurture them and make all necessary decisions, but sometimes they jealously guard every personal right. Either case leads to guilt, diminished self-esteem, and often depression. This sort of behavior is not exclusive to old persons. The five-year-old faced with a new baby once again sucks his thumb. The teenager refuses a date because "my mother won't let me go." The middle-aged man refuses an invitation because his wife would get angry if he accepted. These transient regressions are tolerated in younger persons and should be seen as having a similar cause in old persons.

Old people often substitute material goods for affectional goods. They frequently try to press food, gifts, or money on visitors to ensure their return.

Underlying this behavior is a deep-seated fear that their good regard will not be sufficient reinforcement for repeated visits.

When faced with the awareness of their aging and the loss of personal ties, old persons often become narcissistic, living in the present and showing potent self-centeredness. At this time they are reviewing their lives as well as disengaging themselves from personal ties. Persons at this stage are narcissistic but feel a need to hold onto others to affirm that they are still alive and human. Such persons are apt to become sticky, loquacious, and repetitious; this may alienate others, starting a vicious circle of increased demand and increased rejection and thus leading to a further decrease in self-esteem.

Old people faced with loss often become preoccupied with their bodies. Comments about food, bowels, and operations often make up the bulk of their conversations. These attempts at communication involve no real interchange; true emotions remain cloaked. Old persons may be trying to relieve the anxiety about what is happening to them physically by repeating the nature of their physical changes. However, they thereby isolate even themselves from their anxiety and distress.

A poem written by a seventy-nine-year-old nursing home resident demonstrates the feelings of fear, despair, and depression that often underlie an apathetic or introverted exterior.

> Well, I can't say when you get any older
> Things go to pieces
> What I mean by go to pieces
> Is that everything goes wrong
> You get nervous
> And you get so you can't walk.
> Now I can't read anything
> I want to be happy
> And I want to enjoy my family
> As they are
> But that seems to me
> It's impossible
> So — I take it as it comes.*

The methods of coping discussed above are adaptive ways of dealing with the cognitive, physical, and personal losses of old age. As long as these work to control the anxiety, fear, and depression these losses engender, adequate function will be maintained. When either anxiety persists or organic impairment sets in, diagnosable psychiatric disorders, broadly classified as functional or organic dysfunction, may result.

*Koch, K. *I never told anybody: Teaching poetry writing in a nursing home.* New York: Vintage Books, 1977, p. 200. Copyright ©1977 by Random House, Inc.

### Diagnostic Classifications

The American Psychiatric Association has recently published the third edition of its *Diagnostic and Statistical Manual* (1978), DSM III. The classification scheme of DSM III is considerably different from that of DSM II in that it is multiaxial, i.e., it rates patients on five dimensions or axes.

Axis 1 involves all disorders except personality and specific developmental disorders, which are placed under axis 2. These two axes are essentially an overlap with DSM II. Axis 3 comprises any physical disorders that may be involved in the way the psychopathology manifests itself. Axis 4 is the severity of the psychosocial stresses a person may be exposed to, in a continuum from no stress to extreme stress, such as that due to the death of a spouse, to catastrophic, such as that due to a natural disaster. This diagnostic category was added because of research such as that of Holmes and Rahe (1967) dealing with the effects of stressful life events on psychological function. Finally, axis 5 measures the highest level of adaptive function the person has exhibited in the past year. This is especially important to prognosis in many disorders.

The organic categories of DSM III are expanded and improved over the DSM II classifications. There is no longer a distinction between psychotic and nonpsychotic organic brain syndrome. DSM III instead classifies organic disorders in three general categories: dementias arising in the second half of the life cycle, substance-induced disorders, and organic disorders.

*The Red Cross has many ways of helping disaster victims cope, including counseling to alleviate psychological and emotional stress. Elderly catastrophe victims may have a more difficult time than younger persons adjusting to the changes caused by natural disaster.*

In the affective disorder category various sorts of depression have been consolidated under the label *major depression*. The neurosis section has been dropped and replaced with three new sections: anxiety disorders, somatization disorders, and dissociative disorders. The neurosis category of DSM II grouped together different disorders that are theoretically similar, i.e., are assumed to indicate unconscious anxiety. DSM III strives for a descriptively based system. The specific neuroses have therefore been retained but often renamed.

### Functional Disorders

For a long time mental illness in old age was assumed to be related to brain damage. Psychological symptoms in old people were invariably believed to be caused by arteriosclerosis or senile psychosis, the latter being generally defined as a break with reality precipitated by unknown causes associated with old age. It is now increasingly recognized that depression rather than organic deterioration was often the cause of symptoms. The past twenty years have therefore seen the development of assessment methods useful in distinguishing dementias from affective disorders (Butler & Lewis, 1977; Gurland, 1980).

It has also been realized that even when an organic disorder occurs in old age, it is often acute or reversible. As many as fifty percent of the cases of organic disorder are now thought to be due to acute causes such as drug toxicity, malnutrition, infection, and physical disease (Butler & Lewis, 1977; Sloane, 1980). Even irreversible dementias often have reversible affective or organic components.

### Anxiety Disorders

Classic neurotic and personality disorders are rarely seen for the first time in old age. Old age brings with it anxiety, depression, and somatic complaints, but there are no significant age differences in the ways in which people cope with these difficulties. It has been suggested that old people experience anxiety over loss whereas young persons experience anxiety over meeting life challenges. Despite different causes, however, the symptoms are similar (Simon, 1980).

The normlessness and loss of old age tend to cause anxiety. Old people have many different sorts of anxiety reactions. Acute traumatic anxiety, or anxiety associated with specific events, often occurs in reaction to loss or personal catastrophe. Chronic neurotic anxiety, a carryover from earlier years, often persists as a pattern in old age. Phobic disorders, the displacement of anxiety onto objects or situations that serve as external symbols of internal feelings or concerns, are often present. Obsessive-compulsive behavior is often observed, especially early in organic disorders. Persons with this anxiety disorder suffer from obsessions (thoughts they cannot rid themselves of) and compulsions (rituals they must repeat). This behavior can lead to severe delusions and impairment in persons who are sensorily impaired or isolated (Butler & Lewis, 1977; Simon, 1980).

Another anxiety reaction seen in many elderly persons is helplessness anxiety, which is associated with uncontrolled object loss (Seligman, 1975). Helpless persons feel unable to control their circumstances regardless of what actions they take. Old persons feeling this emotion have often lost a spouse or their health. They are fearful of becoming a burden on others and losing their personal autonomy. They are also afraid of being abandoned if they become ill or deteriorate. Old people, especially those who are ill, often feel depressive anxiety over goals they never attained.

Helplessness and depressive anxiety are more likely to be found in old persons than are the other types of anxiety. It is also not unusual to find old persons in a state of absolute panic in which their defenses have failed completely and they are left only with total fear, preventing normal functioning (Simon, 1980).

Anxiety is a physical as well as a psychological state. People who are anxious feel "nervous." Their heart rates and breathing are often accelerated. Their hands and voices tremble, and their stomachs feel "knotted." These same symptoms may be produced by a variety of physical diseases, such as hyperthyroidism, hyperglycemia, adrenal tumors (pheochromocytomas), and drug or alcohol withdrawal. It is important that these conditions, to which old persons are particularly susceptible, be ruled out before treatment is begun.

Treatment for anxiety disorders involves a comprehensive program of drug therapy, psychotherapy, and environmental supports aimed at eliminating the threat. These methods are discussed in Chapter 11.

### Somatization Disorders

Old people often develop physical symptoms of their psychological distress. This is at least partially due to cohort differences in awareness and discussion of emotional state. Old people today are often uncomfortable discussing their emotions, which they feel are too personal to reveal. Their ways of coping with stress reflect this, as in Briquet's syndrome and hypochondria.

Persons with Briquet's syndrome have multiple recurrent somatic complaints that are not caused by physical illness. Patients frequently see many different physicians because their complaints involve many organ systems. Headache, fatigue, fainting, nausea, vomiting, bowel problems, sexual problems, and allergies occur, often simultaneously. Persons with Briquet's syndrome frequently exhibit conversion symptoms, i.e., physical symptoms that are symbolic of a particular anxiety. An example of a conversion symptom is impotence in a person who feels guilty over his sexuality (Simon, 1980).

Briquet's patients are often depressed, anxious, and suicidal. They are frequently guilty of drug and substance abuse. Their lives are filled with interpersonal difficulties they are unable to cope with. This is an early onset disorder, almost invariably beginning before the age of twenty-five, but is has been found to persist into old age. The disorder is more commonly found in women than in men (Simon, 1980).

Persons with hypochondria, another neurotic somatization, are nervously preoccupied with their own bodies or portions of their bodies, which they believe are either diseased or malfunctioning. These persons are narcissistic in that they have withdrawn psychic interest from objects and other persons in their environment and centered it on themselves, their bodies, and their bodies' functioning. Their anxiety has effectively been shifted from specific areas of psychological distress to some physical ailment that is perceived unconsciously as less threatening.

Hypochondriacs often use their physical symptoms as a means of self-punishment and atonement for their unacceptably hostile or vengeful feelings toward persons too close to them. Their symptoms are often also a means of punishing others they feel have hurt them (Butler & Lewis, 1977; Simon, 1980).

Treatment of hypochondria has had mixed success. Merely explaining to patients that they have no medical condition does not work, nor does diagnosing and treating a bogus disease. Patients treated thus simply develop new disorders. Concern and care for the person in combination with placebo treatment and family therapy have been found to be effective. This takes time, however, and is often not a treatment option (Brink, 1979).

Both Briquet's syndrome and hypochondria are based on the role of sick persons in our society. Persons who are ill are exempt from their normal social responsibilities. Since they are sick through no fault of their own, it is assumed that they have the right to be nurtured and cared for. It is assumed that they have the desire to get well; in fact, they are obligated to get well. It is further assumed that they will seek medical help and cooperate in the process of getting well (Hickey, 1980). Persons with somatization disorders vigorously play all parts of this role but the last. They do not want to get well because the secondary gains of their "illness" are too reinforcing (Simon, 1980).

### Substance Abuse Disorders

Another psychological disorder commonly found in the elderly is drug-use disorder. Alcohol, the most common drug used by adults for its central nervous system (CNS) effect, is consumed extensively even by institutionalized elderly. Nursing homes are increasingly using alcohol as a socialization enhancer, appetite stimulant, and tranquilizer (Simon, 1980), and the incidence of alcoholism in old people is increasing.

Old alcoholics are usually single, divorced, or separated. They are socially inactive and underemployed, and they generally view their health as poorer than the rest of society's. They often see themselves as alienated from society. Old problem drinkers have been classified into two general categories: delayed problem drinkers, persons who do not develop alcohol abuse until the age of fifty or sixty; and decompensated social drinkers, people who begin to drink once they no longer have role requirements to fill (Simon, 1980).

Old people are also found to abuse other prescription and nonprescription drugs, often unintentionally. The abuse of tranquilizers and hypnotics is frequently discovered when a physician requires that a person suffering from chronic anxiety, insomnia, or chronic brain syndrome be withdrawn from all medications as the first step of effective treatment (Brink, 1979).

Persons are considered to be abusing alcohol and drugs when they depend on them to such an extent that the substances interfere with their health, interpersonal relationships, or economic functioning. Elderly substance abusers are not a homogeneous group. Some are young abusers grown old, whereas others are newly abusive. Regardless of the age of onset of abuse, however, the effects of drugs and alcohol are potentially more serious in old than in young persons because of the physical changes that accompany aging. They are also more apt to precipitate depressive reactions in elderly than in young persons and often even become life threatening in old persons (Butler & Lewis, 1977; Simon, 1980).

### Paranoid Disorders

Paranoid reactions occur with increased frequency in old age. These reactions have at their core delusions of self-reference, persecution, grandeur, litigation, jealousy, envy, or supernatural control. Despite the commonness of such beliefs, it is unusual for them to develop suddenly in old persons. Elderly persons who have paranoid ideation are often found to have been "eccentric" for years. Most elderly with paranoid disorders are not impaired in their self-care, function quite well, and are not under any medical care for their delusions (Butler & Lewis, 1977; Post, 1980).

The symptoms of paranoid reactions in most elderly individuals consist of one

*Old people—like some young people—often exhibit single-minded devotion to a cause or group. This usually reflects earlier patterns of involvement.*

or two commonplace delusions, which may or may not be associated with illusions or hallucinations of related content. The personalities of affected persons are usually not disrupted except in a crisis, and the delusions may often be removed by social measures (Post, 1980).

Ms. M., aged seventy-two, was in an acute care hospital recovering from major heart surgery. She had a persistent delusion that CIA agents were spying on her and her roommate. She kept tedious notes on the occurrence of CIA visitations and often regaled the staff with her descriptions of the visits. When carefully examined, her CIA visits were found to correspond to security guard checks of the floor. When this was explained to her, the delusion vanished, although she subsequently became quite depressed; it appeared that she missed the excitement her delusion had offered.

Paranoid reactions often occur in people with the following premorbid personality types:

Quarrelsome-aggressive-hostile
Egocentric-obstinate-domineering
Suspicious-jealous-persecuted
Shy-sensitive-withdrawn (Post, 1980)

Elderly paranoids are often thought to be eccentric, are engaged in such activities as vegetarianism, herbalism, and religious sects, or are totally isolated from interpersonal relations (Post, 1980).

Isolation is a dominant factor in the relationship between deafness and paranoia. Paranoid reactions occur with high frequency in persons who have been deaf since an early age and in hearing-impaired elderly. Hearing-impaired elderly persons with the appropriate premorbid personality make extensive use of projection, hallucinating a new world to fill the void they perceive in the real world. However, the new world is unknown, threatening, and hostile and therefore produces fear. Hearing-impaired elderly thus often lash out or blame persons emotionally or geographically close to them for the fear they feel. Their paranoid reaction allows them to excuse their faults or failures by projecting the cause of these faults on external factors. Figure 10-2 depicts the relation between deafness and paranoia, showing graphically how delusions of persecution and reference can develop in hearing-impaired persons (Butler & Lewis, 1977; Post, 1980; Zimbardo et al., 1981).

Hypnotically induced deafness has been found to lead to an increase in paranoid responses on a number of personality assessment measures (Zimbardo et al., 1981). This suggests that self-validating autistic cognitive systems often lead to unchecked delusions. For many elderly persons such a delusional system is preferable to hearing loss.

Paranoia is typically a symptom rather than a disorder in the elderly, and it often occurs in the absence of any cognitive loss. There is, however, a schizophrenia-like

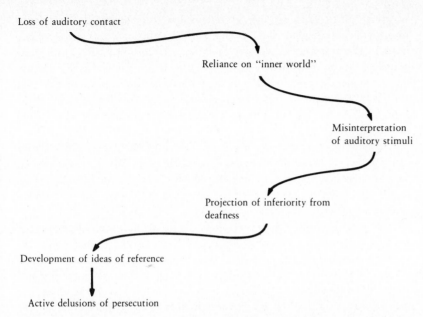

Loss of auditory contact

Reliance on "inner world"

Misinterpretation
of auditory stimuli

Projection of inferiority from
deafness

Development of ideas of reference

Active delusions of persecution

*Figure 10–2  Hypothetical link between deafness and paranoid reactions*

illness called *paraphrenia* that appears late in the life cycle. Patients with paraphrenia are more generally disturbed than persons with paranoia and usually require a physician's attention. They are increasingly distressed by hallucinations and loosely tied delusions (Post, 1980). Full-blown paranoid schizophrenia is also often seen in old age. Patients with this disorder have a narrowly defined area of delusional beliefs that upset them greatly. They often have third-person-singular auditory hallucinations that comment on their actions or even two voices battling over some aspect of their function. Late-manifesting paranoid schizophrenics frequently undergo complete dissolution of ego boundaries and require hospitalization. Paraphrenics and persons with paranoid reactions often improve when they are moved from familiar home surroundings; paranoid schizophrenics do not (Post, 1980).

Paranoid reactions in the elderly are often an indication of terror and aloneness. The paranoid person appears superficially cooperative yet resists treatment and is noncompliant in taking drugs. The patient's trust must be earned before any headway can be made in alleviating symptoms. The general treatment then consists of psychotherapy, administration of anxiety-alleviating drugs, and reduction of the threat from the external environment. Threat reduction is accomplished by clear communication, an empathetic understanding of the frightened person's life, and alternative explanations of what is happening (Busse & Pfeiffer, 1973; Butler & Lewis, 1977; Pfeiffer, 1980; Post, 1980).

## Affective Disorders
Like all functional disorders, affective disorders are not organic but are related to

interpersonal, intrapersonal, and socioeconomic factors that impinge on the person through their psychological or symbolic value rather than by direct physical impact. The affective disorders are the most common psychiatric disturbances found in old age. According to DSM III, they include the following diagnostic entities: major depression, bipolar disorder (formerly manic-depression, depressed and manic types), and cyclothymic disorder (formerly circular type manic-depressive illness). The most likely of these three to occur in old age is major depression.

Depression affects many people each year. Three percent of the total population of the world, one hundred million people, are affected annually by it. The rates are significantly higher for old than for young people (Stenback, 1980). People are not equally disabled by depression, but all to some extent experience dysphoria, slowed thinking, and decreased purposeful activity.

It is not hard to determine why depressive reactions occur with high frequency in old persons. Old age has been described as a season of loss, and depressive reactions, depending on their degree, are appropriate or inappropriate responses to loss. In addition, an intimate relation exists between physical illness and depression. Research indicates that old people can better tolerate the loss of love objects and prestige than a decline in health. Physical disability leads to mobility disruption, which increases social isolation. Isolated persons lose self-esteem and, if they also feel ill or in pain, develop depression (Butler & Lewis, 1977; Raskin, 1979; Stenback, 1980).

The clinical picture of depression varies a great deal, but a core group of *symptoms* is seen in most adults (Raskin, 1979). This core group includes the following:

Abject and painful sadness
Generalized withdrawal of interest and inhibition of activity
Pervasive pessimism
Decreased self-esteem
Poor self-prognosis.

These symptoms are particularly indicative of depression when they differ from the person's normal function and persist without relief day after day.

There are also secondary *signs* of depression that are physical in nature (depression is not confined to the psychological sphere). These signs include

Sleeplessness
Weight loss
Appetite loss
Fatigue
Constipation
Psychomotor retardation or agitation
Daily repeated mood cycles.

Generally, depressed persons feel a profound depression early in the day that lifts as the day continues (Raskin, 1979).

The full list of depressive signs and symptoms is presented in Table 10-5. Research has indicated that old people are more likely to show the signs (e.g., constipation and fatigue) rather than the symptoms (e.g., dysphoric mood and pessimism) of depression (Winokur et al., 1980).

Aside from the signs and symptoms of depression, certain other behaviors often occur in elderly depressives. Depressed persons frequently feel profound guilt over minor or major fantasied wrongdoings. They may become preoccupied with attempts to make restitution or with fear of future punishment. Depressed persons often experience severe anxiety or tenseness. The external signs of such agitated depression are tremulousness, pacing, hand-wringing, clawing at bedclothes, and in institutionalized elderly, attempts at self-mutilation. Suicide is also a risk in severely depressed old people, and depression should therefore be considered a life-threatening disorder.

Depressive equivalents are not unusual in the elderly. These are somatic manifestations, often a pain of unknown origin, without any subjective awareness of depression. Patients "look" depressed but vigorously deny being depressed. Their posture is slumped and they are tearful, and show pacing, hand-wringing, and so on. These patients generally hold high expectations of themselves and are unable to admit personal failure. They see the admission of psychological symptons as a personal failure and would rather be physically ill than psychologically ill (Zung, 1980).

In clinical practice depression is difficult to distinguish from chronic organic brain syndrome in the elderly. Persistent and careful interviewing are often required for it to be detected. Depression may also be confused with unhappiness or existential sadness, which may be a normal response to the situation the old person is in. If the suspected depression is reactive, it is crucial that family and care givers not make a "patient" of the person, i.e., someone who passively receives professional care. The person must believe that it is possible to overcome this state and that the professional's prognosis of recovery is optimistic.

Clinical depression is distinguished from an existential state by the following characteristics (Raskin, 1979):

Symptoms last longer than six weeks.
Significant weight loss occurs.
Sleep is disrupted.
The degree of sadness exceeds the losses sustained.
Worthlessness and guilt are expressed.
The degree of sadness gets worse.

Depression is often confused with a somewhat biased interpretation of normal aging changes and therefore overlooked. However, there is a clear distinction

*Table 10-5  Signs and symptoms of depression in the elderly*

---

*Dysphoric mood*
    Looks sad; mournful or depressed
    Cries easily; eyes moist or tearful
    Reports feeling depressed or blue
    Speaks in a sad, gloomy, or mournful
      voice

*Suicidal behavior and ideation*
    Reports recurrent thoughts of death,
      dying, or suicide
    Expresses wish to be dead
    Says life is not worth living
    Has made suicide attempts

*Pessimism and inadequacy*
    Reports future seems bleak, dark, or
      unbearable
    Reports feeling hopeless
    Is preoccupied with feelings of
      inadequacy
    Has clinging dependency
    Worries continually about something
    Reports feeling indecisive

*Guilt, shame, or worthlessness*
    Blames self for things done or not
      done
    Feels worthless and no good to
      anyone
    Reports feeling inferior to others
    Suffers from troubled conscience

*Anergia or fatigue*
    Feels everything is an effort
    Feels tired, worn out, lacking in energy
    Looks tired and lacking in energy
    Reports waking up feeling tired
    Sits or lies around because of lack of
      energy

*Apathy and social withdrawal*
    Lacks interest in hobbies previously
      enjoyed

*Somatic complaints*
    Headaches
    Constipation
    Dry mouth

Does not enjoy being with others
Is alone most of the time
Spends little free time at recreational
    activities
Has lost interest in TV or radio

*Retardation in speech or behavior*
    Speaks slowly
    Moves slowly and deliberately
    Subjectively feels slowed down in
      movements

*Memory*
    Has trouble remembering recent
      events
    Has trouble remembering past events
      such as from childhood
    Has good memory one day, bad the
      next

*Attention or concentration*
    Has difficulty attending or
      concentrating
    Checks and double-checks every
      action

*Confusion or perplexity*
    Reports feeling confused
    Appears bewildered by events
    Rambles or drifts off topic being
      discussed

*Sleep disturbances*
    *See text discussion*

*Vegetative disturbances*
    Loss of appetite
    Recent weight loss of 10 pounds or
      more

*Sex difficulties*
    No longer shows interest in sex
    Derives little pleasure from sexual
      activities previously enjoyed

Pains in stomach
Pressure in head
Nausea or upset stomach

---

(Source: Raskin, A. Signs and symptoms of psychopathology in the elderly. In A. Raskin & L. Jarvik (Eds.), *Psychiatric symptoms and cognitive loss in the elderly*. Washington, D.C.: Hemisphere Publishing Co., 1979, p. 9).

*Table 10–6   Symptoms of old age contrasted with depression*

| Old age | Depression |
|---|---|
| Worry | Worry cannot be stopped |
| Loneliness | Person shows loneliness when not socially isolated |
| Past regrets | Regrets are general, not specific |
| Inactivity | Inactivity is preceded by lack of interest |
| Halting speech | Speech is preceded by long pauses |
| Slowing | Intention, not action, is slowed |
| Sleep disturbances | Person rises feeling tired with gloomy thoughts |
| Appetite and weight decrease | Appetite and weight decrease although taste is not affected |
| Fatigue | Fatigue is constant, not just after exertion |
| Tremor | Tremor is associated with anxiety |
| Dizziness | Dizziness is not related to posture; person feels light-headed, not spinning |

between the physical signs of old age and depression, as may be seen in Table 10-6 (Gurland, 1980; Winokur et al., 1980).

Depression may be caused by clearly defined organic factors aside from the psychosocial factors discussed earlier. Systemic illnesses such as congestive heart failure; pulmonary, hepatic, or renal insufficiency; or cancer can cause depression. Metabolic disorders such as endocrine or mineral imbalance may cause depression. The altered brain chemistry of neurologic disorders may be associated with depression, as may certain drugs. Table 10-7 lists the causes of organic depressive disorder. In all cases, if the physical disorder or imbalance is reversed, the depression is also lifted.

In summary, depression in the elderly is a life-threatening disorder of complex causation. It affects all spheres of a person's life, and its causes and signs may be easily misinterpreted. Although depression often has symbolic causes in young people, real-life events often contribute to its development in the elderly. Losses in the biological, social, and physical spheres of the old person's life interact in the development of psychological disorders. So too must these spheres be addressed in the treatment of these disorders. Psychological symptoms and their direct causes are an interlocking house of cards. The search for one clue leads invariably to some other, perhaps unsuspected, aspect of the disorder. This is true not only for the functional disorders but also for the organic disorders discussed in the next section.

### Organic Mental Disorders
Organic brain disorders are caused by or associated with impairment of brain tissue function due to various causes. The primary symptom of both reversible and

*Table 10–7   Causes of organic depressive disorders*

*Systemic illness*
   Congestive heart failure
   Pulmonary insufficiency
   Renal insufficiency
   Hepatic insufficiency
   Lupus erythematosus
   Acute intermittent porphyria
   Viral infection
   Pancreatic carcinoma

*Metabolic disorder*
   Hypothyroidism
   Hyperadrenalcorticism
   Hypokalemia
   Hypercalcemia
   Pernicious anemia
   Acute intermittent porphyria

*Neurologic disorders*
   Parkinson's disease
   Intracranial mass lesion
   Huntington's chorea

*Toxic*
   Reserpine
   Alpha methyldopa
   Clonidine
   Propranolol
   Bromide
   Ethanol
   Barbiturates
   Diazepam
   Glucocorticoids
   Digitalis

(Source: Raskind, M.A., & Storrie, M.A. The organic mental disorders. In E. Busse & D. Blazer (Eds.), *The handbook of geriatric psychiatry*. New York: Van Nostrand Reinhold Company, 1980, p. 324. Copyright © 1980 by Van Nostrand Reinhold Company. Reprinted by permission of the publisher)

irreversible organic brain disorders is intellectual impairment, which is sometimes but not always accompanied by hallucinations, delusions, aphasias, emotional lability, or depression.

The irreversible disorders, called *dementias*, include Senile dementia, Alzheimer's type (also known as primary neuronal degeneration), Senile dementia, cerebrovascular type (also known as multi-infarct dementia), Pick's disease, Wernicke-Korsakoff syndrome, Creutzfeldt-Jakob disease, Huntington's chorea, multiple sclerosis, and kuru. The reversible organic brain disorders, called *delirium* or *pseudodementia*, include depression, normal-pressure hydrocephalus, and a host of drug toxicities. It is not necessary to understand each component of these disorders but it is important to see the almost overwhelming array of factors that can present as senility. Delirium that is not recognized as being caused by these reversible factors and is instead assumed to be dementia may progress through lack of appropriate treatment to an irreversible brain disorder.

*Dementia*   Dementias are often insidious, progressive, and life-shortening. They are characterized by disturbed cognition, memory, reasoning, and attention. The symptoms of dementia (Sloane, 1980) are presented in Table 10-8. Demented persons show impoverished and concrete ideation. Their speech shows stereotyped repetitions called *perseverations*. They often show compensative fabrications called *confabulations*, which involve combining memories appropriate to the situation but out of time synchrony with the situation. To the untrained observer these confabulations resemble lies. Disorientation, short-term memory loss, impaired conscience and judgment, and shallow affect are all symptoms of dementia (Sloane, 1980).

*Arteriosclerotic Dementia.*    Despite the common symptoms listed above, the various dementias have very different causes, courses, and responses to treatment. Arteriosclerotic dementia is believed to account for only twenty percent of the cases of senile dementia diagnosed each year. Another twelve percent of the cases are believed to be uncertainly related to vascular disease, including hypertension, multiple infarcts in the cortex, major lesions due to narrow cerebral arteries, and widespread subcortical ischemia (Binswanger's disease) (Terry & Wisniewski, 1977).

The arteriosclerotic dementias are generally acute in onset, follow a stepwise course, and present focal neurological symptoms. The physical focal symptoms were discussed in Chapter 5. The vascular dementias generally show intact personalities, insight until late in the disease course, explosive or unstable emotions, irritability, and patchy cognitive defects. They often occur in association with seizures and high blood pressure (Sloane, 1980).

Table 10–8    *The symptoms of dementia*

Amnesia with attendant reduced learning, retention, and recall of recent events and
    remote past

Confabulation

Lack of initiative and spontaneity

Concrete and impoverished thought

Inability to integrate and think sequentially with attendant tendency to catastrophize

Confusion

Disorientation

Affective disturbances

Suspiciousness and paranoid tendencies

Aphasia

Agnosia (inability to understand nonverbal symbols)

Apraxia (inability to carry out purposeful movements)

(Adapted from: Sloane, R.B. Organic brain syndrome. In J. E. Birren & R. B. Sloane (Eds.), *Handbook of mental health and aging.* Englewood Cliffs, NJ: Prentice-Hall, 1980)

Cerebrovascular dementia follows a variable course of temporary partial remissions followed by exacerbations. These fluctuations make the disorder diffcult to manage. Families and patients hope for a cure; then when an exacerbation occurs, their hopes are dashed (Eisdorfer & Cohen, 1978).

Treatment for the vascular dementias has involved hypotensive medications, thromboendarterectomy (surgery to clear the cerebral arteries of atheromatous deposits), and anticoagulants. These are discussed in Chapter 11.

*Alzheimer's Disease.* In Alzheimer's disease the white matter of the cortex shrinks and the ventricles enlarge owing to the degeneration or loss of as many as fifty-five to sixty percent of the neurons. Brain-reactive antibodies and diminished arborization of the nerve dendrites have also been found. Neurofibrillary tangles, i.e., fibers that irregularly transverse the neuronal cytoplasm, occur, displacing the normal cytoplasmic structures. In such damaged cells the nucleus is intact but displaced and often becomes faulty or nonfunctional (Terry & Wisniewski, 1977).

The nerve filaments of Alzheimer's disease are formed of new protein structures in the body. Three possible causes of such new protein structures have been suggested:

Genetic derepression, i.e., the activation of a previously dormant gene.

Mutation (not a viable explanation, since mutation would affect more cells than are in fact affected).

Slow virus acting as "the means by which new genetic material gains access to the cellular mechanism causing it to synthesize the abnormal new protein" (Terry & Wisniewski, 1977, p. 7).

These new proteins are also associated with increased concentrations of aluminum in the brain. When injected into the brains of susceptible animals, aluminum has been found to induce the formation of nerve filaments similar to those seen in Alzheimer's patients (Terry & Wisniewski, 1977).

The senile plaques found extensively in Alzheimer's patients are composed of degenerated presynaptic terminals and are believed to be caused by immunological abnormalities in the brain. Scrapie, a slow virus, produces similar plaques in mice; the plaques of Creutzfeldt-Jakob disease and kuru are also similar. Both of these latter disorders are caused by a transmissible slow virus in genetically susceptible humans. Perhaps Alzheimer's disease is also caused by a slow virus in genetically susceptible humans. This explanation would account for its prevalence among old persons (Cohen & Dunner, 1980; Terry & Wisniewski, 1977).

Alzheimer's disease follows a steady downward course, as opposed to the stepwise fluctuation of the vascular dementias. Alzheimer's patients show progressive deficits in cognition, self-care, and adaptation, and they die prematurely. In early phases of the disease they show minor changes in affect and cognition. The family of the afflicted person often cannot pinpoint the time of onset. Affected persons realize they have difficulty organizing and keeping track of their life activities, and this realization leads to anxiety, irritability, and depression. These secondary aspects of the disease are treatable. In its later stages, Alzheimer's disease causes restlessness, perseveration, aphasia, affective lability, and finally, lack of knowledge of self, family, and friends. Incontinence, a vegetative existence, and death follow these cognitive deficits (Cohen & Dunner, 1980). There is, however, great variability in the extent and nature of these cognitive deficits as well as in the duration of the illness.

Treatment of the organic brain disorders focuses on institutionalization and chemical intervention. Cerebral vasodilators, psychotropic drugs, and anticoagulants have all been used with varying degrees of success. Hyperbaric oxygenation, i.e., the breathing of pure pressurized oxygen, has been attempted. Reality orientation and behavior modification have also been used. For the most part treatment has been only palliative or, in increasing numbers of cases, directed at maintaining residual skills (Cohen & Dunner, 1980; Sloane, 1980). Treatment issues are discussed in Chapter 11.

*Delirium*    Delirium, or acute brain syndrome, is caused by transient stress in the internal or external environment. A key symptom in delirium is a clouded consciousness with imaginary illusional experiences (i.e., distorted or misinterpreted perceptions), as opposed to the hallucinations and delusions of dementia. Delirium is often accompanied by increased psychomotor agitation, in contrast to the slowing of dementia. Delirious patients look feverish and restless; their demeanor is one of perplexity, as though they are bewildered by what is happening to them, and their attention is unfocused. They are oriented to persons but not to places. They have no insight, and their thought has a dreamlike quality (Cohen & Dunner, 1980; Sloane, 1980).

Delirium often first presents itself at night through "sundowning," or intense confusion, a phenomenon associated with impaired circulatory or pulmonary function combined with disorientation due to a darkened room. Sundowning has been successfully treated by use of a light kept on in the patient's room. Drugs, a common way of dealing with this problem, only appear to exacerbate it. The drug-related aspects of night confusion are discussed in Chapter 11.

The progress of delirium is mixed, as is its prognosis. Most patients show full recovery when the cause of the acute episode is treated. If not treated, however, delirium can progress to dementia or even death if the concurrent disease, toxicity, or imbalance is serious. Compounding the problem is the fact that delirium in the elderly is rarely caused by a single factor.

> A common example is the elderly patient with mild congestive heart failure who is given diuretics and sedative drugs for agitation, thus causing an electrolyte imbalance. (Sloane, 1980, p. 559)

Treatment for delirium consists of correction of the systemic disorder and sufficient oxygen, glucose, and nutrition. A quiet room away from the unfamiliar noise of a general hospital ward, a single familiar sitter, and a well-lighted room also help to remove the symptoms of delirium (Sloane, 1980).

### Differential Diagnosis of Affective and Organic Disorders

The symptoms of depression, delirium, and dementia are very similar. It is important that a patient's functioning be carefully assessed before a diagnosis is made. The distinctions between dementia and depression are detailed in Table 10-9. The main distinctions are in degree rather than in kind. However, depression is likely to be sudden in its onset, whereas dementia is more insidious. Without a careful case history, this distinction is apt to go unnoticed.

The distinction between acute and chronic organic brain syndrome is clouded by the professional bias toward labeling all pathology in old age as "senile," i.e., chronic, irreversible, and untreatable. It is important to distinguish treatability from irreversibility. Even in chronic organic brain disorders adjunctive problems such as depression or an acute overlay may be treatable, and the patient's overall function may thus be improved. Without proper treatment acute brain disorder may cause permanent structural damage and thus become a self-fulfilling prophecy.

Even persons with severely degenerated neurons show great variability in functional capacity. This capacity is largely determined by the nature of the patient's personal and environmental supports (Diamond, 1978; Roth, 1980). In the absence of a supportive environment even a well-functioning person may show sudden deterioration. The converse, of course, is also true.

## Summary

The elderly as a group are more prone than young persons to certain psychiatric disorders, such as depression and organic brain disorder. Age alone, however, does not determine the presence of any psychiatric syndrome. Past mental and physical health, ability to adapt to stress, and environmental supports all determine mental health. There are no psychopathological behaviors that are unique to old age; even "senile dementia" can occur as both symptom and disease entity in young people.

Senility is an overused, misused, and pejorative label. Senility does not occur in all old people, but the behaviors it comprises may occur in some. These same symptoms may also be caused by functional or organic disorders. Senile dementia is the presence of a disease process, not changes caused merely by age. The chances are almost fifty/fifty when such symptoms are seen that they are acute and treatable. However, one should heed the following warning when dealing with psychopathological behaviors in old people:

One way to ensure "senility" is to misdiagnose a case of reversible cognitive disorder and consequently treat the patient as a case of chronic

*Table 10–9   The differential diagnosis between dementia and depression*

| | Dementia | Depression |
|---|---|---|
| Affect | Labile, fluctuating from tears to laughter, not consistent or sustained; may show apathy, depression, irritability, euphoria, or inappropriate affect; normal control impaired, can be influenced by suggestions | Depressed, feelings of despair that are pervasive, persistent; anxious, hypomanic; affect not influenced by suggestion |
| Memory | Decreased attention; decreased memory for recent events; confabulation; perseveration | Difficulty in concentration; impaired learning; decreased attention, with secondary decrease in recent memory |
| Intellect | Impaired, decreased, as tested by serial 7s, similarities, recent events | Impaired, but patient can perform serial 7s and remember recent events |
| Orientation | Fluctuating with varying levels of awareness; patients may be disoriented for time, place | May have some confusion, not as profound as in dementia |
| Judgment | Poor judgment with inappropriate behavior, dress; deterioration of personal habits and personal hygiene; loss of bladder and bowel control | May be poor |
| Somatic complaints | Fatigue; failing health complaints, with vague complaints of pain in head, neck, back | Typical complaints of decreased sleep, decreased appetite, decreased weight, decreased libido, decreased energy, constipation |
| Psychotic behavior | Mainly visual hallucinations, delusions | May occur in psychotic depressions, with mainly auditory hallucination; delusions |
| Neurological symptoms | Dysphasia, apraxia, agnosia | Not present |

(Source: Zung, W. W. K. Affective disorders. In E. Busse. & D. Blazer (Eds.), *Handbook of geriatric psychiatry.* NY: Van Nostrand Reinhold Company, 1980, p. 357. Copyright © 1980 by Van Nostrand Reinhold Company. Reprinted by permission of the publisher)

organic brain syndrome. The medications and the milieu experienced by patients with the diagnosis of chronic organic brain syndrome will certainly combine to fulfill the prophecy. The clinical rule is to rule out and diagnose the pseudosenilities with the expectation that effective therapy will follow.*

*Libow, L.J. Senile dementia and pseudosenility: Clinical diagnosis. In C. Eisdorger & R.O. Friedel (Eds.), *Cognitive and emotional disturbance in the elderly.* Chicago: Year Book Medical Publishers, 1977, p. 87

*Why is it important that multiple causation be taken into account in any consideration of psychiatric dysfunction?*

*How could the psychosocial treatment model be applied in institutions?*

*Why has the U.S. approach toward long-term care been predominantly one of "out of sight, out of mind"?*

*Is it inevitable that institutions strip their residents of their identity?*

*Why are so many of the treatment modalities currently used physical in nature?*

*How does their use of physical or chemical restraints reflect the values of care takers and their institutions?*

M A N Y old persons voice complaints or engage in behaviors that may be symptomatic of breakdown in the individuals themselves, in the social system, or in both. Such indices of dysfunction occur in many persons who never break down. This chapter deals with the types of treatment provided to old people when these problems occur. This treatment may be broadly divided into four categories: psychological intervention, physical or chemical intervention, institutionalization, and community-based or social intervention.

Psychological intervention commonly includes therapies aimed at improving cognitive and/or emotional function. This chapter discusses individual and group psychotherapy, behavior modification, milieu treatment, reality orientation, and other forms of psychosocial therapies offered primarily to institutionalized old persons. Discussion of the second category involves drug therapy, electroconvulsive therapy (ECT), and hyperbaric oxygenation. The chapter also deals with the psychological impact of institutionalization on persons exposed to it for their total care. Finally, a section on social intervention looks at various programs of the aging network (Gelfand & Olsen, 1980) as they affect the mental health of old people.

Several factors must be considered in any discussion of the various forms of treatment offered to mentally impaired old people. First, the elderly are at greater than normal risk for psychological disorders. Their psychological, social, and physical losses precipitate great stress, and their longevity increases the likelihood of time-dependent organic dysfunction. Furthermore, old people are not popular with health professionals, many of whom see the aged as helpless, hopeless, and unworthy of careful treatment and evaluation (Eisdorfer & Cohen, 1978). Finally, there has always been a tendency to relegate old people to the poorest, most hopeless therapeutic modality — one usually based on a philosophy of custodialism and minimal expectations of patient progress (Kahn, 1977).

This chapter critically explores the strengths and weaknesses of mental health interventions and examines the values of society and of the care givers who provide these interventions.

**The Mental Health Professional**

Although there is no logical basis for therapeutic discrimination against the elderly, such discrimination exists. The emotional disorders of old people are not intractable or untreatable, nor are they exclusively found in old age. Fear, frustration, anger, and depression may be found in persons at any stressful life transition, be it retirement, high school or college graduation, or menopause. There are no emotional problems that are peculiar to old age and none from which old persons are free. Why then is there a hesitancy by many mental health workers to work with old clients?

There are two initial barriers for mental health professionals. The first is the belief that the mental health conditions of old people are irreversible and physical in nature and therefore not amenable to psychological intervention. The second is the view that the patient's life is almost over and that the therapist should not "waste" time on a person so close to death (Butler & Lewis, 1977; Kastenbaum, 1978). In fact, psychotherapy may be least wasteful at this point in the life cycle, given that health and general well-being among old persons mean economic and social relief to their families.

The second of these factors is directly related to ageism (prejudice against the old) and gerontophobia (fear of the elderly and the process of personal aging) on the part of the therapist. Therapists of the elderly are often "reluctant therapists" (Kastenbaum, 1978). They see the elderly as being of low financial and social status, and they are afraid that young patients will avoid them because they work with the elderly. They see old clients as requiring only supportive techniques, which are low-level and not worthy of a good therapist. Working with old clients causes many mental health professionals personal distress because it calls to mind their own fears about growing old and facing death. This identification with patients on a personal level, referred to as *countertransference*, is discussed later in this chapter.

Certain myths about clinical practice with the elderly produce barriers against more mental health workers treating elderly clients. These myths are as follows (Butler & Lewis, 1977; Kastenbaum, 1978; Storandt et al., 1978):

The myth of tranquility and unproductivity
The myth of therapeutic unresponsiveness
The brain damage myth
The myth of institutionalization.

### The Myth of Tranquility and Unproductivity

The myth of tranquility and unproductivity is based on the belief that old age is a time of relative peace and tranquility when persons should relax and enjoy the fruits of their labor. Old age is also considered a time of disengagement, or withdrawal, from the environment and persons (Cumming & Henry, 1961). This myth is destructive because it encourages the belief among potential therapists that no mental health problems should exist in old age.

In actuality, old age is a time of increased and potentially more devastating stress than other ages because of the decreases in social sphere and physical abilities that accompany old age. As seen in Chapter 10, depression, anxiety, and paranoia are common in geriatric patients. Moreover, the complex of physical disease, social isolation, and bereavement lead to an increase in the suicide rate, especially among old men.

Old people, like young people, feel the need to create and perform constructive tasks. Some old people choose to disengage upon retirement, but many more first become or continue to be creative. Picasso, Rubenstein, and Fiedler all carried their creative efforts into their eighth decade, and Grandma Moses first became creative then. The forced withdrawal from activity that often accompanies old age can cause mental distress. Old people who put great personal value on a role they no longer fill often suffer from a loss of significance and the fear of becoming a burden on their spouse, friends, or children.

### The Myth of Therapeutic Unresponsiveness
Physicians hesitate to refer elderly patients to psychiatrists because of the view that such clients resist change or are even unable to change. This view also affects the psychotherapist's goals and efforts once therapy is undertaken.

*Many elders satisfy their need to create and be constructive through volunteering.*

In fact, although in their personal lives old people tend to be conservative, mainly owing to economic pressures, they are able to change and successfully adapt to many changes in late life. Retirement, the loss of health or significant others, a geographic move, and the loss of income are all serious life transitions that many old people undergo with only passing disruption. However, false beliefs about the inability of old people to adapt and change carries over into the therapeutic philosophy of many therapists. Psychotherapy has been successfully used with people in their sixties, seventies, and eighties (Gotestam, 1980; Hartford, 1980; Kastenbaum, 1978). This therapy often involves somewhat different techniques with old than with young persons and frequently focuses on particular themes, such as widowhood, illness, bereavement, loss, and significant life transitions. However, these differences do not render it any less successful than therapy with younger age groups.

Therapy with old clients involves activity by the therapist and often is more supportive than insight-oriented in nature. Six general principles apply to therapy procedures with old, frail patients (Kastenbaum, 1978; Pfeiffer, 1980):

Listen attentively to the patient and ensure that communication is adequate. Especially with sensory-impaired persons, engage in eye-to-eye contact and physical touch as a means of ensuring understanding.

Indicate that the aged person you are conversing with has something to teach and is a valuable being.

Avoid false reassurances or platitudes that may serve to close down the flow of emotions relating to life as the old person experiences and perceives it.

Deal honestly with anxiety, grief, and defenses.

Help the old person get rid of illusion and denial as long as the removal of these defenses does not precipitate increased psychic distress.

Discuss death, loss, and the problem of grief, but always in the context of possibilities, restitution, and resolution (Brink, 1979; Garner, 1977).

These are essentially the same principles a sensitive therapist uses with any client, regardless of the client's age. The empathetic therapist works compassionately and carefully to discover the roots of the client's defenses rather than attacking them overtly. The therapist does not allow illness or age to be used as a defense, nor does the therapist make decisions for the client, which would make the client lose autonomy and become helpless. Therapy following these principles has a chance of being highly successful regardless of the age of the client.

### The Myth of Brain Damage

The myth of brain damage is the tendency to think that the main psychiatric problem of all old people is damage to the brain. Alzheimer's disease and multi-infarct dementia are psychological disorders of organic origin, but there are also many functional disorders that affect old people. Anxiety, reactive depression, paranoia, and hypochondria are but a few of these emotionally based disorders.

Age and brain damage do not account for all psychopathology seen in elderly people; fundamental aging processes per se probably play a very small role. Old people frequently display such symptoms as disorientation, confusion, and memory loss, but these may be temporary, reversible, and caused by the environment, or they may occur in conjunction with chronic disorders.

It is important for therapists or mental health workers of any sort not to assume that the symptoms they see in elderly clients are necessarily irreversible. Disorientation and cognitive symptoms may have temporary causes. For example, old persons may be preoccupied with finances, family concerns, or health. They may be suffering from malnutrition or some treatable physical disorder such as congestive heart failure, respiratory disease, or drug side-effects. However, if such treatable alternatives are not explored and the old person as a result is not treated, the acute symptoms may eventually produce a permanent change in function.

### The Myth of Institutionalization

According to the myth of institutionalization, many physicians overemphasize the effects of age, brain damage, and hypochondria and place old patients in long-term-stay institutions such as nursing homes, despite the fact that these patients generally function better at home. The other part of this myth is that families are often forced to institutionalize seriously impaired relatives and then are blamed for rejecting them. This does happen on occasion, but the extent of such rejection is exaggerated (Kart et al., 1978; Sherwood & Mor, 1980).

In fact, many families endure enormous hardships to keep their elderly in the community and their own homes. They shop, clean, and cook for two places, endure the complaints of failing but demanding relatives, and often undergo financial hardship and psychological stress to keep their relatives at home. The decision to institutionalize an old parent is difficult, often requiring professional consultation.

The geriatric mental health worker must assess the family's attitude toward and objective capacity to help sustain the patient. The mental health worker must determine the following facts:

What is the role of the patient in the family?
How objectively does the family see the role of organic decline in the patient's present and future function?
Can the family be helped in their response to the patient?
Can family members become part of a treatment plan?
Are family members fostering childishness and helplessness in the patient?

Family consultation is crucial in and essential to the decision to institutionalize a close relative. Therapists may often find that they are treating two sets of clients —the patient and the family. In such family settings the nature of dependency, the family's perception of it, and the question of senility should be dealt with.

*Senility* is a pejorative term. It is important for family members to understand that what they consider senile symptoms may actually indicate one of three different conditions:

The beginning of a depression, manifested as a state of confusion.
The development of a reversible brain disorder.
The presence of a chronic brain disorder that may either remain stable or progress at various rates of speed (Cohen & Dunner, 1980; Sloane, 1980).

Two of these three conditions may be successfully dealt with by a stay in an acute-care hospital and then a return home. However, chronic brain disorders have no specific treatment other than placement of the patient in a medically and socially prosthetic milieu in which simplification, order, and a balance of care and self-care exist. This treatment, together with supportive drug therapy, may be conducted at home or in an institution.

Given the negative psychological effects of institutionalization, therapists or mental health workers who see institutional placement as the only alternative are doing a disservice to themselves, their clients, and the clients' families.

### The New Ageism

Ageism involves stereotyping of, prejudice against, discrimination against, segregation of, and hostility toward the elderly. Many gerontologists feel that a new form of ageism exists in our society, especially among people who are advocates for and workers with the elderly. This new ageism has four basic characteristics:

It stereotypes "the elderly" as least capable, least healthy, and least alert, despite the insistence that "not all elderly are alike."
It perceives old persons as relatively helpless and dependent individuals who require the support services of agencies and other organizations to function successfully in society.
It encourages the development of services for the elderly without adequate concern as to whether these services reduce the freedom of participants to make decisions about their own lives.
It produces an unrelenting stream of criticism against society and its members for their mistreatment of the elderly, emphasizing the unpleasant existence faced by the elderly (Kalish, 1979).

The new ageism obscures individual and group differences among the twenty-three million persons defined as elderly in our society. It especially ignores the fact that most elderly persons are intact, functioning effectively on their own, and getting along on the income they have. The new ageists make their listeners think that the problems and issues of old age apply to all twenty-three million elderly persons.

The new ageism is based on the "failure models" believed by many workers with the elderly. According to these models, the old person has failed or is going to fail without the services the care provider provides. In the incompetence role model, old people are constantly reminded of how incompetent they are, and in the geriactivist model, a rigid set of rules or standards for appropriate behavior is established and old people who do not adhere to these standards are faulted. The incompetence model is advocated by persons trying to gain federal dollars for their projects. The intent is good, but the outcome is negative in that the elderly may begin to believe that they are in fact incompetent. The work of the advocates of the elderly may thus be as potentially damaging as the actions of persons who express benign neglect toward the elderly or even overt ageism (Kalish, 1979).

It is not clear who is responsible for these failure models. It is possible that federal funding agencies have encouraged them by demanding that service agencies compete for funds and make their needs and clientele appear most deserving. It is possible that gerontologists themselves have perpetrated these models to keep their own programs going or because they are active in their own lives and value this quality in others. Regardless of the origins of these models, however, it is important for mental health workers to consider how they define their clients and not to place restrictive boundaries on what they consider mentally healthy aging. Essentially, we all are responsible for the failure models unless we continually re-examine our values and the way in which we deal with the elderly persons with whom we interact (Kalish, 1979).

Psychologists, physicians, or any service providers dealing with an elderly clientele need to recognize that old age is simply part of the life process. Old persons have a wealth of memories, skills, and experiences that make them unique versions of their younger selves. However, old people as a group experience certain tasks, losses, and problems that may require the special skills of mental health workers. These skills can be taught and may enhance the care provider's ability to work with aged clients.

**Psychological Intervention**

### Patient and Therapist Roles
A good rapport between therapist and client is necessary if the therapist expects to obtain needed information from the client. In order to be open with the mental health worker, the client must feel that

The therapist accepts him or her as a person and is not frightened or disgusted by the physical or mental changes that take place in old age.
The therapist has knowledge of the psychological problems of old age.
The therapist understands the social problems of old age.
The therapist has the professional skills necessary to work with old persons and is empathetic toward their problems (Butler & Lewis, 1977; Pfeiffer, 1980; Tesiny et al., 1978).

The therapist role should be based on accuracy, empathy, depth of contact, and good expectations for treatment outcome, as well as the ability to communicate these to the client (Gotestam, 1980).

It is important for mental health workers to understand that the setting and time of the evaluation also influence its success. It is helpful for old clients to be interviewed at midday, since some clients experience morning confusion or late-day fatigue, which could affect an interview. In order for the therapist to elicit as much information as possible, clients should feel relaxed. However, if they ramble, the therapist should draw them back to the topic by strategic interruptions and focused questions.

The importance of reminiscence in old clients cannot be overstressed. *Reminiscence*, defined as thinking about the past and reflecting, can be used as a positive aid in the interview. It is considered by some researchers to be a part of the normal life review process in the aged (Butler & Lewis, 1977). According to this view, the old person who realizes that death is an imminent possibility uses life review as a way of accepting the successes and failures of the past. Depending upon the person, life review can have mild or extreme manifestations. In the mildest form of review, the person tells stories about the past and verbalizes successes and regrets. In more severe cases life review causes anxiety, guilt, depression, and despair; in extreme cases, if the person cannot resolve problems or accept them, life review may lead to suicide. The most tragic life review is one in which a person decides that life has been useless. However, positive results can also come of the review; the person can take pride in past accomplishments, feeling satisfied and serene (Butler & Lewis, 1977).

Therapists may need to develop other modifications and sensitivities in working with old clients. They may need to be more active than usual in order to delineate and clarify problems as well as find out their causes. Therapists may have to determine whether and how late-life losses can be replaced. They may also have to deal with transference by clients (in which the therapist becomes a surrogate son or daughter) as well as their own countertransference (in which a client becomes a parent or an older version of the therapist) (Gotestam, 1980).

Patients come to the evaluation or counseling session with life review, the death of others, feelings of powerlessness and fear, and reactive emotions in attendance. They must be made to feel that regardless of its exact nature, this psychic "baggage" is theirs and they have a right to it. These emotions reflect choice — the choice to relate to persons and events in whatever way seems most comfortable and appropriate at the time. Therapists must keep in mind that clients are doing the best they can, that they are making choices about their behavior, and that they are responsible for maintaining the interview at a level that is manageable for them. When their limits are exceeded, clients will effectively terminate an interview by avoidance, shutting down, redirecting, or other means (Lowy, 1980; Pfeiffer, 1980).

Regardless of what kind of psychological intervention is chosen, the nature of these two roles remains basically the same. In all settings the therapists is an active listener, and the client is pleased to have the therapist's attention and be understood. The client does not feel judged and has the chance to express feelings freely under conditions of safety. This alone often removes some of the psychological distress a person feels when initially seeking counseling.

### Psychotherapy with the Aging

Therapy for the elderly may be group-oriented or individually oriented. Even deep analytic therapy and complete personality reconstruction have been conducted with elderly persons, although these are usually not advised because of the deep sense of loss their termination causes (Grotjohn, 1955; Kaufman, 1940). Therapy with the aging usually has two main goals: alleviation of anxiety and maintenance (or restoration) of adequate psychological functioning (Gotestam, 1980). In addition, the broad goals of therapy as applied to any client pertain to the elderly as well (Table 11-1). If any disorder typifies old age, it is anxiety caused by the attrition of coping resources and the accrual of stresses. Many old persons are most afraid of loss of self-control and personal autonomy. They, and in many cases others as well, have no faith in their recovery powers. Therefore, old people are ruled by the fear that they will lose their impulse control, and they may thus retreat into states of confusion and incontinence when threatened. Kahn (1977) describes old people with advanced vegetative deterioration, whom he terms *unoriented*. Unorientation differs from disorientation in that the person remembers nonthreatening things (such as the name of the President of the United States) but cannot recall personally relevant things (such as where he or she lives). The unoriented old person is a helpless, panic-stricken victim of a plethora of psychological insults and stresses. Mental breakdown in the elderly is usually linked with periods of panic.

The psychological treatment of such anxiety consists of the client's ventilating feelings of anger, fear, isolation, and rejection. Anxiety-filled old persons need to know that they are not alone in their symptoms, that they are not evil, and above all else, that they are sane (Gotestam, 1980). Insight formation is not necessarily required. It is sometimes therapeutic simply to siphon off the immobilizing tensions by allowing the expression of petty complaints. In therapy old persons should be helped to accept the realities of diminishing physical capacities, personal

Table 11-1    *Broad goals of psychotherapy*

Insight
Symptom relief
Delayed deterioration
Adaptation to present situation
Self-care skills
Activity
Lower level of required care

loss, role changes, and death. Persons must develop a tolerance for loss to maintain optimum psychological function, because loss is the reality of old age.

> The best thing to do, of course, would be to give the elderly new functions in society and thereby assure them of a role and status of a more positive nature. Psychotherapy is a second-best solution which is meant to help the person adjust to the fate of growing old. (Gotestam, 1980, p. 777)

Despite these qualifications, the results of therapy for psychotic and neurotic disturbances of old age have been good, but results of therapy for organic disorders have been far less positive. In all cases, therapists must adapt treatment to the resources of their clients. Supportive therapies, in which therapy becomes a substitute for social contact, have been suggested for the organic disorders. In these cases the understanding and warmth of the counselor, combined with a peaceful environment and an optimal level of stimulation, are beneficial (Gotestam, 1980; Lawton, 1980).

### Group Therapy

The task of therapy is not only to identify the cause of behavioral symptoms but also to plan the level at which intervention will be most feasible or potentially most effective. The previous section dealt with individual psychological treatments focusing mainly on physical disabilities or self-imposed stress. Alternative interventions focusing on the stress imposed by significant others are also available. Group therapy is an example of an alternative capable of reaching more people than the one-on-one model of traditional psychotherapy.

The following illustates the goals of group therapy:

> Generally the approach of group therapy used with older people is to produce reinforcement and support, some growing awareness of the nature of the individual's problems and guidance in finding new ways of dealing with the problems which the individual participant faces. (Hartford, 1980, p. 817)

Group therapy explores present difficulties and past methods of coping in an interpersonal context. Its goals are not significantly different from those of individual psychotherapy or therapy with groups of young people. However, group therapy tends to be used in cases of less severe disorders than individual therapy.

### Activity Therapy

Activity is therapy with aging persons, especially those who are cognitively impaired. The main therapeutic goal of activity therapy is prevention of the deterioration that results from withdrawal and disuse of interpersonal, cognitive, and self-care skills (Eisdorfer & Lawton, 1973). Such therapy is especially important in maintaining the residual skills of institutionalized elderly. It has been found repeatedly that impaired persons need continuing human contacts, social participation, and meaningful work in order to maintain their functioning (Lawton, 1980).

*Activity therapy is especially important in maintaining the residual skills of the institutionalized elderly.*

In 1970 forty to fifty percent of patients in nursing homes were assumed to be severely mentally impaired. Eighty percent of these persons were diagnosed as "senile." A persistent difficulty with such labels as "senility" has been the tendency to provide patients labeled thus with custodial rather than therapeutic interventions. Patients with organic brain syndrome are faced with nondisruptive chronic suffering and are therefore often overlooked in favor of patients who are "management problems." Activity and other group therapies deal with this problem by focusing on adaptation and the patient's use of residual skills.

Without close supervision many patients with senile dementia will hurt themselves or others. Other demented patients are ill but do not require extensive care. Patients with senility require more than mere management. Group therapy provides the means for staff, relatives, and the patient to come to grips with their own feelings about chronic mental disorder (Isaacs, 1977).

In activity-oriented therapy the therapist becomes very involved with the clients. The therapist assumes multiple roles when working with cognitive-impaired elderly, including the roles of social planner, family consultant, recreational and vocational advisor, and friend. In activity therapy patients are helped to change their behavior by a therapist in a setting in which a particular activity provides the focus of the interaction among group members (Hartford, 1980). Individuals grow through the activity's therapeutic focus of music, art, dance, poetry, or discussion of objects.

In interventions with cognitively impaired persons it is important to make the distinction between therapy and prosthesis. True therapy may not be possible in brain-damaged persons, but prosthesis, a decrease in the functional disabilities associated with this damage, is possible (Lawton, 1980). The disability associated with the various senile dementias is irreversible, but the "excess" disability associated with these disorders is susceptible to ameliorization (Kahn, 1977; Lawton, 1980). *Excess disability* may be defined as the extent to which the environment supports or discourages adequate behavior. Institutionalized old people may be deficient in self-care skills such as bathing, feeding, toileting, and dressing not because they do not possess the ability to do these things, but because it is more time-efficient for the institution to have staff members perform these functions for them. Excess disability in institutionalized elderly patients is also caused by encouragement of the avoidance of interpersonal contact. Elderly women are commonly given dolls or stuffed animals, allowing staff members to avoid the responsibility of substituting new relations for lost significant others.

Various specialized group activity therapies have been used predominantly with institutionalized elderly. Reality orientation, remotivation therapy, and milieu therapy are all characterized by the use of verbal and nonverbal expressions of the problems felt by group members. When deteriorated mental processes need bolstering, such programs of perceptual and conceptual retraining may give a sense of mastery and renewed self-esteem to impaired old persons.

*Reality Orientation*    Reality orientation, an increasingly popular treatment derived from behavior modification techniques, uses positive reinforcement to reinstate appropriate behaviors. The target behaviors are usually simple orientation to time, place, and person and sometimes basic personal hygiene or social interaction skills.

In the therapy sessions a staff person trained to use normal conversation techniques rehearses important items with the patients. The setting of such sessions should be constant and free of intervening activities and ambient noise (Lawton, 1980).

The effectiveness of reality orientation sessions has been widely questioned (Lawton, 1980; Sherwood & Mor, 1980). Generally the results of such training are not generalizable, and the gains exhibited in treatment sessions often do not persist after treatment. To succeed, therapy must be tailored to the needs of particular patients and must be continually applied. Staff members need to realize that gains will often be small, if any are made at all, and that reality orientation should focus on tasks that affirm a continued sense of self. All too often staff and patients become dissatisfied and depressed over such sessions—staff because their expectations are too high or they feel the sessions are meaningless exercises, and patients because they feel embarrassed by their inability to respond.

Valid criticisms have been made of reality orientation and its related therapies of validation and remotivation. Patients often show a decrease in life satisfaction and an increase in depressive symptoms because of such sessions. Staff members increasingly go through orientation sessions ritually without concern for individual patients. The content of such sessions is often meaningless, irrelevant, or inappropriate to the institutional life of the patients.

In a nursing home in Buffalo, New York, reality orientation sessions were conducted for five cognitively impaired old patients. The sessions were conducted in the dayroom, where several other activities were also going on. On April fifth, for example, one patient in the group was visited by another staff person during the session, and a TV was playing in a corner of the room. The most striking part of the session on this day, however, was its theme.

The subject of discussion was spring. Posters had been made depicting spring, flowers, and sunshine. Group members were asked questions about the season and what weather was associated with it. Yet at the same time a typical Buffalo spring snowstorm was raging just outside the dayroom's large picture windows. Neither staff nor patients appeared to notice the incongruity.

*Milieu Therapy*    Milieu therapy appears to be one of the most effective types of institutional treatments. This mode involves creation of an environment that is both structured for the desired outcome of improved patient behavior and supportive of learning and formation of a positive self-image. In milieu treatment the staff is closely involved in planning and treating patients, and highly structured activities are performed jointly by staff and patients. Rewards are used for task accomplishment.

Although potentially useful in improving the functioning of institutionalized elderly, milieu therapy has not been tried frequently. It is very expensive and involves large numbers of sensitive, well-trained staff members and a great deal of time. The support and social integration of such therapy acts to improve both staff and patient morale, but further study is needed to determine how effective it is in improving the cognitive functioning of patients (Lawton, 1980).

### Conclusions

Generally, group therapies have been found to improve patient morale and affect when carried out sensitively. Effective therapy appears to involve setting realistic goals, increasing patient interaction, focusing on patient strengths, and building group cohesiveness. The therapist must be flexible, warm, persevering, and patient. Touching and manageable tasks are also crucial. However, in the end it is the therapist's uncritical acceptance of and interest in the patients that lead to the increased self-interest necessary for institutionalized elderly persons to become motivated. The real enemy of such effective intervention is the feeling of futility with which many staff members, family members, and professionals regard any sort of mental health intervention with the elderly (Eisdorfer & Lawton, 1973).

**Physical Intervention**

The goals of various physical interventions in the mental health problems of old people are much the same as those of psychological therapies;

To minimize the suffering of the patient.

To improve the patient's behavior and prevent further deterioration of abilities.

To lessen interpersonal friction by controlling the patient's aggression, sexuality, or agitated behavior.

To assist the patient in taking greater pleasure in the environment (Kapnick, 1978).

However, the means by which these goals are accomplished differ radically in physical and psychological interventions.

Psychological therapies involve the manipulation of affect and cognition by interpersonal communication, whereas physical interventions entail direct changes in certain aspects of the patient's physiological function. Systemic drug therapy involves the administration of chemicals or gases. Electroconvulsive therapy (ECT) involves the administration of electric shock to the brain of the patient in an effort to reset the brain's chemical and electrical activity. Hyperbaric oxygenation involves the breathing of oxygen at increased atmospheric pressure so as to increase the amount of oxygen that reaches the brain. All three of these therapies are designed to improve cognitive or affective function.

ECT and hyperbaric oxygenation are used far less frequently than drugs in treating cognitive and emotional disturbance in the elderly. However, all of these interventions are sometimes used concurrently or consecutively, as illustrated in Table 11-2. Most psychiatrists and psychologists agree that physical interventions should never be given alone to treat psychological disorders. For the well-being and continued healthy functioning of the person's psyche it is wise to offer adjunctive psychotherapy on an individual or group basis (Butler & Lewis, 1977; Pfeiffer, 1980).

Table 11-2   *Recommended treatments for affective disorders*

| Type of affective disorder | Treatment of first choice |
| --- | --- |
| Adjustment disorder with depressed mood | Psychotherapy |
| Recurrent depressive disorder | Tricyclic antidepressant during acute phase; lithium for prophylaxis if patient has a history of hypomania |
| Bipolar affective disorder | Lithium |
| Episodes of recurrent manic attacks | Lithium |
| Depressive disorder, single episode | Tricyclic antidepressants |
| Intermittent depressive disorder | Psychotherapy; tricyclic antidepressants if symptoms are severe |
| Psychotic depression | Antipsychotics; if no response, ECT |
| Atypical depression | Monoamine oxidase inhibitors |

(Source: Walker, J. I., & Brodie, H. K. Neuropharmacology of aging. In E. Busse & D. Blazer (Eds.), *Handbook of geriatric psychiatry*. New York: Van Nostrand Reinhold Company, 1980, p. 109. Copyright © 1980 by Van Nostrand Reinhold Company. Reprinted by permission of the publisher)

## Electroconvulsive Therapy

ECT has traditionally been used in old people with a primary mood disturbance or a combination of early dementia and mood disturbance. ECT in the elderly has been found to improve cognitive performance by improving mood. It is increasingly recommended in the literature as a more effective alternative than prolonged drug therapy in the treatment of depression in the elderly; antidepressants tend to cause cardiotoxicity and drug interaction in susceptible old people (Brink, 1979; Hicks et al., 1980).

The manner in which ECT is given has changed considerably in the last ten years. Currently a patient about to undergo ECT is given a transient anesthesia and a neuromuscular blockade such as succinylcholine. These two drugs dull the patient's awareness of the procedure and prevent the patient's harming himself or herself during the seizure phase of the procedure. The patient's skull is fitted with electrodes, and then a unilateral application to the nondominant side of the brain is given (Hicks et al., 1980). ECT is generally given three times a week until substantial improvement occurs, and then another three or four treatments are given to ensure its effectiveness. In old patients a course of treatment runs from a minimum of six to a maximum of twenty-five with an average of approximately nine treatments for therapeutic success (Kapnick, 1978).

There has been and continues to be considerable resistance to ECT on the part of both patients and the professional sector. Many people question a treatment the exact action of which is unknown, although it has been determined that ECT increases catecholamine synthesis of dopamine and norepinephrine, synaptic transmitter substances that conduct information in the brain (Kapnick, 1978). ECT has also been resisted because of fear of the treatment and the posttreatment confusion and memory loss that occur. There is some validity to these fears. After the first six sessions there is a persistent retrograde loss of short-term memory. This memory loss usually clears within three weeks of the last treatment with no permanent damage. There is concern, however, for elderly patients who show permanent loss of memory and confusion. Especially for elderly demented patients, such a side-effect could be devastating (Kapnick, 1978).

The decision to give a demented or frail elderly person ECT or drug therapy is difficult to make. Drugs have severe side-effects that may produce toxicity, confusion, psychosis, or even death in susceptible old people. In the choice between a routine of ECT sessions and long-term drug therapy with antidepressants or antipsychotics, many geriatricians are currently opting for ECT (Hicks et al., 1980; Kapnick, 1980). Future research on the effects and consequences of these two treatments will perhaps make this decision easier.

### Hyperbaric Oxygenation

Jacobs and her colleagues (1971) were the first to administer pure oxygen under high pressure to elderly cognitively impaired patients. She reported that after administration of 100 percent oxygen at 2.5 atmospheres for 3 hours a day for 15 days, cognitive function improved because of the flow of blood rich in oxygen reaching the brain. These studies have been regarded skeptically mainly because of the inability of other researchers to replicate the results. Moreover, Jacobs's results were relatively short-term in effect. This is not surprising, since the areas of the brain that are damaged by diseases such as Alzheimer's or arteriosclerosis do not require blood and thus will not receive blood-borne oxygen. Jacobs's results may have been due to transient improvement in collateral areas of brain function or, more likely, to a state of euphoria or heightened attention.

### Drug Therapy

People older than sixty-five make up approximately eleven percent of the total U.S. population, but they purchase twenty-five percent of all prescription drugs bought in the United States. Old people take three times as many drugs as all other age groups combined. The average nursing home resident takes eight to ten different drugs a day. Ten percent of all nursing home budgets are spent on medications, many of them sedatives or tranquilizing drugs. Twenty to forty percent of the drugs administered in U.S. nursing homes are administered in error, and thirty thousand nursing home deaths a year are caused by drug miscombinations (Brink, 1979; Pfeiffer, 1980).

These statistics are made grimmer by the realization that since old people are more susceptible than young people to the effects of drugs, they are also more likely to suffer the negative consequences of the drugs they take. Old people's drug-taking behavior is filled with dangerous abuse, misuse, and nonuse (Pfeiffer, 1980). Misuse occurs when a physician inadvertently prescribes the wrong drug or when elderly persons take drugs on their own that interact with other prescription or nonprescription drugs they are also taking. Abuse occurs when an old person voluntarily consumes excessive quantities of drugs for hedonistic reasons. Nonuse occurs when old persons consume old drugs that are no longer effective or take drugs in lower doses and for less time than suggested by their physicians or pharmacists. All of these cases are capable of precipitating a mental or physical health crisis.

The bodies of elderly people undergo changes that affect pharmacokinetics, the way in which drugs are used in the body. The *absorption* rate, the rate at which drugs are absorbed and enter the bloodstream, slows in old people owing to changes in gastrointestinal function. The *distribution* of drugs throughout the body is slowed by the increased fatty composition of the body mass and by decreased albumin in the plasma. Drugs tend to bind to protein (like albumin) in the blood. Only the unbound portions of drugs diffuse into the organs and are eventually eliminated by the liver and kidneys; the bound portions are pharmacologically inactive. The increased fatty composition of the body mass in old persons also means that the proportion of any drug stored in the fat cells of the body and thus available for future action is greater in old than in young people. For drugs to be excreted from the body, they must first be *metabolized* by the liver; liver metabolism essentially converts fat-soluble molecules to water-soluble molecules, which can be excreted. Old people have smaller amounts of metabolizing enzymes in the liver than young people and thus metabolize at a much slower rate. Finally, drugs are *excreted* through the kidneys, which are less efficient in old than in young people. As a result of all of these factors, drugs are absorbed more slowly by old than by young people, but once absorbed, they tend to remain in the body stored in fat tissue for longer periods of time (Brink, 1979; Hicks et al., 1980; Pfeiffer, 1980; Raskind & Storrie, 1980).

Other physical changes affect the drug behavior of old people. Elderly people are more susceptible than young persons to chronic physical debilities, which often occur in combination with each other. This may result in the use of many different types of medicine at the same time. Given that drugs are retained longer, get into the bloodstream more slowly, and accumulate in the liver and kidneys of old persons, there is a danger of mental confusion arising as a result of sedation, misspecification of drug dose, or drug interactions (Brink, 1979).

Perhaps the biggest problem in the mental and physical health of the elderly is *polypharmacy*, the prescription and taking of multiple medications for the same ailment. The dangers associated with polypharmacy are diverse. Two different drugs may interact in some undesirable way. One drug's effects may be potentiated by the second drug so that the level of the effect becomes undesirably high; for example, aspirin taken with anticoagulants can cause internal hemorrhaging, and antacids taken in combination with major tranquilizers can lead to a decrease in the effectiveness of the tranquilizer. Some of these interactions may be life-threatening, and many compromise the quality of life of the elderly persons subjected to them (Brink, 1979).

Table 11-3 lists the five major categories of drugs used by elderly patients as well as the positive and negative effects of these drugs. The impact of these drugs on the psychological function of old persons taking them is discussed below.

*Major Tranquilizers*    Major tranquilizers are used to treat psychotic disorders in the elderly. As seen in Table 11-3, they act to decrease hallucinations, delusions, and thought disorders (Kapnick, 1978). However, they may also cause drowsiness, sedation, parkinsonism, and hypotension. Treatment with any of these antipsychotic drugs involves the risk of tardive dyskinesia, regardless of the dosage, duration of treatment, patient's age, or diagnosis. Tardive dyskinesia is an extrapyramidal late-onset neurological disorder involving stereotyped, rhythmic, involuntary movements in any part of the body. It fluctuates in severity over time, disappears during sleep, and increases with emotional arousal (Sovner, 1978). Tardive dyskinesia is prevented primarily by weekend drug holidays, a drug-free period after one year of continuous drug therapy, and discontinuation of antiparkinsonism drug adjunctive therapy as soon as possible. For most patients parkinsonism and akathisia (involuntary restlessness) do not recur after three months of antiparkinsonism drug use (Sovner, 1978).

It is common practice to combine an antiparkinsonism drug such as trihexphenidyl or benztropine mesylate with major tranquilizer to counteract the tendency of the antipsychotic to produce extrapyramidal symptoms, such as tremor and

*Table 11–3    Actions of drugs on old people*

| Action | Desired effects | Undesirable side-effects |
|---|---|---|
| Major tranquilizers | Decrease hallucinations, delusions, and thought disorders | Cause drowsiness, sedation, parkinsonism, and hypotension |
| Minor tranquilizers | Relieve anxiety without excess drowsiness | May produce physical and psychological dependence |
| Antidepressants | Produce psychic energization and emotional lift | May produce physical and psychological dependence, may contribute to central nervous system poisoning |
| Stimulants | Reduce fatigue and depression | Are frequently abused and may cause psychological dependence |
| Sedatives and hypnotics | Increase sleep | Have a high abuse potential; may cause physical and psychological dependence; produce a withdrawal syndrome that may be life threatening; may produce confusion and paradoxic excitement |

(Adapted from: Kapnick, P. Organic treatment of the elderly. In M. Storandt, I. Siegler, & M. F. Elias (Eds.), *The clinical psychology of aging.* New York: Plenum Press, 1978)

rigidity, and to lower the convulsive threshold. Another side-effect of antipsychotics is depression, so patients often take an antidepressant also. However, this "drug cocktail" can have extremely serious side-effects.

Major tranquilizers such as chlorpromazine, thioridazine, fluphenazine, and haloperidol are frequently used for old persons. Thioridazine is the choice of most geriatricians because of its relatively benign side-effects. The secondary behavioral features of dementia (e.g., paranoid states, nocturnal confusion, agitation, hostility, impulsivity) are fairly amenable to drug therapy. Late-onset continued schizophrenia and paraphrenia are also amenable to major tranquilizer therapy. The general rule for geriatric patients on major tranquilizer therapy, however, is to use one-fourth to one-third the adult dose once a day at bedtime in combination with drug-free weekends. Even with these safeguards old people are likely to develop akathisia, akinesia (generalized slowing of facial movements and fattened facial expressions), dystonia (uncontrolled muscle movements), and tardive dyskinesia (Kapnick, 1978).

*Minor Tranquilizers*   Negative life events in old age can cause stress, which, if unresolved, leads eventually to neuroendocrine imbalance. Cerebral ischemia, loss of neurons, and decreased mental capacity may then occur (Lehman, 1977). Given that neuronal loss occurs only near the end of this process, social and drug intervention imposed early may halt or reverse the process.

Minor tranquilizers such as diazepam and chlordiazepoxide are useful in controlling acute anxiety or panic reactions. When used for three to four days, they physiologically reduce anxiety and thus allow effective coping mechanisms to develop (Pfeiffer, 1980). As shown in Table 11-3, however, these drugs may also lead to physical and psychological dependence. Furthermore, they may slow the patient down and increase confusion, thereby leading to increased anxiety and aggression and the need for more or stronger drugs to control these new symptoms (Kapnick, 1978).

Anxiety in old people is often due to real events rather than intrapsychic conflict. Supportive therapy is therefore superior to drugs, given the severity of their side-effects.

*Antidepressants*   Since depression is one of the major psychiatric disorders of late life, antidepressant medication is frequently prescribed for old people. The tricyclics with their anti-anxiety component are often prescribed for old people, and monoamine oxidase inhibitors (MAOIs) are also frequently used. These drugs are potent and should be used only for clinical depressive syndromes—not just for feelings of sadness, upsetedness, anxiety, or distrust — and then only in combination with psychotherapy (Pfeiffer, 1980).

The antidepressants have extremely negative side-effects, i.e., central nervous system (CNS) toxicity, hypotension, and sedation. Many are also known to produce confusion even in small doses. MAOIs tend to interact with certain foods, the list of which may be overwhelming to an old person. However, MAOIs may also be the right biochemical agent to treat depression.

In cases of manic affective disorder lithium carbonate is often prescribed. Since renal function decreases in old age, there is an increased danger of lithium toxicity, the symptoms of which include nausea, stomach pain, vomiting, weakness, thirst, and sleepiness. The use of diuretics in combination with lithium further increases this risk (Brink, 1979).

*Stimulants*  Lethargy is often seen in old people as a secondary symptom of depression or in association with cognitive loss. Stimulants such as dextroamphetamine, methylphenidate, and caffeine have been prescribed to counter these symptoms. However, these are likely to overshoot the mark and cause far more extreme symptoms, including tension, restlessness, insomnia, and psychotic symptoms. These drugs should therefore be avoided in the elderly (Hicks et al., 1980; Kapnick, 1978; Pfeiffer, 1980).

*Sedatives and Hypnotics*  Old people, especially those in nursing homes, are often sedated with such drugs as chloral hydrate or flurazepam to make them sleep through the night. However, these drugs interfere with normal sleep patterns and prevent occurence of the dream state of sleep. The consequences of such drug therapy are increased anxiety, paranoid ideation, daytime stupor, and sundowning or night-time delirium. Moreover, all sleeping medication stops working at all if given for more than fourteen days consecutively (Pfeiffer, 1980), although it continues to cloud morning consciousness and decrease memory function. Diazepam (2 mg) given at bedtime is the safest and most effective chemical agent used to produce sleep. Warm milk, wine, and increased daytime activity levels are also effective.

*Iatrogenic Effects of Psychotropic Medications*  A complete listing of psychotropic medications used with old people is provided in Table 11-4. Frequently drugs are given to counter the effects of other drugs, thereby setting the stage for iatrogenic abnormalities. Examples of such treatment-induced disorders follow (Kapnick, 1978):

Tranquilized, oversedated patients often develop chest infections because of decreased mobility.

Insulin and the oral hypoglycemics often lead to severe hypoglycemia, which can cause acute mental changes, including bizarre behavior, disorientation, and coma.

Diuretics may lead to a potassium deficiency (hypokalemia) or sodium deficiency (hyponatremia), both of which cause confusion and delirium.

Since symptoms such as confusion and delirium have a tendency to be considered signs of "senility," an uninformed physician or family member may assume that these changes are irreversible.

*Table 11–4    Generic drugs and their most commonly used trade names*

| Generic | Trade | Generic | Trade |
|---|---|---|---|
| *Major tranquilizers* | | *Antidepressants* (cont'd.) | |
| Chlorpromazine | Thorazine | MAOI | |
| Fluphenazine | Prolixin | Isocarboxazid | Marplan |
| Haloperidol | Haldol | Phenelzine | Nardil |
| Loxapine | Loxitane | Tranylcypromine | Parnate |
| Mesoridazine | Serentil | | |
| Molindone | Moban | *Antimanics* | |
| Perphenazine | Trilafon | Lithium carbonate | Eskalith |
| Prochlorperazine | Compazine | | |
| Thioridazine | Mellaril | *Stimulants* | |
| Thiothixene | Navane | Amphetamine | Benzedrine |
| Trifluoperazine | Stelazine | Dextroamphetamine | Dexedrine |
| | | Methylphenidate | Ritalin |
| *Minor tranquilizers* | | *Sedatives and hypnotics* | |
| Benzodiazepines (antianxiety) | | Nonbarbiturates | |
| Chlordiazepoxide | Librium | Chloral hydrate | Noctec |
| Clorazepate | Tranxene | Ethchlorvynol | Placidyl |
| Diazepam | Valium | Flurazepam | Dalmane |
| Oxazepam | Serax | Glutethimide | Doriden |
| Mephesine-like compounds | | Methaqualone | Quaalude |
| Meprobamate | Equanil | | Sopor |
| | Miltown | Methyprylon | Noludar |
| *Sedating antihistamines* | | Barbiturates | |
| Hydroxyzine | Atarax | Amobarbital | Amytal |
| | Isoject | Amobarbital and secobarbital | Tuinal |
| | Vistaril | Pentobarbital | Nembutal |
| Promethazine | Phenergan | Phenobarbital | Luminal |
| | | Secobarbital | Seconal |
| *Antidepressants* | | *Antiparkinsonism agents* | |
| Tricyclics | | Amantadine | Symmetrel |
| Amitriptyline | Elavil | Benztropine | Cogentin |
| Desipramine | Norpramin | Carbidopa and levodopa | Sinemet |
| Doxepin | Adapin | Levodopa | Dopar |
| | Sinequan | | Larodopa |
| Imipramine | Tofranil | Trihexyphenidyl | Artane |
| Nortriptyline | Aventyl | | |
| Perphenazine and amitriptyline | Triavil | | |
| Protriptyline | Etrafon | | |
| | Vivactil | | |

(Source: Kapnick, P.L. Organic treatment of the elderly. In M. Storandt, I.C. Siegler, & M.F. Elias (Eds.), *The clinical psychology of aging.* New York: Plenum Press, 1978, p. 249)

Psychotropic medications may also cause a kind of CNS poisoning called the *central anticholinergic syndrome*. This is a form of toxicity caused by the ingestion of drugs that decrease choline and acetylcholine activity in the brain. Antiparkinsonism drugs, antidepressants, and major tranquilizers taken alone or in combination cause physical symptoms (paralytic ileus, urinary retention, glaucoma, and tachycardia), peripheral symptoms (facial flushing, blurred vision, and dry mouth), and central symptoms (disorientation, hyperactivity, hallucinations, and seizures). Nose drops, eye drops, over-the-counter sleep and cold medications, and other nonprescription drugs can also have this effect. The central anticholinergic syndrome is reversed by another drug, physostigmine salicylate, given slowly. This drug wears off quickly, but the fact that it has an effect proves that the central anticholinergic syndrome is caused by CNS toxicity rather than by one of the senile dementias. Once this has been established, the other drugs should be decreased or stopped entirely (Hicks et al., 1980; Kapnick, 1978; Walker & Brodie, 1980).

A selective deficiency of cholinergic neurons has been found to be an important component of Alzheimer's disease. Decreased levels of brain choline have been correlated with decreases in memory. These changes are not seen in multi-infarct dementia (Roth, 1980). These findings would suggest that demented patients with Alzheimer's disease, who are most likely to be treated with drugs that have potent anticholinergic action, are especially at risk for the central anticholinergic syndrome.

*Cognitive-Acting Agents*   Senile dementia of various causes occurs in high numbers of old people. In the early stages of the disorder patients are mildly aware of their cognitive deficits, and this awareness increases their anxiety. The impairment becomes obvious in the middle stages; short-term memory decreases, and patients find it difficult to choose the appropriate words in conversation. In later stages severe confusion and disorientation occur. This last stage is treated least successfully. Patients often can't hold a thought long enough to decide what to do with it. They are restless and often appear psychotic (Reisberg et al., 1980).

Various forms of cognitive-acting drugs have been suggested to remedy these changes (Table 11-5). These drugs have not been adequately researched, but current results indicate mixed results at best, with optimum improvement occurring in mildly impaired persons. Most positive results appear to be due to elevated affect rather than a directly cognitive effect (Hicks et al., 1980; Pfeiffer, 1980; Reisberg et al., 1980). For example, Hydergine, which is often used in the management and treatment of institutionalized elderly, was assumed to act as a vasodilator but now appears rather to have an antidepressant effect. Gerovital-3, another "age-reversing" drug, has no cognitive effect but has a mild MAOI effect, which decreases depression and therefore increases performance.

New research is focusing on the decrease in cholinergic enzyme activities that occurs in old age. Deanol, adrenocorticotropic hormone (ACTH), vasopressin, levo-dopa, and lecithin have all been tried with mixed results. More research is

*Table 11-5   Congestive-acting agents*

Cerebral "vasodilators": papaverine (Pavabid): isoxsuprine hydrochloride (Vasodilan): cyclandelate (Cyclospasmol); dihydroergocornine, dihydroergocristine, and dihydroegrocyptine (Hydergine); nicotinic acid
CNS stimulants: caffeine; pentylenetetrazol (Metrazol); pipradol; methylphenidate (Ritalin); amphetamines; and pemoline (Cylert)
Procaine hydrochloride (Gerovital-H3)
Anabolic substances
Cholinomimetic agents
Miscellaneous: hyperbaric oxygen; piracetam (Nootropyl); vitamins; RNA-like compounds; propranolol

(Adapted from: Hicks, R., Funkenstein, H. H., Davis, J. M., & Dysken M. W. Geriatric psychopharmacology. In J. E. Birren & R. B. Sloane (Eds.), *Handbook of mental health and aging.* Englewood Cliffs, NJ: Prentice-Hall, © 1980, p. 762)

needed to make the effects of these agents clear. Also being considered for use in patients with senile dementia are nootropic drugs, designed to work only on confusion. These drugs have no autonomic nervous system effect and in clinical studies have been found to increase cognitive behavior and performance. They also appear useful in mild cerebral insufficiency (Lehman, 1977).

Piracetom (Nootropil) may be useful with mildly demented persons mainly because of its mild antidepressant effect. Comparisons of the effects of these drugs with the effects of the tricyclics and MAOIs are necessary for their respective therapeutic utility and side-effects to be assessed. For severely demented persons cognitive-acting drugs appear to be an expensive and ineffective option.

### Conclusions

Geriatric pharmacy has many problems. In addition to iatrogenic factors, elderly people themselves contribute to these difficulties. They frequently stockpile or borrow medications; they visit several physicians simultaneously and collect multiple medications for the same condition; and if they are confused, they may forget that they have taken drugs and take them again or neglect to take them at all.

For many people drugs are necessary, improving quality of life and allowing continued autonomy. The following statement puts the issue in proper perspective:

> The intelligent solution for the problems of geriatric pharmacology does not lie in withholding all medications from elders but in realistically appraising the potential dangers of each medication, balancing them against the consequences of alternative therapies and closely monitoring all medicated elders for evidence of undesirable reactions.*

*Brink, T.L. *Geriatric psychotherapy.* New York: Human Sciences Press, 1979, p. 101

**Institutionalization**

Care of the elderly in the United States may largely be summed up by "out of sight, out of mind" or "discard after use." As stated earlier, the main mode of treatment for the cognitive and emotional disorders of old people in this century has been custodial care in institutions. From 1900 to 1955 the main site of such care was the state hospital; the current site is the nursing home. Both of these settings allow for treatment based on minimal expectations of cure or remediation. This rapidly degenerates to total care and maintenance (Kahn, 1977).

In 1974 the National Health Survey estimated that there were 3,300,000 mentally ill aged in the United States. This number was greater than the total population of elderly persons in 1900. Two and a half million of these persons were either in mental institutions (111,000 persons) or otherwise out of the mainstream of daily life. One and a half million required home care by family members or some in-home support agency. Another five hundred thousand required constant care at home or in a skilled nursing facility. In 1976 the National Health Survey estimated that forty to fifty percent of all nursing home residents had some form of mental disorder or impairment (Burnside, 1980). Other surveys indicate that as many as fifty to sixty-five percent of nursing home patients have some significant problem with cognition, orientation, or emotion (Eisdorfer & Freidel, 1977).

Table 11-6 shows the primary diagnoses of nursing home patients reported in the 1973–1974 National Nursing Home Survey. The main diagnostic categories as indicated by the highest numbers and rates were senility, stroke, hardening of the arteries, and mental disorders. All of these disorders are psychiatric in nature or lend themselves to severe behaviorial symptoms. Most long-term–care facilities are not prepared to deal adequately with such psychiatric difficulties.

One reason for the high numbers of old people with psychological difficulties being placed in nursing homes is the lack of services in the mental health system or aging network to meet the psychiatric needs of old people. In particular, programs

*The main mode of treatment for the cognitive and emotional disorders of old people in this country has been custodial care in institutions. The current site is the nursing home.*

*Table 11-6   Reported chronic conditions presented as primary diagnosis at last examination for both sexes combined (rates per 100,000)*

| Condition | Total no. of residents | All ages | Under 65 yrs | 65–74 yrs | 75–84 yrs | 85 years and over |
|---|---|---|---|---|---|---|
| Senility, old age, other symptoms and ill-defined conditions | 146,800 | 136.5 | 20.6 | 85.2 | 140.9 | 184.6 |
| Heart attack | 55,700 | 51.8 | * | 41.1 | 53.3 | 64.1 |
| Stroke | 113,400 | 105.4 | 94 | 138 | 120.6 | 81.5 |
| Hardening of the arteries | 241,800 | 224.7 | 36.6 | 151.7 | 237.2 | 293.9 |
| Diseases of the circulatory system other than hardening of the arteries, stroke, and heart attack | 39,400 | 36.6 | * | 31.4 | 39.9 | 40.4 |
| Accidents, poisonings, and violence | 49,300 | 45.8 | 39.6 | 35.8 | 45.8 | 51.4 |
| Mental disorders | 115,800 | 107.6 | 395.8 | 185.1 | 72.1 | 30.5 |
| Diseases of the musculoskeletal system and connective tissue | 73,100 | 67.9 | 48.3 | 58.5 | 70.7 | 74.4 |
| Endocrine, nutritional, and metabolic disease | 48,100 | 44.7 | 44 | 59.5 | 46.9 | 37.1 |
| Diseases of the respiratory system | 22,200 | 20.6 | * | 33.3 | 22.9 | 13.7 |
| Neoplasia | 25,600 | 23.8 | 27.9 | 29.4 | 23.6 | 20.7 |
| Diseases of the nervous system and sense organs | 64,200 | 59.7 | 156 | 78.4 | 49.3 | 35.4 |
| Diseases of the digestive system | 20,500 | 19 | * | 18.6 | 17.9 | 20.1 |
| Infective and parasitic diseases | * | * | * | * | * | * |
| Diseases of genitourinary system | 15,600 | 14.5 | * | * | 16.7 | 15.1 |
| Diseases of the skin and subcutaneous tissues | 6,000 | 5.6 | * | * | 6.1 | * |
| Diseases of the blood and blood-forming organs | 7,600 | 7.1 | * | * | 7.6 | 8.8 |
| Congenital anomalies | 3,100 | 2.9 | 19.1 | * | * | * |
| Other diagnoses | 16,100 | 15 | 22.1 | 15.9 | 15 | 12.6 |
| Unknown diagnoses | 9,600 | 8.9 | * | * | 9.3 | 9.8 |

Final estimates from the 1973–74 National Nursing Home Survey
*Figure does not meet standards of reliability or precision, i.e. relative standard error exceeds 25%.
(Source: National Center for Health Statistics)

to serve senile dementia patients and their families are lacking. The main causes of this lack, as stated, are the individual focus of the medical model of treatment and professional self-interest (Gatz et al., 1980). Another cause has been the inability of the mental health system to adapt to the care of organically impaired persons who require extended or chronic rather than acute psychiatric care. Adding to this problem has been a deficiency in the reimbursement monies used to pay for mental health care. Medicare, Medicaid, or Title XX Social Security Act funds may be used to provide care for mentally impaired old persons, depending on the sort of care they are receiving. Because of these different sources of reimbursement monies, the aged mentally ill fall both under the mental health system and under the system that provides services for the aged in general. This causes a conflict in which neither system wants to be responsible for the mentally ill aged but also does not want to yield any of their turf to the other (Gatz et al., 1980). This reimbursement problem has led to poor consultative ties between the mental health system and the skilled nursing facilities in which many of the mentally impaired elderly are housed (Cohen, 1980). Consequently the quality of care provided for geriatric psychiatric patients has deteriorated during the last twenty-five years.

Institutional care for the elderly may be broken down into four levels, depending on the severity of the problem and the type of diagnosis:

1. Skilled nursing facilities for patients requiring the highest level of nursing care.
2. Health-related facilities for patients requiring minimal nursing care.
3. Personal care or adult homes, where patients are assumed to need no nursing care but are provided with help in their daily activities (domiciliary care is often included in this level of care).
4. Psychiatric care for inpatients with psychological difficulties as their main diagnosis.

The division of health services for old patients into such levels is meant to allow for appropriate treatment and thus optimal function with the least possible loss of autonomy. However, studies have shown that approximately fifty percent of all geriatric patients are inappropriately placed, usually in the direction of increased custodial care and decreased autonomy (Gatz et al., 1980; Kahn, 1977).

Of even greater concern than the inappropriate placement of older persons in various custodial settings are the psychological effects of reduced autonomy and custodialism. The negative effects of institutionalization on psychosocial functioning are discussed below.

### The Negative Effects of Institutionalization

The decision for an old person to enter an institution is usually not easy for the person or the person's family, even if the institution is of high quality. Nor do the problems end once the decision is reached. In 1967 the average stay in a nursing home was one year, with most cases of "discharge" being caused by the death of the patient. The reasons for these high death rates are complex. As can be seen in Figure 11-1, the percentage of patients who remain in the hospital or are dead two years after admission varies considerably according to diagnosis. Patients with senile dementia, acute dementia, or arteriosclerotic dementia die in significantly higher numbers than other patients. These patients are also more likely to be placed in a skilled nursing facility than in a psychiatric hospital.

It would be easy to say that the death rates in nursing homes are high because very sick patients or patients with life-threatening diseases go there. This is even

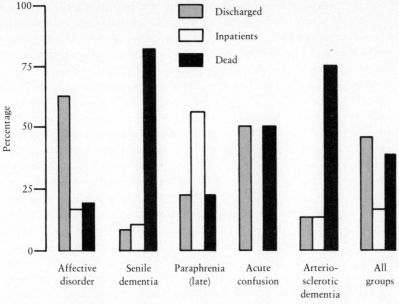

Figure 11-1 Percentage of patients discharged, remaining in hospital, or dead 2 years after admission to Graylingwell Psychiatric Hospital

(Source: Roth, M. Senile dementia and its borderlands. In J. O. Cole & J. E. Barrett (Eds.). *Psychopathology in the aged.* New York: Raven Press, © 1980, p. 207)

partially true. However, in a disturbing series of research studies Blenkner (1968) found that the old people who received the most services from agencies and professionals also had the highest rates of institutionalization and death. Such findings provide support for Kalish's (1979) discussion of the new ageism. Professional intervention may damage clients, especially if it is carried out too quickly and without regard for the clients' needs (Burnside, 1980).

> Intervention needs to be kept to a minimum and should be based on current data about the aged. Intervention should not be based on the personal needs of the intervener. (Burnside, 1980, p. 722)

Many intervention programs are efforts to deal with the secondary symptoms created by therapy. For example, the reality orientation and activities programs of many institutions are often necessitated by the excess disabilities caused by institutional care rather than by any disorder (Kahn, 1977).

### Institutionalism

One of the main psychological concomitants of institutional placement is a syndrome called *institutionalism* (Butler & Lewis, 1977). This syndrome is marked by erosion of the personality, overdependence, and loss of interest in the outside world, as well as an expressionless face and automatic behavior. Institutionalism is an attempt by the patient to deal with the depersonalization that total-care institutions encourage in the name of efficiency. Staff attitudes toward chronic-care patients, such as infantalization, desexualization, and avoidance also erode self-esteem and self-concept. Rigid routines, loss of decision-making responsibility, the lack of privacy, and the lack of affectionate, supportive relationships frequently found in institutional settings may lead to behavior similar to the symptoms of organic brain syndrome even in unimpaired persons (Kahn, 1977; Whanger, 1980).

The environmental docility hypothesis (Lawton, 1980) suggests that as cognitive competence decreases, factors in the external environment become more important determiners of behavior and affect; a small change in the environment thus has a greater effect on organically impaired old persons than on mentally competent persons. In a study of proxemics (the behavioral use of space and its communicative function) DeLong (1970) found that as the level of sensory reception in old persons decreased, the importance of touch increased. Old persons with organic impairment tend to communicate with others at a closer distance than normal; this makes staff members uncomfortable and leads them to avoid organically impaired patients (Lawton, 1980). When staff members in long-term–care institutions are forced to interact with mentally impaired elderly residents in close proximity, as when dressing, bathing, or feeding them, they tend to use distancing mechanisms. These mechanisms include rough handling of the patient, conversation with someone other than the patient, arching of the body away from the patient, and avoidance of eye contact. Such body signals all communicate an avoidance message (Lawton, 1980; Burnside, 1980).

Institutional living often involves a complete denial of personal territory or privacy. It also involves segregation for impaired old persons. Such segregation is a regular procedure in long-term–care facilities because the presence of persons with organic brain syndrome has been found to increase the anxiety levels of intact persons, perhaps owing to the fear of losing mental control. However, effective modeling and conversation can occur only between organically impaired patients and intact persons, not between organically impaired patients alone. Without such integration, further deterioration of cognitive abilities will occur in patients with organic impairment.

Age-integrated wards have also been found to be superior to age-segregated wards. Group cohesion, in which patients help their more feeble peers, appears only in integrated wards. In settings with only very old people, individuals lose even their identity as old persons (Kahn, 1977). The emotional blunting and cognitive deficits of senile dementia no doubt contribute to the psychosocial sterility of an age-segregated ward, but the lack of staff response and the environmental flatness of institutions also play a role. In the absence of disease, an impoverished environment, or poor nutrition, the nervous system has the potential to oppose marked deterioration with aging (Diamond, 1978). However, when a poor environment and disease are combined, deterioration inevitably occurs.

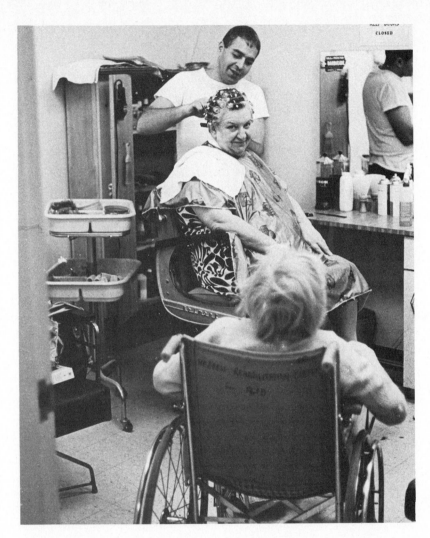

*Institutional living often involves a denial of personal territory or privacy. Many institutions help residents adapt successfully and retain their individuality.*

## The Social Breakdown Syndrome

Gruenberg (1967) first discussed the social breakdown syndrome, a depersonalization disorder in which institutionalized elderly persons come to see themselves as useless and helpless. This syndrome is another example of symptoms resulting from management procedures used to treat primary mental disorders (Kahn, 1977).

Until recently the effect of the social environment on the aging process was underestimated. It is now clear that social environments constitute the cultural backdrop against which elderly persons test their adaptability. Three elements determine the outcome of social and interpersonal situations:

Normative expectations for the context, i.e., what society views as appropriate behavior.

Capacity for interactions, i.e., past patterns and abilities in interpersonal situations.

The subjectively evaluated correspondence between expectations and performance (Eisdorfer & Lawton, 1973).

If all of these factors are in balance, the person feels a sense of well-being, but as people age these factors often change at different rates and are in a state of disequilibrium. People increasingly come to depend on a supportive environment rather than their own resources in manipulating unfavorable situations. In this sort of psychological climate it is possible for self-concept and even total function to be affected by the views of others. This is especially true for institutionalized elderly persons whose main source of affirmation is the paid staff who care for them.

In the social breakdown syndrome role loss, ambiguousness, and loss of significant others lead old persons to question their self-worth. This causes them to become dependent on external labeling and the societal view of them as incompetent or obsolete. If believed, such negative labeling leads to atrophy of skills, self-labeling as incompetent, and increased susceptibility to self-questioning. At this point the vicious cycle starts over again, as seen in Figure 11-2, only with the person's functional capacity already compromised. The social breakdown process may culminate in psychological or physical death.

Some persons profit from social exchange in the institutional setting. Institutionalized persons have often been marginal members of society. Many were relatively dependent personalities during their lives outside, and the institutional setting fulfills their dependency needs. The total care provided by an institution entails an alteration of societal demands and may be therapeutic for old persons who could not compete successfully in the larger society, such as the single-room occupant or the chronic schizophrenic. Life in an institution may actually increase the self-concept of these marginal persons (Sherwood & Mor, 1980; Kart et al., 1978).

### Conclusions

Criticism of the nursing home industry during the 1970s led to renewed concern for quality care and the adoption of high legal standards for care. This in turn led to increases in the cost of care. The outcome has been visibly improved physical standards for many nursing home patients but perhaps little more. Some facilities still have extraordinarily high moribidity and mortality rates, inadequate staffing, and even patient abuse. However, even the facilities that provide good care for their elderly patients foster a process that strips residents of their identities. Although quantity of life is increased, quality of life is often poor (Kart et al., 1978).

Institutionalism and social breakdown syndrome effects are endemic in nursing

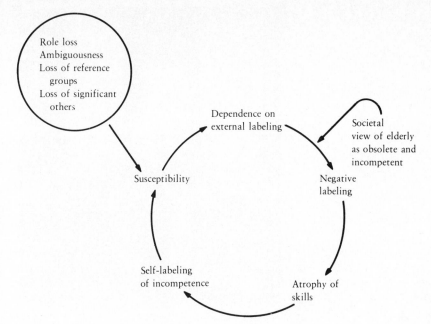

*Figure 11–2   The social breakdown syndrome*

home patients. Few attempts have been made to promote the growth of new relationships to take the place of old ones that have been lost in the process of growing old or sick. Social integration of long-term–care patients is essential; social isolation may exacerbate already existing symptoms or create new, negative ones. In institutions conflict, identity, and autonomy are all suppressed. The sterility and orderliness of institutional dayrooms may hurt social interaction rather than foster environmental interest. As institutions assume responsibility for the total care of their residents, feelings of powerlessness and isolation on the part of their residents also increase. Unfortunately, given current health trends, such conditions are likely to persist well into the foreseeable future.

Custodial care need not be pejorative. It can include the application of psychiatric principles and the use of adjunctive, rehabilitative services. Old patients should participate as much as possible in establishing the ground rules for their living situations. Choice, or at least its illusion, is important in preserving self-concept and autonomy. Physical structuring of space should provide freedom and safety for the wandering or confused person. Finally, whether the old person remains at home or is placed in an institution, contact with persons close to him or her can be the single most important factor in both life satisfaction and self-concept. Interpersonal contact, regardless of with whom, signifies to old persons that they are not totally isolated, that they are not discarded, and that they are still valued. These are perhaps the most important factors determining the "healthful" impact of an institutional environment.

*Interpersonal contact signifies to old persons that they are neither totally isolated nor discarded and that they are still valued. Institutions can help promote contact by encouraging visitors.*

**Community-Based Social Intervention**

Large numbers of old people are now surviving to old age in a time when needed health care, social care, and the financial resources necessary to provide such services are limited. The number of people in poor health increases with age. Many impaired old persons eventually enter long-term–care institutions. Those who live with families are more likely to remain in the community.

Nursing homes, chronic-care hospitals, and other long-term–care institutions are sometimes used as solutions to the problems of impairment by both family members and primary-care physicians even in cases in which all that is needed is limited periods of care during the day or occasional periods of respite for the family. However, a number of federal, state, and locally funded programs are designed to provide the supports necessary to keep frail elderly persons in their own homes.

### In-Home Services

In-home services are designed for persons who live in their own houses or apartments. In-home services can be grouped into three general categories

Intensive or skilled service, i.e., nursing
Personal or intermediate care
Homemaker-chore or basic services.

This multiservice pattern can thus be tailored to individual clients' needs. Since they are offered in the homes of clients, in-home supports extend the functional

*In-home support services extend the functional ability of old persons and help them continue to be a part of the family and community.*

abilities of their clients and help them continue to be part of their families and communities (Gelfand & Olsen, 1980).

In-home services are geared toward preventing unnecessary institutionalization by shortening the length of hospital stays, speeding recovery, and preventing inappropriate institutionalization. In many cases home health care is significantly less expensive for clients than other alternatives. Nevertheless, funding for in-home services continues to be below the demand for such services, especially for services not reimbursable through available funding sources (Gelfand & Olsen, 1980). Moreover, the available funding sources have different eligibility requirements and pay for different aspects of home care. Thus, in-home services run the risk of placing elderly clients between two competing agencies in terms of reimbursements for services rendered.

### Adult Day Care

Adult day-care centers offer an alternative to in-home care. These day-care centers are designed to provide assistance in daily independent functioning to mentally or physically impaired old persons. In 1974 the Department of Health and Human Services (formerly the Department of Health, Education, and Welfare) defined *day care* as a program

> provided under health leadership in an ambulatory care setting for adults

who do not require twenty-four-hour institutional care and yet, due to physical and/or mental impairment, are not capable of full-time independent living. (U.S. Health Resources Administration, 1974, p. 1)

Frequently day care is used for persons discharged from nursing homes or psychiatric hospitals, as well as for elderly persons living in their own homes, in foster homes, or with families. Researchers have noted that the residents of nursing homes often lived alone before entering an institution, whereas the users of day care live with families. This suggests that day-care clients have better access to social, economic, and health supports than do residents of long-term–care institutions (Gelfand & Olsen, 1980).

### Programs of the Older Americans Act

The Older Americans Act (OAA) is an age-specific program targeted for old adults. It was passed initially in 1965 and reauthorized in 1981. The OAA is designed to help old persons by providing funds to states for service, training, and research. The goals of the OAA, seen in Table 11-7, are laudable but difficult to achieve (Gelfand & Olsen, 1980). Nevertheless, several OAA programs that have been implemented have proved useful to old persons. They have not been as helpful in serving the frail elderly, however. No formal evaluation has been conducted of the overall impact of the OAA programs.

Title III of the OAA outlines social services, nutritional programs, and senior centers to be provided to old persons.

*Social Services*   The social services of the OAA are defined as health care, transportation, housing assistance, tax counseling, residential repairs, homemaker services, and an ombudsman program (designed to safeguard the health and rights of old persons living in long-term–care settings). For the most part these services are to be provided to persons who do not qualify for programs with other sources of funding.

*Table 11-7   The goals of the Older Americans Act*

An adequate income
Best possible physical and mental health
Suitable housing
Full restorative services
Opportunity for employment without age discrimination
Retirement in health, honor, and dignity
Pursuit of meaningful dignity
Efficient community services when needed
Immediate benefit from proven research knowledge
Freedom, independence, and the free exercise of individual initiative

*Nutritional Program*   The intent of the nutritional program of the OAA is to provide well-balanced meals and social interaction to old persons. Two programs are included in this category: congregate meal sites, which provide one hot meal at least five days a week, and home-delivered meals. The main intent of the program is to encourage congregate dining; old persons who are not home-bound or in extreme transportation difficulty do not qualify for home-delivered meals (Gelfand & Olsen, 1980).

*Senior Centers*   The senior centers authorized by the OAA are designed not to be independent entities but rather to serve as multipurpose settings in which various programs of the OAA may be carried out. For example, they often serve as congregate dining sites, counseling centers, health clinics, and even educational centers. They were envisioned by the planners as the physical focus of all community programming involving the elderly segment of the population.

### Additional Programs for Elderly Adults

A number of programs, including federal programs, exist for old persons (Table 11-8). However, there is a tremendous disparity between the number of programs that exist and the number that are currently available to old persons. The federal programs include the Social Security Act, Supplemental Security Income, Medicare, and Medicaid. The Supplemental Security Income (SSI) Program and the Medicaid program are not based on entitlement but rather on economic need. SSI

*Senior centers serve as multipurpose settings in which various social, medical, and educational programs are carried out.*

Table 11-8   Representative federal programs for the elderly

Housing programs
    Section 202 housing
    Low-rent public housing

Income maintenance
    Civil Service Retirement
    Old Age Survivors Insurance (Social Security)
    Supplemental Security Income Program
    Veterans pension program

Employment
    Foster Grandparents
    Retired Senior Volunteer Program (RSVP)
    Service Corps of Retired Executives (SCORE)
    Volunteers in Service to America (VISTA)
    Older Americans Community Service Employment Program

Health Care
    Grants to states for medical assistance programs (Medicaid)
    Program of health insurance for the aged and disabled (Medicare)
    Veterans domiciliary care program
    Veterans nursing home care program

Social service programs
    Education programs for non-English-speaking elderly
    Food stamps
    Legal Services Corporation
    Multipurpose senior centers
    Nutrition program for the elderly

provides income maintenance for the aged, blind, and disabled, whereas Medicaid pays health costs for the medically indigent. Medicaid is often the source of reimbursement for extended long-term care after a person's own money has been exhausted (Gelfand & Olsen, 1980).

Title XX of the Social Security Act also allocates federal funds to states to provide social services as they see fit. The main purpose of these funds, however, is to help old persons maintain independent, self-sufficient lives in the community. Some persons eligible for SSI are mandated to receive additional services such as home management, homemaker services, housekeeper/chore services, housing improvement, and health-related services. These services are clearly meant to halt inappropriate institutionalization of old, financially impoverished persons (Gelfand & Olsen, 1980).

### Conclusions

Many frail old persons need help getting help. The proliferation of social programs to assist the elderly is positive in that it indicates a concern with the social, economic, and health-related problems of the aged. However, the high number of programs, their different eligibility requirements, and their different funding sources (sometimes even for the same program) make the maze difficult for old persons to find their way through. The fragmentation of programs and confusion of regulations are especially indecipherable to those old persons who need the programs most, the mentally and physically impaired elderly. This maze of programs has led the Federal Council on Aging to conclude,

> The present haphazard array and the uneven availability of health and social services creates additional need for persons, already functionally impaired to a considerable degree, who cannot broker their own services and benefits. (Federal Council on Aging, 1978, p. 30)

**Summary**

Older persons tend to be at greater than normal risk for psychiatric difficulties. Mental health intervention, whether psychological, physical, institutional, or social, does not adequately meet the needs of mentally impaired old persons. In many cases the therapies themselves create negative behavioral patterns, such as excess disability, institutionalism, and the social breakdown syndrome. In some cases they make a helpless client or "patient" of the person. However, in other cases—often too few—they lead to independent function and increased life satisfaction for the old persons receiving them.

For any of these interventions to work, three criteria must be met:

Diagnosis and therapeutic intervention for both mental and physical disorders must be carried out early.

Primary prevention focused on increased education, medical care, and counseling early in the life span must be developed and implemented.

The availability of existing services must be improved (Gaitz & Varner, 1980).

A comprehensive mental health program for old adults as presented in Table 11-9 is needed. Such a program would integrate all elements of the aging network in a coordinated plan of caring for the mental health needs of the elderly. At present the social service, protective service, health, legal, and mental health systems do not interact at all.

In addition, persons who work with the elderly must realize the importance of empathetic concern, a stimulating environment, problem-oriented therapy, and ambulatory treatment (Gotestam, 1980). Without these mental health intervention will continue to be fragmented, inefficient, and potentially harmful to persons seeking it, and old persons will continue to receive the least adequate and most

*Table 11-9   Comprehensive mental health program for old people*

| Disorders | Treatment modalities | Services | Settings for intervention | Liaisons, affiliates, coordination |
|-----------|----------------------|----------|---------------------------|-------------------------------------|
| Depression | Individual | Outpatient | Mental health | Area agency on |
| Psychosis | therapy | Inpatient | clinics | aging |
| Organic | Group therapy | Partial | Medical clinic | Community |
| brain | Family therapy | hospitalization | Hospitals | health clinics |
| syndrome | Pharmacotherapy | Emergency | Nursing homes | Social service |
| Alcohol | Counseling | Consultation | | agencies |
| abuse | Special | Traveling team | Congregate | Local housing |
| Crises | techniques | Other | living settings | authority |
| Troubled | Other | | | Volunteer |
| transitions | | | Senior centers | organizations |
| Other | | | Patient's home | Churches |
| | | | Other | Other |

(Source: Gaitz, C. M., & Varner, R. V. Preventive aspects of mental illness in late life. In J. E. Birren & R.B. Sloane (Eds.), *Handbook of mental health and aging.* Englewood Cliffs, NJ: Prentice-Hall, ©1980, p. 979.)

hopeless type of mental health care available (Kahn, 1977), regardless of the sheer number of intervention programs available on an individual, local, state, or federal level.

M A N Y gerontologists or other persons interested in the processes of aging feel uncomfortable including material on death and dying in their courses on adulthood and aging. These persons feel that death and dying are a separate discipline warranting treatment in their own right under the heading of "death education," or "thanatology." Still others feel that the association of death with aging has been at least a partial contributor to the ageism in evidence in our society today. If this is true, academics who teach thanatology in aging courses may actually foster ageism or at least fear of the aging process in their students.

There is however, another point of view. According to this view, the predominant one among academic gerontologists, a major transition facing people in their later years is the change from being a healthy person to being a dying person. A person in our modern society fortunate enough to survive through childhood and grow to maturity will most likely live to old age and face death in that segment of the life span. Death and the bereavement it brings to survivors is therefore a reality for aging persons. This adaptive challenge may also be faced by younger persons, but it occurs in old age with greater frequency than at any other time in the life cycle; to paraphrase Longfellow, the young person *may* die, whereas the old person *must* die.

Death is a novel experience for the person who is dying, though it may be routine for the doctors, nurses, and other professionals who care for that person. The absence of human awareness often robs dying persons of a dignified death. The prolonged existence of terminal patients lacks dignity in the eyes of survivors and care takers. Our culture gives no other universal experience more avoidance, less preparation, or as much distress as we do death (Cutter, 1974). Although the subject of death seems grim, its problems and challenges are only made worse by avoidance. Preparation for death can be a life-long enterprise freeing a person to give daily life the best value. The key to resolving the conflict over the inevitability of death is to understand that dying, like other aspects of the life cycle, can be a period of personal growth and fulfillment despite physical deterioration. Death has been included in our life schedule from the day we were born and as such is not surprising, frightening, or dreadful, but simply an event, like birth, presenting a novel challenge to our adaptive capabilities.

This chapter presents the psychological aspects of death and dying. Anticipation and fear in both the dying person and the survivors are discussed, and the responses of young and old people to the thought of death are considered. The chapter also presents the specific needs of dying individuals and the problems confronting the bereaved survivors. Finally grief work as a normal aftermath of death is discussed and the adaptive challenge it places on the human organism considered.

## The Changing Face of Death

Death has become an alien, secret experience in modern industrial society. We separate ourselves from the dying person as if, by doing so, we could safeguard our own immortality. In today's youth-oriented society death and dying are systematically denied as natural steps in the life cycle. Since death occurs most often in isolation in some institutional setting, its reality is obscured by its very remoteness. This is illustrated by the existential philosopher-author Simone de Beauvoir: "All

*On a worldwide basis, the majority of deaths occur in children under the age of five.*

men must die, but for every man his death is an accident and, even if he knows it and consents to it, an unjustifiable violation." This statement reflects the changing face of death in the twentieth century.

Over the last fifty to sixty years there has been a shift in the nature of the causes of death. This shift may be seen as the culmination of a trend that started in the late eighteenth century of increasing life expectancies at birth for each generation. Rapid increases in average life expectancy were then seen in this century as childhood disease and infant mortality were conquered and public health projects such as sewage and water treatment instituted. Although such rapid increases in life expectancy may never again be realized in the developed countries of North America and Europe, death in these countries is increasingly encountered in old age. Worldwide, however, the majority of deaths occur in children under the age of five (approximately fifty percent), with the remaining deaths scattered across all other age groups (McHale et al., 1979). Even in the United States the highest numbers of deaths occur in persons under the age of five and over the age of forty-five.

In the early part of this century death in the United States was apt to occur in a haphazard way anywhere in the life span. Children died of childhood infectious diseases, adolescents died of rheumatic fever or tuberculosis, mothers and infants died in childbirth, and men died of various causes or just "old age," as the obituaries read. Figure 12-1 presents the different patterns of death in 1900, 1940, and 1975. The patterns indicate several major changes in those seventy-five years. The 1900 death rate for diseases of early infancy had been cut two thirds by 1975. Over that same period cancer had quintupled; so had heart disease, which today accounts for the largest percentage of deaths. By 1975 flu and pneumonia had been cut to one fourth of their 1900 levels. Kidney disease, tuberculosis, and infectious diseases such as gastroenteritis no longer account for any significant percentage of deaths.

Since 1900 there has clearly been a shift in the nature of dying. About ninety percent of adult deaths today are due to diseases of the heart, cancer, and strokes, all chronic illnesses that tend to progress slowly from onset to termination. After diagnosis these diseases may run from three to twelve months before the patient becomes "terminal." Increasing numbers of persons have a fatal disease for several years before death occurs. The effect of such prolonged dying on the patient, the family, and their medical care takers is discussed later in this chapter.

The encounter with death is thus considerably different, and the death rate significantly lower, in modernized cultures than it was and is is preindustrial and nonmodernized cultures. As can be seen in Figure 12-2, the death rate in the United States has been steadily decreasing since 1900. The extent of this decrease is considerably greater in more than in less developed countries. Death rates in the past were dramatically higher at birth, in infancy, and in childhood than they are today, and average age of death was lower (Marshall, 1980; Williamson et al., 1980).

Our society's patterns of death have undoubtedly had a significant effect on our cultural and personal ways of dealing with death. When deaths occur in massive

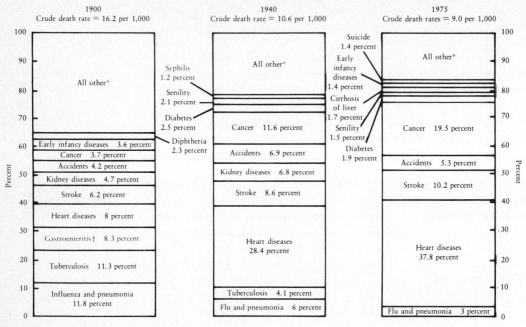

*No disease in this category represents more than 2% of all deaths.
†Inflammation of the stomach and intestines.
(Source: Population Reference Bureau (n.d.))

*Figure 12-1   Major causes of death in the United States, 1900–1975*

numbers, thoughts of death may be constant, and death may thus become an important part of a family's and society's rituals and awareness. The causes of death used to be much less predictable than they are today; for example, one could not accurately foretell such events as famine and plague. This lack of predictability caused death to be considered an outsider, something beyond the control of human beings (Marshall, 1980).

Today, however, death is more predictable and has to a large extent been relegated to institutional settings. Institutionalization of the dying patient makes the institutional medical staff, who interact most frequently with the patient, a significant part of the dying person's life. Such institutionalization also removes death from our everyday lives. An advantage to this is that we as individuals do not have to confront death personally. A disadvantage is that the grace and dignity of death at home is often lost.

Hospitals as they function today tend to prevent graceful death. Death is intensely personal, and a person's reaction to the news of impending death is often determined by the setting in which dying takes place. A person's fear of death as unnatural and alien is accentuated if that person is in an unfamiliar place such as a hospital or nursing home.

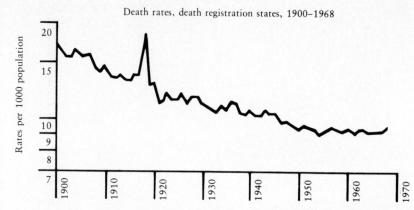

*Figure 12–2 Crude death rate per 1,000 population: United States, 1900–1968*

(Source: Schulz, R. *The psychology of death, dying and bereavement*. Reading, Mass.: Addison-Wesley, 1978, p. 45)

Because of the mortality trends described above, we as a culture tend to not think about death until it strikes us personally. When it touches us, therefore, we have often made no psychological, economic, or social preparation for it. This denies us the opportunity to orchestrate our demise in a way that will make the experience one of growth for us as well as for those who live on.

In part because of our modern life-sustaining technologies, death has become difficult to define. Three sorts of death can occur:

1. Clinical death, in which spontaneous respiration and heart beat stop.
2. Brain death, which occurs as a consequence of clinical death.
3. Biological or cellular death, which is essentially the death of various organ systems within the body and the last of the three to occur (Schulz, 1978).

Clinical death may not constitute irreversible death; resuscitation is often possible in this phase. Brain death may also not lead to irreversible death of the human organism, but it may cause loss of the "person." Without oxygen brain cells die in four to six minutes. The cortex dies first, and with it die voluntary acts, memory, and thought. The midbrain and brainstem follow. A person whose cortex and midbrain have died will be in an irreversible coma with only vegetative functions left. With intravenous feeding the person may be kept alive indefinitely, since the brainstem allows breathing to occur unaided (Korein, 1978; Schulz, 1978). Should biological death occur, no amount of intervention will bring the body back to function.

The issue of brain death was brought to public attention by the case of Karen Anne Quinlan, who went into an irreversible coma after consuming a combination of sedatives and alcohol. Karen's parents sought a court injunction to have her removed from respirator support, which was maintaining her, so that she might die in peace. After a lengthy legal battle she was removed from the respirator, but

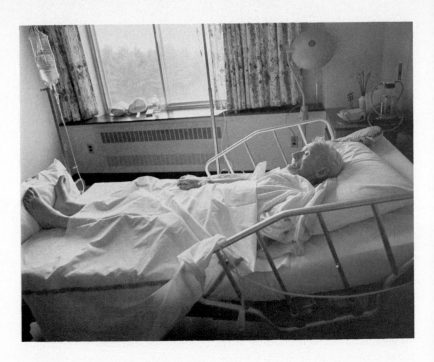

*Today, death has to a large extent been relegated to institutional settings.*

because her brainstem still functioned she was able to breath unassisted. She is still alive many years after the court battle and has been placed in a skilled nursing facility. During this time she has remained unresponsive.

Other cases similar to the Quinlan case were reported in a discussion of the apallic syndrome, a disorder in which severe total or almost total irreversible destruction of the cortex (pallium) occurs in association with severe anoxia, or oxygen deprivation (Ingvar et al., 1978). Patients with the apallic syndrome have been documented to live for seventeen or more years in irreversible coma (Ingvar et al., 1978).

The tragic nature of such prolonged coma raises broad ethical questions about quality of life, euthanasia, and the use of extraordinary means to maintain life. Patients are unaware of decreased quality of their lives, but the psychic pain felt by family members and care takers is profound.

With the advent of such life-sustaining machines as heart-lung machines and respirators, the brain appears to be the only system not directly supportable by machines (Schulz, 1978). Brain death has therefore emerged as a popular criterion on the basis of which to assess organismic death. In 1968 the Harvard Ad Hoc Committee to Examine the Definition of Brain Death formulated a definition of irreversible coma that was a combination of the following four criteria:

Unreceptivity or unresponsivity
No movements or breathing

No reflexes

Flat electroencephalogram (EEG) for twenty-four hours.

The last criterion was added because a flat EEG may be produced by certain reversible events, among them low body temperature, alcohol use, and heroin/barbiturate/tranquilizer overdose. Of 503 persons in irreversible coma studied, only 44 persons recovered, and these were people with reversible flat EEGs associated with the factors listed above (Ad Hoc Committee, 1968; Schulz, 1978).

Many researchers argue that the Harvard criteria are outmoded. Medical ethicists and philosophers ponder the notion of "cerebral death," or the state that exists when the cortex is irreversibly destroyed and the patient is unconscious but breathes unaided. In this sort of death the organism is alive but the individual, self, or person is irretrievably lost. If cerebral death were the legal definition of death, persons such as Quinlan would be technically dead.

A discussion of the ethical issues involved in the distinction among various sorts of brain death is beyond the scope of this book. However, it is not difficult to see how some definitions of death could lead to active euthanasia of cerebrally dead persons or old people with organic brain syndromes who are no longer themselves. The notion has even been broached of "neomortuaries," where the bodies of brain-dead persons could be kept functioning to allow preservation of organs needed for transplants. The persons who will make decisions on such matters in the future will have a profound responsibility.

**Death in the Individual**

Symbols of death are often grim or frightening — the cloaked skeleton, the pale rider, the grim reaper, or "nothing." The death of an individual may be frightening or unacceptable, but it is at least comprehensible. Death occurring to multitudes spontaneously is stupefying. The twenty-five million persons killed in Europe by the Black Death, the six million Jews exterminated by the Nazi Holocaust, or the three hundred thousand Japanese annihilated by the "small" atomic bomb dropped on Hiroshima are such huge numbers that we tend to think of the victims as objects rather than as many individuals similar to friends and relatives we know and love.

Death is very personal; we may rage against it, as Dylan Thomas suggested, deny it, or accept it, but our reaction always relates to ourselves and those we value. Death occurs to persons, to individuals who deal with it in their own unique ways. However, members of different age groups and social classes may also have common fears about, expectations about, and experience with death.

### Attitudes Toward Death

It is a common fallacy that the elderly, especially institutionalized elderly, think about death frequently and with a great deal of anxiety or fear. Several studies indicate that old persons are less anxious and fearful about death than young

*Death in the abstract is often presented in symbols, such as that of an old man with a scythe.*

persons (Kalish & Reynolds, 1976; Marshall, 1980; Riley, 1970). Perhaps old persons find death more salient but not stressful or frightening because of more death rehearsals or greater acceptance of their personal finitude (Kalish & Reynolds, 1976).

In a survey research project Riley (1970) found that fifty-three percent of all U.S. citizens surveyed agreed with the statement "Death always comes too soon." The majority of persons in our society grow old and die with this negative belief. Many people also feel that death occurs too soon for themselves and for old persons they love, but they expect other old persons to die. This attitude is typified by such statements as "Too bad he died, but then, he *was* eighty!"

As a society we profess a belief in personal immortality. However, it appears that the elderly share this belief in far fewer numbers than younger persons (Marshall, 1980). In addition, among subjects surveyed in various studies it was found that the higher the educational level, the better the acceptance of death as a personal event and the less the fear associated with it (Riley, 1970).

Significant age differences exist in the extent to which plans for death such as wills and the purchase of cemetery plots are carried out. In general, the older a person is, the more likely that person is to have made out a will, purchased a cemetery plot, made funeral arrangements, or made arrangements for someone to handle his or her affairs (Kalish & Reynolds, 1976). The only major point of agreement among all the age groups surveyed was on the need for life insurance.

Research suggests that old people have a more practical reaction to death than young persons and thus fear it less. Kalish and Reynolds (1976) have suggested several reasons for this. First, society places a low value on quality of life in old age. To the extent that an old person shares this attitude, the costs of giving up life decrease. Second, persons who live to old age may not feel that death is cheating them of time. Finally, persons in old age are socialized to accept their own deaths through the deaths of spouses and peers.

Old persons have been found to fear dishonor, pain, and loneliness more than death (Marshall, 1980). They have reached an awareness of their own finitude and have personalized death. They are aware that time is finite and that the time they have until death is far shorter than the time they have had since birth (Neugarten, 1977). Many persons make these realizations through the life review process (Butler, 1963). Natural reminiscence and the working through of unresolved conflicts are a means of reintegration for old persons, especially those who have a confidant to share in the process. Life review not only gives old persons a sense of closure and wholeness but also allows them to prepare for death.

For many persons life review brings with it the knowledge that death is appropriate for their stage of the life cycle. Death is preferable to inactivity, which they may foresee will increasingly be a part of their future. Death is also preferable to the loss of the ability to be useful and more desirable than becoming a burden on one's children. It is preferable to the loss of mental faculties or to progressively deteriorating health or discomfort. For many old persons death thus becomes a desired companion (Marshall, 1980).

For most people, young and old, it is the attendant consequences of death that are fearful and undesirable: suffering, humiliation, interruption of goals, and negative impact on survivors (Schulz, 1978). Nevertheless, once they reach the terminal stage of an illness, many persons come to desire death for reasons just as compelling: removal of severe pain, mental distress, or isolation; the belief that life is no longer meaningful; the desire for a dignified death; the desire to control how and when one dies; the finances involved in extended periods of illness (Schulz, 1978). Once death is personalized, regardless of the age of the dying person, the struggles against and fear of it are resolved, and it is quietly accepted (Kastenbaum, 1979; Marshall, 1980; Schulz, 1978).

### The Process of Dying

Just as each individual has an emotional response and makes an adjustment to dying, so too are the trajectories of dying distinct for each person and illness. A dying trajectory is the form and length of the dying process. Dying has been divided into three phases: an acute phase, in which the individual becomes aware of impending death; a chronic living-dying phase, in which the person's anxiety is reduced but emotions run from hope to determination to acceptance; and a terminal phase, in which the person begins the process of withdrawing from the world (Hultsch & Deutsch, 1981; Pattison, 1977). As can be seen in Figure 12-3, the acute crisis phase and the terminal phase are the shortest stages of the dying process.

The death trajectory is affected by a number of factors, including the person's adaptive capacity, the nature of the person's supports, and the sort of illness involved. Figure 12-4 presents various sorts of death trajectories, each of which requires different adaptive skills from the dying person, the family, and the care takers. Patterns involving either reversals of expectancies or extended dependencies, such as the vacillating, suspended sentence, entry-reentry, or lingering trajectory, are especially difficult for the patient and the significant others. A sudden decline from presumedly good health shortens the chronic phase of dying and ultimately requires less adaptation by the dying person. However, it places extra demands on the survivors in their grief work.

Regardless of the nature of the dying trajectory, the question of the appropriateness of the death arises (Kastenbaum, 1979). According to Weisman (1980), in an appropriate death the person dies in a manner he or she would have chosen, i.e., in a manner consistent with the person's life and values. In contrast, in an appropriated death control of the manner of dying is removed from the person by circumstances outside the person's control. Most deaths of elderly persons today occur in institutional settings. Eighty percent of all old persons spend their last days in hospitals or skilled nursing facilities (Kastenbaum, 1979). For the most part these deaths are not appropriate, because the efficiency and sterility of institutional care take control of death out of the hands of the dying person.

### Individual Reactions to Death

Individual reactions to impending death have received increasing amounts of research attention. Perhaps one of the best known approaches to this topic is that of Dr. Elisabeth Kubler-Ross, a Swiss-born psychiatrist who has spent a great deal of

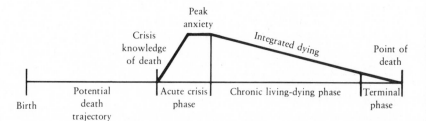

*Figure 12–3   Phases of dying*

(Source: Hultsch, D.F., & Deutsch, F. *Adult development and aging.* New York: McGraw-Hill Book Company, 1981, p. 355. Copyright © 1981 by McGraw-Hill Book Company. Used with permission of the publisher)

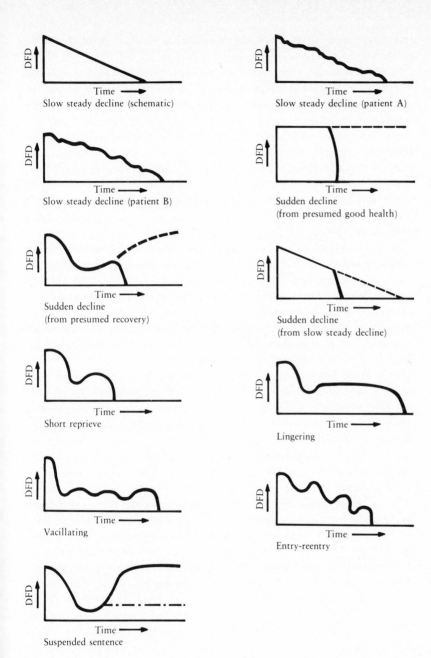

*Figure 12–4    Dying trajectories*

*DFD: Distance from death
(Source: Williamson, B., Munley, A., & Evans, L. *Aging and society.* New York: Holt, Rinehart & Winston, 1980)

time with terminal patients. Kubler-Ross's work has given us great insight into the feelings and problems of dying patients.

Kubler-Ross (1969) states that a patient's confrontation with a diagnosis of malignancy is difficult and poses problems for psychological adaptation. She believes that the physician must share the diagnosis with the patient in a way that encourages hope, that stresses that the person will not be abandoned, and that allows for continued open communication. Patients need to know the truth about their condition; they lose confidence in doctors who lie to them or do not help them face the seriousness of their own illnesses. Kubler-Ross's methods of terminal care require confidence and trust, which can exist only when there is truth between the patient and the care givers. She acknowledges that regardless of whether they have been formally told, most terminal patients are aware of their status (Kalish, 1970; Kubler-Ross, 1969).

Care givers disagree on the amount of information they feel should be disclosed to patients and the manner in which it should be disclosed. Dying persons are usually more aware that they are dying than most family members and care providers believe (Hultsch & Deutsch, 1981), but they are also often unable or unwilling to share this knowledge with others even if they know the others are aware of their condition (Kalish, 1970). This leads to mutual silence, which prevents closure on many important aspects of the dying person's life and emotional needs (Kalish, 1970; Kubler-Ross, 1969).

Often dying persons suspect that something is seriously wrong with them because of changes in the way in which family and care providers treat them. In some cases physicians, nurses, or family members give terminal patients explicit information about their condition. The initial response to this information may be fear, anger, or denial, but with time terminal patients deal with these emotions and plan for death. Patients who receive no explicit information often become increasingly anxious during the course of their illness as everyone works to keep up the process of denial.

Persons who have received no explicit information about their physical state often get clues from looks, questions, and whispers. They are then faced with the task of dealing with illness with incomplete data on outcome. They are often unsure how to treat their bodies' inability to get well or the changing pain experience they undergo. Generally the prognosis becomes clearer as other persons' responses change; for example, an increase in the number of long-distance telephone calls or out-of-town visits a patient receives suggest that the illness is not a normal one. Changes in medical care procedures or bodily signals often suggest to patients that the explanations being offered are not sufficient. Often something as subtle as a change in the tone of the conversation when terminal patients mention their future may indicate that their future is in question (Kalish, 1970).

Weisman (1972) suggests that dying patients have a sort of "middle knowledge" about their illness. They are aware that they will not recover, but they vacillate between believing and not believing it. *Middle knowledge* refers to the acknowledgment of dying patients of only a portion of the total available knowledge of what their sickness means. This knowledge sometimes approaches full acceptance of death but at other times is quite narrow. The way in which patients deal with the uncertain certainty of their dying varies considerably from person to person, age to age, and illness to illness. In her interviews with sick patients Kubler-Ross (1969) found five stages on the path to death (Fig. 12-5). The first stage is that of denial and isolation, which buffer the shock of the news of impending death. Denial is followed by anger and the feeling, "Why me and not someone else?" This second stage is difficult for the patient's family and the care providers to cope with because the patient's anger is displaced in all directions, most frequently against those with whom he or she is emotionally or physically the closest. Dying persons find grievances everywhere. If respected, understood, and given attention and time, they soon reduce their angry demands. However, if others become angry with them in return or if they are left alone for long periods of time, the situation often worsens.

The third stage is the bargaining stage. At this point patients try to reach an agreement that will postpone the inevitable. Dying persons bargain with themselves, family members, doctors, and God, although the bargains made with God are often kept a secret. The fourth stage, depression, begins when the dying person can no longer deny the illness owing to surgery or hospitalization. Anger is replaced by a great sense of loss. Often this depression is due to the inability the patient feels to face impending death; dealing with vital issues and personal affairs continually reminds the patient of what he or she must leave behind. The emotion encountered in this stage is for the most part anticipatory grief. The person mourns the loss of beloved objects and persons. Patients should not be denied this essential part of the process of dying. Without the freedom to express grief, dying persons must cover

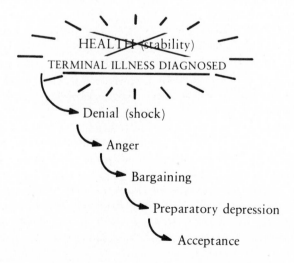

HEALTH (stability)
TERMINAL ILLNESS DIAGNOSED

Denial (shock)

Anger

Bargaining

Preparatory depression

Acceptance

*Figure 12-5  Kubler-Ross's stages of dying*

up their authentic emotions and once again engage in pretense. Final acceptance of death and integrity of life are easier for the terminal patient who is allowed to express sorrow over these impending losses. The dying person should not be told not to be sad.

The fifth and final stage of dying is acceptance. This is not a happy stage but is rather void of feelings, "the final rest before the long journey" (Kubler-Ross, 1969, p. 113). It is a time during which the family often needs more help and understanding than the patient. Dying persons at this stage have found some peace and acceptance, and their circle of interest therefore diminishes. They want to be left alone and not be bothered with problems of the outside world. At this stage communication becomes more nonverbal than verbal; dying persons often appreciate someone sitting quitely with them and holding their hand. They are reassured to know they are not being abandoned or forgotten when nothing more can be done (Kubler-Ross, 1969).

Although Kubler-Ross's stage theory of dying was a ground-breaking effort in the field of thanatology and broadened awareness of the dying process, it has not achieved universal acceptance (Kalish, 1970; Kastenbaum, 1979; Marshall, 1980). Most of Kubler-Ross's patients were young, only three were middle-aged, and none was elderly. The age of the patients sampled may well account for the nature of the emotions shown by them. As seen earlier in this chapter, attitude toward death varies with age, with young persons feeling fear or denial and elderly persons feeling unconcern (Marshall, 1980). Old patients may not show the intense anger described by Kubler-Ross (1969). Furthermore, it is not clear whether Kubler-Ross's patients had official knowledge of their "terminal status" when they were interviewed. Additionally, many studies are constructed on the assumption that people fear death, and lack of fear of death is thus interpreted as denial. It is unclear whether Kubler-Ross's patients were experiencing denial or harmonious acceptance of death (Marshall, 1980).

Other methodological criticisms may be made of Kubler-Ross's work. The nature of a person's illness may well affect the nature of that person's death experience. As seen earlier in this chapter, death trajectories may vary considerably. Persons on a vacillating course are likely to have a different emotional response to their illness from persons on a steady, swift downward course. Moreover, different illnesses produce their own emotional concomitants. Head and neck cancer produces different emotional responses in patients and their families than liver cancer; dying of emphysema, with its many alternations from acute crisis to remission and back again, is far different from dying from some acute disorder such as pneumonia or myocardial infarction. A final criticism is that what Kubler-Ross describes are not stages but rather means of coping with psychological trauma. They do not occur in a universally sequential order, nor are they irreversible. It has also not been proved that all dying persons go through any or all of them by necessity.

Regardless of these criticisms of her work, Kubler-Ross (1969) has made great contributions to the care and awareness of the needs of the dying person. She has stressed the need for communication, warmth, and touch in staff and family members. She has pointed out that dying is a trauma for the living as well as the dying and has advocated treatment of the whole family. The family plays a significant role, and their reactions to the situation contribute a great deal to the patient's response to illness. One of Kubler-Ross's greatest contributions has been the caveat "Treat the person, not the disease."

### Tasks of the Dying Person

Weisman and Kastenbaum (1968) suggest that patients entering the terminal phase of life can be separated into two groups on the basis of their response to impending death: those who are aware of death and accept it by withdrawing from daily activities and those who are aware of death but stay busy in daily activity. Regardless of these differences, dying persons share many needs and tasks.

The dying need to control pain, retain dignity or feelings of self-worth, and receive and give love and affection. Once pain is controlled, the focus shifts to the need for dignity and self-worth. Dignity can come from the patient's participation in decisions affecting the duration and outcome of the illness. Control over the terminal phase of one's life is as important as control over earlier parts of the life span. Individuals who feel unable to control their lives feel hopeless and helpless as a result (Schulz, 1978). The loss of control resulting from decreasing mobility and financial competence, loss of roles, and loss of freedom from institutionalization is psychologically as well as physically devastating (Seligman, 1975).

The individual plays an important role in the timing of death by either postponing or accelerating it (Shneidman, 1980a). Control may be direct or indirect; suicide is direct control, whereas eating and drinking too much is indirect control. Many dying persons also play a psychological role in their own death. This is illustrated by Weisman and Worden (1975), who studied cancer deaths among persons with identical illnesses. Given approximately the same treatment and initial physical status, some patients survived for long periods of time whereas others survived for only brief periods of time. Patients with cooperative, mutually responsive relationships with others survived for significantly longer periods of time than patients without such relationships. Patients who felt apathy, depression, and death wishes and had longstanding, mutually destructive relationships with others lived for a shorter time than expected on the basis of physical status alone.

For many persons institutionalization presents the ultimate loss of control. When this environmental loss is combined with the sense that one's body is failing and the anticipatory grief of dying, one may die "before one's time," perhaps because the will to live is replaced by the will to die. The following case illustrates this notion:

> A seventy-six-year-old former horse trader, gambler, and adventurer . . . had been admitted to the hospital in 1957 in a state of severe emaciation and

with signs of taboparesis. His physical condition improved with treatment, but he remained confined to a chair or to a walker. He also had chronic urinary infection, which proved resistant to treatment. His peevish, complaining attitude, constant demands, competition with and provocation of other patients, and cunning attempts to test the personnel made him a management problem. At the same time, several members of the team had a certain liking for this unusual patient. He showed strong, though ambivalent, attachment to the nurse, the charge aide, and the physician. It was possible to handle him only by a well-coordinated, rigid system of privileges and controls.

After the [geriatric ward] fire (which produced no injuries but necessitated a three-week move for repair), this patient was transferred to the neurological ward where the former special privileges (such as providing him with cartons of milk at certain hours each day) and controls could not be maintained. The patient appeared dejected and sad. He did not express his bitter anger as usual and hardly answered when addressed. Two weeks after the fire, he was found dead and the diagnosis was probable myocardial infarction. Autopsy was not performed.

Though the patient had been undernourished and feeble, there was nothing to indicate a critical condition and his death came as a complete surprise. Death was classified as "unexpected."*

Any illness, whether the common cold or cancer, affects mental functioning. The pain and discomfort of illness decrease psychic energy, and sick persons often become introverted because they do not have the energy to spend on secondary matters (Kastenbaum, 1979). In the elderly this introversion may be mistaken for "senility." It is important to maintain good communication with elderly dying patients, because their decreased sensory abilities, combined with the distress and distraction of their inner bodily signals, make cognitive functioning difficult to maintain. Elderly persons who are dying need to interact with significant others to maintain their mental functioning (Kastenbaum, 1979).

Dying persons feel they are in a world of their own. If they feel they are being abandoned, they may become angry, apathetic, or depressed. Elderly persons often stop eating because they are depressed. Common approaches to this problem include intravenous feeding, psychoactive medication, or letting the person die. All of these approaches are insensitive in that they omit the psychological factors leading to the behavior. The inner world of terminally ill old persons is often more real than the sick room. Dying persons in fact live in two realms. They are often aware, a few months or weeks before their death, that death is approaching. Terminal drop, the cognitive changes associated with death discussed in Chapter 7,

---

*Aleksandrowicz, D.R. Fire and its aftermath on a geriatric ward. *Bulletin of the Menninger Clinic*, 1961, 25(1), 23–32. Copyright 1961 by the Menninger Foundation. Reprinted with permission

often sets in and may provide a premonitory warning. Persons then often begin to give away valuable goods, advice, or memories to family members in the need to gain closure and leave a legacy (Kalish, 1970; Kastenbaum, 1979).

This is a difficult time for family members. They feel a need for leave taking but often do not know how to approach it. This lack of knowledge may translate itself into an inability to do or say anything, or it may lead to a poignant moment that becomes indelibly etched into the memory of the family member.

> The last time I saw my father, I guess I knew it might be the last time. We talked a little about this and that. Nothing important. It was as if we both had agreed to keep it that way because we both knew and we knew that we knew.
>
> As I started to go, I started rearranging his pillow and blankets. I don't know why. I found myself saying, "Good night! Sleep tight!" just the way he used to say that to me when I was a little girl and he would be tucking me in. I don't know what made me do that and I was afraid I had done something wrong, said the wrong thing.
>
> But Daddy just looked at me with the nicest expression on his face, a private little smile there. And he repeated it and finished it: "Good night! Sleep tight! Don't let the bed bugs bite!" That was my Daddy. And that's a moment I won't ever forget.*

The need for such closure and communication is as real for dying persons as it is for family members. The touching and memories shared in such interchanges reaffirm to dying persons that they are valuable, that their lives have had meaning, and that they have left a legacy. The leaving of a legacy is but one task of a dying person. There are several more that in many ways are similar to the tasks associated with illness-related stress discussed in Chapter 5.

Dying persons must arrange a variety of personal affairs, such as writing a will, purchasing a cemetery plot, and seeing to the care of children or a spouse. They must deal with death as it affects them and their survivors. To assure the quality of their remaining life, regardless of the amount of time left them, they must plan for their medical care and allocate their energy, time, and money. They must anticipate future pain and discomfort and deal with the fear of loss of autonomy associated with it. They must cope effectively with their own death encounter. They must decide whether to slow down or accelerate their own dying process. Finally, they must adjust to the sick or dying role (Kalish, 1970).

These are not easy tasks for any person. They are made easier by supportive family members or confidants but harder by the process of institutionalization, which often appropriates death. It is important for health care providers to be aware of the psychological processes experienced by dying persons. It is also

---

*Kastenbaum, R. *Growing old: Years of fulfillment*, Life Cycle Series (L. Kristal, Ed.). New York: Harper & Row, 1979, p. 118

essential for them to be aware of the potentially harmful aspects of the environment in which persons die. Death in a hospital setting produces a far different set of
benefits, realities, and tasks for the dying person than does death in a less rigid
setting such as a home or hospice.

**The Setting of Death**

As said earlier in this chapter, eighty percent of all elderly persons die in an
institutional setting. The benefit of death in such a setting is that society as a whole
is protected from the sights of death and dying. However, because care functions
are performed by nonfamily members in this special setting, family participation is
peripheral at best. The role of caring family members is often taken over by health
care providers whose medical training frequently includes desensitization toward
death. Medical personnel also often avoid dying patients.

Kastenbaum and Aisenberg (1972) state that persons involved with a dying
patient tend to emotionally isolate the patient. They treat him or her in a routine,
efficient manner devoid of personal concern. Inadequate communication among
the people intimately involved with the patient's well-being, e.g., the doctors,
nurses, and aides, render care of the total person impossible.

Health personnel often feel great anxiety when dealing with dying persons. For
their own mental stability they frequently use psychological distancing mechanisms, such as a brisk, abrupt manner, avoidance of eye contact, and avoidance of
touch. Doctors often look upon terminal status as a failure. Medical training
focuses on saving lives and acute care; chronic and terminal care focus on pallia-
tion. This often makes doctors and nurses faced with a dying person feel like
helpless bystanders when in fact no part of the life cycle requires more sensitive help
than this final stage.

Kastenbaum and Aisenberg (1972) cite three main reasons why medical personnel and family members often distance themselves from dying persons. First, they
see dying persons as somehow socially inferior. This unconscious attitude grows
out of the values our society places on productivity, youth, and achievement. Dying
is seen as a personal inadequacy to be avoided at all costs. Second, most persons,
medical professionals included, do not know what to do or say when dealing with
the dying or bereaved. They do not know what is appropriate behavior because
they have been denied opportunities to learn how to comfort persons facing the last
phase of their lives. Finally, contact with dying persons often forces them to
confront their own unresolved fears or uncertainties about dying.

The fact that medical personnel are frequently younger than dying persons may
also influence their manner of interacting (Kastenbaum & Aisenberg, 1972; Riley,
1970). Young people often see death as a sign of personal failure and an external
menace to be overcome. In contrast, elderly persons see death as part of an internal
process that should be embraced. Generally society and the health care professions
stress the overcoming orientation; this places them in an ambivalent position with
respect to the patients for whom they must care.

Life expectancy has been increasing and is expected to continue to increase, although, as seen in Chapter 2, these trends may be reversing. The medical world's success in postponing death and reversing circulatory death has led to the expectation that doctors may delay death indefinitely. According to our social ethic, any life is better than no life, even if we must live with a machine instead of a vital organ. This attitude presents another barrier to a death with dignity and autonomy. Often the use of life-sustaining machines results in the prolongation of dying rather than the extension of a meaningful life. Patients are robbed of a dignified death, burdens are imposed on survivors, and valuable resources are wasted.

Physicians often have mixed feelings as to what the optimal treatment of terminal patients is. In *Vital Signs: The Way We Die in America* (Langone, 1974) one doctor says,

> I feel there are times when we must let the patient go, particularly from a surgical standpoint, when we find there is a totally incurable disease such as cancer. . . . I am not justified in prolonging life by surgery or supportive treatment beyond what in the past would have been a natural death if the condition is not remediable. (Langone, 1974, p. 160).

However, a doctor who removes life-support machines risks the danger of a malpractice suit. Furthermore, physicians are committed by oath to preserve life, and the death of a patient is thus a failure of healing ability. Studies have suggested

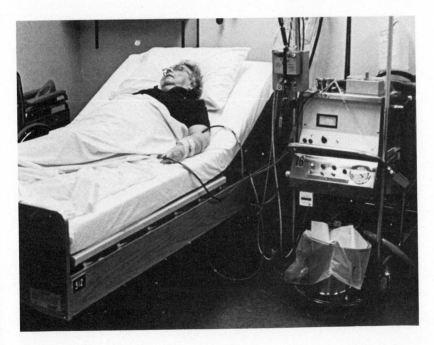

*The use of life-sustaining machines may result in the prolongation of dying rather than in the extension of a meaningful life.*

that medical students and physicians fear death more than any other professional group; perhaps this aversion to death is what impels them to preserve life (Mannes, 1973).

Doubts and fears about death in the medical staff working with terminal patients are also a deterrent to an appropriate death. Doctors and nurses tend to spend less time with terminal patients than with patients whose prognosis is good. Nurses take significantly longer to answer the bedside calls of terminal than of other patients. Most nurses try to remain professional, objective, or scientific. When a patient brings up the subject of death, they respond with reassurance ("You're doing fine"), denial, fatalism ("We're all going to die") or discussion ("What makes you feel that way?"), or they change the subject. They make these inappropriate responses because of inadequate training in terminal care, emotionality, or the fear of making a mistake. Enormous attention is given to the techniques of life prolongation but not to the provision of comfort. As Jeanne Quint, nurse and social scientist, has stated, "It is difficult to strive to keep the patient alive at all costs and at the same time help him die in a dignified and comforted manner" (Quint, 1967).

There is growing awareness in society of the possible conflict between life-prolongation techniques and an appropriate death. Many persons are turning to such documents as the "living will" stating their desires for medical care (Fig. 12-6). Such forms are intended to ensure that the patient's intentions will be taken into account in the total pattern of terminal care. Although such documents are not legally binding, they are considered appropriate and salient by the physician (Kastenbaum, 1977). Physicians engaged in terminal care are faced with two difficult questions: whether terminal patients should be told about their condition, and whether the focus of treatment should be on alleviating discomfort or on prolonging life, the two of which are often incompatible. The living will helps the doctor make these difficult decisions.

### Hospice Care

Perhaps the first consideration in the case of a terminal patient should be the possibility of dying at home. At home respect for the patient's unique identity is retained, and care is provided by persons who respond sensitively. Families deciding to follow this course, however, often need medical and emotional support and, if the terminal phase persists, occasional respite from the demanding nature of terminal care. The hospice approach to terminal care makes an appropriate death possible.

A hospice has been defined by the Subcommittee on Health and Environment of the U.S. House of Representatives as

A program which provides palliative and supportive care for terminally ill patients and their families, either directly or on a consulting basis with the patient's physician or another community agency such as a visiting nurse association. Originally a medieval name for a way station for pilgrims and

*To my family, my physician, my lawyer, my clergyman*
*To any medical facility in whose care I happen to be*
*To any individual who may become responsible for my health, welfare, or affairs*

Death is as much a reality as birth, growth, maturity and old age—it is the one certainty of life. If the time comes when I, _____ , can no longer take part in decisions for my own future, let this statement stand as an expression of my wishes while I am still of sound mind.

If the situation should arise in which there is no reasonable expectation of my recovery from physical or mental disability, I request that I be allowed to die and not be kept alive by artificial means or "heroic measures." I do not fear death itself as much as the indignities of deterioration, dependence, and hopeless pain. I therefore ask that medication be mercifully administered to me to alleviate suffering even though this may hasten the moment of death.

This request is made after careful consideration. I hope you who care for me will feel morally bound to follow its mandate. I recognize that this appears to place a heavy responsibility upon you, but it is with the intention of relieving you of such responsibility and of placing it upon myself in accordance with my strong convictions that this statement is made.

Signed _____

Date _____

Witness _____    Witness _____

Copies of this request have been given to _____

_____

Figure 12–6
The living will

(Source: Euthanasia Education Council)

travelers where they could be replenished, refreshed and cared for; used here for an organized program of care for people going through life's last station. The whole family is considered the unit of care and care extends through the mourning process. Emphasis is placed on symptom control and preparation for and support before and after death, full scope health services being provided by an organized interdisciplinary team available on a twenty-four hours a day, seven days a week basis.*

Hospices originated in England with St. Christopher's Hospice outside of London. The goals of hospices include relieving patients from the distressing symptoms of their disease, providing security in a caring environment, providing sustained expert care, and assuring patients and their families that they won't be abandoned (Craven & Wald, 1975). The emphasis of the hospice is on relieving pain and other symptoms as well as providing an emotional climate that will give a

*Congressional Report of the Ninety-Fourth Congress, 1976

sense of security during the last days and weeks of a person's life. The patient and family together are considered the unit of care. By being included in the treatment program, relatives have the opportunity not only to work through their own relationships with the patient but also to perform practical services for the dying such as meal preparation. This minimizes feelings of guilt during bereavement. Friends and relatives are also encouraged to consult with the staff during their period of bereavement (Saunders, 1965).

The hospice approach to treatment of the terminally ill has now begun in the United States. The National Cancer Institute is supporting a hospice in New Haven, Connecticut, modeled after St. Christopher's in London. Other communities around the United States and across the world are supporting hospice alternatives to traditional hospital care of the dying. Some of these efforts are in-hospital, others are independent of any hospital or nursing home, and still others are conducted by teams coming into the patient's home. Regardless of the setting of hospice care, the philosophy is always the same: to make the terminal phase of life as free of mental and physical pain as possible (Saunders, 1965).

Pain is one of the most significant causes of anxiety in dying persons. Hospice care involves the liberal use of opiates to control pain. Although opiates are highly addictive, nothing works as effectively for severe pain, and addiction should not be of concern in terminally ill persons. In a hospice opiates are used in small doses at an earlier stage than at most hospitals. Hospices use an antipain "cocktail" called *Brompton's mixture*, a mixture of morphine, cocaine, gin, syrup, sugar, and chlorpromazine syrup. According to Saunders (1965), the dosages of morphine may then be decreased over a period of time once the patient's fears and anxieties about pain are relieved. Other aspects of the pain-control regime are also strongly psychosocial in nature:

> The complement to a pain-control program is a loving and caring atmosphere created by the constant attention rendered by the staff and volunteers who, along with friends and relatives, spend much time just listening to the patients and holding their hands. Visiting hours are not restricted as in hospitals, so that families and friends spend as much time with the patient as they desire.*

For the terminal patient love and affection are usually expressed by physical contact such as touching and holding. Touching is an important part of the patient-staff member relationship in hospice care. The staff is encouraged to sit with patients and touch them as well as listen and follow the patients' own approaches to their dilemmas with assurances that they will not be abandoned.

A basic component of the hospice plan is delivery of care at home for as long as possible, with back-up inpatient beds provided at the hospice, which is an

*Schulz, R. *The psychology of death, dying and bereavement*. Reading, MA: Addison-Wesley Company, 1978, p. 80. Copyright © 1978 by Addison-Wesley Company. Reprinted with permission

attractive, home-like, deinstitutionalized setting. The hospice plan acknowledges that most terminally ill patients prefer to spend their remaining days in familiar surroundings and among their families. Often a point is reached, however, when the family can no longer cope with a patient's condition at home and the patient must transfer to an inpatient facility, if only for a short time. For example, terminal cancer operates in such a way that symptoms occasionally get out of control and the patient must be brought in to the hospice for what is called *respite care*. The patient is later returned home. Meanwhile, the family gets a reprieve from constant care of the patient and the mental and physical fatigue such care produces in them. However, the inpatient facility is used only when it is absolutely necessary and the patient has the choice.

The following case illustrates the difference between the care a patient receives in a hospice and the care provided in a traditional hospital or nursing home setting.

> Dorothy McBride, a seventy-seven-year-old divorcee who had cancer of the liver, decided to die at home. Her family took total responsibility for feeding and bathing her and administering her pain-killing mixture every four hours. Hospice teams visited Dorothy once a week. Although it was difficult for the family and they could not have endured the process without the support of the hospice personnel, it gave Dorothy a dignified death and provided satisfaction for her family.

It is difficult for a family to learn to live intimately with a person who is dying. It is not easy for the dying patient and the family to manage their emotions. However, an appropriate death with dignity is often possible only in this sort of supportive setting.

The subjects of euthanasia and suicide inevitably arise in any discussion of death. Both euthanasia and suicide usually involve death by voluntary choice at a self-appointed time. Suicide is self-inflicted, voluntary death; euthanasia is the act of painlessly putting to death a person suffering from an incurable disease or severe disability (Williamson et al., 1980). Although the means and vehicles of these two types of death are different, both kinds often accomplish the same goal in the elderly: being able to die with dignity at a time when life is devoid of dignity.

**Euthanasia and Suicide**

### Euthanasia

As long ago as 1624 John Donne, Dean of St. Paul's cathedral in London, wrote an essay in support of euthanasia asking whether it was logical to

> conscript a young man and subject him to the risk of torture and mutilation in war and probable death, and refuse an old man escape from an agonizing end. (Mannes, 1973, p. 72)

Others have also tried to support euthanasia, but attempts in 1947 to enact legislation permitting voluntary euthanasia within strict limits were struck down in the New York State Legislature even though the bill was underwritten by two thousand physicians and fifty-four clergymen.

Euthanasia has been divided into *passive euthanasia*, in which life-sustaining measures are withdrawn from a seriously ill person, and *active euthanasia*, in which something is done to hasten death artificially, as through the injection of a lethal dose of a drug. Euthanasia is not always "clean"; a physician may carry out euthanasia, for example, by refusing to use antibiotics in treating the pneumonia associated with terminal cancer. Antibiotics are usually not considered heroic measures, whereas heart-lung machines and respirators are. Experts in medical ethics feel that suicide and euthanasia often overlap.

Advocates of euthanasia stress the need for a "good death," i.e., a death with dignity in which the person controls his or her autonomy by dying voluntarily before that autonomy is lost. Critics of euthanasia usually focus on involuntary euthanasia and raise the specter of the Nazi Holocaust as an example of what might occur. Others fear attempts at financial gain by physicians or greedy family members. Still other critics stress that euthanasia might be used as a means of obtaining scarce organs for transplantation. The arguments are persuasive on both sides (Williamson et al., 1980).

Patient autonomy and the right to die with dignity are important issues. However, these concerns may be in conflict with sound medical decision making and optimal patient care. It is important even in cases of terminal care that all aspects of the patient's psychosocial environment be considered before any decision to discontinue treatment is made.

### Suicide

Shneidman (1980a) suggests that death certificates include a cause item about people's intentions toward their own deaths, i.e., show what role their psychology played in their dying. With this suggestion in mind, Shneidman (1980a) proposes four categories of death intention:

1.   High imputed lethality, in which a person commits suicide.
2.   Medium imputed lethality, e.g., neglect, carelessness, or disregard of a prescribed medical regime.
3.   Low imputed lethality, which differs from (2.) only in degree, not in kind.
4.   Absence of imputed lethality. (Williamson et al., 1980)

Suicide as envisioned by laypeople usually falls only into category (1.) above; for professionals, it also falls into categories (2.) and (3.).

Suicide is a human act of self-inflicted, intentional cessation of life (Shneidman, 1980a). Different causes of suicide have been described by different theorists. Durkheim, for example, felt that suicide was a result of society's strength or weakness of control of the individual. He discussed three different types of suicide: altruistic, in which death is required by society, much like the deaths of Japanese kamikaze pilots in World War II; egoistic, which occurs in persons who have few ties to the community and answer only their own needs; and anomic, which occurs when the accustomed ties between a person and society are suddenly shattered (Shneidman, 1980d).

The suicide of elderly persons may fit into any of these three categories. Old persons who commit suicide because they see themselves as falling beneath the standards of society would be considered altruistic suicides. Single-room occupants who drink themselves to death would be considered egoistic suicides. Elderly persons who kill themselves after the death of a spouse would be classified as anomic suicides.

Freud, in a far less cited theory, claims that suicide is murder of the introjected love object. According to this view, people commit suicide because of fear of, hate for, or hostility toward a desired love object. Rather than killing the external object, they kill their image of it and thus permanently remove its potential to hurt them. In the process, however, they also kill themselves (Shneidman, 1980d).

In addition to theories about causes of suicide, there are various myths about suicides, and the existence of such myths may render society ineffective to halt the occurrence of suicide. One of the most common fallacies is that persons who talk about suicide do not commit suicide. Another is that suicide happens without warning. Others include the fable that suicidal persons are fully intent on dying and that suicidal persons are mentally ill or psychotic (Shneidman, 1980d).

Because of the common view in our society that old age is a time of tranquility and decreased stress, suicide rates are not expected to be high in old age. Statistical evidence, however, suggests that they are. Suicide rates for nonwhites are generally lower than for whites. For white females, nonwhite females, and nonwhite males the suicide rate is generally U-shaped, with rates increasing until midlife and declining or staying the same thereafter. For white males, however, the rate increases with each decade of life, the highest rate occurring among men over eighty-five.

White men who have recently lost their wives, live alone, and are afflicted with some chronic illness appear to be especially at risk for suicide. Suicide threats and depression in the elderly should never be taken casually.

**Interventions for Bereavement and Grief**

Dying, like any other life transition, may be considered a crisis for the persons involved, whether they are dying or experiencing the death of a loved one. Death presents a further crisis for the survivors, i.e., for those who are bereaved, because usual methods of problem-solving often do not work in the death situation. This frequently leads to a period of upsetedness or disorganization in which many abortive, not necessarily constructive, attempts at adaptation are made.

Current methods of dealing with bereavement and grief are based on crisis theory, as discussed above, and on the work of Erich Lindemann. Lindemann was a physician who provided psychiatric help to the family members of victims of the

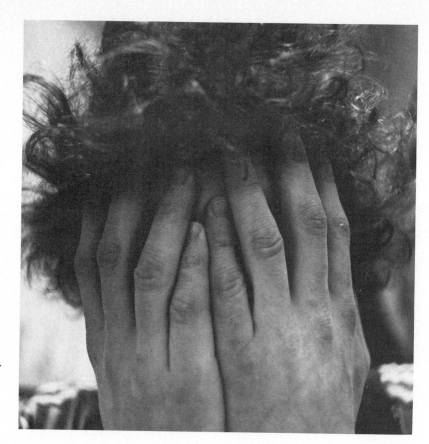

*Death presents a crisis for the survivors, for whom usual problem-solving methods often do not work.*

fire that swept through the Coconut Grove nightclub in Boston on the night of November 28, 1942. Four hundred ninety-three people died in that fire, most of them crushed in panic around the only two operating exit doors. Lindemann helped the survivors of the fire and the families of those who had died and chronicled his findings (Kastenbaum, 1975).

The bereaved had uniform reactions to grief. They described waves of bodily distress lasting twenty to sixty minutes and including tightness in the chest, a lump in the throat, lack of muscular power, and an empty feeling in the abdomen. The survivors learned that these waves were precipitated by various events such as mentioning the name of the deceased victim or hearing the name of the victim mentioned by others. Often the survivors found themselves avoiding such situations to avoid the psychological pain they produced.

The bereaved also suffered from changes in affect. They felt a sense of unreality and emotional distance from other people. They were frequently preoccupied with the image of the deceased, and this image was often accompanied by feelings of guilt, i.e., survivors often felt that they had somehow neglected the victim or somehow contributed to the victim's death.

The survivors often indicated that they felt a loss of warmth in relationships with other people and were frequently overcome by anger and hostility. They complained of being unable to conduct and maintain an organized pattern of activity and of lacking energy for activity. Survivors often developed a strong dependence on anyone who could stimulate them to a pattern of activity.

As time passed the survivors readjusted to the world without the deceased. They achieved a psychological separation from the deceased and were able to form new relationships. The major obstacle to this healthy adjustment to bereavement was unwillingness to express the intense emotional distress connected with the experience. Lindemann found that if he could facilitate that expression of grief, there would often be a rapid relief of tension and reconstruction of normal daily patterns. If this grief were not allowed to express itself, survivors would often exhibit a morbid, possibly life-threatening, grief reaction.

Morbid grief reactions as described by Lindemann include postponement of grief and distorted reactions of grief such as the following:

Overactivity without a sense of loss
Development of symptoms previously held by the deceased
Psychosomatic disorders
Extreme hostility toward specific persons
Agitated depression
Tension, insomnia, feelings of worthlessness
Self-accusation
Suicidal impulses or actual suicide.

Most survivors performed the grief work successfully with minimal outside intervention. For those who evidenced morbid grief reactions professional intervention was needed.

Since Lindemann's pioneering work grief, bereavement, and loss have been studied in various mass disasters, such as the 1972 Hurricane Agnes floods in Pennsylvania, the 1972 Buffalo Creek flood in West Virginia, and the 1974 Indiana tornadoes. In all cases patterns similar to those first described by Lindemann have been found in the bereaved. Similar dynamics work in the process of grief whether one person or several hundred are involved.

Successful adjustment to grief due to loss of a loved one by death depends on a number of factors. One factor involved is whether the bereaved person was able to communicate with the deceased before death occurred. Survivors are better off if they were able to communicate with the dying person, for example to resolve old problems, before the death occurred. Also, to the extent that the bereaved are able to perceive the patient's acceptance of death, they may be better able to make that adjustment themselves. Failure to communicate with or understand the dying process leads to guilt about, anger toward, frustration with, and even rejection of the deceased.

Bereaved survivors may die prematurely owing to grief. The death rate for surviving relatives is unusually high for the year following the death of a loved one. Surviving spouses are more vulnerable than other relatives. Men are especially likely to commit suicide or die of natural causes after the death of a spouse.

However, most people do not have such an extreme psychological response to bereavement. Most persons go through a period of one or two years in which they feel psychic distress upon mention of the deceased person's name, upon seeing a picture of the person, under various other circumstances. During this period their ability to function is impaired but not typically pathological. The most important need of persons feeling normal grief is to realize that they are not abnormal or "crazy." They need to know that grief work is a difficult, distressing, and normal process.

Certain basic principles of grief management are helpful to professionals or family members involved closely with the bereaved. It is important, for example, to help the bereaved express their grief and find new patterns of rewarding interaction. They must be helped to review their relations with the deceased and verbalize their feelings of guilt. The traditional responses of comfort, invocation of divine will, and promises of later reunions offer many people consolation but not help in working through the difficulties they encounter in grieving. To a certain extent these traditional responses limit conversation to "safe" topics, effectively closing future communication about what the bereaved person is really feeling.

Thanatological counseling has certain broad differences from normal psychotherapy. The goals are different because the therapy is time limited, both for the dying person and for the survivors. Psychological comfort, stability, and the tying off of loose ends are essential foci of such therapy. The rules of therapy with a dying person are different. A deeper relationship must develop than is countenanced in any other professional relationship. Should the patient survive, this contract must of course be renegotiated; furthermore, the relationship is ever as deep with the survivors as with the dying person (Shneidman, 1980d).

Therapy with the bereaved often focuses on benign intervention. The therapist is not passive but rather acts as an ombudsman for the patient and the family. Working through psychological difficulty is a luxury for those who will survive, not for the dying person. Therefore, although the anticipatory grief of the dying and the reactive grief of the survivors have things in common, there are essential differences in the manner of counseling dying persons and survivors.

**Summary**

Death in the elderly — its reality, anticipation, and attendant emotional consequences — is different from death in young people. With age comes a growing awareness that death is near, and as health status declines, the finitude of death is welcome to many old persons. The awareness of death and their personal

*Dying is something we human beings do continuously, not just at the end of our physical lives on earth. . . .*

mortality often prompts old people to embark on a process of life review or reminiscence, which provides some wholeness or integrity to the lives they have lived.

Once the dying process is actively encountered, dying persons must reconcile their desire for autonomy and an appropriate death with the realities of their family constraints and the health care they must receive. The various tasks dying persons must complete, such as accepting the sick role and planning for their limited future, are different for persons dying at home and persons dying in the hospital. In either case the needs and wishes of dying persons with respect to relief of pain, autonomy, and the use of heroic measures to prolong life must be dealt with by family members and health professionals. If they are not, death may be appropriated from the dying person and may thus be more of a psychological trauma than it need be. If the process of dying is legitimated for the dying person and the problem of impending death is successfully resolved, life in its final phase may be a bittersweet enjoyment different only in degree from that of earlier life transitions.

Dying is something we human beings do continuously, not just at the end of our physical lives on earth... through a willingness to risk the unknown, to venture forth into unfamiliar territory, you can undertake the search for your own self — the ultimate goal of growth. Through reaching out and committing yourself to dialogue with fellow human beings, you can begin to transcend your individual existence, becoming as one with yourself and others. And through a lifetime of such commitment, you can face your final end with peace and joy, knowing you have lived your life well.*

*Kubler-Ross, E. *Death: The final stage of growth.* Englewood Cliffs, NJ: Prentice-Hall, 1975, p. 145

Abrahams, J.P., & Birren, J.E. Reaction time as a function of age and behavioral predisposition to coronary heart disease. *Journal of Gerontology*, 1973, *28*, 471–478.

Achenbaum, W.A. *Shades of gray: Old age, American values and federal policies since 1920*. Boston, Mass.: Little, Brown, 1983.

Adams, G.F. *Essentials of geriatric medicine*. Oxford, Great Britain: Oxford University Press, 1978.

Adams, R.D. The morphological aspects of aging in the human nervous system. In J. E. Birren & R.B. Sloane (Eds.), *Handbook of mental health and aging*. Englewood Cliffs, N.J.: Prentice-Hall, 1980.

Adelman, R.C. Macromolecular metabolism during aging. In C.E. Finch & L. Hayflick (Eds.), *Handbook of the biology of aging*. New York: Van Nostrand Reinhold, 1977.

Ad Hoc Committee of the Harvard Medical School to Examine the Definition of Brain Death. A definition of irreversible coma. *Journal of the American Medical Association*, 1968, *205*, 85–88.

Adler, W. H. An autoimmune theory of aging. In M. Rockstein, M.L. Sussman, & J. Chesky (Eds.), *Theoretical aspects of aging*. New York: Academic Press, 1974.

Aleksandrowicz, D. R. Fire and its aftermath on a geriatric ward. *Bulletin of the Menninger Clinic*, 1961, *25*(1), 23–32.

American Psychiatric Association. *Diagnostic and statistical manual of mental disorders* (3rd ed.). Washington, D.C.: American Psychiatric Association, 1980.

Arenberg, D., & Robertson-Tchabo, E. A. Learning and aging. In J. E. Birren & K. W. Schaie (Eds.), *The handbook of the psychology of aging*. New York: Van Nostrand Reinhold, 1977.

Back, K. W. Personal characteristics and social behavior: Theory and method. In R. Binstock & E. Shanas (Eds.), *Handbook of aging and the social sciences*. New York: Academic Press, 1976.

Baltes, P. B., & Nesselroade, J. R. The developmental analysis of individual differences on multiple measures. In J. R. Nesselroade & H. W. Reese (Eds.), *Life-span developmental psychology: Methodological issues*. New York: Academic Press, 1973.

Baltes, P. B., & Schaie, K. W. (Eds.). *Life-span developmental psychology: Personality and socialization*. New York: Academic Press, 1973.

Baltes, P. B., & Schaie, K. W. The myth of the twilight years. *Psychology Today*, 1974, *7*(10), 35–40.

Baltes, P. B., & Willis, S. L. Toward psychological theories of aging and development. In J. E. Birren & K. W. Schaie (Eds.), *Handbook of the psychology of aging*. New York: Van Nostrand Reinhold, 1977.

Baric, L. Recognition of the "at-risk" role: A means to influence health behavior. *International Journal of Health Education*, 1969, *12*, 24–34.

Barrow, G. M., & Smith, P. A. *Aging, ageism and society*. St. Paul: West, 1979.

Bartus, R. T., Dean, R. L., Beer, B., & Lippa, A. S. The cholinergic hypothesis of geriatric memory dysfunction. *Science*, 1982, *217*, 408–417.

Bayley, N., & Oden, M. H. The maintenance of intellectual ability in gifted adults. *Journal of Gerontology*, 1955, *10*, 91–107.

Bengtson, V. L., Kasschau, P. L., & Ragan, P. K. The impact of social structure on aging individuals. In J. E. Birren & K. W. Schaie (Eds.), *Handbook of the psychology of aging*. New York: Van Nostrand Reinhold, 1977.

Berkowitz, B. Changes in intellect with age: IV. Changes in achievement and survival in older people. *Journal of Genetic Psychology*, 1965, *107*, 3–14.

Berkowitz, B., & Green, R. F. Changes in intellect with age: V. Differential change as functions of time interval and original score. *Journal of Genetic Psychology*, 1965, *107*, 179–192.

Birren, J. E. *The psychology of aging*. Englewood Cliffs, N.J.: Prentice-Hall, 1964.

Birren, J. E., & Botwinick, J. The relation of writing speed to age and to the senile psychoses. *Journal of Consulting Psychology*, 1951, *15*, 243–249.

Birren, J. E., Butler, R. N., Greenhouse, S. W., Sokoloff, L., & Yarrow, M. R. *Human Aging*. Washington, D.C.: Public Health Service Publication No. 986, 1963.

Birren, J. E., & Morrison, D. F. Analysis of the WAIS subtests in relation to age and education. *Journal of Gerontology*, 1961, *16*, 363–369.

Birren, J. E. & Renner, V. J. Research on the psychology of aging: Principles and experimentation. In J. E. Birren & K. W. Schaie (Eds.), *Handbook of the psychology of aging*. New York: Van Nostrand Reinhold, 1977.

Birren, J. E., & Sloane, R. B. (Eds.). *Handbook of mental health and aging*. Englewood Cliffs, N. J.: Prentice-Hall, 1980.

Birren, J. E., Woods, A. M., & Williams, M. V. Behavioral slowing with age: Causes, organization and consequences. In L. W. Poon (Ed.), *Aging in the 1980s: Psychological issues*. Washington, D. C.: American Psychological Association, 1980.

Bjorksten, J. Crosslinkage and the aging process. In M. Rockstein, M. L. Sussman, & J. Chesky (Eds.), *Theoretical aspects of aging*. New York: Academic Press, 1974.

Blazer, D. The epidemiology of mental illness in late life. In E. W. Busse & D. Blazer (Eds.), *Handbook of geriatric psychiatry*. New York: Van Nostrand Reinhold, 1980.

Blenkner, M. The place of the nursing home among community resources. *Journal of Geriatric Psychology*, 1968, *1*, 135–144.

Bondareff, W. Neurobiology of aging. In J. E. Birren & R. B. Sloane (Eds.), *Handbook of mental health and aging*. Englewood Cliffs, N. J.: Prentice-Hall, 1980.

Botwinick, J. *Cognitive processes in maturity and old age*. New York: Springer, 1967.

Botwinick, J. *Aging and behavior.* New York: Springer, 1973.

Botwinick, J. Intellectural abilities. In J. E. Birren & K. W. Schaie (Eds.), *Handbook of the psychology of aging.* New York: Van Nostrand Reinhold, 1977.

Botwinick, J., & Storandt, M. Cardiovascular status, depressive affect and other factors in reaction time. *Journal of Gerontology,* 1974, *29,* 543–548.

Botwinick, J., West, R. & Storandt, M. Predicting death from behavioral test performance. *Journal of Gerontology,* 1978, *33*(5), 755–762.

Brink, T. L. *Geriatric psychotherapy.* New York: Human Sciences Press, 1979.

Bromley, D. B. An approach to theory construction in the psychology of development and aging. In L. R. Goulet & P. B. Baltes (Eds.), *Life-span developmental psychology: Theory and research.* New York: Academic Press, 1970.

Bromley, D. B. *The psychology of human aging* (2nd ed.). New York: Penguin Books, 1974.

Bühler, C. Genetic aspects of the self. *Annals of the New York Academy of Sciences,* 1962, *96,* 730–764.

Burnside, I. M. Symptomatic behaviors in the elderly. In J. E. Birren & R. B. Sloane (Eds.), *Handbook of mental health and aging.* Englewood Cliffs, N. J.: Prentice-Hall, 1980.

Busse, E. W., & Blazer, D. The theories and processes of aging. In E. W. Busse & D. G. Blazer (Eds.), *Handbook of geriatric psychiatry.* New York: Van Nostrand Reinhold, 1980.

Busse, E. W., & Pfeiffer, E. (Eds.). *Mental illness in later life.* Washington, D. C.: American Psychiatric Association, 1973.

Butler, R. The life review: An interpretation of reminiscence in the aged. *Psychiatry: Journal for the Study of Interpersonal Processes,* 1963, *26,* 65–76.

Butler, R. N., & Lewis, M. I. *Aging and mental health.* St. Louis: C.V. Mosby, 1977.

Canestrari, R. E., Jr. Paced and self-paced learning in young and elderly adults. *Journal of Gerontology,* 1963, *18,* 165–168.

Cohen, D., & Dunner, D. The assessment of cognitive dysfunction in dementing illness. In J. O. Cole & J. E. Barrett (Eds.), *Psychopathology in the aged.* New York: Raven Press, 1980.

Cohen, D., & Eisdorfer, C. Serum immunoglobulins and cognitive status in the elderly. I. A population study. *British Journal of Psychiatry,* in press.

Cohen, G. D. Prospects for mental health and aging. In J. E. Birren & R. B. Sloane (Eds.), *Handbook of mental health and aging.* Englewood Cliffs, N. J.: Prentice-Hall, 1980.

Conrad, C. C. When you're young at heart. *Aging,* 1976, *4*(258), 11–13.

Corso, J. F. Presbycusis as a complicating factor in evaluating noise-induced hearing loss. In D. Henderson, R. P. Hamernik, D. S. Dasanjh, & J. H. Mills (Eds.), *Effects of noise on hearing.* New York: Raven Press, 1976.

Corso, J. F. Auditory perception and communication. In J. E. Birren & K. W.

Schaie (Eds.), *Handbook of the psychology of aging.* New York: Van Nostrand Reinhold, 1977.

Costa, P. T., McCrae, R. R., & Arenberg, D. Enduring dispositions in adult males. *Journal of Personality and Social Psychology,* 1980, *38,* 793–800.

Coyle, J. T., Price, D. L. & DeLong, M. R. Brain mechanisms in Alzheimer's disease. *Hospital Practice,* November 1982, pp. 50–58.

Craik, F. I. M. Age differences in human memory. In J. E. Birren & K. W. Schaie (Eds.), *Handbook of the psychology of aging.* New York: Van Nostrand Reinhold, 1977.

Craven, J., & Wald, F. Hospice care for dying patients. *American Journal of Nursing,* October 1975, pp. 1816–1822.

Crowley, C., & Curtis, H. J. The development of somatic mutations in mice with age. *Proceedings of the National Academy of Sciences,* 1963, *49,* 626–628.

Cumming, E., & Henry, W. E. *Growing old.* New York: Basic Books, 1961.

Cunningham, W. R., & Birren, J. E. Age changes in human abilities: A 28 year longitudinal study. *Developmental Psychology,* 1976, *12,* 81–82.

Curtis, H. J., & Miller, K. Chromosome aberrations in liver cells of guinea pigs. *Journal of Gerontology,* 1971, *26,* 292–294.

Cutler, N. E., & Harootyan, R. A. Demography of the aged. In D. S. Woodruff & J. E. Birren (Eds.), *Aging: Scientific perspectives and social issues.* New York: Van Nostrand Reinhold, 1975.

Cutter, F. *Coming to terms with death.* Chicago: Nelson-Hall, 1974.

DeLong, A. J. The microspatial structure of the older person. In L. A. Pastalan & D. H. Carson (Eds.), *The spatial behavior of older people.* Ann Arbor: University of Michigan Press, 1970.

DeVries, H. A. Physiology of exercise and aging. In D. S. Woodruff & J. E. Birren (Eds.), *Aging: Scientific perspectives and social issues.* New York: Van Nostrand Reinhold, 1975.

Diamond, M. C. The aging brain: Some enlightening and optimistic results. *American Scientist,* 1978, *66,* 66–71.

Diamond, M. C., Rosenzweig, M. R., Bennett, E. L., Lindner, B., & Lyon, L. Effects of environmental enrichment and impoverishment on rat cerebral cortex. *Journal of Neurobiology,* 1972, *3,* 47–64.

Dollard, J., & Miller, N. E. *Personality and psychotherapy.* New York: McGraw-Hill, 1950.

Doppelt, J. E. & Wallace, W. L. Standardization of the Wechsler Adult Intelligence Scale for older persons. *Journal of Abnormal and Social Psychology,* 1955, *51,* 312–330.

Douglas, K., Arenberg, D. Age changes, cohort differences, and cultural change on the Guilford-Zimmerman Temperament Survey. *Journal of Gerontology,* 1978, *33,* 737–747.

Dusek, J. B. *Adolescent development and behavior.* Palo Alto, Calif: Science Research Associates, 1977.

Dusek, J. B., Kermis, M. D., & Monge, R. H. The hierarchy of adolescent interests: A social-cognitive approach. *Genetic Psychology Monographs*, 1979.

Eisdorfer, C. The WAIS performance of the aged: A retest evaluation. *Journal of Gerontology*, 1963, *18*, 169-172.

Eisdorfer, C., & Friedel, R. O. *Cognitive and emotional disturbances in the elderly*. Chicago: Year Book Medical Publishers, 1977.

Eisdorfer, C., & Lawton, M. P. *The psychology of adult development and aging*. Washington, D. C.: American Psychiatric Association, 1973.

Eisdorfer, C., Nowlin, J., & Wilkie, F. Improvement of learning in the aged by modification of autonomic nervous system activity. *Science*, 1970, *170*, 1327-1329.

Eisdorfer, C., & Wilkie, F. Stress, disease aging and behavior. In J. E. Birren & K. W. Schaie (Eds.), *Handbook of the psychology of aging*. New York: Van Nostrand Reinhold, 1977.

Elias, M. F., Elias, P. K. & Elias, J. W. *Basic processes in adult developmental psychology*. St. Louis: C. V. Mosby, 1977.

Engen, T. Taste and smell. In J. E. Birren & K. W. Schaie (Eds.), *Handbook of the psychology of aging*. New York: Van Nostrand Reinhold, 1977.

Erickson, R. P. Sensory neural patterns and gustation. In Y. Zotterman (Eds), *Olfaction and taste*. Elmsford, NY: Pergamon Press, 1963.

Erikson, E. H. *Childhood and society*. NY: W. W. Norton, 1950. (First Edition)

Erikson, E. H. *Childhood and society*. New York: W. W. Norton, 1963.

Etholm, B., & Belal, A., Jr. Senile changes in the middle ear joints. *Annals of Otology, Rhinology, & Laryngology*, 1974, *83*, 49-54.

Federal Council on Aging. *The frail elderly*. Washington, D. C.: Federal Council on Aging, 1978.

Finch, C. E., & Hayflick, L. (Eds.). *Handbook of the biology of aging*. New York: Van Nostrand Reinhold, 1977.

Flavell, J. H. Cognitive changes in adulthood. In L. R. Goulet & P. B. Baltes (Eds.), *Life-span developmental psychology: Research and theory*. New York: Academic Press, 1970.

Foulds, G. A. & Ravens, J. C. Normal changes in the mental abilities of adults in age advances. *Journal of Mental Science*, 1948, *94*, 133-142.

Fozard, J. L. The time for remembering. In L. Poon (Ed.), *Aging in the 1980s: Psychological issues*. Washington, D.C.: American Psychological Association, 1980.

Fozard, J. L., & Costa, P. T. Age differences in memory and decision-making in relation to personality, abilities and endocrine function: Implications for clinical practice and health planning policy. In M. Marios (Ed.), *Aging: A challenge for science and social policy*. London: Oxford University Press, in press.

Fozard, J. L., Wolf, E., Bell, B., McFarland, R. A., & Podolsky, S. Visual perception and communication. In J. E. Birren & K. W. Schaie (Eds.), *Handbook of the psychology of aging.* New York: Van Nostrand Reinhold, 1977.

Friedrich, D. D., & Van Horn, K. R. *Developmental methodology: A revised primer.* Minneapolis: Burgess, 1976.

Fries, J. F., & Crapo, L. M. *Vitality and aging.* San Francisco: W. H. Freeman & Company, 1981.

Gaitz, C. M., & Varner, R. V. Preventive aspects of mental illness in late life. In J. E. Birren & R. B. Sloane (Eds.), *Handbook of mental health of aging.* Englewood Cliffs, N.J.: Prentice-Hall, 1980.

Garner, H. H. Somatopsychic concepts. In R. P. Marinelli & A. E. Dell Orto (Eds.), *The psychological and social impact of physical disability.* New York: Springer, 1977.

Gatz, M., Smyer, M. A., & Lawton, M. P. The mental health system and the older adult. In L. W. Poon (Ed.), *Aging in the 1980s: Psychological issues.* Washington, D. C.: American Psychological Association, 1980.

Geldard, F. A. *The human senses.* New York: John Wiley & Sons, 1966.

Gelfand, D. E., & Olsen, J. K. *The aging network: Programs and services.* New York: Springer, 1980.

Gilbert, J. G. Memory loss in senescence. *Journal of Abnormal and Social Psychology,* 1941, *36,* 73-86.

Gotestam, K. W. Behavioral and dynamic psychotherapy with the elderly. In J. E. Birren & R. B. Sloane (Eds.), *Handbook of mental health and aging.* Englewood Cliffs, N.J.: Prentice-Hall, 1980.

Goulet, L. R., & Baltes, P. B. (Eds.). *Life-span developmental psychology: Research and theory.* New York: Academic Press, 1970.

Granick, S., & Patterson, R. D. *Human aging II: An 11-year biomedical and behavioral study.* Washington, D.C.: U.S. Government Printing Office, 1971.

Gregory, R. L. *The eye and the brain.* New York: McGraw-Hill, 1967.

Grotjohn, M. Analytic therapy with the elderly. *Psychoanalytic Review,* 1955, *42,* 419-427.

Gruenberg, E. M. The social breakdown — Some origins. *American Journal of Psychiatry,* 1967, *123,* 481-489.

Gurland, B. J. The assessment of the mental health status of older adults. In J. E. Birren & R. B. Sloane (Eds.), *Handbook of mental health and aging.* Englewood Cliffs, N.J.: Prentice-Hall, 1980.

Gutmann, D. L. An exploration of ego configurations in middle and later life. In B. L. Neugarten et al. *Personality in middle and late life.* New York: Atherton Press, 1964.

Gutmann, D. L. Dependency, illness and survival among Navajo men. In E. Palmore and F. C. Jeffers (Eds.), *Prediction of life-span.* Lexington, Mass.: D.C. Heath, 1971.

Gutmann, D. L. Parenthood: A key to the comparative study of the life cycle. In N.

Datan & L. Ginsberg (Eds.), *Life-span developmental psychology: Normative life crises.* New York: Academic Press, 1975.

Gutmann, D. L. The cross-cultural perspective: Notes toward a comparative psychology of aging. In J. E. Birren & K. W. Schaie (Eds.), *Handbook of the psychology of aging.* New York: Van Nostrand Reinhold, 1977.

Louis Harris & Associates. *The myth and reality of aging in America.* Washington, D.C.: National Council on the Aging, 1975.

Hartford, M. E. The use of group methods for work with the aged. In J. E. Birren & R. B. Sloane (Eds.), *Handbook of mental health and aging.* Englewood Cliffs, N.J.: Prentice-Hall, 1980.

Hartley, J. T., Harker, J. O., & Walsh, D. A. Contemporary issues and new directions in adult development of learning and memory. In L. W. Poon (Ed.), *Aging in the 1980s: Psychological issues.* Washington, D.C.: American Psychological Association, 1980.

Harwood, E., & Naylor, G. F. K. Recall and recognition in elderly and young subjects. *Australian Journal of Psychology*, 1969, *21*, 251–257.

Havighurst, R. J. History of developmental psychology: Socialization and personality development through the life-span. In P. B. Baltes & K. W. Schaie (Eds.), *Life-span developmental psychology: Personality and socialization.* New York: Academic Press, 1973.

Hayflick, L. The cellular basis for biological aging. In C. E. Finch & L. Hayflick (Eds.), *Handbook of the biology of aging.* New York: Academic Press, 1977.

Hickey, T. *Health and aging.* Monterey, Calif: Brooks/Cole, 1980.

Hicks, R., Funkenstein, H. H., Davis, J. M., & Dysken, M. W. Geriatric psychopharmacology. In J. E. Birren & R. B. Sloane (Eds.), *Handbook of mental health and aging.* Englewood Cliffs, N.J.: Prentice-Hall, 1980.

Holmes, T. H., & Rahe, R. H. The social readjustment rating scale. *Journal of Psychosomatic Research*, 1967, *11*, 213-218.

Horn, J. L. Organization of data on life-span development of human abilites. In L. R. Goulet & P. B. Baltes (Eds.), *Life-span developmental psychology: Research and theory.* New York: Academic Press, 1970.

Horn, J. L., & Donaldson, G. On the myth of intellectual decline in adulthood. *American Psychologist*, 1976, *31*, 701-719.

Horn, J. L. & Donaldson, G. Cognitive development. II. Adulthood development of human abilities. In O. G. Brim & J. Kagan (Eds.), *Constancy and change in human development: A volume of review essays.* Cambridge, Mass.: Harvard University Press, 1980.

Hornykiewicz, O. Parkinson's disease and its chemotherapy. *Biochemical Pharmacology*, 1975, *24*, 1064-1065.

Hultsch, D. F., & Deutsch, F. *Adult development and aging.* New York: McGraw-Hill, 1981.

Ingvar, D. H., Brun, A., Johansson, L., & Samuelsson, S. M. Survival after severe cerebral anoxia with destruction of the cerebral cortex: The apallic syndrome. In J. Korein (Ed.), Brain death: Interrelated medical and social issues. *Annals of the New York Academy of Sciences*, 1978, *315*, 184-214.

Isaacs, B. Comprehensive care of the cognitively impaired elderly. In C. Eisdorfer & R. O. Freidel (Eds.),*Cognitive and emotional disturbance in the elderly.* Chicago: Year Book Medical Publishers, 1977.

Jackson, M., & Wood, J. L. *Aging in America: Implications for the black aged.* Washington, D.C.: National Council on the Aging, 1976.

Jacobs, E. A., Alvis, H. J., & Small, S. M. Hyperoxygenation: A central nervous system activator? *Journal of Geriatric Psychiatry*, 1972, *5*, 107-121.

Johoda, M. *Current concepts of positive mental health.* New York: Basic Books, 1958.

Jarrett, R. J. The treatment of mild, late-onset diabetes mellitus. *British Journal of Hospital Medicine*, 1973, *16*, 200-204.

Jarvik, L. F., & Blum, J. E. Cognitive declines as predictors of mortality in twin pairs: A twenty-year longitudinal study of aging. In E. Palmore & F. C. Jeffers (Eds.), *Prediction of life span.* Lexington, Mass.: D. C. Heath, 1971.

Jarvik, L. F., & Falek, A. Intellectual stability and survival in the aged. *Journal of Gerontology*, 1963, *18*, 173-176.

Jones, H. E., & Conrad, H. S. The growth and decline of intelligence: A study of homogeneous population between the ages of ten and sixty. *Genetic Psychology Monographs*, 1933, *13*, 233-298.

Kahn, R. L. Perspectives in the evaluation of psychological mental health programs for the aged. In W. D. Gentry (Ed.), *Geropsychology: A model of training and clinical services.* Cambridge, Mass.: Ballinger, 1977.

Kahn, R. L., & Miller, N. E. Adaptational factors in memory function in the aged. *Experimental Aging Research*, 1978, *4*, 273-290.

Kalish, R. A. The onset of the dying process. *Omega*, 1970, *1*, 57-59.

Kalish, R. A. The new ageism and the failure models: A polemic. *The Gerontologist*, 1979, *19*(4), 398-402.

Kalish, R., & Reynolds, D. K. *Death and ethnicity: A psychocultural study.* Los Angeles: University of Southern California Press, 1976.

Kapnick, P. L. Organic treatment of the elderly. In M. Storandt, I. Siegler, & M. Elias (Eds.), *Clinical psychology of aging.* New York: Plenum Press, 1978.

Kart, C. S., Metress, E. S., & Metress, J. F. *Aging and health: Biologic and social perspectives.* Menlo Park, Calif.: Addison-Wesley, 1978.

Kasl, S. V. The health belief model and behavior related to chronic illness. *Health Education Monographs*, 1974, *2*, 433-454.

Kastenbaum, R. Is death a life crisis? On the confrontation with death in theory and practice. In N. Datan & L. Ginsberg (Eds.), *Life-span developmental psychology: Normative life crises.* New York: Academic Press, 1975.

Kastenbaum, R. *Death, society and human experience.* St. Louis: C.V. Mosby, 1977.

Kastenbaum, R. Personality theory, therapeutic approaches and the elderly client.

In M. Storandt, I. Siegler, & M. F. Elias (Eds.), *The clinical psychology of aging*. New York: Plenum Press, 1978.

Kastenbaum, R. *Growing old: years of fulfillment,* Life Cycle Series (L. Kristal, Ed.). New York: Harper & Row, 1979.

Kastenbaum, R., & Aisenberg, R. *The psychology of death*. New York: Springer, 1972.

Kaufman, M. R. Old age and aging. *American Journal of Orthopsychiatry,* 1940, *10*, 73–84.

Kausler, D. H. *Experimental psychology and human aging*. New York: John Wiley & Sons, 1982.

Kelly, G. A. *The psychology of personal constructs*. New York: W. W. Norton, 1955.

Kenshalo, D. R. Age changes in touch, vibration, temperature, kinesthesis and pain sensitivity. In J. E. Birren & K. W. Schaie (Eds.), *Handbook of the psychology of aging*. New York: Van Nostrand Reinhold, 1977.

Kirikae, I. Auditory function in advanced age with reference to histological changes in the central auditory system. *International Audiology,* 1969, *8*, 221–230.

Kir-Stimon, W. Counseling with the severely handicapped: Encounter and commitment. In R. P. Martinelli & A. E. Dell Orto (Eds.), *The psychological and social impact of physical disability*. New York: Springer, 1977.

Kleemeier, R. Intellectual changes in the senium. In *Proceedings of the social statistics section of the American Statistical Association*. Washington, D.C.: American Statistical Association, 1962.

Koch, K. *I never told anybody: Teaching poetry writing in a nursing home*. New York: Vintage Books, 1977.

Kohlberg, L. Continuities in childhood and adult moral development revisited. In P. B. Baltes & K. W. Schaie (Eds.), *Life-span developmental psychology: Personality and socialization*. New York: Academic Press, 1973.

Kohn, R. R. Heart and cardiovascular system. In C. E. Finch & L. Hayflick (Eds.), *Handbook of the biology of aging*. New York: Van Nostrand Reinhold, 1977.

Korein, J. (Ed.). Brain death: Interrelated medical and social issues. *Annals of the New York Academy of Sciences,* 1978, *315*.

Krmpotic-Nemanic, J. Presbycusis and retrocochlear structures. *International Audiology,* 1969, *8*, 210–220.

Kubler-Ross, E. *On death and dying*. New York: Macmillan, 1969.

Kubler-Ross, E. *Death: The final stage of growth*. Englewood Cliffs, N.J.: Prentice-Hall, 1975.

Lachman, J. L., & Lachman, R. Age and the actualization of world knowledge. In L. W. Poon, J. L. Fozard, L. S. Cermak, D. Arenberg, & L. W. Thompson (Eds.), *New directions in memory and aging: Proceedings of the George A. Talland Memorial Conference*. Hillsdale, N.J.: Lawrence Erlbaum, 1980.

Langone, J. *Vital signs: The way we die in America.* Boston: Little, Brown, 1974.

LaRue, A. An overview of measures of cognitive functioning: Comparative performance of depressed, organic and normal aged patients. Paper presented at the Annual Meeting of the Gerontological Society held in Dallas, Texas, November, 1978.

Lawton, M. P. Psychosocial and environmental approaches to the care of senile dementia patients. In J. O. Cole & J. E. Barrett (Eds.), *Psychopathology in the aged.* New York: Raven Press, 1980.

Lehman, H. C. The use of medication to prevent custodial care. In C. Eisdorfer & R. O. Friedel (Eds.), *Cognitive and emotional disturbance in the elderly.* Chicago, Ill.: Yearbook Medical Publishers, 1977.

Lesnoff-Caravaglia, G. (Ed.), *Health care of the elderly: Strategies for prevention and intervention.* New York: Human Sciences Press, 1980.

Libow, L. J. Senile dementia and pseudosenility: Clinical diagnosis. In C. Eisdorger & R. O. Friedel (Eds.), *Cognitive and emotional disturbance in the elderly.* Chicago: Year Book Medical Publishers, 1977.

Lieberman, M. A. Psychological correlates of impending death: Some preliminary observations. *Journal of Gerontology,* 1965, *20,* 181–190.

Lieberman, M. A. Observations on death and dying. *Gerontologist,* 1966, *6,* 70–72.

Light, K. C. Slowing of response time in young and middle aged hypertensive patients. *Experimental Aging Research,* 1975, *1,* 209–227.

Light, K. C. Effects of mild cardiovascular and cerebrovascular disorders on serial reaction time performance. *Experimental Aging Research,* 1978, *4,* 3–22.

Lowenthal, M. F. Toward a sociopsychological theory of change in adulthood and old age. In J. E. Birren, & K. W. Schaie (Eds.), *Handbook of the psychology of aging.* New York: Van Nostrand Reinhold, 1977.

Lowy, L. *Social work with the aging.* New York: Harper & Row, 1979.

Lowy, L. Mental health services in the community. In J. E. Birren & R. B. Sloane (Eds.), *Handbook of mental health and aging.* Englewood Cliffs, N.J.: Prentice-Hall, 1980.

Lozier, J. Accommodating old people in society: Examples from Appalachia and New Orleans. In N. Datan & L. Ginsberg (Eds.), *Life-span developmental psychology: Normative life crises.* New York: Academic Press, 1975.

Maas, H. S., & Kuypers, J. A. *From thirty to seventy.* San Francisco: Jossey-Bass, 1975.

MacMahon, B., & Pugh, T. J. *Epidemiology: Principles and methods.* Boston: Little, Brown, 1970.

Maddi, S. R. *Personality theories: A comparative analysis.* Homewood, Ill.: Dorsey Press, 1980.

Maddox, G. L. Themes and issues in sociological theories of human aging. *Human Development,* 1970, *13,* 17–27.

Makinodan, T. Immunity and aging. In C. E. Finch & L. Hayflick (Eds.), *Handbook of the biology of aging.* New York: Van Nostrand Reinhold, 1977.

Mannes, M. *Last rights.* New York: William Morrow, 1973.

Marsh, G. A. Perceptual changes with aging. In E. W. Busse & D. G. Blazer (Eds.), *Handbook of geriatric psychiatry.* New York: Van Nostrand Reinhold, 1980.

Marshall, V. W. *Last chapters: A sociology of aging and dying.* Belmont, Calif.: Wadsworth, 1980.

Mausner, J. S., & Bahn, A. K. *Epidemiology.* Philadelphia: W. B. Saunders, 1974.

McHale, M. C., McHale, J., & Streatfield G. J. *Children in the world.* Washington, D. C.: Population Reference Bureau, 1979.

Miller, J. H., & Shock, N. W. Age differences in the renal tubular response to antidiuretic hormone. *Journal of Gerontology,* 1953, *8,* 446–450.

Monge, R. H. Developmental trends in factors of adolescent self-concept. *Developmental Psychology,* 1973, *8,* 382–393.

Monge, R. H., & Gardner, E. J. *A program of research in adult differences in cognitive performance and learning: Backgrounds for adult education and vocational retraining. A Final Report.* Washington, D.C.: Department of Health, Education, & Welfare, 1972.

Monge, R., & Hultsch, D. Paired-associate learning as a function of adult age and the length of the anticipation and inspection interval. *Journal of Gerontology,* 1971, *26,* 157–162.

Monte, C. *Beneath the mask: An introduction to theories of personality.* New York: Holt, Rinehart & Winston, 1980.

Moos, R. H., & Tsu, V. D. The crisis of physical illness: An overview. In R. H. Moos (Ed.), *Coping with physical illness.* New York: Plenum Medical Book Company, 1977.

Muller, H. F., Grad, B., & Engelsmann, F. Biological and psychological predictors of survival in a psychogeriatric population. *Journal of Gerontology,* 1975, *30,* 47–52.

Murray, R., Huelskoetter, M. M., & O'Driscoll, D. *The nursing process in later maturity.* Englewood Cliffs, N.J.: Prentice-Hall, 1980.

Murrell, F. H. The effect of extensive practice on age differences in reaction time. *Journal of Gerontology,* 1978, *25,* 268–274.

Nash, J. *Developmental psychology: A psychobiological approach.* Englewood Cliffs, N.J.: Prentice-Hall, 1978.

Nesselroade, J. R., & Harkins, S. W. Introduction to methodological issues. In L. W. Poon (Ed.), *Aging in the 1980s: Psychological issues.* Washington, D.C.: American Psychological Association, 1980.

Neugarten, B. L. Personality and aging. In J. E. Birren & K. W. Schaie (Eds.), *Handbook of the psychology of aging.* New York: Academic Press, 1977.

Neugarten, B. L., & Datan, N. Sociological perspectives on the life cycle. In P. B. Baltes & Schaie K. W. (Eds.), *Life-span developmental psychology: Personality and socialization.* New York: Academic Press, 1973.

Neugarten, B. L. et al. *Personality in middle and late life.* New York: Atherton Press, 1964.

Neugarten, B. L., Havighurst, R. J., & Tobin, S. S. Personality and patterns of aging. In B. L. Neugarten (Ed.); *Middle age and aging.* Chicago: University of Chicago Press, 1968.

Neugarten, B. L., & Weinstein, K. K. The changing American grandparent. *Journal of Marriage and the Family,* 1964, *26,* 199–204.

Newman, B. M., & Newman, P. R. *Personality development through the lifespan.* Monterey, Calif.: Brooks/Cole, 1980.

Oden, M. H. The fulfillment of promise: 40-year follow-up of the Terman gifted group. *Genetic Psychology Monographs,* 1968, 77, 3–93.

Okun, M. A. Adult age and cautiousness in decision: A review of the literature. *Human Development,* 1976, *19,* 220–233.

Okun, M. A., Siegler, I. C., & George, L. K. Cautiousness and verbal learning in adulthood. *Journal of Gerontology,* 1978, *33,* 94–97.

Orgel, L. E. The maintenance of the accuracy of protein synthesis and its relevance to aging. *Proceedings of the National Academy of Sciences,* 1963, *49,* 517.

Overton, W. J., & Reese, W. W. Models of development: Methodological implications. In J. R. Hesselroade & H. W. Reese (Eds.), *Life-span developmental psychology: Methodological issue.* New York: Academic Press, 1973.

Owens, W. A. Age and mental abilities: A longitudinal study. *Genetic Psychology Monographs,* 1953, *48,* 3–54.

Owens, W. A. Age and mental ability: A second follow-up. *Journal of Educational Psychology,* 1966, *57,* 311–325.

Palmore, E. B. Physical, mental, and social factors in predicting longevity. *Gerontologist,* 1969, *9,* 103–108.

Palmore, E. B. *Normal Aging. I.* Durham, N. C.: Duke University Press, 1970.

Palmore, E. B., & Cleveland, W. Aging, terminal decline, and terminal drop. *Journal of Gerontology,* 1976, *31,* 76–81.

Pattison, M. *The experience of dying.* Englewood Cliffs, N.J.: Prentice-Hall, 1977.

Peck, R. C. Psychology developments in the second half of life. In B. L. Neugarten (Ed.), *Middle age and aging.* Chicago: University of Chicago Press, 1968.

Pfeiffer, E. Psychopathology and social pathology. In J. E. Birren & K. W. Schaie (Eds.), *Handbook of the psychology of aging.* New York: Van Nostrand Reinhold, 1977.

Pfeiffer, E. Pharmacology of aging. In G. Lesnoff-Carovaglia (Ed.), *Health care of the elderly.* New York: Human Sciences Press, 1980.

Pfeiffer, E. The psychosocial evaluation of the elderly patient. In E. W. Busse &

D. Blazer (Eds.), *Handbook of Geriatric Psychiatry*. New York: Van Nostrand Reinhold, 1980.

Post, F. Paranoid, SZ-like and schizophrenia states in the aged. In J. E. Birren & R. B. Sloane (Eds.), *Handbook of mental health and aging*. Englewood Cliffs, N.J.: Prentice-Hall, 1980.

Quint, J. C. *The nurse and the dying patient*. Chicago, Ill.: Aldine, 1967.

Rabbitt, P. Changes in problem soving ability in OA. In J. E. Birren & K. W. Schaie (Eds.), *Handbook of the psychology of aging*. New York: Van Nostrand Reinhold, 1977.

Raskin, A. Signs and symptoms of psychopathology in the elderly. In A. Raskin & L. F. Jarvik (Eds.), *Psychiatric symptoms and cognitive loss in the elderly*. Washington, D.C.: Hemisphere, 1979.

Raskind, M. A., & Storrie, M. C. The organic mental disorders. In E. W. Busse & D. Blazer (Eds.), *Handbook of geriatric psychiatry*. New York: Van Nostrand Reinhold, 1980.

Reichard, S., Livson, F., & Peterson, P. G. *Aging and personality: A study of 87 older men*. New York: John Wiley & Sons, 1962.

Reiff, T. R. Biomedical aspects of aging and their relation to geriatric care. In G. Lesnoff-Caravaglia (Ed.), *Health care of the elderly*. New York: Human Sciences Press, 1980.

Reimanis, G., & Green, R. Imminence of death and intellectual decrement in the aging. *Developmental Psychology*, 1971, *5*, 270–272.

Reisberg, B., Ferris, S. H., & Gershon, S. Pharmacotherapy of senile dementia. In J. O. Cole & J. E. Barrett (Eds.), *Psychopathology in the aged*. New York: Raven Press, 1980.

Reitan, R. M. The relationship of the Trail-Making Test to organic brain damage. *Journal of Consulting Psychology*, 1955, *19*, 393–395.

Riegel, K. F. The prediction of death and longevity in longitudinal research. A twenty-year longitudinal study of aging. In E. Palmore & F. C. Jeffers (Eds.), *Prediction of life span*. Lexington, Mass.: D. C. Heath, 1971.

Riegel, K. F. Developmental psychology and society: Some historical and ethical considerations. In J. R. Nesselroade & H. W. Reese (Eds.), *Life-span developmental psychology: Methodological issues*. New York: Academic Press, 1973. (a)

Riegel, K. F. Dialectic operations: The final period of cognitive development. *Human Development*, 1973, *16*, 346–370. (b)

Riegel, K. F. An epitaph for a paradigm. *Human Development*, 1973, *16*, (1–2), 1–7. (c)

Riegel, K. F. History of psychological gerontology. In J. E. Birren & K. W. Schaie (Eds.), *Handbook of the psychology of aging*. New York: Van Nostrand Reinhold, 1977.

Riegel, K. F., Riegel, R. M., & Meyer, G. A study of the drop-out rates in longitudinal research on aging and the prediction of death. *Journal of*

*Personality and Social Psychology,* 1967, *4,* 342–348.

Riley, J. W., Jr. What people thing about death. In O. G. Brim, Jr., H. E. Freeman, S. Levine, & N. A. Scotch (Eds.), *The dying patient.* New York: Russell Sage Foundation, 1970.

Riley, M. W., Foner, A., Moore, M. E. Hess, B., & Roth B. K. *Aging and society: An inventory of research findings.* New York: Russell Sage Foundation, 1968.

Robertson-Tchabo, E. A., Arenberg, D., & Costa, P. T. Temperamental predictors of longitudinal change in performance on the Benton Revised Visual Retention Test among seventy-year old men: An exploratory study. In F. Hoffmeister & C. Muller (Eds.), *Brain function in old age: Evaluation of change and disorders.* New York: Springer-Verlag, 1979.

Rockstein, M., Chesky, J., & Sussman, M. Comparative biology and evolution of aging. In C. E. Finch & L. Hayflick (Eds.), *Handbook of the biology of aging.* New York: Van Nostrand Reinhold, 1977.

Rockstein, M., & Sussman, M. *Biology of aging.* Belmont, Calif.: Wadsworth, 1979.

Rosenman, R. H., & Friedman, M. The central nervous system and coronary heart disease. In P. Insel & R. Moos (Eds.), *Health and the social environment.* Lexington, Mass.: D. C. Heath, 1974.

Roth, M. Senile dementia and its borderlands. In J. O. Cole & J. E. Barrett (Eds.), *Psychopathology in the aged.* New York: Raven Press, 1980.

Salthouse, T. A. Age and memory: Strategies for localizing the loss. In L. W. Poon, J. L. Fozard, L. S. Cermak, D. Arenberg, & L. W. Thompson (Eds.), *New directions in memory and aging: Proceedings of the George Talland Memorial Conference.* Hillsdale, N.J.: Lawrence Erlbaum, 1980.

Saunders, C. The last stages of life. *American Journal of Nursing,* 1965, *65,* 70–75.

Schaie, K. W. Cross-sectional methods in the study of psychological aspects of aging. *Journal of Gerontology,* 1955, *10,* 91–107.

Schaie, K. W. Methodological problems in descriptive developmental research on adulthood and aging. In J. R. Nesselroade & H. W. Reese (Eds.), *Life-span developmental psychology: Methodological issues.* New York: Academic Press, 1973.

Schaie, K. W. Rigidity-flexibility and intelligence: A cross-sectional study of the adult life-span from 20 to 70 years. *Psychology Monographs: General and Applied,* 1958, *72*(9), 1–26.

Schaie, K. W. Translations in gerontology — From lab to life: Intellectual functioning. *American Psychologist,* 1974, *29,* 802–807.

Schaie, K. W. Intelligence and problem-solving. In J. Birren & R. B. Sloane (Eds.), *Handbook of mental health and aging.* Englewood Cliffs, N.J.: Prentice-Hall, 1980.

Schaie, K. W., & Labouvie-Vief, G. Generational vs. ontogenetic components of change in adult cognitive behavior: A 14-year cross-sequential study. *Developmental Psychology,* 1974, *10,* 305–320.

Schiffman, S. Food recognition by the elderly. *Journal of Gerontology,* 1977, *32*(5), 586–592.

Schiffman, S., & Pasternak, M. Decreased discrimination of food odors in the elderly. *Journal of Gerontology,* 1979, *34*(1), 73–79.

Schonfield, A. E. D. Learning, memory and aging. In J. Birren & R. B. Sloane (Eds.), *Handbook of mental health and aging.* Englewood Cliffs, N.J.: Prentice-Hall, 1980.

Schulz, R. *The psychology of death, dying and bereavement.* Reading, Mass.: Addison-Wesley, 1978.

Seligman, M. E. P. *Helplessness: On depression, development and death.* San Francisco: W. H. Freeman, 1975.

Selye, H. *The stress of life.* New York: McGraw-Hill, 1956.

Shanas, E., & Maddox, G. L. Aging, health and the organization of health resources. In R. H. Binstock & E. Shanas (Eds.), *Handbook of aging and the social sciences.* N.Y.: Van Nostrand Reinhold, 1977.

Sharp, G. L., Butterfield, W. H. J., & Keen, H. Diabetic survey in Bedford. *Proceedings of the Royal Society of Medicine.* 1964, *57,* 193–202.

Sherwood, S., & Mor, V. Mental health institutions and the elderly. In J. Birren & R. B. Sloane (Eds.), *Handbook of mental health and aging.* Englewood Cliffs, N.J.: Prentice-Hall, 1980.

Shneidman, E. S. The death certificate. In E. S. Shneidman (Ed.), *Death: Current perspectives.* Palo Alto, Calif.: Mayfield, 1980. (a)

Shneidman, E. S. Suicide. In E. S. Shneidman (Ed.), *Death: Current perspectives.* Palo Alto, Calif.: Mayfield, 1980. (d)

Shock, N. W. Biological theories of aging. In J. E. Birren & K. W. Schaie (Eds.), *Handbook of the psychology of aging.* New York: Van Nostrand Reinhold, 1977. (a)

Shock, N. W. Systems integration. In C. E. Finch & L. Hayflick (Eds.), *Handbook of the biology of aging.* New York: Van Nostrand Reinhold, 1977. (b)

Siegel, J. S. Prospective trends in the size and structure of the elderly population, impact of mortality trends and some indications. *Current Population Reports,* 1979.

Siegler, I. C. The terminal drop hypothesis: Fact or artifact? *Experimental Aging Research,* 1975, *1,* 169–185.

Siegler, I. C. The psychology of adult development and aging. In E. W. Busse & D. Blazer (Eds.), *Handbook of geriatric psychiatry.* New York: Van Nostrand Reinhold, 1980.

Simon, A. The neuroses, personality disorders, alcoholism, drug use and misuse, and crime in the aged. In J. E. Birren & R. B. Sloane (Eds.), *Handbook of mental health and aging.* Englewood Cliffs, N.J.: Prentice-Hall, 1980.

Sloane, R. B. Organic brain syndrome. In J. E. Birren & R. B. Sloane (Eds.), *Handbook of mental health and aging.* Englewood Cliffs, N.J.: Prentice-Hall, 1980.

Sovner, R. *Tardive dyskinesia: Diagnosis and management.* East Hanover, N. J.:

Sandoz Pharmaceuticals, 1978.

Spieth, W. Slowness of task performance and cardiovascular diseases. In A. T. Welford & J. E. Birren (Eds.), *Behavior, aging and the nervous system.* Springfield, Ill.: Charles C. Thomas, 1965.

Spirduso, W. W. Reaction and movement time as a function of age and physical activity level. *Journal of Gerontology,* 1975, *30,* 435–440.

Stenback, A. Depression and suicidal behavior in old age. In J. E. Birren & R. B. Sloane (Eds.), *Handbook of mental health and aging.* Englewood Cliffs, N.J.: Prentice-Hall, 1980.

Storandt, M., Siegler, I. C., & Elias, M. F. (Eds.). *The clinical psychology of aging.* New York: Plenum Press, 1978.

Strehler, B. L. Introduction: Aging the human brain. In R. D. Terry & S. Gershon (Eds.), *Neurobiology of aging.* New York: Raven Press, 1976.

Surwillo, W. W. The relation of simple response time to brain wave frequency and the effects of age. *Electroencephalographic Clinical Neurophysiology,* 1963, *15,* 105–114.

Terry, R. D., & Gershon S. (Eds.). *Neurobiology of aging.* New York: Raven Press, 1976.

Terry, R. D., & Wisniewski, H. Structural aspects of aging in the brain. In C. Eisdorfer & R. O. Friedel (Eds.), *Cognitive and emotional disturbance in the elderly.* Chicago: Year Book Medical Publishers, 1977.

Tesiny, D. J., Newman, E. I., & Brockett, R. G. *Basic adult services: A model curriculum.* Albany, N.Y.: School of Social Welfare, 1978.

Thomae, H. Personality and adjustment to aging. In J. Birren & R. B. Sloane (Eds.), *Handbook of mental health and aging.* Englewood Cliffs, N.J.: Prentice-Hall, 1980.

Tomlinson, B. E., & Henderson, G. Some quantative cerebral findings in normal and demented old people. In R. D. Terry & S. Gershon (Eds.), *Neurobiology of aging.* New York: Raven Press, 1976.

United Nations. Guidelines for national policy. In *The aging: Trends and policies.* New York: United Nations, 1975.

U.S. Department of Commerce. Social and economic characteristics of the older population. *Current Population Reports,* 1979, *85.* (a)

U.S. Department of Commerce. *Population profile of the U.S.: 1981.* Washington, D. C.: U. S. Bureau of the Census, 1979.

U.S. Department of Health, Education, & Welfare. *Health United States 1976–77.* Washington, D.C.: Public Health Service, 1977.

U.S. Department of Health, Education, & Welfare. *Health United States, 1978.* Washington, D.C.: Public Health Service, 1978.

U.S. Department of Health, Education, & Welfare. *Health United States, 1980.* Washington, D.C.: Public Health Service, 1980.

U.S. Health Resources Administration, Division of Long-Term Care. *Guidelines and definitions for day care centers under PL 92–603.* Washington, D.C.: Government Printing Office, 1974.

Upton, A. C. Pathobiology. In C. E. Finch & L. Hayflick (Eds.), *Handbook of the biology of aging.* New York: Van Nostrand Reinhold, 1977.

Verwoerdt, A. *Clinical geropsychiatry.* Baltimore: Williams & Wilkins, 1975.

Walford, R. L. *The immunological theory of aging.* Baltimore: Williams & Wilkins, 1969.

Walker, J. I., & Brodie, H. K. Neuropharmacology of aging. In E. W. Busse & D. Blazer (Eds.), *Handbook of geriatric psychiatry.* New York: Van Nostrand Reinhold, 1980.

Warren, L. R., Wagener, J.W., & Herman, G. E. Binaural analysis in the aging auditory system. *Journal of Gerontology,* 1978, *33*(5), 731–736.

Waugh, N. C., & Barr, R. A. Memory and mental tempo. In L. W. Poon, J. L. Fozard, L. S. Cermak, D. Arenberg, & L. W. Thompson (Eds.), *New directions in memory and aging.* Hillsdale, N.J.: Lawrence Erlbaum, 1980.

Wechsler, D. *The measurement of adult intelligence.* Baltimore: Williams & Wilkins, 1939.

Weg, R. B. Changing physiology of aging: Normal and pathological. In D. S. Woodruff & J. E. Birren (Eds.), *Aging: Scientific perspectives and social issues.* New York: Van Nostrand Reinhold, 1975.

Weisman, A. D. *Death and denial.* New York: Behavioral Publications, 1972.

Weisman, A. D. Common fallacies about dying patients. In E. S. Shneidman (Ed.), *Death: Current perspectives.* Palo Alto, Calif.: Mayfield, 1980.

Weisman, A. D., & Kastenbaum, R. The psychological autopsy: A study of the terminal phase of life. *Community Mental Health Journal,* 1968, Monograph No. 4.

Weisman, A. D., & Worden, J. W. Psychosocial analysis of cancer deaths. *Omega,* 1975, *6*, 61–75.

Welford, A. T. Motor performance. In J. E. Birren & K. W. Schaie (Eds.), *Handbook of the psychology of aging.* New York: Van Nostrand Reinhold, 1977.

Whanger, A. D. Treatment within the institution. In E. W. Busse & D. Blazer (Eds.), *Handbook of geriatric psychiatry.* New York: Van Nostrand Reinhold, 1980.

White, R. W. Motivation reconsidered: The concept of competence. *Psychological Review,* 1959, *66*, 297–333.

Williamson, J. B., Munley, A., & Evans, L. *Aging and society.* New York: Holt, Rinehart & Winston, 1980.

Winokur, G., Behar, D., & Schlesser, M. Clinical and biological aspects of depression in the elderly. In J. O. Cole & J. Barrett (Eds.), *Psychopathology in the aged.* New York: Raven Press, 1980.

Wohlwill, J. F. *The study of behavioral development.* New York: Academic Press, 1973.

Woodruff, D. S. Biofeedback control of the EEG alpha rythmn and its effect on reaction time in the young and old. (Dissertation, University of Southern California, 1972).

Woodruff, D.S. A physiological perspective of the psychology of aging. In D.S. Woodruff & J. E. Birren (Eds.), *Aging: Scientific perspectives and social issues.* New York: Van Nostrand Reinhold, 1975.

Wrong, D. H. *Population and society (4th ed.).* New York: Random House, 1977.

Zarit, S. H., Miller, N. E., & Kahn, R. L. Brain function, intellectual impairment and education in the aged. *Journal of the American Geriatrics Society,* 1978, *21*(2), 58–67.

Zimbardo, P. G., Anderson, S. M., & Kobat, L. G. Induced hearing deficit generates experimental paranoia. *Science,* 1981, *212*(6), 1529–1531.

Zung, W. W. K. Affective disorders. In E. W. Busse & D. Blazer (Eds.), *Handbook of geriatric psychiatry.* New York: Van Nostrand Reinhold, 1980.

Atchley, R. C. The life course, age grading and age-linked demands for decision-making. In N. Datan & L. Ginsberg (Eds.), *Life-span developmental psychology: Normative life crises.* New York: Academic Press, 1975.

Beattie, W. Designing systems of care—Planning: Issues and perspectives. In E. Pfeiffer (Ed.), *Alternatives to institutional care for older Americans: Practice and Planning.* Durham: Center for the Study of Aging and Human Development, 1973.

Bengtson, V. L., & Treas, J. The changing family context of mental health and aging. In J. E. Birren & R. B. Sloane (Eds.), *Handbook of mental health and aging.* Englewood Cliffs, N. J.: Prentice-Hall, 1980.

Cole, J. O., & Barrett, J. E. (Eds.). *Psychopathology in the aged.* New York: Raven Press, 1980.

Comalli, P. E., Jr. Life-span changes in visual perception. In L. R. Goulet & P. B. Baltes (Eds.), *Life-span developmental psychology: Research and theory.* New York: Academic Press, 1980.

Datan, N., & Ginsberg, L. H. (Eds.). *Life-span developmental psychology: Normative life crises.* New York: Academic Press, 1975.

de Beauvoir, S. *A very easy death.* London: G.P. Putnam's Sons, 1966.

Eisdorfer, C. Paranoia and schizophrenic disorders in late life. In E. W. Busse & D. Blazer (Eds.), *Handbook of geriatric psychiatry.* New York: Van Nostrand Reinhold, 1980.

Eisdorfer, C., & Stotsky, B. A. Intervention, treatment and rehabilitation of psychiatric disorders. In J. Birren & K. W. Schaie (Eds.), *Handbook of the psychology of aging.* New York: Van Nostrand Reinhold, 1977.

Everitt, A. V., & Huang, C. Y. The hypothalamus, neuroendocrine and autonomic nervous systems in aging. In J. E. Birren & R. B. Sloane (Eds.), *Handbook of mental health and aging.* Englewood Cliffs, N. J.: Prentice-Hall, 1980.

Fiske, M. Tasks and crises of the second half of life: The interrelationship of commitment, coping and adaptation. In J. E. Birren & R. B. Sloane (Eds.), *Handbook of mental health and aging.* Englewood Cliffs, N. J.: Prentice-Hall, 1980.

Granick, S., & Patterson, R. D. *Human aging II: An 11 year biomedical and behavioral study.* Washington, D.C.: Government Printing Office, 1971.

Habot, B., & Libow, L. The interrelationship of mental and physical status and its assessment in the older adult: Mind-body interaction. In J. E. Birren & R. B. Sloane (Eds.), *The handbook of mental health and aging.* Englewood Cliffs, N. J.: Prentice-Hall, 1980.

Herr, J. J., & Weakland, J. H. *Counseling elders and their families.* New York: Springer, 1979.

Insel, P. M., & Moos, R. H. (Eds.). *Health and the social environment.* Lexington, Mass.: D.C. Heath, 1974.

Kalish, R. A. *The dependencies of old people.* Ann Arbor, Mich.: University of Michigan Division of Gerontology, 1969.

Koestenbaum, P. *Is there an answer to death?* Englewood Cliffs, N. J.: Prentice-Hall, 1976.

Kramer, M., Taube, C. A., & Redick, R. W. Patterns of use of psychiatric facilities by the aged: Past, present and future. In C. Eisdorfer & M. P. Lawton (Eds.), *Psychology of adult development and aging.* Washington, D. C.: American Psychiatric Association, 1973.

Kuypers, J. A., & Bengtson, V. L. Social breakdown and competence: A model of normal aging. *Human Development,* 1973, *16,* 181–201.

Medvedev, Z. A. Caucasus and Altay longevity: A biological or social problem? *The Gerontologist,* 1974, *14,* 381–387.

Medvedev, Z. A. Aging and longevity: New approaches and new perspectives. *The Gerontologist,* 1975, *15,* 196–201.

Moody, R. A. *Life after life.* New York: Bantam Books, 1976.

Moos, R. H. (Ed.). *Coping with physical illness.* New York: Plenum Medical Book Company, 1977.

Poon, L. (Ed.). *Aging in the 1980s: Psychological issues.* Washington, D.C.: American Psychological Association, 1980.

Rabins, P. V., Mace, N. L., & Lucas, M. J. The impact of dementia on the family. *Journal of the American Medical Association,* 1982, *248,* 333–335.

Raskin, A., & Jarvik, L. F. *Psychiatric symptoms and cognitive loss in the elderly.* Washington, D.C.: Hemisphere, 1979.

Salthouse, T. A. *Adult cognition.* New York: Springer-Verlag, 1982.

Troll, L. E., Miller, S. J., and Atchley, R. C. *Families in later life.* Belmont, Calif.: Wadsworth, 1979.